# JACQUES THE FRENCHMAN

Memories of the Gulag

Jacques Rossi is one of Stalin's most well-known victims. Author of *The Gulag Handbook*, a fascinating encyclopedia of the Soviet forced labour camps, Rossi spent twenty years in interrogation, prison, and Gulag detention. Born to a prominent Polish father and French mother, the young Jacques became attracted to communism as a blueprint for radical social reform. He spent years in the communist underground in interwar Europe, agitating for the revolution, but he was arrested during Stalin's Great Purges in 1937. This book represents a conversation between Jacques Rossi and Michèle Sarde which weaves together personal reflections and historical analysis.

Rossi's remarkable life (1909–2004) spanned the twentieth century and sheds important light on the tumultuous history of Europe – the appeal of communism in the interwar period and beyond, the mentality of party members, the effects of mass repression, everyday life in Stalin's Gulag, and the problem of rights for former prisoners during the Khrushchev era. As he abandoned his internationalist communist beliefs, Rossi increasingly identified as French, embracing the name his fellow prisoners gave him in the Gulag, "Jacques the Frenchman." Rossi's reflections on his own political beliefs, his frustrations with those who could not accept the truth of his brutal experiences in the Soviet Union, and his life as a witness to one of the twentieth century's worst crimes offer a fascinating history of Stalinism and its legacies.

JACQUES ROSSI was a Polish-French writer and polyglot. Rossi was best known for his book *The Gulag Handbook*.

MICHÈLE SARDE is a French writer and professor emerita at Georgetown University.

GOLFO ALEXOPOULOS is a professor of History at the University of South Florida and founding director of the USF Institute on Russia.

KERSTI COLOMBANT is a French translator.

# Jacques the Frenchman

*Memories of the Gulag*

JACQUES ROSSI AND MICHÈLE SARDE
EDITED BY GOLFO ALEXOPOULOS
TRANSLATED BY KERSTI COLOMBANT
PREFACE BY MICHAEL DAVID-FOX

UNIVERSITY OF TORONTO PRESS
Toronto Buffalo London

© University of Toronto Press 2020
Toronto Buffalo London
utorontopress.com

*Jacques, le Français*
© Le Cherche Midi, 2002

ISBN 978-1-4875-0604-9 (cloth)       ISBN 978-1-4875-3318-2 (EPUB)
ISBN 978-1-4875-2406-7 (paper)       ISBN 978-1-4875-3317-5 (PDF)

---

**Library and Archives Canada Cataloguing in Publication**

Title: Jacques the Frenchman : memories of the Gulag / by Jacques Rossi and Michèle Sarde ; edited by Golfo Alexopoulos ; translated by Kersti Colombant ; preface by Michael David-Fox.
Other titles: Jacques, le Français. English
Names: Rossi, Jacques, author. | Sarde, Michèle, author. | Alexopoulos, Golfo, editor.
Description: Translation of: Jacques, le Français. | Includes bibliographical references and index.
Identifiers: Canadiana 20190186593 | ISBN 9781487524067 (paper) | ISBN 9781487506049 (cloth)
Subjects: LCSH: Rossi, Jacques. | LCSH: Political prisoners – Soviet Union – Biography. | LCSH: Concentration camps – Soviet Union. | LCSH: Political persecution – Soviet Union. | LCSH: Soviet Union – History – 1925–1953.
Classification: LCC DK268.R675 A313 2020 | DDC 365/.45092 – dc23

---

University of Toronto Press acknowledges the financial assistance to its publishing program of the Canada Council for the Arts and the Ontario Arts Council, an agency of the Government of Ontario.

  Canada Council   Conseil des Arts
        for the Arts     du Canada

Funded by the    Financé par le
Government      gouvernement
of Canada        du Canada

*for Regina*
*for Marie-Cécile, Sophie, and Véronique*

If I had to sum up the twentieth century, I would say that it raised the greatest hopes ever conceived by humanity, and destroyed all illusions and ideals.

Yehudi Menuhin, quoted in Eric Hobsbawm, *Age of Extremes*

What we need to understand are not what people were forced to submit to, but what they sought to do – not only as perpetrators of evil, but also as fighters against evil, as resisters, and as rescuers of human lives.

Tzvetan Todorov, *Hope and Memory*

# Contents

*Preface* ix
MICHAEL DAVID-FOX

*Introduction* xi
GOLFO ALEXOPOULOS

The Meeting  3
MICHÈLE SARDE

**Part 1: Before**

1. Never Again  11
2. The Established Order  18
3. The Future of the Worldwide Proletariat Is More Important than One's Career!  26
4. The Fugitive  36
5. Secret Agent  43
6. Let Them Stuff Themselves with Caviar! They Won't Grow Old!  59
7. Early Indications of an Announced Arrest  69
8. The Trap  77

**Part 2: During**

9. From the Dog House to the Train Station  89
10. We Don't Torture Foreigners  99
11. Confess, Filthy Fascist!  106

12 On Interrogations   113
13 Everyday Life at the Butyrka Prison   120
14 The Story of a Blind Man and Coffee with Milk   128
15 The Verdict: Now We're Going to Put into Practice Marxist-Leninist Theory   136
16 Destination Unknown   142
17 Transit: May Your Memory Be Your Only Travel Bag!   150
18 An Operatic Voice on the Yenisei   158
19 Dudinka: The End of the World   168
20 The Polar Night   175
21 Surviving   184
22 Yes, I Am a Communist and You Are Too; Only Between Us There Is Barbed Wire   192
23 How Jacques the Frenchman Ceased to Be a Communist   200
24 The Friends of the People   207
25 Continuing in Spite of Oneself   215
26 The Rebel: The First Hunger Strike   226
27 In the Central Prison of Alexandrovsk   233
28 The Beginning of the End   241
29 "I *Choose* Samarkand"   249

**Part 3: After**

30 "Sir, You Are Dripping Snow on My Floors!"   261
31 In Central Asia: The Man Who Came from a Country with No Collective Farms   270
32 To Comrade Khrushchev [Stop] I Jacques Rossi [Stop] a Free Citizen [Stop] Am Starting a Hunger Strike [Stop] with No Time Limit and Until Death   279
33 Communist Poland: Origins of *The Gulag Handbook*   288
34 Seeing Paris Again   295
35 Life after Communism   305

**In Place of an Epilogue: Paris, Autumn 2001**

Afterword to the English Edition: A Man of Secrets   325
MICHÈLE SARDE

*Notes*   331

*Index*   339

# Preface

MICHAEL DAVID-FOX

The Jacques Rossi Memorial Fund for Gulag Research was the brainchild of Elisabeth Salina Amorini, who has long been animated by the desire to further scholarly research on the Gulag, and the initial steps to found it were taken by my predecessor at Georgetown University, the late Richard Stites. As explained in the pages that follow, the extraordinary life of Jacques Rossi was for a time connected to Georgetown, and the origins of this extraordinary book date to Rossi's fortuitous 1982 meeting at the university with Michèle Sarde, now professor emerita of French. It is therefore fitting in many ways that the Jacques Rossi Fund was able to sponsor the translation and publication of this English-language edition.

I became director of the Jacques Rossi Fund in 2012–13 and began planning an inaugural international conference, "The Soviet Gulag: Evidence: Interpretation, and Comparison." When this was held at Georgetown in April 2013, Sarde delivered a keynote address entitled "Jacques Rossi: An Education in the Gulag." Present in the audience was Golfo Alexopoulos of the University of South Florida, who was taking part in a round-table discussion about the state of scholarly research on the Soviet camp system. Rossi's contributions to Gulag scholarship, particularly his *Gulag Handbook: An Encyclopedia Dictionary of Soviet Penitentiary Institutions and Terms Related to the Forced Labor Camps*, published first in English and Russian and later in French, were well known to scholars. Indeed, one of the historians at the conference was Russia's foremost historian of Stalinism, Oleg Khlevniuk. His essay recounted how he had personally met Rossi in Paris and later used Rossi's work in the book that resulted from the conference proceedings.[1] However, the full story of Rossi's biographical trajectory – not to mention his more intimate recollections about his time in the camps, told in riveting fashion in the current work on which Sarde and Rossi so successfully collaborated – has remained unknown even to the vast majority of specialists in Russia, North America, and elsewhere. More to the point, a broader English-speaking public will only now be able to read about his remarkable twentieth-century odyssey. As a result of this second fortuitous meeting at Georgetown between Sarde and Alexopoulos, the path towards the present book was first set.

The mission of the Jacques Rossi Fund is to support scholarly research relating to the Gulag, broadly conceived. To that end, it sponsors competitive research grants available to Georgetown students at all levels, from undergraduate to doctoral, as well as conferences, talks, outreach activities, and publications. Both this English edition of *Jacques, le français* and a Russian edition, published by NLO Press in Moscow in 2019, were sponsored and facilitated by the Jacques Rossi Fund. Expenses such as the able French-English translation by Kersti Colombant were supported by additional donations by Elisabeth Salina Amorini, whose support for both this project and the Rossi Fund itself never wavered.

The present English-language edition benefitted greatly from the editorial work of Golfo Alexopoulos, whose introduction explains how the import of the present volume goes even beyond the valuable light it sheds on the Gulag and the Soviet system. It is, as she recognized immediately, the story of an at once quintessential and highly unusual twentieth-century life. The account of Rossi's commitment to and disillusionment with communism is an international story; his experiences as a foreigner inside the Soviet Union, as "Jacques the Frenchman," his moniker in the camps, were highly cross-cultural. Ultimately, the book is a record of his personal and political battles over memory and conscience. In her valuable "Afterword to the English Edition," Michèle Sarde adds additional details about her collaboration with Rossi and the nature of their interactions. As she emphasizes, Rossi's entire life's journey had made him a "man of secrets." It was their rapport and partnership over many years that helped peel away the secretive layers surrounding his memories. As a result, Rossi's experiences and his reflections, set in their historical context, are available to us all.

# Introduction

GOLFO ALEXOPOULOS

The present work is a conversation between friends, Michèle Sarde and Jacques Rossi, one a writer and professor of French literature at Georgetown University and the other a survivor of the Stalinist forced labour camps or Gulag. The exchange focuses on Jacques's remarkable and improbable life that spanned the twentieth century, from his aristocratic upbringing in Poland to his work as a Soviet spy in interwar Europe to his Gulag detention, and finally his search for home in France and the United States. Not only a chronicle of the Gulag, this book is a memoir of the Soviet socialist movement. Author of the groundbreaking and highly influential *The Gulag Handbook*, Rossi reflects on the Soviet project, Stalinism, and the forced labour camp system, as well as belief and disillusionment among diverse socialists in Eastern Europe, Russia, and the West. The book is a history of Stalinism through the eyes of its ardent defender and sharp critic – the same person, only at different life moments.

The dialogue distinguishes this work from other memoirs, as the narrative is shaped in part by the penetrating questions of the interlocutor. Crucial elements of Jacques's past emerged only slowly, as the trust between friends and Michèle's gentle probing brought to the surface stories that Rossi had kept buried. He was indeed "a man of secrets," as she writes in her afterword to this volume. There are many insightful memoirs of the Gulag and the Soviet experience, where the writers craft

---

I would like to express my deepest appreciation to Michèle Sarde for entrusting me with this wonderful project and for her generous support. I am very grateful to Elisabeth Salina Amorini and Michael David-Fox for making this edition possible. The anonymous reviewers and copyeditor for the University of Toronto Press provided important suggestions that improved this book. I thank them and our editor, Stephen Shapiro, for their invaluable assistance.

the story themselves and select what to reveal and what to leave unexplored.[1] This book is different. Michèle pushed Jacques to express the uncomfortable, and the result is a rich and honest account of a life profoundly affected by Stalinism. For example, a decade after the collapse of the Soviet Union, Jacques finally admitted that prior to his arrest he had worked as a Soviet spy. He kept this secret deeply hidden, and it emerged only in the course of extended conversations with Michèle. "Even he was surprised when he told me the truth," she writes.

Throughout Jacques Rossi's long and remarkable life, he went from being one of Soviet socialism's staunchest defenders to among its most persecuted victims, and finally, one of its most eloquent critics. This is a story of one man's journey from communist activist to prisoner, from believer to witness. Jacques examined, at times uncomfortably, his own experiences of belief, indignity, trauma, and shame, as Michèle carefully elicits these sensitive details. The narrative takes the reader from Poland to Spain to the Soviet Union, back to Poland, France, and the United States, through some of the twentieth century's critical moments – the rise of fascism, the Spanish civil war, Stalinist terror, Khrushchev's de-Stalinization at home and in Eastern Europe, the Cold War, the collapse of the Soviet Union, and memory of post-communism. As a young man growing up in interwar Poland, Jacques Rossi rejected his aristocratic upbringing, as it appeared to be a sterile and brutal vestige of a bygone era. Instead, like many young Central European intellectuals of his generation, he became drawn to Marxism and its promise of social justice. Youthful enthusiasm for radical political and social change was not uncommon among his class at the time.[2]

Jacques possessed an idealistic commitment to the Soviet Union and the dream of a communist future, and spent much of his young adulthood adopting various false identities as he worked in espionage for the Comintern and the Soviet Red Army. Years later, he would describe himself as a foolish young man, who was "headstrong and stupidly stubborn" when confronted with information about Stalinist purges or political repression. While the Western press provided critical coverage of Soviet forced collectivization, he refused to accept what he believed at the time constituted vicious slander against the Stalinist regime. Jacques worked as an operative in the communist underground in interwar Europe, travelling on different passports between countries – Germany, Spain, Belgium, and France. In Berlin, he enrolled in the Beaux-Arts and acted in plays. In Moscow, he took classes on Marxism and philosophy. He did not form close friendships in his youth but led the solitary life of a committed communist operative. Jacques recalled denouncing a man who condemned a Gulag project, and later hearing about the man's subsequent arrest. He seemed sure that the arrest was not the result of his denunciation, but the reader is left wondering. By his own admission, Jacques would have done anything to advance the cause to which he was so deeply committed. He also insisted that he was always an unimportant low-level functionary, despite ample clues in the present work that appear to contradict his self-assessment.

Zealous communist believers like himself made easy victims, Jacques asserts. They were too trusting of the regime. He and others who worked in the communist underground in interwar Europe willingly returned to Moscow at the height of Stalin's purges in the late 1930s, despite indications that their arrest was imminent. Like many who were charged with so-called counter-revolutionary crimes, Jacques wrote numerous petitions against his arrest and proclaiming his innocence. But as the months in confinement turned into years, and as he moved from prisons to camps meeting many people like himself, he gradually ceased to believe. Such a change of heart was not unusual among former prisoners, although some remained steadfast in their beliefs despite their ordeal.[3] Jacques became critical of his younger self. He characterized his earlier blind commitment to the "unrealizable utopia" as not only naive but one that inescapably leads to "crime and lying." It was hard for him to identify the exact moment when he stopped believing, when he "changed like animals that lose their skin, their feathers or their carapace," but it took many years.

Jacques spent some of the most important years of his life in the camps. He was twenty-eight years old when he was arrested in Moscow and not yet thirty when he was sent to the Gulag in 1939. After a brief release, he returned to the camps during the wave of purges in the late 1940s, when many former prisoners were rearrested and given longer sentences – fifteen, twenty, and twenty-five years. Historical works on the Gulag have been published since this book first appeared in French, and they enhance what is recounted here.[4] Yet Jacques not only provides insight on the Soviet forced labour camp system, but he connects his pre-Gulag, Gulag, and post-Gulag experiences. His observations and commentary often surprise. A fellow inmate and close friend betrayed him, yet another prisoner he hardly knew refused to denounce him. The Stalinist camps detained a remarkable diversity of prisoners, largely Russian and non-Russian Soviet citizens, but also a number of Yugoslavs, Albanians, Englishmen, Austrians, Greeks, Chinese, Koreans, Japanese, even Americans. Jacques also noted that he rarely observed pure sadism among the camp guards. Those working in the camps could not act independently. He blames the system for the cruelty that he believed largely involved individuals trying to protect themselves.

Like Aleksandr Solzhenitsyn and others, Jacques came to believe that the Gulag constituted the fundamental expression of the Soviet order. It was the system that was criminal and not necessarily the people it employed. He called this "institutional sadism." In his view, "the Gulag was part of the Soviet communist system," the same system to which "I had been ready to give my life a thousand times over." Although he admits that rules and regulations varied according to the year and the camp, there were certain constants, like one captured in the Gulag proverb "When you carry your head under your arm, then you'll be exempted from work." He rejected the notion that the Marxist-Leninist project had simply gone astray under Stalin, and was "convinced that this project is an illusion that can only lead to disaster." According to Jacques, the purpose of Soviet oppression and exploitation was to find scapegoats for the unrealized and unrealizable utopia, to frighten the public into submission, and to generate prison labour. On the Nazi-Soviet comparison, Jacques is unambiguous. He observed many similarities between the twentieth century's two totalitarianisms and lamented that "Soviet crimes were never publicly condemned like the Nazi crimes."

Long after he left the camps and prisons, Jacques Rossi called prisoners in the Soviet Union his "brothers" and reminded Michèle that his deep desire to combat social injustice was what drew him to the communist movement in the first place. He found it troubling that Soviet society treated ethnic Russians considerably worse than foreigners, and that women faced so much discrimination, despite the official party rhetoric of equality. He deplored Soviet-style classism and the disparities between the everyday lives of the party rich and the ordinary Russian poor. The resilience of Soviet citizens and their ability to endure hardship greatly impressed him. Jacques's narrative lacks an anti-Russian undertone, as he often spoke with compassion of the masses of ordinary Russian criminal offenders in the camps. He fondly recalled the old women in Krasnoyarsk who watched with sympathy as prisoners were marched through their town, and the Tajik and Russian professors who carried his frail body to the police station after his hunger strike in Samarkand. Jacques told the story of a guard who took the risk of entering his cell late at night during his hunger strike in order to offer him homemade food. He refused the gift, yet deeply regretted having offended the man and rejected his courageous act of kindness. These were the moments that often struck him the most – the surprising and courageous acts of compassion in an environment of fear and cruelty.

Like hundreds of thousands of political prisoners, Jacques was released from the camps during Nikita Khrushchev's de-Stalinization campaign. The new Soviet leader gradually dismantled the Gulag following the death of Stalin in 1953.[5] As an ex-prisoner, Jacques was forbidden to settle in the major cities, but the authorities could not tell him which cities were unrestricted. Life shifted now from the brutal to the absurd. He had to stumble upon a city on his own after multiple attempts. This way, the regime could avoid mention of forced exile and claim that the former prisoner himself "chose Samarkand." The ex-prisoner discovered to his surprise that he was given Soviet citizenship without his consent. Unlike most former inmates, Jacques was born and raised outside the Soviet Union. Prior to his arrest, he was a Polish citizen, but he had been working as a spy under various aliases. He strenuously objected to his Soviet citizenship, but the regime may have forced it on him to mitigate the security risk involved in having former prisoners and state enemies living abroad.[6]

Jacques's resistance prompted a long battle to return to France, the place he identified as home. Remarkably, he managed to jump the fence at the French embassy in Moscow, but then could not bring himself to ask for asylum. His ordeal might have ended there had he not been burdened by feelings of guilt. He refused to seek favours and assistance from a French capitalist government that he had once devoted himself to overthrowing. It seemed wrong "to take advantage of the French ambassador's generosity and create problems for him by begging for political asylum." Jacques's sense of dignity and his conscience are striking, but his behaviour was also dictated by a burden that he carried, a belief that he was himself at least partly responsible for his own suffering. Rather than seek political asylum at the French embassy, Jacques followed Soviet instructions and made his way to Samarkand. He was told that he must first register there as a former prisoner before he could petition for repatriation.

Local authorities in Samarkand simply refused, and Jacques found himself stuck there, working at an institute translating articles. Nonetheless, he appreciated his life there. He liked the fact that Muslim society had not been completely displaced by Soviet culture, and he enjoyed the traditional cultural celebrations, the cuisine, the music, and the weather. He could have spent the rest of his life in Samarkand, he says, but he wanted to return to his beloved France. This turned out to be especially difficult because Jacques had no family there. Eventually, he attempted to leave the USSR as a citizen of Poland and overcame the bureaucratic resistance to his request by going on hunger strikes.

Jacques finally left the Soviet Union for Poland in 1961 at the age of fifty-two and after spending roughly twenty years in Soviet prisons and labour camps.

Few historical accounts provide such insight into the status of foreigners in Stalin's and Khrushchev's USSR as well as the difficult process of repatriation. Jacques spent decades in Soviet camps and prisons, but his experience following release is no less informative than his life as an inmate. He decided to write *The Gulag Handbook* because, as Michèle explains, the linguist took great interest in the peculiar language of the Gulag's recidivist criminals. One of the most valued books on the history of the Stalinist camps, *The Gulag Handbook* constitutes an encyclopedia of both official Soviet terms and prisoner jargon, with detailed explanations and cross-referencing.[7] Jacques used his exceptional memory, aided by memorization techniques, to remember hundreds of words and phrases (official and colloquial) that he encountered in the camps. He sought not only to compose a dictionary of Gulag slang, but to teach the public about the Stalinist forced labour camp system. According to Michèle, he kept notes during his time in detention because he knew that this monstrosity could happen again. Jacques felt the need to educate others about the camps, especially given his own naivety: "I felt that my mistake had been so profound, so serious that I had the obligation to warn the world so that such mistakes could be avoided."

Jacques's memory, his sense of mission, and his education helped him to survive the Gulag. He was highly literate, so camp officials recruited him at times to prepare reports. In this way, he was at times spared the most punishing physical labour – in mining, forestry, and construction. His knowledge and love of languages helped him too. Sometimes he served as a translator, interpreter, and mediator. At times he tutored in English. He had skills as an artist, so he could do portraits of camp supervisors, employees, and prisoners, including a few hardened criminal offenders who were so flattered by Jacques's portraits that they offered him protection. Jacques did set design for the camp theatre and worked as a draftsman, doing architectural or engineering drawings for the planning department. His astonishing memory helped when he needed to recall places and names, and the precise addresses of friends in Moscow, Poland, or Japan. He read and studied a great deal, and he found his fellow prisoners fascinating. He believed that being a Frenchman was advantageous because he lacked any Soviet family that could be used for blackmail. He maintained that he did not have to denounce anyone or inform on anyone, which could have earned him enemies among the prisoners. Jacques states that he was never badly beaten and was in relatively good health during his time in detention. Interestingly, he claims that he was only "an indirect witness" to the worst in the camps. When in prison following his arrest, he could not bear to hear the moans of the tortured, as if he refused to acknowledge them. But what he witnessed affected him nonetheless. Years passed before he could speak about mass starvation in the camps. To survive, he said, one needed to remain mentally sharp, be lucky, and "lie endlessly."

Life in the West presented its own distinct challenges. Jacques struggled to find understanding and support among intellectuals on the political left, his natural circle of friends. Some of them worried that the right would exploit his experience for their own political gain. As Jean-Paul Sartre told his friend Albert Camus, "Like you, I find these camps intolerable, but I find equally intolerable the use made of them every day in the bourgeois press."[8] French editors who were interested in publishing Jacques's *The Gulag Handbook* feared that doing so would advance the interests of traditional anti-communists. Others questioned the truth of his testimony or maintained that "it is not right to reveal facts that are embarrassing to the USSR, which contributed so greatly to liberating Europe from fascism!" For many intellectuals in the postwar years, as Tony Judt explained, "Philo-Communism, or at least anti-anti-Communism, was the logical essence of anti-Fascism."[9] Given their attraction to Marxism, many of his closest friends listened to his experiences with distinct unease. His dear friends Emma and Harry, an American couple and old communists, found his testimony unpleasant and even in some sense wrong, as they believed such information served the cause of their political adversaries.

According to Jacques, leftists in the West were initially very interested in his personal story, but later they began to avoid him because, in his view, "I represented a living witness to their hypocrisy." Despite revelations about the Gulag, Jacques's communist friends in the West refused to let such information shake their faith. They wanted to believe that "everything was the fault of Stalin." One insisted that the Gulag was by far the most humane system for re-educating social deviants, as the Soviet regime had claimed. At least initially, French intellectual circles were reluctant to accept him, even if later they embraced him completely. According to Jacques, they knew better, they had the information available to them, and yet they "continued for the sake of their own reputation or because of intellectual complacency to praise that wicked system!" Jacques remained very critical of Western intellectuals who defended the Soviet system despite ample evidence of its crimes. Perhaps this bothered him so profoundly because he had done the same when he was younger. As fellow traveller Arthur Koestler noted, "Each of us carries a skeleton in the cupboard of his conscience; added together they would form galleries of bones more labyrinthine than the Paris catacombs."[10] In the course of this life, Jacques developed a profound sense of guilt and shame concerning his old beliefs. In his view, he was "very responsible for the erroneous project" to which he had committed his life. He blamed himself for overlooking the unpleasant realities that did not conform to his worldview. Later, he asserted that he and other former communists were complicit in Stalinist crimes because they denied them for so long. This explains why, despite all he endured, he did not consider himself a victim, but rather a witness. The voice in this highly original work shifts artfully between Michèle and Jacques, and what emerges is a story of the Gulag and post-Gulag experience that is unlike any other. For Jacques was a Frenchman, and this identity shaped his ordeal profoundly.

JACQUES THE FRENCHMAN

Memories of the Gulag

# The Meeting

> In life there are unexpected meetings. This courteous, almost ceremonial man had a life whose tragedy defies our imagination.
> Alain Besançon, preface to *Le manuel du Goulag*

He knocked firmly yet discretely. It was the fall of 1982 at Georgetown University in the capital of the United States. It must have been late in the afternoon because I remember that I had just lit the lamp on my desk. I was finishing a day filled with too many classes, meetings, committees, and visits from students. I was in a hurry to go home.

Behind the door stood an unexpected visitor, a frail man with an angular face and black piercing eyes who introduced himself in French with the courtesy of traditional France. He was sorry to inconvenience me. He simply wanted, on the advice of Aurelia Roman, one of my colleagues of Romanian origin, to find out if it would be possible to teach several French classes in our department.

At that time, Jacques must have been seventy-three years old. He was dressed the same way I would always see him since that day: pants and a jacket in shades of grey, which looked like nothing worn by my colleagues at the university. I attempted to avoid his question: I was not the department head who assigned classes, but I could certainly recommend a candidate. For that purpose, I had to know whether he was "qualified." Qualified! Did I really say that word, or have I reinvented it almost twenty years after the meeting?

Jacques Rossi did not smile. Much later I would know him to be very ironic when referring to himself and to the world around him. He answered that he was qualified because he was French and spoke French, and indicated that I could have a look at his résumé if I wanted to.

We were still at the door when he handed me his résumé, three typed pages, written in English. I stepped back towards the light of my desk lamp and he took a step forward. In fact, I looked at his document in a bureaucratic way, quickly trying to see what was meaningful, what was useful. The section on education immediately caught my attention with this phrase: "Survival Studies, the Gulag Archipelago 1937–1957." The two preceding lines mentioned another kind of study: "Fine Arts Graduate, Berlin, Akademie am Hardenberg Platz and École des Beaux-Arts, Paris, 1923–1934, and Oriental Civilizations (Chinese and Indian History and Languages), Sorbonne and ELOV, Paris 1929–1936."

I kept this résumé and I am looking at it as I write these lines. It began by stating his objectives: "I would like to extend my stay in the United States, by a temporary appointment at an institution of higher learning which would permit me to earn a living by teaching and giving lectures in the different fields that I know first-hand. I am also looking to take advantage of this respite in an atmosphere of intellectual freedom in order to publish a scientific reference work dedicated to the Soviet labour camps of which I have first-hand knowledge."

Born in 1909, Jacques Rossi spent twenty years of his life in the Gulag. The Gulag had been his school, his university, his experience, his career, and the object of his research. This is what he claimed in his résumé.

Stunned, I fell into the chair reserved for students and visitors and showed him to the other chair. That evening we did not speak a lot about French classes or about the Georgetown Jesuits who had offered him asylum in their library so that he could finish writing what would become *The Gulag Handbook*, a work of first-hand knowledge of the Gulag. On the contrary, we talked about the Gulag right away, and only about that. Jacques spoke about the Gulag in his inimitable way, full of humility and panache, lucidity and biting black humour.

From that evening on, Jacques tried to make me understand one of the secrets of his survival. No, he did not consider himself an innocent victim. A tough communist, a member of Comintern who had chosen to actively collaborate in the destruction of the capitalist world, he had been lucky to find a school of truth in the Gulag. No, the price to be paid for having followed a myth is not onerous. If you insisted, he would have been almost thankful for it.

I would like to say that I immediately understood Jacques's denial, on which he always insisted so strongly. However, I would be lying. I started by seeing in Jacques a victim and above all a survivor of the camps. This is more understandable if I add that, as the granddaughter of deportees, I am extremely sensitive to this topic. I waited for years, waited for any kind of information, and even after, when adults knew that there was no more hope, I continued to wait for my grandfather and grandmother to return from the Nazi camps, convinced that one evening they would knock on the door of our Parisian apartment, like Jacques Rossi had done that evening on the door of my office.

There was affinity, confidence, and friendship that linked Jacques and me together from that very first second, even before I had done a more thorough study of his résumé in which I could see that this man who was so slight and yet so strong must have seen the face of Gorgon and come back.

But being Jacques's friend did not stop me from imagining things about him. Based on tales, passionately listened to and deformed, over the years I created a legend for myself about Jacques's life, which the media sometimes relayed when it started to speak about him. In this legend, which this book should help to demystify, Jacques would be the rejected child of a noble family, whose French mother married a Polish aristocrat whom Jacques calls "the stepfather" (see my afterword). Exiled in Poland with his dearly beloved mother, who died when Jacques was only ten, he became aware of social injustice through the class relationships that manifested themselves in the domains and properties of the distant stepfather. At sixteen he became a member of the illegal Polish communist party; soon after he was arrested and detained for several months. Upon coming out of prison, he became a liaison agent for the Comintern. During the Spanish Civil war, while on a mission for the Spanish Republicans, the young Rossi was called to Moscow and comrade Stalin had him arrested. He was about twenty-eight years old when he was arrested and condemned to the Gulag. He left the Gulag after Stalin's death, twenty years later.

This premature sketch that I had of Jacques and his history when I first knew him (but did not know his life) would be modified and become more precise fourteen years later in 1999, when we recorded his testimony. We were once again in Washington, during the azalea season. Jacques was then ninety years old; he had come back, as a known author, to the place where he had worked to finish his book and passionately hoped for its publication. I learned that Jacques was accustomed to these repeat visits. He had returned as a free and celebrated man to Norilsk in the Arctic some forty years after his long detention in the camps of that Siberian city, built by prisoners like him. *Revisiting* is the English term that so well captures both Jacques's journey and the work we accomplished together on his story.

At first, he wanted this work to be presented as fiction, and he proposed that I write a novel based on his life. That is why he came to a writer rather than to a historian. In his complex and very secretive existence, so rich in events and in meetings, he knew that there was the risk of omission, of simplification and of silence. He knew that all memories have their limitations and that he was reaching ninety. He considered that because of the millions of sacrificed lives, it was not appropriate to grant his own person particular and special attention. Above all, he affirmed that his private life belonged only to him.

However, the force of his testimony made any attempt at a fictional rendition completely inadequate. It became obvious that the truth of such a man required that no artifice be used. There was no reason to replace one subjectivity by another. A man, as André Malraux stated, is not what he hides but what he is. And according to the truthful phrase of Tzvetan Todorov, "even without being preoccupied in the same way by the concern for truth, the speech of a witness enriches that of the historian."[1]

Some people have the vocation to be witnesses and some to be artists. For Jacques, the methodical work of remembering had begun early. After years of detention, Jacques the prisoner well understood that the member of the Comintern and Jacques himself were not two distinct people that the system had confused by mistake. He opened his eyes to the other prisoners, his companions, and to the nefarious system that had transformed everyone into convicts. He lived to record and absorb. In a universe where paper and pencil were forbidden objects, where the slightest writing could mean a lengthening of one's confinement by several years, he relied on an exceptional memory to record his observations. He used it on a daily basis when he was in solitary confinement. And when the regime became less strict he wrote quick notes on tiny pieces of paper, which he managed to hide from the frequent searches.

A year after he left the Soviet Union in 1961, in a Poland that was communist but less strict than the USSR, he transferred his memories into writing and drafted hundreds of memoranda. This precise work would lead to *The Gulag Handbook*, a kind of encyclopedic dictionary describing in detail the prison universe that he knew so well, in order to understand via the Gulag system "the true essence of communist totalitarianism." That work, written with the dry passion of precision, which would have delighted the novelist Marguerite Yourcenar, was published in Russian in London in 1987, then in English in New York in 1989, in Russian in Moscow in 1991, in Japanese in 1996, in Czech in 1999. Its author had to wait about ten years after its first publication to see his work published in Paris in his native language in 1997. But hadn't he himself waited patiently more than four decades before entering "the world of his ancestors," Avenue of the Resistance in Montreuil?

It is also this story of patience that we tried to grasp in the thirty or so tapes that contain the essential part of our meetings. Now as I write these lines, at the beginning of 2000, Jacques is still waiting patiently. He is waiting for me to write the story that he asked me to write, based on our conversations. Essentially based on listening, my role in this task will be first that of a questioner and a narrator. In this tragedy, which uses catharsis with its techniques of terror and pity, I will alternate identifying myself with the chorus and with the spectators. Confronting this former prisoner of the Gulag who is testifying, I will assume the roles of those who were irresponsible, of those who did not want to know. One after the other, I will be the spoiled child of our coddled society, the leftist intellectual, the accomplice in the prosecution of Nazi totalitarianism, more publicized and better known than its opposite and complement, Soviet totalitarianism. These are the faces that Jacques needs to confront in order to exorcise the pain that is even more agonizing because it goes beyond his person and represents that of the millions of prisoners in the Gulag hell.

In spite of this constant and necessary confrontation, the narration is the result of a close collaboration. The nature of our pact did not authorize the distance that permits a narrator to employ other criteria to evaluate the choices of his or her witness. This book is not an autobiography of Jacques Rossi because it is written by another person and because certain details of his private family life remain in his secret garden. It is not traditional historical biography because it is primarily inspired by the vision the witness has of himself. Nor is it a novel because nothing has been invented. It is, above all, the story of a life where the voice of the witness is translated, as accurately as possible, with the modulation, the intonation, and the rhythm of his voice, and also its silences.

The story told here is that of a man who, starting from what he calls a vision, knew how to constantly expand his experience of self-understanding. It is the story of a man who never sank into despair, despite having spent twenty years and more of his life in the jails of an inhumane system, which he himself had defended with humanistic zeal. It is the story of a man who not only survived horror, but resisted it.

Through his Gulag experience, Jacques tenaciously constructed an identity capable of survival and resistance. His was the journey of an idealist, whom the system did not manage to corrupt or destroy. Along the way, he refused to compromise himself. This narration will probably be one of the very last living testimonies of Soviet totalitarianism from the 1930s, and one of the rare works written by a Frenchman. We decided together to title it *Jacques the Frenchman*, using the name that his companions in the Gulag gave to this foreign communist. It is intended for a readership that will have the opportunity to learn first hand what other human beings experienced in that era. Thus, the journey of Jacques Rossi joins that of other witnesses born at the dawn of the twentieth century and whose exemplary destiny enlightens that somber period, a period that did not make them disappear like millions of others nor imposed silence upon them. Jacques is one of the great transmitters of experience from one century to the next.

Michèle Sarde

# PART 1

# Before

In place of the old bourgeois society, with its classes and class antagonisms, we shall have an association, in which the free development of each is the condition for the free development of all.

Karl Marx and Friedrich Engels,
*The Communist Manifesto*

# 1 Never Again

> My unique consolation when I went up to go to bed was that my mother would come and kiss me when I was in my bed.
> Marcel Proust, *À la recherche du temps perdu, vol. 1: Swann's Way*

My mother and I were good friends. Talking about her is very difficult for me because really she was the only person in my life until I was ten who was my best friend. We didn't need to talk. We only needed to be next to one another. We looked at each other sometimes. We knew. It was much later, when I was a clandestine worker, that I discovered this complicity. When I was in the clandestine service, I had to collaborate with communists in countries whose language I did not speak: Hungary, Norway, Finland. In this job I had to send messages, a small package and a box to an unknown person. When I exchanged a glance in the street, I felt it immediately: here is someone who is on my side. We are both committed to a very important mission, the only one that counts. I had the same feeling with my mother. We didn't need to talk. When she played board games with me, when we played cards for example, she was there among other people, men, women, sometimes only women. Suddenly I noticed that I was making a mistake. She turned around. Our eyes met. She had a slight smile. It was the same complicity. Was it because we were not in our own country? At home we spoke French. My mother never knew how to speak Polish. She could mumble it a bit. Even when I was very small I was already her translator into Italian and German and other languages when she went shopping or during trips in Europe or when she needed to speak to the domestic help. And then naturally in Polish with the grooms at the stables when we went to see the horses, I was the interpreter.

> I remember too, on the property of the father in Poland, after the hunt, a reception with aristocrats, neighbouring landowners, and on the porch a pile of wild boars, pheasants, and deer. Later there was a party with lots of commotion. I was in bed. And I felt an urgent need to see my mother. So I called, not too loudly because I didn't really dare to scream. I was far from the grand room but she heard me, and she came in just to give me a kiss. She leaned over me. Her hand touched my hair. She was not in a hurry. She left quickly but not in haste. I remember it so well. It was eighty years ago but I remember it perfectly. From that complicity, that awareness that she was someone from whom, even in the secret work of the Comintern, I would not have had secrets.

Jacques wants to modify this last phrase. He wants to replace it with the notion that he was lucky that his mother disappeared long ago, and he did not have to hide anything from her. From this first version or lapse, we can nonetheless see that even in the clandestine nature of the secret service, this determined person working for the Comintern never spoke. Jacques, the prisoner of Butyrka prison who resisted difficult interrogations, believed that he could trust only one person, his mother. Leontine Charlotte Goyet was born in Bourg-en-Bresse, Ain, in 1877. She died in Poland when little Jacques was about ten, around 1920.

> She was so beautiful. I looked at her like one looks at the Mona Lisa. Mona Lisa, because of her discreet smile, which she kept even as she became sicker and sicker until she stayed in bed all the time … There always remained beauty in her eyes. And I looked at her like a believer looks at pictures of the Holy Virgin. Mother was tall, well, not so tall, but of course taller than I was. She had dark eyes, dark wavy hair with a part in the middle, and regular features. There was such music in her voice. When I looked at her it was pure pleasure.

Jacques held this mother, whom he dreamed of during the unending hours, weeks, and years of imprisonment, as the main object of his affection. He does not want to talk at length about most of the other women he knew in his life, but he speaks easily about his mother. She is also his reference when explaining his capacity to adapt to unknown situations. "It seems to me that for my mother and myself life was there and we took it".

And life, between 1909, the date of Jacques's birth, and 1918, the end of the Great War, was a voyage across Europe, from Italy to Sweden, from Vienna to Madrid, from Berlin to London, to Salzburg, to Lucerne, to Geneva, to Lausanne, to Bern, and even to Norway and Finland during the Russian occupation. His earliest memories of childhood are probably of Bourg-en-Bresse because that is "the town where my mother was born" and perhaps Lyons, "because when I search my memory I remember those typical streets of a certain neighbourhood in Lyons; high ceilings in the houses and memories that later I identified as details of the Tête d'Or park and the streets around Notre-Dame de Fourvière."

But above all, the first years of Jacques's childhood were marked by luxurious wanderings, coming and going from grand hotels to palaces, from rich apartments to small palaces, an existence typical of wealthy European families at the end of the century. He who would be confined for so many years in narrow cells remembers only one dwelling – in passing – in Paris near the Luxembourg Gardens. He remembered how he got to the house from the gardens. Perhaps from the rue de Fleurus: "It was the street that went directly to the garden, a kind of prolongation of that street and it was on the right because we didn't walk a long time and just before entering the garden, we had to cross a street, probably the rue Guynemer." But he remembers with precision the pool in front of the Senate where he sailed his toy boat, the alley with the ponies and the donkeys.

And then the image stops. The memory is frozen. He is in the Luxembourg Gardens around 1916. He was barely seven. He was accompanied by his nanny because the governess, with superior standing, did not have any contact with the external world of the lower classes. A soldier approached them with his azure blue uniform. He spoke to the nanny. The garden was full of these men who wore uniforms but who were no longer soldiers. Some of them dragged their feet; others walked with crutches. There were also double amputees who moved forward on small platforms, pushing on the ground with wooden paddles. The child was impressed. It was the first time that he saw a man who had no legs. Another time he was struck by a terrible face, that of a blind man whose eyes had disappeared from his face. After the man was wounded by a grenade, an eye hidden by skin had been put back as carefully as possible. As for the other eye, it was no longer in its place; it was only an empty hole, while another horizontal slit marked the absence of his lips.

These people with no legs, no arms, who are they, the child asked? He heard the sombre answer: "They are the wounded of the war." So, while the nanny let herself be courted by a soldier, little Jacques observed. For a certain time he had heard many conversations where the mysterious word "the war" was uttered, as well as the expressions that adults used all the time: "Never again."

> I kept in my memory, in my ears: "Never again!" "The war to end all wars!" It was really dramatic, like Greek theatre; not only the intonation of the voices of these adults, but also their eyes. I tried to

copy them; I imitated their style ... These gestures, these eyes looking skyward, sometimes their hands; I realized to what extent it was serious. If later I believed in communist ideals, it was also because they promised to end all wars!

War was that black cloud which frightened adults. He studied at length the illustrated pages of drawings and prints in *L'Illustration*. The portrait of an invalid, it was almost pretty in the magazine. Nothing like the terrifying men in the Luxembourg Gardens. The child also liked to draw. Eighty-five years later he could still recall the box of crayons and his erasers. Later, he was a student at the Beaux Arts. In the Gulag, he would be able to use his talent. He often made portraits of his fellow prisoners.

The mother who watched her five-year-old artist could hardly imagine what his destiny would be. Nonetheless, for her and because of her, he developed aptitudes that later became useful in the secret service and during his deportation: the gifts of languages and drawing, the love of books and writing, and an incredible memory. Very early, his mother taught him to write and read and the basics of mathematics. Since he was considered too fragile, he was not sent to school. When he was six he knew his letters and numbers. All by himself, he took an interest in the alphabets of the languages to which he was exposed. He copied the Russian alphabet from the illustrated *Larousse*. He looked for similarities in the letters of different alphabets. He discovered that, contrary to French, in some languages for every sound there was only one character. In mathematics, sadly, he was always slow: "Today when I go shopping, I always give my wallet to the cashier so that she can take the coins and bills from it. Because I have difficulty counting and when I have to pay I confuse twenty-cent coins and francs."

He learned to read very quickly and read the children's book series *Bibliothèque Rose*. He remembers the beauty of the volumes, gold on the back with their hard covers and their illustrations made from copper plates. His stepfather studied architecture in Germany, and Jacques thought that he went to visit worksites in all the countries of Europe. He believed it because he saw his stepfather make copies of architectural plans. At a time of no copying machines, copies of architectural plans were made by exposing them to the sun, then by dipping them in a kind of bath in very large tubs. Sometimes Jacques was allowed to help, and that pleased him greatly.

During this waltz through Europe, his playmates changed constantly, just as his companions in the Gulag would change. He adapted quickly and soon spoke several languages. At home, of course, his mother and the one Jacques sometimes called the "stepfather," sometimes the

"Polish father," and who was officially Jacques's father, if not (perhaps) his biological father, spoke French.[1] The father also spoke German, his native language in which he had studied, English – he had a cousin in London – and Russian, in spite of his antipathy as a Polish patriot for that language. The child spoke mainly French but also German with his Alsatian maternal grandmother, who sometimes visited them in Paris when they stayed there a while.

In Riga in Latvia, little Jacques managed to play in Russian and German. Once, in Budapest, he had difficulty communicating in Hungarian, but there were some children who could jabber in German. He would visit some of these places again some twenty years later as a wandering secret agent for the Comintern. As an agent, he pursued the destruction of this world, the very world that created him and from which he benefitted as a child.

It was a luxurious existence. The staff was numerous. Jacques, however, could distinguish between the domestics of the house and those of hotels. He lived his early childhood surrounded by nurses and maids who later were replaced by more distant tutors and governesses. The nannies contributed to his linguistic experience. They were French, Swiss, and Austrian. He remembers a nanny in 1912 and 1913 with different eyes who taught him to sit on the floor; he learned years later that she was from Laos.

> A long time later, around 1950, I was in a high-security prison in eastern Siberia and I was put in a cell with Japanese men. The habit of sitting cross-legged saved my legs because in those freezing cold prison cells, having your feet on the ground meant getting rheumatism. I have always had very cold feet. The Japanese had permission to sit on their beds. The others couldn't. This special treatment did not constitute extraordinary generosity. After the Second World War, the Russian communists thought that they could sell those war prisoners back to Japan for political gain. Since this way of sitting was their tradition, I benefitted from it thanks to my Laotian nanny.

This child of the rich was frail and in poor health. He was not allowed to run or swim or skate. Only sledding was permitted. He might get too hot. He might catch a cold. And what if he perspired? In Siberia, he dug out the frozen trunks of trees, but in his youth he could not play with other children because he was considered too fragile. He was taken to Alexandria, which at that time had an international reputation for having fresh air that was beneficial for people with lung diseases. It was just before the outbreak of the First World War. Jacques was not yet five.

He remembered the dark skin of the Egyptians, their red fezzes and their shiny moustaches, and the fact that it was summer and his mother came with him. His health would not improve until 1927–28, when at the age of sixteen to seventeen he had his first experience with a Polish prison. How does one explain how this child raised in luxury could adapt so well to the most difficult of life experiences?

> I consider it a privilege to live, and I have never looked elsewhere for privilege. Of course, I have been in very difficult situations. In prison, I tried to improve my condition. However, we only sleep in one bed at a time; we only eat three times a day and, above all, we will be alone in our coffin. We cannot have twice that or thrice that. This is true. The hole in the ground will always be but one hole. Above all, I had the privilege of seeing misery first hand and witnessing the misery of millions of people. This often led me to ask the question, when I lived in better conditions, when I ate well: What right do I have to this better life?
>
> One time in the Butyrka prison, I managed to stick a match into the wall. I hung my shirt on this match because when we slept next to each other, we would sweat and it was disgusting to always wear the same wet shirt. It was an extraordinary comfort to hang my shirt above my head on the wall thanks to that match, which I managed to keep in place with some bread. Wet bread holds as well as cement. This match held for a long time. Luckily, the guards did not complain. At night, I was naked and soaked in sweat, but in the morning at least I could wash a bit in the showers and put on my dry shirt. This kind of comfort, you see, I looked for it in every possible situation. And, yes, your comfort, you the coddled ones, it bothers me. It's true that I got out of the Gulag, but that doesn't mean that it is finished. I know that the Gulag as I knew it no longer exists. Now there are Russian prisons and other prisons. But the prisoners are still my brothers. Don't forget that I became a communist because of social injustice.

In the sixties, when Jacques came back to France from Poland for short stays, he researched his legal identity with the help of his friends. According to his birth certificate, Jacques H. (whose name appeared as Franciszek Ksawery or François Xavier) was born in Breslau, formerly Wratislavia, in Silesia, on 10 October 1909. Breslau was then part of Germany and would not become part of Poland until 1945, when it became Wroclaw. Jacques also discovered that his mother, the French woman Leontine Charlotte Goyet, was the daughter of a carpenter and that the witnesses at her birth in 1877 were a blacksmith and a cabinetmaker. His legal father appeared as Marcin H. Thus the initial of Jacques's last name, which he does not consider his own and reluctantly reveals.

How does one reconcile Jacques's humble origins with the image of the grand lady dressed for a ball that the child looked at from the top of the marble stairs of a luxurious residence? Certainly, there were at that time misalliances and love marriages that could explain how Marcin H., heir of a rich family of landowners and businessmen, could have married the daughter of labourers. But Jacques was not indifferent to this discovery. He offers some clarity by evoking his Alsatian grandmother, whom he always knew as the widow of his cabinetmaker grandfather, and who was a lady's companion when she left to join her daughter in Poland after the war. After his seventy-year battle for justice and the abolition of class privileges, Jacques identifies himself only with this mother who was prematurely taken from him. In fact, Leontine died shortly after Marcin H. decided, out of patriotism, to go back to his family in recently independent Poland. Sylvia or Sylvie, his sister, and Piotr or Pierre, his brother, were, according to him, the biological children of Marcin H.

The 1919 Versailles treaty established an independent Polish Republic, and in Warsaw, Jozef Pilsudski became the head of state. At the conclusion of the 1920 Russo-Polish war, the Riga treaty declared the re-establishment of the Polish borders that had existed before partition. Between 1926 and 1935, Pilsudski exercised power, and beginning in 1930 he became more authoritarian. Books can confirm the historical facts that one remembers, but the confirmation of personal facts depends mainly on memory. Jacques would become angry when I insisted on verification of these personal facts. "I didn't have a notebook! ... What happened fifteen years ago, I can easily tell you, I'll find the notebook. But when I was ten, I didn't have a notebook!"

# 2 The Established Order

Not all that see have their eyes open, nor do all those see that look.
Baltasar Gracián, *The Art of Worldly Wisdom*

It was in Poland, when Jacques was about twelve, that he had his first revelation concerning social injustice. During a promenade in a carriage with his Scottish governess, they stopped to look at a field of wheat, corn, and barley. Suddenly a peasant woman interrupted the lesson, grabbing the child's hand to kiss it. He pulled his hand back abruptly. The governess who was standing behind him and was much taller than he began lecturing him: "Don't. This is the established order! Don't do that. Here we abide by the established order!"

The child was troubled. Usually Miss Dunlop, the Scottish governess, was strict but fair. And usually she explained things. For example, when there was a reception at the house, the gentlemen placed their hats on the sideboard that was by the wall in front of the big mirror in the entrance hall. The top hats had to be placed upside down, the top of the hat on the sideboard. Why? Because if, by mistake, the maid had not dusted with care, the dust would dirty the border of the hat, and the head of its owner would get dirty. Another example: eggshells. One had to crush them in one's plate before Jan cleared the table. Why? Because they could fall when he took the tray to the kitchen, and this would embarrass him needlessly. "So we crushed the egg shells! I was hurting no one by doing so and being helpful. But the established order? For the child that I was you can understand that the hand kiss was both unbecoming and repugnant. First, it was humiliating for that peasant woman, an old lady! Plus she was dirty. She worked in the fields …"

The move to Poland was a break in Jacques's childhood. For him it was like exile in the domain of Marcin H., with whom he did not get along. In the beginning, he shared this exile with his mother. After her death, despite the presence of other children, he missed her terribly. He spent time with his stepfather, whom he called "father" and with whom he used the formal "you" in the language they spoke between them (Polish or French). "The Polish father was formidable and a master. It was obvious that he had important responsibilities. As a child I did not know what they were, but I observed him and I was offended. All that respect, all that grandeur!"

The family of Marcin H. had several houses. There was notably one that was called the "palace." The villa was not as great as Versailles, but it looked like the White House, with columns, many rooms, kitchens, and quarters where the servants lived. Miss Dunlop had a private suite: "Nowhere was it labeled *private*, but we considered it to be private." Jacques sometimes played with the children of the property manager who was responsible for the house and lived nearby with his family in a beautiful house.

Life in Poland became settled. First the family lived in a hotel in Warsaw. They felt patriotic euphoria for a Poland that was finally free. Then they lived in a large apartment and later in the country where his stepfather had, so it seemed, duties as the administrator of Kutno before becoming the director of the Urban Department at the Ministry of Higher Education. There were also vacations in France. The Polish maids took the child regularly to mass. However, he does not remember having gone with his mother or with his stepfather, who only went for official ceremonies.

> They were not very religious. At that time in Poland, churches were not heated in winter and I was very sensitive to having cold feet as a child, so I did not like to go to church. However, I liked the teachings and the personality of Jesus. I had the feeling that he had sacrificed himself for the cause of justice, so that we all could be equal. Afterwards, contrary to my communist comrades, I was never hostile to religion. There is such barbarism in human beings, in each one of us! Religions in different civilizations have softened that barbarism a bit. For me, well, I have still not solved the problem: I do not know where the world comes from. If I am told that God created it, yes, but where does God come from? I still do not know the origins of DNA and how the first molecule was created. And time? When did time start? I have no idea. But this is the least of my concerns, because I have known misery. The unhappiness of billions of humans is my primary concern. With my friend Marie-Isabelle, who is a believer, we do not speak about God, but about human beings. She is studying theology in Strasbourg.

When she comes to Paris, which is rare, I accompany her from one train station to another. She has never tried to convert me. I have respect for people who believe in ideals without imposing them on others.

In Poland at school, Catholic teachings were obligatory. When I went to high school at twelve or thirteen, I took catechism classes. I had heard communism spoken about without really understanding it, and it intrigued me. So one time, after class I asked the priest a question:

What is Marxism? I was very curious to hear his answer. He took my question very seriously. He looked at me straight in the eye. I think I remember exactly what he said to me, and it was seventy-five years ago: "Marxism is something invented by the Jew Marx in order to destroy the apostolic and Roman Catholic church." I was surprised by that answer. This priest was very sincere but also very narrow-minded, and I quote his answer with such interest because several years later, around 1927, when I was sixteen or seventeen, I asked the secretary of my clandestine Polish cell the same question but about fascism. It was after Mussolini's march on Rome and people were talking about it in Poland, but I didn't know a lot about it. He was a young proletarian, and like my priest, he became very serious. And pointing his index finger at me like a professor, he answered: "Fascism is like an iron broom which capitalism uses to sweep away all the gains of the proletariat." At that moment the priest's answer came back to me. And I was doubly unsatisfied.

Between his mother and his Polish father, Jacques remembers that there was a certain "complicity" and that they called to each other in the garden of the villa, whistling the beginning of an opera aria. Marcin H. was an important bureaucrat in independent Poland when the authoritarian regime of Pilsudski was established in 1919. Jacques drew a distinction between that regime and a "dictatorship." When he was very small Jacques asked his maid one day why she hadn't bought what they had set out to buy. "She responded, 'We don't have enough money.' I thought, No problem! We were in front of one of those banks that at the time displayed bills and coins. And I thought that we were going to that bank to buy money because we didn't have any."

Until his mother's death, Jacques didn't go to school. He was taught by tutors, one of whom was Russian, from a family that had fled the communists in 1920. The tutor was supposed to teach him mathematics, but he spoke mainly about Bakunin and Plekhanov. A very serious young woman taught him history. Jacques remembers other tutors who checked his school notebooks and that his "father" made very severe comments about those notebooks.

Little by little, the son of a wealthy man grew to see himself as the son of a family within an authoritarian and hierarchical society. During a train trip alone when he was twelve or thirteen he was disgusted by the state of the bathrooms at the train station. He risked soiling his lovely leather suitcase.

> What could I do? I was not going to put it on the floor in the pee … there were two policemen on the platform. So, very politely, like I had seen my stepfather do, I asked them: "Please be nice and watch my luggage while I go to the bathroom." I considered it normal that policemen would help everyone. They answered me politely. I looked like the son of important people and with important people one never knows! This small service was not part of their official duties. Their duties consisted of starting an inquiry in case the suitcase was stolen.

Other realities, however, seemed less and less normal to the pre-teen living within a family of many rules, like the servility of the underclass as illustrated by the hand kiss of the peasant woman. The same happened with the coachman. The child loved this fifty-year-old who spoke so well about horses, who knew so many human truths, and spoke to him with such wisdom. "But as soon as father appeared I discovered with surprise the distance that separated us. The coachman took off his cap. He did not salute but his attitude changed. For example, if he were sitting, he would stand up. Obviously, I felt more like an equal with the coachman than with my stepfather, and when he took off his cap to answer questions or orders from his master, I felt I was on the side of the coachman."

Then there were the maids who pampered him on the sly. When Marcin H. appeared again, everyone froze with appropriate gestures. The young boy learned this double game that would help him later when he worked underground. "It consisted of appearing to be what I was not and carrying secret messages." Human warmth, especially after the death of his mother, came from those maids. Jacques remembered their warm hugs, their care, and particularly the ordeal of the meals:

> At dinner, a child had to eat everything that was put on his plate. He had to eat everything. Luckily, one of the maids at my father's home knew what I didn't like. She would remove what I didn't like from my plate and swallow it. I remember that I was unhappy when she couldn't do it. The meal did not continue. Everyone stopped eating and waited while I ate, staring at me. I cried. I swallowed. I don't know how that woman managed to help me, but I am grateful to her even to this day.

When his accomplice was not serving at the dinner table, sometimes the child could not swallow. He was stubborn. He resisted. Then he was punished and sent to his room. The door was not closed, but he did not have permission to leave his room. The Scottish governess came in regularly to see if he had changed his mind.

> "How are things? Where are you?"
> The child did not give in.
> "I'm here. I'm staying here!"

It is probable that this stubbornness was a trait that became worse after the death of his mother. His mother's illness remains a vague memory for him. One day she was not at breakfast. From that day forward, he visited her in her room with the governess.

> It was a bit like in a film, where you see your mother in bed. She kissed me, said two or three words. She did not move and that worried me. I was afraid of the stuffy atmosphere, with the blinds closed, the soft noise, and the smell of medicine. There was nearly always a nurse in white. When a doctor rang, we ran to the door. They were always elegant men, with black ties, wing collars, and glasses on a chain, who spoke gravely and whom even the governess listened to with respect. After the visit they went and talked in Polish with father.

One morning, he was not taken to see his mother. Several days later, he was told that she had left. No one ever told him that she had died. He has no memory of her burial. A bit later, the Polish maid told him to take off his jacket. She had to put a mourning band on his arm. He had seen people around him wear mourning bands in memory of those among them who had died. He thought that it was a sign. Deep inside he *knew*. He had known the minute they told him that his mother had left. But he didn't ask any questions.

Compared to others, he was a difficult child. He even calls himself "mean," but he doesn't use the word "rebellious." "What does that mean, rebellious? I often read in the press about rebellious children. Rebel against Stalin, yes. That is worth the effort. But rebelling in a situation with no risk? That's inconsequential. The person is only trying to get attention."

After the death of his mother, the family moved to the country, where Marcin H. had been appointed prefect. For the first time, he sent his son to a public secondary school. The enrolment in a Polish high school posed several bureaucratic problems because Jacques did not have a primary school certificate. These problems were quickly resolved thanks to his father's connections with the director. At the high school, the boy got bad grades in every subject except drawing. His father became angry. He used the horse whip that hung in the entrance hall and which he used when he went riding.

> He was not sadistic about it. I didn't have to lower my pants. He simply held the report card and he asked me: "Does a Polish student have the right to get bad grades in Polish language class?" I thought and then I answered, "No."
> "Does a French person have the right to get bad grades in French class? Does a Catholic have the right to get bad grades in catechism?" And so on. "Could one get a bad grade in gym?"
> Except in drawing, where I was always good, the answer was consistently no. As with Marxism or Leninism or Catholicism, where everything was known ahead of time, the answer could only be yes or no.

Jacques recognized that he made fun of the pronunciation of his French teacher, a woman who had learned the language of Moliere in Poland. He also hated authority, especially that of his father and that of all the other children. He was the only one who was spanked. "Especially during the summer at the family home there were cousins, brothers, and my sister. All the children were treated the same way except for me. Father's mother hit with the back of her hand. I remember the deformed arthritic ring finger on her right hand. I was the only one who got the slaps and the horse whip, proof that I was difficult and different from the others."

As for the Alsatian grandmother who joined the family in Poland, she does not seem to have consoled him at all after the death of her daughter. She was thin and energetic. She had blotchy skin, grey hair, and she wore steel glasses. Jacques remembers her as being very strict and wearing a bunch of keys at her belt that permitted access to the locked closets. She had the position of manager and firmly directed the staff, who feared her. At the same time, since she did not speak Polish, she had difficulty speaking to the staff. "She could pronounce their names, and for everything else she just pointed."

With the child, she spoke French and tried to teach him German, but Jacques insisted on his French patriotism. It was the period when France was trying to get Alsace and Lorraine back. The grandmother suffered living in Poland, especially after the death of her daughter, whom she did not survive for long. For her, as for Jacques, a curtain of "foreignness" isolated the home of the father from the rest of the world. One day the child surprised his grandmother, who was taking a box filled with papers out of a closet. On seeing a photo of Marcin H. when he was young, she exclaimed: "How could Leontine fall for a man like him!" This remark and others persuaded Jacques that Marcin was not his father. Another indication: Silvia and Piotr spoke French also but with an accent, with a rolled *r* that their little brother pronounced perfectly. Really, though, the son of Leontine did not need proof. He had his own convictions. Very quickly, another woman appeared in the life of the father and the family. The boy rejected her in spite of all her attempts to charm him. "Stepmother was pretty, a charming person, with a heart. But in spite of her efforts, I behaved like a frightened cat." Jacques admits that the staff liked their new mistress very much: "That could be felt. A child feels that." However, this Polish stepmother could not stand the disciplinary sessions with the horse whip. At the end of one of them, Jacques overheard her telling her husband: "If you do that again, I will leave the house."

With Aunt Marie, the sister of Marcin H., Jacques had more pleasant exchanges. Before the independence of her country, this patriot had taught in some private associations to give young Poles training to fight against the oppression of the Russian occupier. After 1919, Aunt Marie became a teacher of natural science in a secondary school. She was single and was said to be severe but fair. She had inherited a small property from her parents in an area quite far from Warsaw, formally occupied by the Russians, in Noskow, not far from Kalis, where she was a gentlewoman farmer. She was helped by two employees who worked on the land. Young Jacques spent vacations there with other children of the family. The aunt had a small herd of two cows, two horses, an orchard, and a vegetable garden where she employed her talents as a botanist. She had a beautiful two-storey main house, plus other buildings and stables. Jacques liked to stroke the horses and even ride them, although as a child he was considered too fragile to ride. He asked his Aunt Marie many questions about nature, which he was passionate about. She had the refined character of the Polish intelligentsia of the time. She spoke French, German, and English. Above all, he trusted her. She was the one who spoke about Jacques's real father, whose name was Rossi and who had been an officer in the navy and had drowned.

Jacques's life, like that of most human beings, is marked by enigmas, secrets, and masks that he cannot or does not know how to pierce. This is the way it was with the name and identity of his "real" father, which he took as his own. In the Gulag, he would be called Jacques Robertovitch Rossi alias Franciszek Ksawery H. Jacques's birth certificate, after his French naturalization and reintegration, dated 9 August 1999, states that he was permitted to be called Jacques Rossi following a decision of the Warsaw municipal council on 4 August 1962. "Jacques Rossi" could be the name of his real father, as Jacques sometimes suggests, or the borrowed identity that the secret agent temporarily adopted when he was arrested.

As for Marcin H., he was of German Jewish origin, from a Berlin family that at the end of the nineteenth century had bought land, factories, and companies in Poland, in the region of Warsaw and Lodz during the Russian occupation. The "Polish father" was part of that group of Jews that converted to Christianity and became Polish. Their patriotic zeal for Poland and hostility towards Russia was expressed with ardour. In addition, his Protestant aunt and her Catholic brother were committed to a free Poland. Marcin H.'s mother was a member of a community of Jewish women who embroidered a flag for a company of Polish anti-tsarists during the insurrection of 1863. This unique flag, which was later hung in a museum in Warsaw, was shown with pride to little Jacques.

Nearly eighty years after the events that separated him from the Polish father, and in spite of his distant memory of him, Jacques insists on paying homage to a man who was "correct" with him and did not skimp on his education, although they could never have a meaningful conversation. As for the French father, he left his son only a first name, a surname, and, according to Jacques, certain Italian characteristics. These short pieces of information are the only recollection of a paternal figure that Jacques always dreamed about.

# 3 The Future of the Worldwide Proletariat Is More Important than One's Career!

> Man is born free, and everywhere he is in chains. One thinks himself the master of others, and still remains a greater slave than they.
> Jean-Jacques Rousseau, *On the Social Contract*

I accepted the authority of the communist party, Marxism, and Marx and Engels. However, I liked Engels more than Marx because I understood what he wrote better. The philosophical and ethnographic aspects interested me more than the economic aspects. I had chosen my master. As a former good communist, I regret having preferred Engels because a good communist does not choose his authority according to his temperament. He respects Marxism-Leninism without asking questions. In fact, I chose nothing. I was chosen by the party.

I was sixteen or seventeen after the coup of Pilsudski in 1926. The communist party was illegal and you wouldn't go and become a member of an illegal clandestine party. It was the party that found you and considered you appropriate and capable. Like the Freemasons. And so I was contacted.

During adolescence, Jacques's awareness became sharper. Once he left the narrow world of his family where the only people he could observe were the staff and the peasants on the land, he opened his eyes to the world. While he was still in high school, a classmate, the son of a train conductor, invited Jacques to his house. Their high school was a public school with a diverse population. Jacques was surprised to see that the house of the train conductor had only two rooms, that the three children slept in the same room, and that the kitchen was also the living room. Above all, there was a smell, a smell that bothered the young, fragile boy: "You know, the toilets were between two floors." However, the son of the train conductor did better at school than the son of a rich family. He was the one who explained mathematics to Jacques, who had difficulty understanding math.

Slowly but surely, Jacques opened his eyes. Like the image of the young Buddha that he would later admire, he left the large garden of the family villa that was like a palace by climbing over the wall, and discovered reality. In addition to gaining practical experience, the student with the poor grades devoured his father's library, a large room whose books, even with ugly bindings, attracted the future student of the Beaux-Arts. Jacques's visits to the library were discreet: Marcin H. didn't like to have his books disturbed. When his father had guests, he wanted to be able to find a book in its usual place to look something up. After a discussion at coffee time, he wanted to be able to find a precise quote or the name of its author. How could one imagine that a child who came home with such bad grades could be drawn to reading difficult works? Without the knowledge of his father, the adolescent read Rousseau very early, before the governess first confronted him with the argument of "the established order." He also read Voltaire and Diderot, from whom he learned the concept of systematic doubt. "But it was when I went to my Polish friend's house, the son of the train conductor where there was no thick carpet, and no staff, that I began to doubt the established order." In the meantime, he was expelled from high school because, in a paper at the end of the school year, he wrote about a subject that was considered subversive – the responsibility of the state and the wealthy.

> It was a poetical-political variation on the theme of the four seasons. I had written and developed the metaphor that the summer season symbolized the adults of the Republic and that the spring season symbolized youth. Without knowing it, I had copied a quote of the communist party. The director, a very proper man, came to the house and spoke seriously with my father and his wife. No, my father was not too furious that time. He was faced with a *fait accompli*. I will always say that he was correct with me, never trying to avoid expenses for my education. But we got along poorly. He had erroneous ideas and he was always right because he used his knowledge and erudition to demolish me with his arguments, which I could not oppose. Today, in the same way, I say, you can't have a discussion with Jehovah's Witnesses or with old communists.

Once again his father's wife came to his rescue. "She was the one who came and settled me in Poznan in 1927, in a very good family. I enrolled at the Applied Arts School while at the same time continuing my clandestine activities for the party, far from the tutelage of the Polish father. At that time, I was about 17."

Among his acquaintances during that period were the three Karpinski sisters, who also attended the Applied Arts School. Poznan is located in western Poland, but the Karpinski family came from eastern Poland, a region formally occupied by the Russians. They were very committed to the fight for independence. The family belonged to that minor nobility that had been completely ruined, the one that the poet Mickiewicz spoke about in the nineteenth century and whose daughters milked cows with their gloves on. The three sisters rented a big room in a bourgeois house and invited their friends, with whom they reinvented the world during their discussions. Jacques compares this group of young people to the youth of 1968, who were "not unlike my friends and myself." The idol of these young people was an authentic son of peasants who studied economics at the university. He enchanted his friends with stories of peasant life that he drew from his experience. Jacques never forgot the old woman who had kissed his hand in the past because he knew that his new friend could have been her son.

It was probably in this milieu that Jacques caught the attention of the KPP, the Polish communist party, which was clandestine at that time. He was easily recruited:

"You, you have the privilege of being able to study. The proletariat of this nearby factory does not have this privilege. It would be only fair to let the workers benefit from what you have learned."

He started, on the advice of the party, by joining the TUR (the Workers' Universities Association), and with great enthusiasm he taught general civilization, history, and geography to about twenty workers. Some of them were older than he and barely knew how to read and write. The meetings took place in the evening after work in a popular bar where his new students would come to drink beer. After class, they discussed a bit. Jacques asserts that he learned a lot from his "students."

Then, after a certain amount of time, almost all the members of the TUR joined the PPS-Left, the Polish socialist party, which was permitted under the authoritarian government of Pilsudski. Reflecting, Jacques notes that Pilsudski's regime was not fascist. After a trial period, Jacques was very proud to learn that he could become a member of a tiny cell of the clandestine communist party. It had three to six members maximum and met in a private apartment. The member in charge summarized the situation of the proletariat. The topics under discussion were social injustice and the lies of capitalism and its governments. The first task that the party proposed to them was to become members of an organization run by the socialist party, a teaching association for workers, called SWIT. To recruit new members the SWIT militants put on plays, works of Broniewski, Mayakovsky, Stande, Wandurski, and others. The actors and the audience were workers. The shows took place in cafes or in meeting rooms. "We never had the means to rent a real theatre. We made the posters ourselves and we counted on word of mouth to attract an audience. There were never more than a hundred people. Among them were off-duty police officers who were recognizable by their manner, but we didn't bother them." Jacques and a few of his comrades were one-man shows. He was the director, the stage manager, the choreographer, the set designer, and even the writer, when they didn't have a text.

In fact, he wrote one play whose subject was "Never Again," that standard phrase that had impressed him so much as a child. In 1927 the war had been over for almost a decade, but it was nevertheless still the topic of conversations.

> I remember a play where we had all the victims who had fallen in battle come out of their tombs and we had them curse capitalism, which we believed was responsible for so much bloodshed. They danced a kind of ballet on the stage from right to left, from left to right. When they passed each other, they would shout profanities against the imperialists' war. We drew from revolutionary authors whose works had been published, such as *I Burn Paris* by Bruno Jasienski.

The censors only intervened, when they did, after the work had been performed, *post factum*. Then the police made an appearance and certain published texts or certain texts written by neophytes such as Jacques were censored. The author paid for his audacity and was arrested for several days, but not sent to prison. They were deep into the Pilsudski regime, which Jacques and his friends at that time called fascist. However, that regime resembled what Jacques himself would experience in the communist Soviet Union. "Furthermore, in this allegedly fascist regime there were leftist socialist representatives and opposition Ukrainian and Belarus representatives." The hidden objective of this theatrical activity consisted in attracting socialist militants to the illegal communist party through skilful propaganda. Jacques managed to have his twelve worker students join, and this group became the core of a communist youth cell.

> I was the one who convinced them and who prepared them to become communists. After that they were asked, each one individually, to become members. They were all very proud, as I was, because

we believed it was the only way to obtain social justice. In such a clandestine party, no one had documents or a card. One's word was enough. When we organized the election of the secretary of the cell, a comrade from the party who had come to give a speech asked: "Whom do you choose as secretary?" Of course, we proposed unanimously the comrade who had come to make the speech but whom we saw for the first time. Everything was fixed in advance. And that person was always elected.

Afterwards, my group was divided into three cells of three to six people maximum. Each time we had to vote, there was a comrade who came from the party to be elected. Later in Russia, I saw the same show, and I understood the mechanism after 1929, when I attended those democratic elections of which the Soviets were so proud. However, there too a member was always especially sent who would begin with the sacred formula: "Listen comrades, we propose the candidacy of comrade Petrov or Ivanov." Obviously, we never knew who the "we" was. "Who is in favour?" The comrade started by raising his hand. Then all those who did not join him were immediately identified. Their names were written down. Later, during the interrogations of 1937, several comrades told me that the fact that they hadn't raised their hands five or six years earlier during the vote for the first secretary of their cell had been held against them.

During the cell meetings, there were animated discussions, mainly based on the leftist press, such as the *Internationale Presse-Korrespondenz*, published in German before the rise of Hitler. It consisted mainly of articles written by communists in what was then the still-free Weimar Republic. This kind of publication with contributions from well-known communists or sympathizers provided intellectual and revolutionary agitation for these clandestine militants. Jacques and his comrades read the articles with passion, discussed them, and agreed with them, convinced that they were reading the truth. "When we were clandestine in the communist party, it was a different kind of secrecy than in the international secret service. Later, I had to hide my opinions, hide myself with other identities, and behave like a courageous little bourgeois person, so as not to attract attention. But in the clandestine Polish CP, I was a lowly militant and I engaged in communist propaganda with the risk of being caught." Of course, he got caught. "With a friend, I threw leaflets over the wall of a Polish army barracks during the night. It was the fifteenth Uhlan regiment made up mostly of Ukrainians. At the time, we were not worried. But later, I was caught in a trap and my place was searched."

The leaflets were intended for Ukrainians from the eastern part of Poland who did their military service in Poznan, a western town. The party believed a war would likely break out between Soviet Russia and the imperialistic countries, including Poland, and that the young draftees should be prepared. The leaflets called on these young Ukrainians, in the event of war with the Soviet Union, to turn their arms against their oppressors, who were Polish landowners, manufacturers, and capitalists. The young Ukrainians were encouraged to fraternize with their brothers, the Russian peasants and workers. The police seized about sixty pounds of leaflets.

"In every country, it was considered a serious crime to call on soldiers to betray their oath of allegiance. That is serious!" The police searched the room of the young militant and found some of the same paper that had not been used and a basic mimeograph machine, and asked him, "Who gave you this machine?"

He had a story ready. A young girl that he had met in a park had given him a small box. He did not know what it contained. The girl did not come back. Finders keepers. Looking back, Jacques is surprised by the patience of Pilsudski's police and the fact that they did not harm him. At the same time, he knew that they could get nothing out of him. The two other members of the group, including the instigator of the operation, were arrested. Jacques was only the last link in the chain. There were lots of raids by the police, who knew the weaknesses of the clandestine communist party in Poznan. It was a region that was traditionally conservative and where there were few party cells. "I was sure that the police who questioned me knew that I was the son of an important person. But I also knew from my friends that in Poznan the police were usually restrained. We were in that part of Poland that had formerly been governed by Germany, where the disciplined police harassed only in certain cases. However, in the eastern, formerly Russian part, the police beat people up regularly."

Thus Jacques began his first stay in prison, a prison whose relative merits he continually praised compared to his experiences later. "During my first months of confinement, I looked out the window, which had bars but not opaque glass as in Russia. I could see through the bars. I composed poems with verses like: *You are the ones who are behind the bars, I am the one who is free.*" The young idealist was hardly depressed by that first incarceration. At least that was how he viewed it seventy years later. "I took risks and I paid the price for them."

The guard when he arrived in his first cell filled out the form, indicating family name, first name, birth date, and crime. Crime? He had not been judged yet, but the guard carefully noted, "communist." The young man protested vigorously.

> "Being a communist is not a crime!"
> And the guard replied calmly, "It's not you who will teach me that!" I asked for clean laundry and I received it. I could do whatever I wanted. I had paper and pencils. I had the works of Lenin brought to me, published in Polish by a Polish editor under the regime of Pilsudski. For the first time in that Polish prison, I started to study Lenin. Much later, after my years in the Gulag, I returned to Poland, a Poland that was then communist. During the hundredth anniversary of the birth of Lenin in 1970, I remember an exhibit of Lenin's works in all the languages of the world, even in Tamil and in Swahili. But I could not find the Polish edition from the Pilsudski period. "Be quiet comrade! We shouldn't shout out everywhere that we could read Lenin in the prisons of that filthy fascist Pilsudski!"

Jacques was called before the judge Hab., who asked him to stand in front of him.

> First I stood up, and then I remembered that I didn't have to bow to that authority so I sat down again. The judge did not react. I explained to him vehemently that the present society deserved to be overthrown, to which he responded ironically:
> "Young man, you who have so much sympathy for the people, do you actually know how much two pounds of potatoes cost?"
> Pilsudski's judge managed to make me be ashamed of my ignorance.
> "You who are fighting for the working class, you do not even know the price of bread?!"
> What shocked me the most was that, upon my return to Poland in 1961, I learned that the judge, who had been dead for two years, had faithfully served the communist regime as he had served the previous regime. This was normal for a man who, unlike a young twit like myself, had always known the price of a pound of potatoes!

Jacques had been in prison for some time when his guard announced the visit of a young cousin. She was none other than one of the workers who had acted in a play of his. In the visiting room where he received her, she threw herself at him, kissed him, and spoke to him like a close family member about some imaginary aunt Babette while giving him a sausage (which he had always hated) and milk. Jacques was proud of the actress, who now played the role of a first cousin. "The Soviets would have refused this visit since their rules forbid visits of close family listed in one's file: no aunts, cousins, or grandmothers. I was delighted to be kissed by a pretty girl who also gave me a bag of food." The guard barely listened and the two young people continued acting. "We followed the advice of the party: condemn the cops and swear with no shame. She was a member of the proletariat and I was the son of a rich man. But there was that complicity between us and I had the impression that from my 'fascist' prison, my ideas were spreading ..."

The proletarian "cousin" sometimes came back to see him in prison. The same "fascist" regime supplied him with an appointed lawyer who had just finished his studies and was slightly older than Jacques. The lawyer came to see him.

"How do you view your defence?"
"I don't need any defence. My cause is just."
The lawyer was not a communist. If he had been, he could never have practised law. However, he took my defence seriously. In his speech, he objected eloquently. "How can you condemn this young romantic who is only taking up, once more, the tradition of the French Revolution?" The Poles had just solemnly commemorated this revolution on July 14, with France, a friendly country. The argument moved people but did not convince them.

Then another lawyer, someone his father knew, came to see him, and said: "You know, dear sir, that as a lawyer, I cannot defend a political prisoner. But I will help you behind the scenes."

He pulled strings and helped the young lawyer with advice, for example, regarding the request for witnesses. "All the people that I had proposed as witnesses were cited. They confirmed that I was a good student at the school of Applied Arts. There was no comparison between these and Soviet trials that gave sentences for twenty-five years without listening to the witnesses presented by the accused!"

The trial took place on 20 and 21 October 1928. Jacques was sentenced to nine months in a fortified prison. He preferred the fortified prison to a real prison because there he did not lose his rights of "honour" (which were not exactly his civil rights). Thus a sentence to the fortress did not stop him from studying or being an officer, for instance, had he been in the military. Normally, he would have been sentenced to one year or perhaps one and a half years. But he wasn't even eighteen, the youngest of the three accused, and came from a good family. The longest sentence would be three years. One day, a long time later, he revisited his cell in the Poznan prison in front of the cameras of German television.

It is rare for a former prisoner to insist that he was well treated in prison. But Jacques was not like other prisoners. Compared with the other prisons he would know, the prison of Pilsudski looked like Eden:

> Well before I was arrested, the party hammered into me that, in case of a trial, I was to deny everything in general and in detail, lie without scruples, and try to destroy the depositions of the prosecution witnesses. In the beginning, I was put in a cell all alone. I was taken down from the fourth floor for a walk outside, which would last an hour. In Soviet prisons, by contrast, the walk lasted only fifteen or twenty minutes. I took several steps alone in the courtyard, a hero who suffered for the universal cause of social justice.

Once, Jacques disdainfully refused a guard's request for a favour. It concerned a stool, built in one of the workshops on the ground floor where the common law prisoners worked, but not the political prisoners.

> The guard could not touch the stool because the person who accompanied a prisoner could not carry anything. He asked me politely: "Sir, would you please help me and carry this stool that was built for the guards up to the third floor?" I thought to myself – I am a political prisoner and I am not going to work for the guard. I refused. He did not yell at me. And the stool stayed there.
> 
> I heard that in these same so-called fascist Polish prisons, during the important trials in Moscow when Zinoviev and Bukharin were condemned, a communist political prisoner asked the prison administration to remove from the library the books of the recently condemned. Can you imagine his nerve? He was the political prisoner of a regime opposed to communism and he had the audacity to ask the director of that same prison to remove books that no longer had the approval of the communist party. He dared to make that request!

One day, before the fake cousin visited him, Jacques was informed that he had a visitor. Who could it be? Jacques did not have family in Poznan.

> I saw my father arrive. He was very serious and, as always, very elegant. The chief guard said to him politely, "Here he is, sir." This chief guard was about fifty. He probably had the same job in the same prison when it was run by the Germans before 1918. He was a fat,

simple man, with a red face, a big belly, and a curled-up mustache in the style of the German emperor Wilhelm II. This decent guard stood to the side, discreetly, with his keys. I don't remember the conversation at all. I only remember a remark that my father made at the end: "Don't you realize that you are ruining your life? What will become of you if at your age you are already in prison? If you don't care about your own career, you should at least care about mine!" Then I said with great pride, "The future of the world's proletariat is more important than one's career!" He was astounded. I remember the look he exchanged with the chief guard, who was standing in a corner, his legs spread apart, his hands behind his back with his ring of keys. These two men, the minor bureaucrat and the important gentleman (vice minister or something like that), each looked at one another with amazement. Both men were asking themselves what could be done with such a fool. It was a scene of fraternity where class differences seemed to disappear. I witnessed a small moment of human truth.

After that exchange, Jacques never saw Marcin H. again. He entered many prisons, but in the course of some thirty-five years, he would never again cross the threshold of one of those rich homes where he had spent his childhood. He would no longer tread upon the thick carpets that had not managed to stifle the sound and the fury of the servants. Marcin H. died, according to Jacques, during the German occupation, and Jacques imagined that until the end he knew that the prodigal son was fighting for a cause more important than his father's career. As for Jacques's university studies in Poznan, they ended with the young subversive being expelled. Jacques would not see Piotr and Silvia again and would see Aunt Marie only after he left the Gulag. During those years, she suffered under the communist regime and finished her days living in one room.

When Jacques left prison in 1928, he was convinced that family and filial attachments were all bourgeois sentimentality. The worldwide revolution would sweep away all those miserable ties. As for him, he would not go back to those who "drink the blood and sweat of the proletariat." Never again, no never!

# 4 The Fugitive

> What combination of adventures was bringing him back into his life?
>
> Gustave Flaubert, *Madame Bovary*

Jacques did not stay nine months in the fortress. At the end of six, he was freed. Of course, he did not go home to the bastion of imperialism and capitalism. The University of Poznan had expelled him, but he continued his studies at the Beaux-Arts in Krakow, where he took sculpture classes with Professor Laszko. "I remember going to a friend's house in Krakow who, like me, was a communist and a young man with an influential father. The housemaid started to clean our shoes as was the custom, and I was about to protest when my friend gestured to me not to take offence. I obeyed, conscious of the risk that such a nonconformist reaction could pose for our revolutionary organization."

In order to contact comrades in Uzhhorod, the party decided to send him to Czechoslovakia, a country that was democratic at that time and where the communist party was legal. The young man did not go alone, but went with two other young Poles who had been involved in the same trial in Poznan: Zenon, a medical student, and Rada, the daughter of counts and landowners in the Ukraine before 1917. She was a little older, probably thirty-four at the time.

The trio entered Czechoslovakia illegally through the town of Zakopane in the Tatras mountains. After walking a long time in the mountains, in the middle of a forest, they discovered a sign in Slovak that they managed to read: *Nefajčiť* (No smoking). What joy! They knew that they had crossed the Polish border into Slovakia without a problem. They had been told that not far from there, in a well-known tourist resort near the border, they would find a party cell. That evening, they arrived at Košice, the departmental capital of Slovakia, where they were to take the train for Uzhhorod the next morning. They didn't know where to spend the night. Lacking experience, they decided to sleep in the train station, where the police arrested them after asking for their papers. They were very proud of their valid train tickets, but this was not enough. The Slovak police politely took the three illegal Poles to prison in the county town office of Košice, where they spent the next several days.

At that time in Košice, a trial was taking place concerning cannibalism. The three revolutionaries knew nothing about it. They were, however, in the same prison in Košice as the cannibals. The trio only wanted the political asylum that they had requested. Rada was held in the women's section, Jacques and Zenon in separate cells. The latter learned from vagabonds and petty thieves with whom he shared his cell that gypsies had assassinated a slightly chubby priest whose fat they then prepared to eat. This affair was sensationalized and attracted journalists from around the world, but Jacques was unaware of anything.

One day, the guard came for him. Jacques didn't know why but the guards put a bandage on him and then a bandana around his head. He was taken into an office. Through the door, he could hear animated voices and laughter. The guard knocked politely. They went in and Jacques saw a large room. There was a bureaucrat who looked very important and there were several other people around a table, one of whom was a priest.

> When I was introduced someone said, "That's him!"
> Then the priest whose back had been turned to me when he came in, turned around, looked at me, and shook his head: "No! That's not him!"
> The cannibal was thin like me and wore a kind of turban around his head. I had been saved thanks to the good priest, who, unlike his colleague, had managed to escape the clutches of the cannibal. I will always be grateful to him. I still remember that atmosphere where everybody was telling funny stories and laughing heartily. Suddenly that priest became serious, stared at me, and did not recognize the aggressor of his colleague. I can still hear him say: "No. That's not him!"

Years later, in the Gulag, Jacques would again be in a cell with frightful cannibals who did not hurt him. Was it just destiny winking at him? Meanwhile, the three young people did not obtain political asylum. They were not condemned, but they were deported without trial – not to their own country, the Poland of Pilsudski, but to nearby

Hungary, which was under the rule of the formidable anti-communist Admiral Horthy. An off-duty police officer was ordered to accompany them to the Hungarian border in a small train.

> The train had two wagons, a locomotive with a steam engine, and the civil servant who, when we got there, took us off the train and announced: "Here we are. This is the other side. You see those apple trees? Over there is the Hungarian border. If you come back to Czechoslovakia you will be arrested. It is in your best interest to cross over to Hungary!"
>
> We knew what awaited us in Hungary and we were terrified. The policeman hurried us along: "Go now!" We understood that he wanted to go home to his wife and kids. It was evening. The train only made one round-trip journey each day and it was going to leave without him. In addition, he was alone with no other policeman around. This was democracy, all right! Contrary to totalitarian regimes that had cops everywhere!
>
> We promised him everything he wanted. Of course, we were going to leave Czechoslovakia! Moreover, what would we do in this desert where only one house could be seen? We only asked him to let us rest a few minutes on the grass. In spite of his job, he had decided to return home. He got back on the train and he left!
>
> In the same wagon there was a Jew, a peddler, who had gotten off with us. He had a bundle hanging from a stick in which he carried all kinds of things. I remember his head with its long curls and his pale face. In Eastern Europe, Jews wore very long black coats, boots, and a yarmulke. He had overheard our conversation with the Czech policeman. He spoke to us in Yiddish and I answered because I spoke German. I explained that we were political exiles, that we had asked for asylum and that those bastards wanted to deport us. He warned us, in Yiddish, not to go to Hungary because he came from there and he knew that all the vagabonds who were deported from Hungary were being sent back to Czechoslovakia – once, twice, even three times – and that eventually their dead bodies turned up somewhere. The Hungarian border was where the policeman had shown us the apple trees. Beyond it, there was a small creek that we were not supposed to cross. He advised us to walk along the border until we got to a Slovak village, six miles further on. There, the communists would welcome us.
>
> This Jew, a miserable peddler, was not a communist at all. He had nothing to do with these political emigrants, but he had seen that the Czech police were deporting us, and he wanted to help us. He

was putting himself in danger and taking a risk by doing so. He was a very young man, perhaps twenty-two, twenty-three at most, who lived near the border, so poor that the economic threat that he posed by coming into Czechoslovakia was zero. The Jewish people had lived as a diaspora for thousands of years and some of them sympathized instinctively with those who were in need. We did not have the same opinions. Not one of us spoke his language. Yet he took a risk by helping us with his advice!

The peddler disappeared. The young people started on their long and uncertain journey. They saw a cross near the road and decided to spend the night behind it, hidden in the grass. Completely worn out, they fell asleep. During the night, they heard the noise of a cart's squeaking wheels and voices that came to them through the humid air and the tall grass where they were lying. Jacques, the language specialist, could hear the voices distinctly but couldn't understand what was being said. Memory of prison was still very fresh. What if they were the gypsies? The young revolutionaries were scared. Of course, they knew they were thinner than the chubby priest. Then the conversation seemed quieter. Listening carefully, they could distinguish the squeaking of badly oiled wheels of two carts from which the strangers called out to one another calmly. Finally, after they came closer, the voices moved away. The "cannibal" gypsies left. Perhaps the strangers had been neither gypsies nor cannibals.

The three fugitives slept until dawn and started walking again when a man appeared with a rifle and gestured to them. It was a Czech border guard. The trio tried to make him take pity on them. They presented themselves as persecuted Polish political activists. As proof, they showed him the legal document that they had with them. The border guard understood a little Polish. He looked at them, said nothing, and then asked:

"Have you had dinner? My wife made too much borsch yesterday. You can eat some of it."

The three youths washed up in the small, clean house where the wife of the border guard welcomed them with the hot soup. Rada, who spoke Ukrainian, made herself understood by the couple.

We talked. We saw small objects in the room that I recognized from the walls of Polish museums. These objects were made from bread and were characteristic of Tsarist prisons. Many Polish prisoners who had been Russian prisoners prior to Poland's independence brought these objects back with them. They were artistically modelled from the bread of the prisoners. The dough of Russian bread was like clay: grey and heavy. In Soviet prisons, I would see chess games made from this same dough, but never objects made with such artistry.

We asked the border guard whether he had ever been in Russian prisons, but he didn't answer. We never heard the end of that story. We devoured our borsch. We warmed up, and we were treated to big slices of bread. At the end of the meal, the Czechs repeated what the Jew had told us. Not far away, there was a village with a communist organization. Perhaps there, we would be helped. Then he took us to the border. There, with a sweeping gesture of his hand, he showed us Hungary on the left, while at the same time explaining to us, very quietly, how to avoid it. That was what he did in case someone saw him with us. He didn't want to be caught himself. On the left there was Hungary, and on the right the apple tree and the rock, and farther on, a village with communists.

We followed his advice. We went to the right, and very quickly found the village. In the village, which was called Smolnik, there was the tavern, with small branches in the shape of a sickle and hammer painted by hand on the facade. We went in and we asked for the owner.

"Are the comrades here?"

"They are working. You will see them tonight."

"Tonight? We have nothing to do until then. We are illegal Polish comrades."

The owner was impressed, and he sent his son to get the person in charge, a peasant, the secretary of the party organization, who came right away.

The three young people were welcomed like heroes by the communists, who were, in fact, Hungarian. They toasted their comrades who were persecuted by police everywhere in the world. They gave them food and drink. The three stayed in the inn until the evening.

When it was night, the feeling of danger came back, even though there was no risk. With a thousand precautions, they took us to a barn. For these lucky people who lived in a law-abiding country, who did not know police repression, our presence was really a sensational event. We stayed in the hay for a long time, because the organization had contacted another organization that had contacted another one, I think, all the way to Prague. Our new comrades did not know what to do or how to act. We stayed five or six days, and only left the barn at night for the most urgent needs. Everything had to be secret.

It seemed the whole village was in cahoots, as practically all the inhabitants were members of the organization. They were so proud of this responsibility, like the courageous French when a dissident Russian arrived in France. He was spoiled and he was courted. The French hosts wanted to absorb a little bit of the dissident's heroism cheaply, but it was a heroism that cost them nothing.

The Slovak villagers and the Hungarian communists spoiled their young revolutionaries, who had been persecuted in fascist Poland. During that summer, there was even a communist Hungarian poet who came from Budapest to enjoy a stay in the country, a free country. He came and visited them in the hay.

Suddenly he appeared at the top of the ladder when Rada was half naked. It was very hot. He saw her blouse and skirt near the entrance. And with a nice gesture, he threw her her clothes and turned his back at the same time. It was like at Versailles, good manners in a pile of hay. He was a revolutionary poet, recognized by the Hungarian republic even though he was a revolutionary. He was a member of the Petőfi club, which would play an important role in the events of 1956.

The young Hungarian poet came back several times to the barn to talk with Jacques and his friends. Rada was always dressed when he arrived, but the two boys just wore their underpants. Finally, the order arrived from the Central Committee in Prague, and the three accomplices were accompanied to the Czech capital by a comrade, who watched over the safety of clandestine youth. In Prague, there was panic once more.

Above all, we had to be careful not to get caught. We got in a tram to go to the address that we had been given. Zenon found a seat in the front. Rada and I were in the back. When the tram began going around a large square, we saw a group of policemen jump onto the trolley, two in the front and three in the back. Those who had just boarded in the front moved a bit further back into the trolley. On the left, near the door, was our comrade. All of a sudden, when the trolley lurched, a policeman lost his balance, and then he kept his balance holding onto Zenon's shoulder. Zenon did not move. I was afraid. We felt ourselves surrounded, with two cops in front and three behind. I almost jumped off. However, the policemen had just boarded this tram because they were in a hurry. If we had jumped off, we would have been caught for nothing. Fear is a bad advisor.

In Prague, while Rada had found other shelter, Jacques and his friend were lodged in the apartment of a worker from the Red Help, an organization that helped prisoners and militants. They lived with a Bulgarian and an Albanian. After five days, their Czech comrades decided to send them to Germany. The trip from Czechoslovakia to Germany before Hitler's rise to power posed no problems. Sometimes security took place on one side of the border and sometimes on the other side. The right time had to be selected and it was important not have any luggage. At rush hour, hundreds of workers crossed the border in tight groups. Jacques and his friends had been careful to dress like the others, so as not to attract attention, and crossed chatting with their Czech comrades who accompanied them. In the German border town, they were given train tickets for Berlin where Red Help, run by the powerful German communist party, took care of political immigrants, in a Germany that was still the free Weimar Republic.

It was 1929. Jacques would never see his travel companions again. Zenon went back to Poland and was arrested. Later, he finished his studies in medicine. As for Rada, she left for the USSR where she was probably swallowed up by the universe that Jacques would later know so well. Many years later, he heard her name mentioned by a police interrogator in eastern Siberia.

Looking back on these youthful adventures, enlightened by distance and experience, the former prisoner is still surprised by the human solidarity that was shown by the generous Jewish peddler and the Czech border guard. "When I returned to communist Poland after the Gulag, I wanted this story to be known. I thought, naively, that the Czech communist authorities could have compensated the border guard for his revolutionary act of long ago. In the sixties, I tried to contact the Czech embassy, in vain. All individual and spontaneous requests were viewed with suspicion."

In Berlin in 1929, Jacques found a Polish comrade again through an intermediary of the German communist party. He helped him to get a job with the Comintern's international secret service that communicated with the Soviet spy services and whose goal was to overthrow capitalism and establish Marxism-Leninism on the entire planet. During many years with different identities and secretive missions, he would clandestinely cross the same borders that he crossed earlier as a rich kid and then, sometimes, as an illegal communist – from Berlin to Vienna, Brussels to Copenhagen, Milan to Paris and elsewhere.

# 5 Secret Agent

The Communist International is the international party for proletarian insurrection and dictatorship. In nearly all the countries of Europe and America, a period of civil war results from class war. Communists cannot in these conditions trust bourgeois legality. It is their duty to create a clandestine organization everywhere, parallel to legal organizations, and capable of accomplishing its duty for the Revolution when the decisive moment arrives.
          Manifesto of the Second Congress of the Comintern

In Berlin, with the help of the Czech communists who had organized the trip of the young Polish communists, Jacques contacted the German communist party. It organized a meeting for him with his former Polish communist party chief in Poznan. That man, it turned out, was an agent for the Comintern. In the early 1930s, Berlin became Jacques's home base. He started by working at the headquarters of the powerful communist party that was located in the house of Karl Liebknecht. His activity as a "sitting editor" or *sitz redakteur* consisted of editing *Glos Ludu* (The Voice of the People) for the German communist party. It was a weekly in Polish and for Polish seasonal workers living in Germany. "In the Weimar Republic, censorship sometimes occurred after publication. The newspapers were first sent to the kiosks to save time, and then they were sent to the police two hours later. When the *sitz redakteur* was censored, this person, being on the lowest rung of the ladder, so to speak, went to prison for several days."[1] Being a militant hardly paid, so Jacques accepted financial help from his extended family in Poland in order to survive.

 In Berlin, his public persona was that of a student enrolled in the Beaux-Arts who amused himself by acting in plays, in addition to other activities. From 1930, the Polish delegation of the KPP transferred him to a clandestine section. He had other activities, notably "technical" missions in Europe, Germany, Belgium, and France.

> The comrade who was responsible for me introduced me to another contact with whom I would work in the future. The new comrade spoke German with an accent. Once, he used several Russian words that he pronounced perfectly. I then realized where he was from. However, I was disciplined. I never asked questions! My activities were purely technical. I would deliver a book or communicate an address to a comrade in various European cities.

In the service of the Communist International, Jacques would spend long periods of time in various European capitals – Milan, Copenhagen, London, and Geneva. That was not counting a trip to the capital of the promised land. In 1929, a meeting was organized for him with a Polish friend in Moscow. It was in the beginning of the thirties that Jacques remembers meeting in Prague Milena Jesenská, Kafka's friend, and a bit later at the Lux hotel, where many Comintern officials stayed, Margerete Beber-Neumann, whom he would see again in Moscow with her companion Heinz Neumann. None of them could imagine at the time that they would all be swept up in the Great Terror or the Great Purges of 1937. "Only the big shots stayed at the Lux hotel, but at that time the minor messengers could still visit there. That was how I contacted important people."

During this time, Jacques lived freely in the Weimar Republic between his many trips. In 1933, Hitler was called to power by Hindenburg, and thereafter proclaimed the dissolution of the Reichstag. Following their electoral victory, the Nazis had a majority in the government as of 5 March. On 2 June, the government sent the SA against the SPD and the BVD in Berlin. Jacques left Nazi Germany. From then on, between short or long missions for the clandestine services, he lived in Moscow and took classes on Marxism and philosophy.

"Neither at that time nor later did I consider myself a spy. My country, whose interests I served, risking my life as an information agent, was the Savior of Humanity." As a citizen of the world, the young idealist trained himself in the culture of his adopted country. It was a culture of secrets, of partitioning, and of obscure missions in which he avoided recognition. The obligation not to know became more and more important and it became a habit and a way of life for Jacques. Yet knowledge and information could become dangerous for the cause and for the agent. His slightest reactions were probably scrutinized by his bosses, who were constantly watching him. One would assume that these bosses knew of this young communist's commitment, as it was clearly displayed by his intellect and ability to reason. His superiors must have tested his exceptional memory, his virtuous courage and loyalty, tests that even produced in him a certain stoicism. Choosing the men who would work for the cause was of vital importance. Jacques also had the advantage of being at ease among people, and he had a capacity for physical seduction and the valuable intelligence required of an information officer. The constraints of living in secrecy developed in him practical skills and a particular attention to detail, which would later help him to survive the Gulag.

One of his memories exemplifies his professional secret life. During a mission Jacques, under a false Swedish passport, carried secret documents from Genoa to a harbour on the eastern Mediterranean. While boarding the cruise ship, he learned from a steward that he was going to be able to speak with a Swedish "compatriot," one of the other passengers. Jacques was petrified at the thought of having his identity revealed by an authentic Swedish citizen, so he pretended to be sick during the entire voyage and stayed in his cabin. He tried to avoid having to speak the language of Queen Christine. Years later, in the Butyrka prison, Jacques tried to distract a prisoner who had been badly tortured during a night of interrogation by telling him stories. His story of the cruise managed to make the poor tortured man stop frowning.

"The other Swede was me!"

Despite the impact of these anecdotes, Jacques insisted that the duties he was given in the clandestine service were insignificant.

> When I left the communist world for good, that is to say, from the big Gulag, and I had returned permanently to France, some Soviet experts wanted to know exactly what I had done because they were convinced that the work of the Comintern was very special and that I had had important responsibilities. But I had done exactly what messengers do in large cities in France. The difference was that I worked for the OMS in the international relations division. It was secret and it was serious. I did nothing more than work as a messenger. I was what was called a "courier." I ignored the contents of the documents that I carried, but I was convinced that each one of these missions brought us closer to *joyous tomorrows*.

The other reason for Jacques's "ignorance" of the secrets of the Communist International was perhaps that during all those years of secrecy, he did not work exclusively for the Comintern.

Life in the underground fascinated this young fanatic, who was proud to serve the world-wide revolution. For a twenty-year-old, life as a secret agent was amusing and stimulating. Of course, it also required skill and luck.

> I was never caught, but almost. One time in 1933, I found myself in a group where there had been arrests by the French police. I was supposed to meet someone who had not come to the meeting place. I went then to the second meeting place that had been arranged in case the first was a failure. No one was there! I could not contact my boss. I met him in cafes. I wasn't allowed to know his address or his identity. I finally learned that he had been arrested by the French police. He was tried for conspiracy and imprisoned long enough to miss the Great Purges. When he got out he was treated like a hero. This boss was my only contact with the CP. We did not have permission to have the slightest contact with the top bosses.
>
> I had the impression that there weren't many of us working for the Comintern, but that all of us were loyal, no matter the ordeal. I once met an Austrian comrade whom I knew from Moscow at the corner of the rue Soufflot and the Boulevard Saint-Michel, near the old Capoulade. We saw each other, but we didn't smile. We didn't even blink. He was called back to Moscow and was executed. It's true that he had more responsibilities than I had. Much later, I met his widow and his son.

From Paris, Jacques remembers an authentic former communard, an old man with a white mustache who was a bit deaf and who functioned as a mailbox for the organization.

> It was the FCP that told him to work for us without him knowing exactly what he would be doing. For him we were, above all, communists from countries where the party was illegal. One day, I went to his home to figure out a way to distinguish our mail from his. We decided that the word "party" would be underlined in a particular way on the envelopes that were for us. When I left I insisted: "All of this, of course, stays between us. It's secret. You don't talk about it to anyone."
>
> He agreed vigorously, held out his hand with an air of conspiracy, and shook my hand again on the landing. While I went down the stairs, he leaned over the railing and started to yell because he was deaf. "OK comrade, it's secret! I won't say anything to anybody!"

From Paris, Jacques was often sent on missions to Switzerland.

I have the impression – but I could be mistaken – that Switzerland was one of the centres of the organization. One time, unarmed, I had to escort a young comrade in the train from Vienna and who was carrying a lot of money hidden in a small leather cushion that was used in the train compartments to prop up one's back. Everything went very well and, following our orders, we met at the same table in the restaurant of the Basel train station. Suddenly, my young comrade shrieked:

"My cushion! I left it in the train!"

I looked at a porter who came towards us: "She left her cushion in the train. It is very dear to her. It's a present from her grandmother!"

The porter asked what train it had been left in and ten minutes later we had the cushion back with its treasure. I did not report the incident, but she must have spoken about it. The Comintern relied on discipline, and we had all internalized that discipline. However, it was rare that we were asked to transport money. In this particular case, it was probably urgent. In general, the Comintern financed its affiliate parties through more or less fictitious organizations run by the Soviets and the European or American crypto-communists.

In France, I had several contacts, one of whom was a worker who was to provide a back-up plan in case of a problem, and an industrial engineer favourable to our cause who at the time had a private airplane, which impressed me. Meanwhile, I had a kind of "accident at work." In Belgium, I was responsible for a small network of artisans, especially bookbinders, who made books with double bindings that permitted transporting certain secret documents. Suddenly, I could not pay them. So I asked the owner of the airplane for the fifteen thousand francs I needed to rebuild my network. He refused outright. So I asked my proletarian comrade, who said he needed ten days to mobilize his friends, who were all workers like him. On the designated day, the money arrived.

All the missions involved a similar task: deliver a small object in which secret information was carefully hidden. Well, that is what I thought because I never knew if it was a message or what the message meant. I only knew that the object I was carrying contained a secret that had to be protected in case of an accident. Nothing more! The routine was this: I had information about the person I was supposed to meet and where, as well as whether it was a double meeting, and on what day it would occur. If that didn't work, I was given an alternate date and place, and if that didn't work, I waited for a meeting with the boss, who had to make a decision. I was proud of what I did. Today, I recognize my own stupidity. But then I was risking my life. Everything depended on what kind of a policeman caught me because, depending on the political regime, they were more or less brutal. For example, the Hungarian police force was known for its extreme severity, contrary to the Czech police that I encountered in Košice, to my wonderful surprise.

The Communist International or Comintern had as its objective the establishment of communism, "the only just system," in all the countries on earth. The two systems, capitalism and communism, could not exist together. Coexistence, we all knew, was unacceptable as long as capitalism remained stronger. Founded in 1919 by Lenin, the International regrouped all the Marxist-Leninist parties around the world. It was a very important and savvy organization. Lenin had the idea to place the worldwide workers' movement under his wing, after the Bolshevik coup d'état in 1917, and then after the First World War. In a very short time communist parties were organized with members coming from socialist and social democratic parties like the French CP created after the Tours Congress of 1920.

The headquarters of the Comintern was located in Moscow because it was considered the "most important workers' and peasants' country in the world," and protected from the capitalist police. There was no risk that the headquarters would be spied upon by the class enemy. Theoretically of course, the CP of Moscow was under the authority of the Comintern. In reality, it was the opposite. Very quickly, everyone understood that the Russian [Soviet] communist party controlled the Comintern. The Central Committee of the Soviet communist party, in other words, the Russian [Soviet] government, controlled all the communist parties in the world, and all the communist parties in the world were operatives for Moscow.

Moscow possessed the role of both capital of an imperialistic and nationalistic country and the centre of a political movement with international aspirations, that hoped to achieve social justice in the entire world. Slowly, without the knowledge of the majority of communist militants, the party's grassroots, the Comintern became an instrument of Soviet imperialism.

Why do I speak at such length about this? In order to emphasize that when the French communist party was called "a foreign party," it was true. Of course, the communist parties in countries like France, England, and Germany before Hitler's rise to power had their own congresses and chose their own central committees and secretary generals. In reality, all secretary generals in any communist party had to be approved by the political board of the Soviet communist party, that is to say, first by Lenin, then by Stalin. This continued until the collapse of the Soviet Union. Georges Marchais [leader of the French communist party, 1972–94] could remain in his position as long as Moscow accepted him. For Robert Hue [who led the French communist party, 2001–03], after the fall of the Soviet Union it was different, because today the French communist party no longer receives subsidies from Moscow and is therefore independent. Officially, however, for tactical reasons, the Comintern was disbanded in 1943, during the Second World War when the USSR was an ally of democratic countries. In fact, it continued to exist under the name Cominform (the Communist Information Bureau). The spy agencies, in my time, depended on three organizations: the Comintern, the Red Army (the PKKA), and the OGPU-NKVD, that is to say, the political police. In general, each agency was quite autonomous, but sometimes agents were lent or transferred from one agency to another. For example, I was recruited by the Comintern, but I realized later that I had been "lent" to the Army – always with protection. Geographically, the agencies were divided into three regions in the world: the East, Europe, and the Americas. Africa, at the time, was perceived as too distant.

Within the Comintern, there were national sections (English, French, German, and others). I indicated that the special organization to which I was assigned was called in Russian the OMS, an acronym for "the Department for International Relations." Young people worked there who were considered "trustworthy," reliable, disciplined, and polyglot. That was my case. I knew many languages and I left on missions with different passports. It was useful "to speak the language of one's passport," as they would say at the Comintern.

In fact, two categories of documents were used. The "little" passport "for crossing a border" was used for leaving the Soviet Union to go to a nearby country, for example, Finland or Sweden. If the mission lasted a long time there, I met a comrade whom I usually didn't know, in a café or another public place. He would give me a completely different passport. The most important thing was not to travel with the first passport, which had stamps from the Soviet Union. The second passport, the "real one," was often established with the name of a real person. Only the photo was changed. As the bearer of this passport, I had to know the complete identity of the person who had lent me his name: his family, the place where he had studied, the events in his life, and all kinds of details. Each time, I learned his life by heart. When I stayed in a hotel during these missions I filled out the registration form according to that information. At any moment, a search could take place in any street, in any city: people like Jacques Dupont, John Smith, or Juan Gonzalez actually existed.

At the Soviet border, if a customs officer stamped the back of the page where the photo was, the passport could no longer be used by another person. One time, I became insolent and tried to show the customs officer on which page he should put the stamp. I only wanted to facilitate the technical task of my comrades. The customs officer reacted badly and talked to his boss about it. The boss made me get off the train. "You know, these fake passports, we know all about them."

I explained to him which service I worked for and asked him to call a certain comrade at the international spy agency in Moscow, which is what he did. I wasn't too worried, because we were virtually in Russia [the Soviet Union], the Holy Land for me.

But I had to wait for two days in a hotel before I was given my papers back with a cordial handshake. The spy services of the Comintern had completely certified the origin of my passport, but the border guard wanted to show his zeal and insisted on demonstrating his vigilance.

And so life continued, first in the service of the Comintern, then in the service of another agency, which lasted about nine years for Jacques. Nine years of voyages with diverse identities and nationalities, nine years of organized wandering, serving a unique goal. When returning from a mission, Jacques would turn in one passport and receive another ID, which he then used in Soviet territory. A false identity could last a month or years. Jacques knew that he could play this role until the end. Hadn't he formerly invented characters when he wrote and directed plays for the revolution? In that era before computers, verification was not easy. With a North or South American passport, for example, it was difficult to get caught. The European police lacked the ability to verify effectively whether a person was known in a given country. Jacques, as a good agent, knew only the name of his superior in the hierarchy but knew nothing else about him, while his boss knew everything about Jacques. A short time ago, a journalist asked if that period in his life had been a happy one. Jacques answered that he had been happy because he was doing something that he considered useful for all of humanity. He agrees when I suggest that this was a time when he lived closest to his "dream," and adds that, at the time, he never questioned what he was doing: "I believed without any doubt that the world-wide revolution was near."

> One night in Hitler's Germany, I was brutally awakened by the railroad police, who asked for my papers. I was lying on a bench in second class, my feet on a piece of newspaper. Like the Germans, I am a bit obsessive. That time I was travelling on a Finnish passport, a language that I didn't speak but this was not considered a problem because so few people speak it. Minutes passed. The German police continued to examine my fake passport and although I appeared confident, I was not. Then they gave it back to me without a word. What a relief!

Jacques insisted on the secrecy of the operations. He did not try to know everything because he wasn't supposed to know. He remained firm in his conviction that he possessed no political responsibility and usually did not know what he was carrying, whether documents with revolutionary instructions or microfilms.

> I was not a leader. I was at the bottom of the ladder. I got to the meeting place. I met the person whom I recognized by particular signs. Typically, I did not know the person. Either the person gave me something or I gave the person something. We chatted a bit to appear like everybody else and then we both went our separate ways.
> I was only an instrument, but one that was proud to serve the Great Cause of Social Justice. I was a small screw in a big machine. I visited towns. I went to respectable restaurants and hotels. I saw very important men who earned a lot of money, who smoked big cigars and paid with checks written from accounts with very sufficient funds, while I, the modest agent working for the Comintern, considered myself more important than they. I was part of the movement that was driving the world toward Total Freedom, while they were just sad little members of the bourgeoisie. However, although I believed this, I remained very discreet. I showed off, but only when I was alone.

As a full-time militant, Jacques was paid by the organization. Every time he got some money, he was asked to provide a receipt. He also prepared invoices for his expenses without having to provide justification. Given his love of conspiracy, he enjoyed creating documents the size of a match box, but this would annoy the comrade in charge of finances. Clandestine work involved many risks. One always had to have a cover.

The professions that involved travel, for example, a journalist or businessman, were useful. For longer trips, studying provided an ideal cover for a young man. Jacques was passionately interested in Eastern civilizations. He was perhaps the only one of his comrades who took advantage of his studies and did not merely consider them a cover for his political work. He attended the School of Oriental Languages in Paris. He also studied in Berlin, Cambridge, and Moscow. At the School of Oriental Languages, he received his diploma under an assumed name.

> I think I remember the name of that person, but I don't know what happened to him. I didn't look for him either. He was a communist sympathizer who was not permitted to join the party so as to avoid being caught as a communist. That would have compromised him. But I only used his name. However, if I betrayed him, he could be arrested. For example, when I received my diploma from the School of Oriental Languages, the young man whose name I was using did not know. I had instructions not to contact him and he had instructions not to be involved in politics. Only once did I have the opportunity to know the person who gave me his name. He was a modest merchant who was proud to serve the cause in this way while he continued to work at his job.

This identity based upon a shared blind commitment seems unimaginable. One person was engaged in action; the other only provided his name. Two people who had never seen each other, two people who would never see each other, depended upon this game of mirrors for life and for death. Did this split personality produce any uneasiness? For Jacques the problems caused by these shared identities were swept away by discipline and his will to serve the only cause that mattered. Perhaps this young fanatic, who later would tell his unlucky friends about the novels that he had read, was sensitive to the romanticism of his own life. In any case, even more than some of his friends, he strictly respected his instructions. He was not at all a James Bond.

> When you were clandestine, you didn't have the right to have personal relationships. That was the rule. Each meeting could hide a potential trap. I was twenty, and for the nine years that I spent in the clandestine services, during missions that could be very long, I avoided all lasting personal contacts, all intimate acquaintances, all meetings outside of the revolutionary duties, out of fear of being betrayed. I had a very solitary life and it was only much later when I found myself in the Gulag that I discovered to my surprise that I could

be liked by others. For the first time, I met people who smiled at me and who wanted to talk to me. In my clandestine life, I scrupulously respected the rules of compartmentalization.

The life of young agents was spiced with danger and superficially resembled that of today's businessmen or international civil servants. They went to fancy hotels and good restaurants. They had to be well dressed, got reimbursed for taxis, and received a good regular salary. Their bosses instilled in them the strict discipline of secret agents and instructed them concerning the smallest details of local cultural customs, in order not to attract attention: what percentage of the taxi fare for the tip, where the lower-class neighborhoods were, and which neighbourhoods of the city should be avoided in order to remain safe. Above all, an agent was trained to lose the person shadowing him and to recognize his "contact."

I knew how to identify and get rid of a shadower. I also knew that there were those who were more clever than I was. To get rid of them, I had to know the city well. The solution was very simple (it can still be seen in movies): it was the subway. I jumped into the subway car just before the doors closed. The same thing with the tramway. Just at the moment it started to move, I got on. Usually we knew which buildings had an entrance on one side and an exit on the other. If I felt I was being followed, I stopped when I turned a corner and I pretended to tie my shoelaces. The shadower understood that I knew he was there. There were many other practical tricks of the trade. Sometimes I did not succeed because the spy was more intelligent than I was. I understood as time passed the extent to which democracies were defenceless because they offered too many opportunities to their adversary who wanted their demise. The relations between Soviet diplomats and the rest of the world were like a game between a cheater ready to do anything and a poor honest guy. The peoples of democracies were idiots against the Soviets.

The system relied on controlling the agents without making errors, which in practice excluded double agents.

The Soviets constantly watched their secret agents. They were surrounded by a network of informers. They were followed. Yes, the agents were even followed abroad. I was never asked to do that work. There was probably a special category of agents trained to spy on the others. A comrade had discovered this type of shadowing by our own colleagues. In the beginning he thought it was the local police. Later, he understood that he was being followed by a Soviet agent. Years later in the Gulag he met his "shadower." They became friends, relieved to find each other alive rather than shot. Compared to this, British intelligence services were a joke, a spy agency that hired Russian spies like Philby and Company!

This need to "sniff out" everything meant that our bosses almost never made mistakes and controlled their network of minor secret agents, by systematically organizing meetings even when there was nothing to do, in order not to lose contact with them. When I left to study in Cambridge for a semester, I told my boss, because my boss had to know everything. They completely ignored sex or love affairs, and such affairs were very rare. Otherwise they were aware of everything about me: if I was studying, if I was doing research for myself in a library, everything that had to do with me. I had absolute confidence in my boss. He was a good communist like me who sincerely believed in our victory. He was humane. Later I understood that you couldn't be a good communist if you weren't capable of carrying out, no matter what, an order from the party, including the most inhumane order. My last boss in the intelligence service was a Russian who had fought in the civil war. He never told me about it, but I understood that because of certain allusions he made. In the Gulag, I met someone who confirmed that. I considered my boss a hero, like a Catholic for whom the boss would have been one of the twelve disciples.

Yes, the gift of "sniffing things out" exists. For example, more than twenty years later, when I was under house arrest in Samarkand, during the fifties, I passed someone in the street whom I immediately felt was suspicious. Ten steps later, not one more, not one less, I turned around. He did too. He was a KGB agent in plain clothes. I had to wait three more years to have confirmation of my suspicions when the same man gave me my certificate of rehabilitation in 1959. From the first moment both of us were suspicious of one another!

Once the agent's package had been delivered and the mission was accomplished, or while waiting for new instructions, what did an agent do? The days were long. So Jacques walked around in the town and "breathed in the air." He was free to get to know all the cities, Italian, Spanish, and Austrian cities, beautiful places, which he would later describe in great detail from memory to his companions in captivity: "It is so wonderful to walk freely in a city!" He went to museums. He read books, no matter what. At that time he adored literature and poetry. Now, he has changed. He remembers, in Italy in the twenties, how he bought *Fascism* by Mussolini and *The Divine Comedy*, works that were permitted by his bosses. He lingered in bookstores in the Indology and Sinology sections. Did he write poetry? "My God. No, I didn't write anything, because writing would have been betrayal …"

"Young men love girls, and I still love girls!" Sometimes he met one, one who accepted him. Jacques does not really like to speak about these relationships.

> I find it indecent to speak about the woman who had confidence in me by giving herself to me. I consider any kind of talk about this subject like a betrayal of this gift that demands discretion and respect, even if I am sure that no one could find that woman seventy years later. These are memories about which I could write another book. Not now. Later. I am only ninety.
>
> I must say, I am attracted to certain kinds of asceticism. Friends often tell me that I lead the life of a monk. Because I refuse to have furniture, they think I am poor. One person says to me: "Oh, I have a big dining room table …" I have to be very firm so that he does not give me his table as a gift. I like my room that is very big because it is very empty. There is only a mattress on the floor. Recently I added a bookcase for my books and a TV. That's all.

Several times Jacques spoke again about his attraction to Eastern philosophy. When he was very young and before he knew anything about Marxism and Leninism, he was passionate about Buddhism that teaches about forgetting oneself, renunciation, and compassion. Without a doubt these values are the reason for his love of oriental languages. He returned to this after the communist cause had died for him. Today, as in the past, he practices certain forms of stoicism, which is an expression of his inner self.

Jacques is really too much of a gentleman not to fear for those who try to get too close to him: "We were really afraid because we knew that we were doing revolutionary work by trying to overthrow bourgeois capitalistic regimes. We were trying to kill them and they would defend themselves by killing us. We had to do everything possible not to be caught. The well-being of all humanity was much more important, in any case!" In the name of humanity's well-being what sacrifices, even crimes, was Jacques prepared to commit so long ago? One day he wrote: "If I had been told to jump off the Eiffel Tower to serve the cause, I would have done it without a moment's hesitation. Just like Prometheus, I wanted to steal fire from the gods for mankind's sake and was ready to pay the price for it."[2]

With such conviction concerning his ultimate objective, no means were condemned, not even informing on others. I asked Jacques about the state of his conscience: "Did you have the right to do this?" This is how he answered:

> Once we were sure that only communism would save humanity, we would denounce even our own comrade, our own brother, if we thought he was betraying the communist cause. I denounced one of my comrades because he had made very critical remarks about some communist projects, specifically about the construction between 1927 and 1933 of an enormous dam on the Dnieper. Concerning the famous *Dneprstroi* built by tens of thousands of labourers who worked with simple wheelbarrows like ants, he said: "Only slaves can work like that!"
>
> And I had other doubts about him. He had been my comrade before, but then I had suspicions about him. My doubts tormented me. How could I tolerate such questioning of everything that I believed? So I denounced him.
>
> I did not see that comrade for a long time. I learned later that he had been arrested well before I denounced him. Probably he had not been careful and others had been shocked. It is a consolation to know that it was not my denouncing him that had sent him to the Gulag. This is a minor consolation because I was really sure that anyone who was opposed to the realization of the communist grand idea, even if that person was one's own mother, was an enemy to be destroyed. I did not fear my death or the death of others. I could have been directly responsible for his death. It turns out that that was the only time I denounced someone, and it had no consequences. I was lucky. I killed no one. I did no dirty work. I was never driven into a corner.
>
> Certainly I was a minor secret agent, not involved in important matters. Through my travels, through certain leaks that I intercepted, I knew for a fact that the totalitarian Soviet system had as its goal a worldwide conspiracy. I committed a crime by having worked for a system that exterminated millions of human beings. I collaborated with the Soviet system with no intention of killing, however. I was a collaborator, and I weigh my words saying that. I am guilty of involuntary homicide. For that crime, I was punished.

Later I would realize that my comrade was right. This slavery had nothing to do with Marxism-Leninism. I could have had blood on my hands because I was ready to do anything. I did not fear death nor the torture that I experienced at the hands of the fascist police. I believed in Lenin. And on the subject of morality Lenin gave this definition: "Ethics is anything that serves the interest of the proletarian class" or, translated from communist language into good French: "Ethics is anything that suits us." I was completely convinced of that. Since capitalism was so hypocritical and dangerous it had to be destroyed at any price. Everything was permitted in order to destroy it. In the ethics of Lenin there were no crimes, nor were there any criminals.

A criminal once said to me: "In front of a crook, I behave like a crook, in front of a man, I behave like a man." Well, today I believe that one cannot be a human being and a crook at the same time.

However, during the thirties, the secret agent had neither doubts nor misgivings. If he didn't manage alone to understand something, his bosses, who were like "conscience directors," easily swept away his scruples. In Moscow, on a bench in the Kremlin park, he was reading *l'Humanite* when a man came up to him: "You must be French since you are reading that newspaper. I am Belgian. I have just been released from the camps. I am waiting to go back to Belgium." Jacques recalled, "He told me his story as a communist, sent to the Gulag under a false accusation. I cannot say that I did not listen to him politely. I easily convinced myself that there had been an error!"

The little-known history of the Comintern states, however, that "in rapid order, various sections of the Comintern began to recruit intelligence agents for the USSR. In some cases the people who agreed to undertake this illegal and clandestine work were genuinely unaware that they were working for the Soviet secret services, including the GRU, the Foreign Section (*Innostrannyi otdel'*; INO) of the Cheka-OGPU, and the NKVD."[3] Imperceptibly, and without being aware of it himself, he insists, Jacques went directly to work for a Soviet intelligence agency. Around 1933 he had an appointment in the military office in Moscow. He understood that he had become a secret agent for military information on behalf of the Red Army. From then on he would serve as a classic Soviet spy, and it is in that function that he was sent to Spain. This is how he was caught up in the Great Purges. Jacques revealed this fact to me much later. He told me about it during our subsequent conversations, a long itinerary of truth unveiling. Even he was surprised at the very moment of this confidence: "I had to wait until April 24, 2001, ten years after the fall of the Soviet Union, to be able to admit that I had worked for the Soviet spy agency."

Together we measured the strength of the intoxicating power of secrecy: how for Jacques – and for others – it became second nature, to the extent that even after the fall of the Soviet Union and his return to the free world, the former agent wrote his notebook of Parisian addresses in a secret code. These men were damaged by their training, practice, and experience and had developed the vital instinct of methodical and systematic observation of secrets in the smallest details. For them, answering the simplest of questions like "What did you do today?" could prompt them to freeze up completely. The Gulag would reinforce this syndrome because in order to survive one had to lie. Transparency was at the heart of this testimony. In the name of truth, this former secret agent tried to share with the public some of his secrets, which he had carefully kept for sixty years. However, even with this belated information, Jacques did not have a lot to reveal about the mysteries of the secret Comintern, for which he worked directly for a short time only when he was still very young.

# 6 Let Them Stuff Themselves with Caviar! They Won't Grow Old!

> When we wanted to say "spies" we said: "those mortals on whom the State counts for vigilance."
>
> Alfred de Vigny, *Lettre à Lord xxxx*

If during the missions vigilance couldn't be relaxed, in Moscow it was different. The agents felt "at home," "at our home," "in the family home," with other comrades, secret messengers, and secret agents, and they could relax. Nonetheless, the young agents were not placed randomly in the dachas where they rested. They were carefully selected according to the service they performed, in order to avoid any foreign indiscretion from their "family." In fact, it was by chatting with these other young men like himself that Jacques realized that some of them had long-term relationships with women outside their network. Those were risks that he refused to take. For a clandestine agent, any friendly or intimate meeting could conceal a trap. I asked Jacques about double agents, possible traitors within the spy service.

> With traitors one never knows because in 1937 when everyone started to get arrested, everyone was thought to be a traitor. During my clandestine missions I was sure that my comrades were honest. The fact that during our shared experience I had not found any errors, any mistakes, was proof for me. As for those who were arrested as traitors, it cannot be determined whether they were real betrayals or programmed arrests, as was often the case in the USSR, even before 1937. I believe that some of them could have betrayed if they thought they were not serving a good cause. That was theoretically possible. However, I am not sure whether those who were designated as traitors at the time I was in the clandestine service were traitors

for good reasons or were called traitors within the framework of eliminating the so-called saboteurs of the grand cause, as I was much later. It is impossible to answer for each case.

Between missions Jacques was lodged in a dacha near Moscow with his colleagues, about whom he knew nothing and would know nothing other than that they were serving the same cause in the intelligence service. There the young men could talk about anything, but the main topic of conversation was politics and their shared conviction that they would change the world. "We spoke about theory but never about our missions because the missions were secret." They were no more talkative about their identities or those of others or the rank they held in the hierarchy.

We knew that within the framework of the international relations section, we were serving the grand cause of the worldwide revolution. We also knew who was at the head of these agencies and who was the boss of our boss. That was all. The complicity among us, the young people working for the Comintern, took the place of confiding in each other. I could be close to comrades who came from faraway regions in China, for example.

In these dachas between missions, they arrived and left without notice. One morning at breakfast, Willi, Grete, or Peter would no longer be there. No one would ask questions. Returning from each mission abroad, Jacques went directly from the train station in Moscow to the office of his agency and met his boss. A meeting date was arranged. If he had to leave in the near future he went to a hotel for foreign tourists. He would adopt the style of a decent young bourgeois man because in the hotels there could be capitalist spies. His agency would tell him if he had to leave immediately or if he had to contact other comrades in other agencies, which could take weeks or even months. If the stay in Moscow had to be extended because there was no immediate or urgent mission, the young man was transferred to one of these dachas for secret agents near Moscow, where he would stay until his next mission.

The dacha was run by a Russian comrade perhaps on a mission, who functioned as administrator and whom they met sometimes during one stay or another. The dacha was co-ed and among good communists there was freedom. "There, we could have relationships with women. Jealousy in theory did not exist. It didn't always work out that way, but at least there was a pretence of freedom. Everything depended on the mood and on the person. However, the women slept with whomever they wanted."

Questioned about the official sexual mores of the Soviet Union, Jacques insisted that everything depended on the necessity of silence. "By sleeping together or, worse, by being in love, secrets could be revealed." If a Soviet civil servant or dignitary had a mistress, he was likely to betray. He became dangerous, and sometimes he was eliminated in the name of "morality," which was more a question of fear than of ethics. In the dachas, "sleeping together" between secret agents was permissible. The ideological and militant family practised endogamy, and sex was only taboo outside the dacha.

On the subject of the women he met there, Jacques remembered the famous, beautiful Alexandra Kollontai whom he knew only indirectly, the Italian Angelica Balabanova whom he saw only once, and the German Clara Zetkin who was a member of the German communist party. "Kollontai was a woman of superior intelligence who managed not to be assassinated in 1937." There were, of course, women of proletarian origins, but often these women were intellectuals and came from important families, idealists in search of personal and collective freedom for themselves, for all women, and for society. Jacques remembered Greta, a German with aristocratic origins, whose family had put her in a convent because of her rebellious character. A meeting with a group of young revolutionaries led her to join the German communist party, which was legal before Hitler came to power. There she was noticed and then contacted by the Comintern.

There were a lot of Germans in this closed circle of secret agents, and also citizens of Eastern Europe. Jacques remarked that, in general, citizens of countries where the communist party was legal were less stressed by the rules of clandestine living than the others. However, there were few French or English people. "Those who spoke several languages, like me, did not always reveal where they came from. No one spoke about themselves. In fact, in the Gulag, it would be the same. Every prisoner had the mentality of a spy."

In the dachas of the intelligence agencies, the language of the majority was spoken. Sometimes it was German, sometimes Chinese. Many of the foreign agents did not master Pushkin's language very well but tried to learn it. I asked Jacques if the number of dachas was limited and if he always went to the same ones. He told me that in the Soviet Union everything that was officially illegal but contributed to the plot to eliminate capitalism had an unlimited budget. In the dachas, the secret agents were well fed compared to other people in the Soviet Union. They received better housing, too. Sometimes they shared a room with two, three, or four people, but there were also individual rooms. Men and women were separated, but there were also rooms for couples, married or not. Jacques even knew families with children, with links to the Comintern from birth. The average age was rather young. The secret agents were rarely more than thirty or thirty-four.

This community, in spite of or perhaps because of its ideology, was not immune to pettiness. The idleness, the diversity, the strictness of the instructions sometimes disturbed those young people, who had accepted the absolute sacrifice of their lives. There was less adrenaline produced while killing time in a dacha than on a perilous mission in which one faced death. So their essential personalities re-emerged quickly. These samurai of the secret bureaucracy, lost for a while in comfortable villas, had their problems, their antipathies, and their gossiping. They were able to slander others and even to denounce them. These young idealists had not completely rid themselves of petty bourgeois individualism. They did not always behave like "good communists." A certain Czech comrade of Jacques demanded the right to own things. "This Czech was the oldest. He was perhaps thirty. A little fat. We were discussing the future communist society and he said: 'But anyway, I need to have my own clean place.'"

Can one be a communist and at the same time covetous, or even just meticulous? The answer is certainly no. Because being jealous when in love, loving food, being stingy or possessive, they were all reasons for sabotage and were considered ideological sins. At that time, internal denunciation did not have serious consequences. The worst that could happen was that those who caused problems were transferred to another dacha. This method would be used later during the Great Purges of 1937, for example, when the accused and those who were accusing him could no longer remember the details of daily life in the dachas. A mere rumour would send a secret agent to the Gulag with no trial at all.

Only the Chinese, more reserved by tradition, did not spread gossip, but they did slander. Jacques became friends with a Chinese peasant whose language he spoke. The man was called back to Moscow suddenly and never came back. Months later it was revealed that he was a traitor. Years later Jacques would learn that he had been arrested because he was a spy. Five roommates, Chinese like himself, and good communists like the others, had heard him talk in his sleep and denounced him. The moral: "If you ever go to the Soviet Union do not talk while you are dreaming."

Jacques went to Moscow for the first time in 1929, that is, twelve years after the 1917 Bolshevik revolution. He met many people who were true communists like himself, who believed blindly that the communist dream would be realized.

At that time in Russia there were still very old people who had fought in the war against the tsar, those who genuinely believed in the reality of a communist utopia. They were honest people, convinced that a big effort was needed, one more effort. Of course, there were enormous challenges with the noble cause. The bourgeoisie fought back. It gathered power to sabotage the communist project. People like me were ready to make sacrifices: "Come on, still one more effort, comrades, before victory!"

Later, I would see them disappear, those men and women who had fought in the October revolution and the coup d'état of the twenties. The newcomers who replaced them did not have the same enthusiasm. They were civil servants and bureaucrats who did their jobs, were paid a salary, and above all had privileges. Being a member of the party and having a responsibility in the party led to enormous advantages. They were another breed, for sure!

I have invented a word to describe the Soviet Union of that period. The word is "Stratistan." Strata are layers separated one from the other. And "stan" is the suffix of the names of certain authoritarian countries, such as Afghanistan, Pakistan, and Uzbekistan. This word truly describes the Soviet system, above all during the twenties. You could live in the same house, the same building, but be part of another world. For example, in 1929 when I was in Moscow for the first time, I went to see some immigrant friends. They lived in a building with several apartments for important civil servants. My friend who was a Bulgarian worker told me that he found rare food in the garbage like white bread, chunks of butter, or chocolates. (Of course, there were no garbage disposals!) These rare bits of food had been thrown away by very important civil servants who lived in the same building. At that time, when a building was built ten percent of the apartments were reserved for the executives of the Communist party, for the Army, or for the OGPU, the former KGB. Later, whole neighbourhoods were reserved for them, and those who were members of the nomenklatura were not mixed with simple citizens, as they lived a very different life. That was Stratistan!

This stratification, this walling off, I also found it in the camps. Isolation could vary greatly, and even the degrees of isolation. In 1955, I was part of a convoy that went towards the west to a transit prison in the Urals, at Sverdlovsk. In that transit prison, I met a prisoner who had never heard of the Second World War.

During his first visit to Moscow in 1929 Jacques met men and women who still remembered speeches by Lenin and Trotsky.

We had endless discussions about various political or ethical problems, but the discussions stopped quickly when someone would quote an appropriate citation from one of the masters of Marxism-Leninism: Marx, Engels, Lenin, or Stalin. At the same time, I met a young Russian worker who asked me all kinds of questions about "Guiougo," a French author that he read with a passion. I was very ashamed not to know this "Guiougo" and I asked him the title of his favourite book by that author. He answered in Russian, *Notre Dame de Paris*. I was astonished that this poor proletarian had read Victor Hugo. At that time, my new friends still quoted freely a phrase of Clausewitz: "In every mountain range there are several passes; a general's genius consists in choosing the best one." When I went back to Moscow several years later, that quote had been replaced by one of Stalin's, a saying that "in a given situation, there is only one solution, which only comrade Stalin knows."

The university studies undertaken by the young secret agent served only one purpose for his bosses: providing a cover. "I chose oriental studies because they were a passion of mine; so the studies were a cover and a passion." This was how Jacques, even while continuing his undercover work, obtained a diploma from the Oriental Language School of Paris. In the beginning, he lived near the school, at Rue de Lille, in student housing. Later he was allocated a studio apartment in the sixteenth arrondissement of Paris. Actually he was not assigned an apartment; he was told which arrondissement he should live in and he found an apartment there. His behaviour was always guided by the need not to draw attention to himself. He had drinks in bars like everyone else, but not too often. He had discussions with his friends without confiding in them. He prepared very carefully for his exams, which he passed. He was considered a serious student, despite his many absences.

In fact, he started his studies in 1930 and finished them only in 1936. At one time, his frequent absences led to a letter from the school asking him the reason for those absences.

When I went to explain to them, they said to me:
"Sir perhaps you have problems. We are ready to help you find work."
It was really touching. I tried to reassure them. Work! I had too many missions, one after the other. During my studies in oriental languages, I had been sent to mainly Scandinavian countries and as a substitute for someone to northern Africa. But when I was not travelling, I was very diligent.

At the Oriental Language School, Jacques studied Persian and Chinese as well as the languages of India: Urdu and Hindi.

I never finished my studies of Persian, but in Samarkand, the country of the Tadjiks who speak Persian, I managed to make myself understood a little. Of the dozen languages that I spoke all my life, Chinese is the one that I worked on the most systematically. I can still speak it a little. However, since I don't use it or read it or write it, it is fading. I can talk one-on-one with someone but not follow a conversation. As for Urdu, I still only know the basics. Recently, they restored the facade of the building where I live in Montreuil. Through the open window, I heard not the words but the music of Urdu. When the workers arrived on their platform on the scaffold in front of my open window, I spoke to them in Urdu. They were very surprised!

Jacques's résumé in 1982 listed, other than the languages mentioned above, French and Polish, his native languages, plus the languages of his studies: Russian, German, English, Spanish, and Italian. Around 1932, he studied for a semester in Cambridge, where he took a class with a renowned specialist in the history of India.

At Cambridge and at Oxford, students lived in houses of two, three storeys, with small apartments. There I shared an apartment with a young man from Mumbai and afterwards with an Englishman. Of course, I was not involved in politics, and if it came up in a conversation I spoke like everybody else. However, it was the period when sons of good English families were becoming fascinated by Marxism-Leninism. They would become future Russian spies. I remember having met the famous Philby. However, I knew other sons of good families, like him, who were complete revolutionaries, which at the time delighted me. Obviously, when I spoke with them, I pretended to have nothing to do with the communist world. I avoided spending too much time with them: as a secret agent I knew too well that the attention of the police should not be focused on me. So there were no discussions other than casual ones. In neutral territory like in a classroom, before or after the professor's lecture, they would start to talk and I listened. I do not think that at the time they were secret Soviet agents because their superiors would have forbidden them to reveal themselves by talking like that before or after class. They had a hardline Marxist-Leninist discourse and they were better educated than I was, above all in matters related to theory.

Hearing those British sons of the wealthy who believed, like I did, in the revolution reinforced my convictions that the revolution would come tomorrow, or maybe in just two or three years at most. I was as naive as Soviet power that, at least in the twenties, seemed to believe that the worldwide revolution was forthcoming. In the beginning, the Soviet justice system gave sentences that were relatively short, because they thought that the communist worldwide victory was at hand. As the socialist horizon receded, the length of the sentences increased. I wrote in *The Gulag Handbook* about how in the first years of the Bolshevik regime, sentences were not precise in time and there were formulas such as "until the end of the civil war," "until he repents," and "until the victory of the worldwide revolution." The maximum sentences in 1921 were limited to five years, but they would be extended to twenty-five years in 1937. From the beginning of the twenties a prisoner was never sure he would be freed at the end of his sentence. The practice of imposing a new sentence under any pretext, even sometimes before the end of the first sentence, became more and more common.

During his stay in Cambridge, Jacques still had his eyes fixed on the red line that led directly to the worldwide revolution for which he worked with all his energy. Later, when he stayed in the Soviet Union waiting for a mission, he would take classes at the Narimanov Institute of Oriental Studies in Moscow. There, he continued to improve his knowledge of the same languages he studied while in Paris.

I found that many students had no scholastic training. And for a good reason! Having fought in the civil war and then having participated in the rebuilding of the country, they hadn't gone to secondary school or they hadn't finished secondary school. I was surprised to hear a Russian student of Turkish say to me:
"You know, in Turkish, as in Russian, there is a subject, a verb and an object."
He was very proud of his discovery!

The European training of Jacques, thanks to the Soviet intelligence agencies, would be highly effective. Later, all those languages would help him to survive in the Gulag. Sometimes he would translate. Other times he would communicate with prisoners who came from abroad. In Samarkand, his knowledge of Persian helped him greatly. This knowledge combined with his travels gave the young man great insight into different mentalities and lifestyles. It enabled him to adapt to unimaginable conditions for a child of wealthy parents who was considered too fragile to be sent to school. "Languages expand the mind, they spark your curiosity. They allow you to understand different cultures and civilizations, like this friend who was learning Turkish and discovered that grammar was similar in many languages." Jacques's knowledge of languages, however, had a downside. It would lead to the worst suspicions and was used to support accusations that the young agent was a foreign spy, even later as a prisoner of the Gulag Archipelago.

On his résumé, Jacques summarizes his years from 1929 to 1936 as follows, downplaying his language studies: "An illegal student and apprentice of the Comintern. Transferred to the legal German communist party (KPD) and studied fine arts in Berlin. Ordered to the Technical Division of the Comintern. Studied Oriental civilizations in Paris (Sorbonne, ELOV). Educational work and travels through Europe were all undertaken at Comintern direction and with names different from my birthname."

Between twenty and twenty-six the young agent for the Comintern, who had quickly become a Soviet spy, lived a dangerous existence that would please any young idealist who dreamed of action. Obeying obscure orders, not having a fixed home or a fixed country or a circle of friends and family, he was far removed from any ordinary human reality. In 1936, he wasn't sent on missions, but he worked at the Frunze Military Academy in Moscow, where he taught conversation classes.

> It was a prestigious military academy where Soviet officers took language classes, in addition to other courses. A large number of the lowly messengers of the Comintern were students at this university and went on missions between their classes. I remember that in my class, one of the topics of conversation was the interrogation of a prisoner of war. First I played the role of the Soviet prisoner officer; then it was the turn of the student. A student answered: "But we are never prisoners." In fact, I learned that Stalin added a clause to the military code according to which Soviet soldiers never surrendered.

Shortly before he was arrested, Jacques stayed at Sochi on the Black Sea in a sanatorium for the privileged with other comrades from the international espionage agencies, three of whom were Chinese.

> The special agents were really well fed, and every morning at breakfast at our table for four there was a jar of caviar. I ate it absentmindedly, for I was used to this kind of food at my stepfather's. When it was empty the waiters filled it up again. During the day we were idle. I was the

only one who spoke Russian, and I walked around the sanatorium talking with people. One day I started a conversation with a worker, a real Stakhanovite. He started to tell me about his daily life and how he liked the sanatorium where bread tickets were not needed like in the rest of the Soviet Union. First surprise! I did not know that the Soviets had a system of ration cards. The second surprise was when I learned that he had never seen caviar, which we ate in such quantity so freely every day. That evening I spoke to my three friends, who knew at least that caviar was a luxury food, which should not have been served to us every morning. They were as indignant as I was to learn that the Soviet people, whom we venerated, were not treated the same way that we were treated. The four of us went to see the head doctor who managed the sanatorium, and I, the spokesperson for the group, asked him in Russian to no longer serve us caviar. The director was a man of a certain age who must also have been an idealist in his youth. He listened to us seriously and said: "You know, comrades, that the working class is not the party. Here, you are the guests of working-class people who have decided to provide you with the best conditions because you risk your lives for them. You represent the vanguard, the guides who lead the way for the future of the working class. Perhaps the Soviet workers seem a bit naive for you, but they are the people who want this superior comfort for you."

The next morning at breakfast, the jar of caviar was still there on our table, but we never ate it again. I recall now the emotional expression of the head doctor when he talked to us. It was 1936 and the Great Purges had already started. He must have said to himself: "Let them stuff themselves with caviar! They won't grow old!"

During his years in training, assuming false identities with potentially serious consequences, the clandestine and underground life represented a school of endurance and patience for Jacques. But that was nothing compared to the school that was about to become his own. If for millions of deported prisoners, the Gulag was the hell that Solzhenitsyn described in *The First Circle*, *Cancer Ward*, and *The Gulag Archipelago*, Jacques maintained that the Gulag had been a university for him, an enormous school of truth from which one returns changed and where, contrary to many of his comrades, he left neither his life nor his soul. It was a school from which he brought back a notebook as a guide and memoir of what could still happen again.

# 7 Early Indications of an Announced Arrest

Although the Soviet Union initially intended to avoid an overt role, the Comintern mobilized all its sections for the cause of Republican Spain, using the conflict as a tremendous vehicle for antifascist propaganda, with particularly good results for the Communist movement … As soon as Stalin had decided that Spain presented important opportunities for the Soviet Union and that intervention was therefore necessary, Moscow sent a large contingent of advisers and other personnel to that country.

Stéphane Courtois and Jean-Louis Panné,
*The Black Book of Communism*

Before being swallowed up by the Great Purges like millions of others, Jacques was an astute observer of events that offered signs of what was to come. First, it was the routine actions of the party to eliminate people held responsible for economic failures. Later, it was the successive campaigns of state terror.

But how could this good communist, jailed by Polish fascists, a secret agent ready to sacrifice his life – how could he have doubted what was to come? In fact, until the last moment, until the minute he was arrested, he suspected something. But he had no concerns.

> *Chistka*. In Russian, the same word is used for Stalin's purges with mass arrests and for the purge commissions that preceded them. When I was a young communist I attended a meeting in Russia [the Soviet Union] of the purge commission with other young foreign communists. The idea initially was Lenin's. Since the party was so powerful, it was expected that suspicious elements would try to infiltrate it. Thus purging was necessary. In the beginning, the idea was very democratic. The purge meetings were open to the public. The presence of party members was

required, but the meetings were also open to non-party members. And everybody, party members and non-members, could ask questions.

Our bosses wanted us, the young foreign agents, to attend this democratic Soviet procedure. It took place in military barracks. There was a very old general who had become famous during the civil war when he put down the mutiny of sailors in Kronstadt in 1921. In the large meeting room, the purge commission was seated on a platform. There were three or five members, but always an odd number so that the president could cast the deciding vote. The commission was composed of old Bolsheviks, one of whom was the famous Rosalia Zemlyachka, known for her militancy under the tsars. She was a tiny woman, very thin, with grey hair drawn back, and she wore a very simple dress. It was summer and she was not wearing shoes but simple slippers. She asked this decorated general very hard questions.

The "purged" appeared one after the other. They were asked how long they had been members of the party and sometimes why. Then they were asked many questions to determine if their behaviour had been politically and morally correct. Since the general was so famous, a kind of historical figure, the commission asked him questions that had been agreed upon beforehand. But Zemlyachka did not hesitate to ask this general other questions, and he was three times taller than she was. He told how he had managed his unit of the Red Army. Then she asked him if with all his activities he had time to read theoretical literature. And he humbly answered that tiny little woman, with fear in his voice:

"Yes, I managed to."

He was so intimidated that she asked him another question to reassure him. As a fervent communist I could not believe this spectacle of Soviet communist democracy.

Then came the turn of a captain or commander who was perhaps thirty-five. He went up to the platform. He was standing and he answered the questions of the commission. At the end Zemlyachka questioned him:

"Is the Red Army a national army or an international army?"

The soldier answered:

"National."

And she responded with the voice of a primary school teacher:

"No. International!"

And he answered "international" like a docile student. Later, I learned who that man was. He was a member of the troops that had fought during the civil war in Ukraine. He had been recognized for his heroism. And I saw him completely diminished in front of that tiny woman who represented the infallibility of the party and who decided whether he was a good communist or not.

After the questioning the comrade being questioned left or he was asked to wait. It was a crucial exam for all the members of the party, whether they were floor sweepers or directors of institutions. And in order to impress us the comrades of the group remarked, "Did you see how the big boss yielded, questioned by that woman?"

In general, the interrogation lasted only five minutes. Some more difficult cases took longer. Often the commission made its decision immediately: "You have been excluded from the party. Of course, you have the right to appeal."

In the beginning, such a verdict did not have serious consequences. Years later, during the Great Purges, the files of those who had failed the purge commissions were used to send them to the Gulag or to execute them. Everything could be used and effectively was used when the political police were looking for pretexts. One comrade in Butyrka prison in 1937 had been arrested because in 1927 he had fallen in love with Trotsky's cook. Since Trotsky was very democratic, his cook lived in the family apartment. Unfortunately, the comrade courted the cook in Trotsky's home. Ten years later, when the regime went looking for saboteurs of socialist development, he became a prime suspect. He was arrested and sent to the Gulag.

The young Jacques did not notice these official warnings. Neither did he notice other, more personal warnings. They came from one of his bosses at the information agency for international espionage of the Red Army, which continued to play an important clandestine role in Jacques's life. This man's name was Adam. He was a Polish Jew, older than Jacques – in his forties at the time. He had more experience, having worked in the secret services since 1920. "It was around 1935–1936 in Switzerland in Neuchâtel. Adam had a very high position in the hierarchy while I had a lowly position. He suggested going for a boat ride with me on the lake. When we were far from listening ears, he told me that the bureau chief was not pleased with me. It was a way of telling me that I was in danger."

But Jacques either didn't or couldn't hear the warning. Adam would not have acted differently than Jacques. In 1938, Adam was called back to Moscow from the United States where he was on a secret mission and, knowing the possible consequences, returned. Years later, when Jacques met him in an endless crowd of Gulag prisoners, he asked Adam: "Why is it that you, with your intelligence and your knowledge of the system, rushed back from the United States when

Moscow called you?" And Adam answered: "Listen, all my comrades had been executed, all victims of the Great Purges. I came back to die with them."

Many of these men gave themselves up in desperation while others, for the same reason, chose to admit to crimes they hadn't committed. "When the cause died," Jacques said, "then men chose to die with it." However, Adam did not die in the Gulag. Neither did Jacques. And twenty years later, a freed Adam would help Jacques to acquire rehabilitation.

On their tiny boat where their words were carried away by the wind on the calm waters of the lake of Neuchâtel, how could those two international communists, who had become Soviet spies, have imagined such finality to their preoccupations? In a few months Jacques would be sent to the land of Franco in the middle of the Spanish civil war with a clandestine short-wave radio transmitter. Spain in the years 1936–39 was a laboratory for the Soviets. They would experiment with techniques there that they would later use, especially after the Second World War. Jacques could not know that this mission would be his last.

It is a cliché to say that you cannot run away from yourself. Today Jacques insists on asking himself whether someone had wanted to help him – Adam for example – and had given him that mission in Spain so that he could escape. In fact, years later Jacques said that he discovered that his 1937 mission in Franco's territory did not appear in his KGB file. Someone might have erased all traces of that mission, hoping that the young agent would not answer the funereal order calling him back to Moscow to be condemned and deported. However, a certificate found in the Central State Archives of the Soviet Army, dated 23 August 1960, indicates that Jacques Rossi had "worked" from April 13 until November 1937. No other details were given.

For that kind of mission two people were required: at that time Jacques was about twenty-seven and a certain "Luisa," another secret agent, was twenty-three. Officially, they were husband and wife – a young Spanish-speaking husband and wife from Central America. His wife was ill and her health would benefit from the mild Spanish climate. On the pretext of her illness, she never left her hotel room, which permitted uninterrupted listening day and night to the radio transmitter that was hidden in the room in disassembled pieces. The fake couple was supposedly waiting for an apartment, but they would never move.

Under a false Spanish name, Luisa hid her real identity. She was probably an Austrian from a good family. Jacques did not know anything more about her because they were supposed to come from Latin America, but he surmised: "Behaviour and manners in the details of daily life revealed one's social class and showed whether one was or was not from the proletariat without having to ask questions. I really had the impression that she was Austrian because of her pronunciation. When I used certain expressions in German she understood. I didn't insist on trying to get the truth out of her." In any case, they spoke Spanish together. They had met in Moscow just before leaving for Spain. "We always had that powerful conviction that we were serving a very important cause. Luisa allowed herself to be called the wife of a man that she was meeting for the first time! It was the sense of sacrifice." But the sacrifice turned out just fine for these two protagonists.

> She was pretty and pleasant, my nice little telegraphist. We got along well! I received number-coded messages, which I translated and sent to certain people at given times. If the comrade did not appear, he had another meeting scheduled two days later. Those same comrades sometimes gave me uncoded messages with no meaning, which I translated into a code for Luisa. I had my assigned area, that is to say a liaison with my neighbour on the left and my neighbour on the right who had their airwave radios, their *ratsia*, the Russian abbreviation for radio station (*radio-stantsia*), a term that the secret agents often used.

Some time after arriving in Valladolid, Jacques received a coded cable ordering him to "return to the village" immediately. "Village" meant Moscow, of course. He was surprised. He had been told before he left: "Do not leave your job for any reason without first having been replaced. Otherwise you will create a void." Sometimes a successor was sent without reason. But there was no replacement on the horizon. Jacques decided to wait for the liaison that they only used for a very few minutes once or twice a week in order not to be detected. Two or three days later he sent a cable in order to make sure he understood that he had to "return to the village." The answer was: "Come back immediately." Jacques still did not want to accept this order, but he decided to obey, despite his "wife's" pleading: "We knew that there were a lot of arrests in Moscow. For a good communist, discipline was discipline. A soldier of the revolution obeyed orders and did not discuss them." Yet he knew better. Jacques and his companion read the newspapers of the capitalist and pro-Franco press, which spoke about the mass arrests and trials in Moscow. Of course, Jacques thought it was anti-communist propaganda. But Luisa had her doubts. "Women are usually more intelligent because they follow their intuition. She begged me not to go. She cried. We had become very attached to each other. Being together serving the most noble of causes created bonds. I consoled her as best I could. In any case, I left."

His blindness was such that when the investigating commissar of the Moscow prison asked him whether he knew why he had been arrested, he thought that they were holding against him the fact that he had not denounced Luisa, who wanted to keep him from going back to "the village." Yet Jacques, confronted by this doubting young woman, had not the slightest concern. Apprehension perhaps, but for her more than for himself. He took the boat to France and found his contact in Paris.

> I knew how to find him. I knew by heart the codes and the phone numbers. I waited for the comrade in a bistro with the newspaper we had agreed upon. It was as always. He asked me if the table was free. We chatted a bit. Then we exchanged the password. The comrade knew about my orders and told me to go back to Moscow as soon as possible. I changed my identity and flew to Moscow while the Great Purges were in full swing. Above all, I did not want to know that everyone was being arrested – members of the central and regional party organization, the Comintern, and other agencies.

Jacques has still not forgotten the clandestine radio transmitter and the young spy whose marital bed he shared in Spain for several weeks sixty years ago. He knows neither her family name nor her real first name, and not even her nationality. He would like to see her again and calculates that his ex-fake-wife would be eighty-seven now, if she survived. He hopes that she would have tried to escape and rejoin her family.

> Or she might have been arrested by Franco's police. At least she would have avoided the Gulag. Among those who were captured later by the Soviets there were so few who survived, even if they hadn't been condemned to death. For example, there was Greta Buber-Neumann, whom I met during the thirties. When Stalin turned her over to Hitler within the framework of their alliance treaty, she was thrown into a Nazi camp with other German communist detainees.[1] For a communist to be in a fascist jail was a

glorious honour. By contrast, for the same person, the communist jails were deep pits of despair.

In Moscow, Jacques went to headquarters. His boss, Kraietsky, wasn't there. He hadn't been seen for two days; no one knew where he was. Terror reigned in the offices. There were arrests everywhere. No one dared say out loud that the boss had been arrested. Perhaps he was on a secret mission. Imagining that one could be arrested was tantamount to anti-Soviet propaganda. If those close to a person learned that in fact he had been arrested they trembled in fear that they were next. Jacques entered the building with small presents. It was the custom to bring back small presents for those comrades who did not travel abroad. He brought back trinkets: stockings for the women, lighters and pens for everyone; things that could not be found in the Soviet Union. He always had cordial relationships with the secretaries and the lower-level staff of civil servants at the spy agency. But this time when he entered the building, he was shocked by the change.

> Suddenly, I saw those comrades whom I knew well, who knew me well but who looked at me with glassy stares, like stuffed animals. No expression! Certainly, they recognized me but their looks pierced through me as though I were a wall. That sent a shiver down my spine! They were people I regularly spent time with. To my questions the answers were always monosyllabic: No, yes, no, we don't know. They feared saying something that could be used against them.

However, he introduced himself at the office entrance as usual: said his name and requested to see his superior officer, the statutory practice of an agent coming from abroad. His boss Kraietsky was absent, so he was sent to see someone else, who decided where he would lodge. He was not put out in the street. He was sent to the Intourist hotel, a place for short stays, and told to come back the next day to see "whether his boss was there." The next day, Kraietsky was still not back. Jacques returned the day after and the following days.

Finally, he found another superior officer who set up a meeting five days later. At that time he told Jacques that he was new to the job and he needed some time before he could meet the young agent. Finally, two weeks later, the new boss found the time and started the interview by saying: "I have just been given responsibility for this mess created by Kraietsky, Hitler's agent!"

Jacques didn't need an explanation. He immediately understood that his boss had been arrested. "I started by being indignant. What a jerk, that Kraietski. He seemed like such a good communist. I had been to his dacha, and I knew his little boy. I thought he was a good guy! Nobody can be trusted!"

His replacement, a tall, swarthy Cossack with a ruddy face named Chernomordik, set up another meeting two weeks later. By the time Jacques went to the meeting it was Chernomordik's turn to be arrested. "Once more, no boss. This time I was ordered to appear immediately. I had been waiting for a long time. When I was finally arrested, I almost said, 'phew'! I knew deep down that this adventure could not end any other way."

# 8 The Trap

The first day of imprisonment is hard to bear, whether it be in a cell, in a fortress, or in penal servitude.
> Fyodor Dostoyevsky, *Memoirs from the House of the Dead*

When he arrived in Moscow, Jacques returned to one of the dachas, where he waited for his future to be decided, as he had done between missions. When he learned that a good German friend of his had been imprisoned, he wanted to visit the man's wife and four-year-old daughter to comfort them. He was met by a welcoming order: "Get the hell out of here." Any family with an arrested member knew it was being watched. The arrest of a friend whom one visited could lead to the arrest of the visitor. The purge was contagious like the plague.

However, Jacques did not put off his marriage to Julita, a young Spaniard from a family of Madrid intellectuals who did not work for the Comintern and was not a member of the party. She was a sympathizer whom Jacques had truly fallen in love with. He talks about her as he does about all those with whom he had grown close. In Moscow, Julita took care of Spanish children that the Soviet government pretended it was protecting from the Spanish civil war. Sadly, some of them would be sent to the Gulag. Jacques and Julita had decided on the wedding while they were abroad. It was supposed to take place on what turned out to be the day after Jacques was arrested. The evening before, Jacques and Julita visited their good friends, Emma and Harry, American communists who lived in Moscow, the same people whose doorbell Jacques would ring twenty years later when he got out of the Gulag.

Just before ringing the bell of the apartment, Julita wiped from Jacques's cheek the smudge of red lipstick left by her kiss. Jacques kept that handkerchief. He would keep it in the Butyrka prison until the cloth was worn thin, long after the mark of Julita's lips had completely faded away. In one of the boxes containing several photos that Jacques had kept, there was a portrait of Julita drawn by Jacques in 1956. On the back of the portrait was a message of love she signed at the end of the summer of 1937. Questioned about this little mystery, Jacques's memory wavered. Perhaps he had kept it with his meagre belongings during his wandering in the Archipelago. He also suggested that perhaps twenty years later he had reproduced from memory that message of love from the young Spanish woman.

The day after this visit – it was December 1937 – comrade Natasha B. phoned Jacques from the agency office. He had been out during the evening, but he found a note on his door when he came back. He was to prepare himself for departure. The order was for the next day. He was to present himself with his luggage and follow the instructions that a comrade would give him the next day during the meeting to prepare for the voyage. Jacques tried to contact Julita to tell her that the wedding would not take place the following day as planned, but she was not at home. He carefully prepared his trunk, a luxurious suitcase covered with stickers of European hotels. He was dressed well, in the suit of a rich Latin American tailored in Paris, with suede shoes, one of his dozens of ties and, early that Moscow winter, an English camel hair coat that was light but warm. A felt hat finished off the sober elegance of his outfit. He did not take any Soviet currency, which would have betrayed him abroad. In his pockets he had exactly one ruble and 167 kopecks, meagre resources for twenty years in prison.

The next day, a sinister day in Jacques's memory and whose precise date he does not remember, he meekly went to the NKVD office. There Natasha B., the secretary, a good friend whom he had known for a long time, whom he had flirted with a bit in the past, said to him that he would leave immediately for Franco's Spain. They had received precise instructions from another agency. She said that being called back from Spain had been a misunderstanding. It was too bad because the radio transmitter had been left without an operator and that had to be corrected as quickly as possible.

"You will go with comrade Ivan."

Suddenly, Jacques became aware of the presence of this unknown comrade whom he had not at first noticed. Natasha embraced Jacques and wished him a good trip. With the same friendliness, Ivan took the trunk and Jacques followed. A gorgeous Packard was waiting for them outside with a chauffeur. Jacques could not identify either the car or the driver. However, he thought he knew all the cars of the security police, usually small and Soviet made. He did not know the driver either. The two men got into the car. Jacques would not ask the only question that was bothering him despite his certitude: Where are we going? The conversation was chit chat, pleasant, not serious. Jacques looked out the window, trying to know where he was but never asking that small, piercing, unanswered question: Where are we going?

Finally, the car crossed Dzerzhinsky Square and stopped in front of the entrance to the Interior Ministry of the Lubianka, along a small street. Jacques noticed that it was not the main entrance.

"Get out, comrade!"

He got out of the car. The comrade again politely took his trunk and they entered the hidden doorway that the comrade closed immediately behind them. They were in a small, overheated room. At the back, there was another door guarded by a soldier armed with a bayonet rifle. Although he only met him once, Jacques remembered him with amazing precision. The man had big black eyes, high cheekbones, scars from pox on his cheeks, and wore the pointed hat of the Red Army with a large red star. The comrade-guide presented a paper. The soldier gestured with his head and opened the door. The two men went through that second door.

And suddenly Jacques was alone. He didn't know how the guide had managed to disappear as if he had exited through a trap door. He did not know that later he would see this lieutenant in the office of the investigating commissar. He was alone among his own, the pure and serious communist, the young idealist who had become a Soviet agent, turned in by his own group in the spy agency, standing with his trunk in a room that looked like a customs office. In the Lubianka prison.

I don't know when my guide disappeared. I was already nervous. I wasn't paying attention. In any case, he was no longer there. On the other hand, there were three or four young soldiers in fur hats with strawberry-coloured coats of arms who asked me nicely:

"Would you please open your trunk and empty your pockets?"

These young soldiers were very polite. I didn't know where we were, but what I knew well was that we were in the building of the political police and that we were in a prison, "the big house," as it was called. They asked me to open the trunk and they made a detailed list of everything that was in it. I said to myself that these precautions were necessary when one was going abroad as a spy. I had recently warned a comrade who knew nothing about the USSR and had wrapped his shoes in his suitcase using pages from *Pravda*. A detail like that could betray you! Then the soldiers had me undress and they inspected my clothes. I got dressed again, surprised that they kept my tie. Then they took me to a nearby office and presented me with a detailed list of all my personal possessions and gave me a receipt, which I kept. I sat down on a chair in front of a small desk where there was an ink pot with purple ink. That's traditional in Russia – purple ink, a pen holder, a pen, and a questionnaire. And very pleasantly, they said:

"Would you please fill this out?"

I took the pen. Questionnaires in Russia were an institution, everywhere and always. They were part of the system.

Surname, first name, party membership, date of birth, place of birth, nationality – an entire page of questions that I answered automatically, still not understanding. "Rossi Jacques Robertovitch." I turned the pages containing a multitude of questions. I got to the last page and I read: signature of the accused. Accused! I was accused! I turned the questionnaire over and I reread the title on the first page, which I hadn't even looked at earlier and which stated in capital letters: QUESTIONNAIRE FOR THE ACCUSED. In my anxiety, I had skipped that phrase, which was so obvious on the page. It was as big as a nose in the middle of a face. When people do not accept reality I cite this example! Yes, this was happening to me. Later in prison, I would continue not to hear the moans of the tortured. I had not seen that title written in bold letters. I hadn't wanted to see it, and it was not until the end of the questionnaire that I was forced to understand the word: *accused*.

I jumped up and ran to the door, which I discovered had no door knob but a Judas window. I knocked on the door. Immediately a soldier appeared:

"What is it?"

"Why am I accused?"

Then very calmly and politely, he answered:

"You will learn tomorrow during the interrogation."

Kraietsky, Jacques's superior, was shot. Thirty years later, Jacques would meet Kraietsky's son, a professor at Warsaw University. In 1937, he was a small boy of about seven. He was respected in communist Poland because his father had been assassinated in Moscow, and was rehabilitated as a good communist after the Twentieth Party Congress. The Poles were proud of their courageous militants, whom they pretended were victims of Stalinism and not of Marxism-Leninism.

Julita would be spared. Jacques thought of her during those first hours of despair in the Lubianka prison. Did he regret this act of fate that had at the last minute prevented their marriage? "The NKVD had been very nice to prevent this marriage because, sadly, she would have been very unhappy if we had married." Jacques knew that if he tried to contact her she would have problems. He chose not to contact her. Two years later, when he was in the camps, he gave a letter to a freed criminal offender who was going back to Moscow. In that letter he begged Julita to leave the USSR, if she could manage to get a permit from Soviet authorities. He knew that all the refugees who had been graciously welcomed by the Soviet government found themselves, in fact, caught in a trap. The young woman managed to send a message back to him. The letter reassured him. She convinced him that she would indeed try to leave the Soviet Union. Years later, Jacques learned that she went to live in Mexico. Forty-three years later, during his stay in Washington, DC, in the United States, Jacques, the former fiancé, made an effort to find her, but it was in vain. He would keep her small handkerchief stained by her lipstick that slowly lost the odour and colours of life, as well as a vivid memory that had not faded for over fifty years since that day in August 1937. That was the day he lost his freedom and – what was a thousand times worse for him, he adds – he started to lose the conviction that he had been devoted to the most just of all causes.

Did he ever ask himself during those first moments why he had agreed to come back from Spain, why he hadn't tried to flee, given that he knew of the mass arrests in Moscow?

> I came back to Moscow because I was sure that those who were being arrested were enemies of the people. This phenomenon could not concern me. And as a soldier of the revolution, I did not discuss. I obeyed. Once in Moscow, escape was impossible. First, from a material point of view because when I arrived in the offices of the clandestine services, in conformity with the regulations, I turned in my passport. I couldn't leave the country. Later, I understood that even if I had been able to leave with a passport, all borders would have been closed for me.
>
> But above all, and I repeat – morally, I did not think of that. I was a communist. Escaping would have meant declaring that I was no longer a part of the communist system, the same way that a criminal, rejected by his own, would accept his destiny without complaining. Later, I would see a criminal "condemned" by his peers, all curled up on the ground and shaken by convulsive trembling. He did not try at all to avoid the blows of the axe. Of course, at that time, I couldn't imagine that I could actually be arrested. In my fierce naivety I thought that if by chance I were arrested, "they" would finally recognize that I was a communist one hundred per cent, and they would admit their mistake. Once I had come back to Moscow and was imprisoned, I did not dream of asking myself why I had come back.

I learned that in difficult situations I should not hurt myself more by turning the knife in the wound, because the very professional NKVD (the future KGB) was already there to torture me. I even went further. In my fantasies in prison, I said to myself that if the French or Polish Consul came and demanded my release, I would refuse to speak to them because the people who imprisoned me and myself, we were communists, real communists, and they were dirty capitalists.

Without foreseeing it, without knowing it, Jacques Rossi had just been swallowed up with thousands of his comrades in what history would call the Great Purges or the Great Terror. Decades later the Great Purges would become a long passage in *The Gulag Handbook* by the same Jacques Rossi – witness, victim, chronicler and writer of one of the most terrible episodes of our last century. His *Gulag Handbook* defines the Great Purges as "the period of terror under Stalin between 1936 and 1938, also known as 'the year thirty-seven' or in short form 'thirty-seven.'"

Under Stalin's orders, a special *dvoïka* (or team of two commissars) would compile a list of individuals to be shot. The list included high-ranking people from various segments of society – the party, the military, industry, science, diplomacy, culture, and the press. More than three hundred lists were drawn up with more than three hundred names on each list. As soon as they were signed by Stalin and another member of the Politiburo (most often Zhdanov or Molotov), the political police or NKVD arrested these individuals under false charges. They were forced to confess. The court invariably condemned them to sentences that had been decided before the trials: death or hard labour. In their attempt to make this horrible farce credible, the political police uncovered vast networks of completely innocent accomplices. This pattern of collective punishment led to an avalanche of arrests.

Long after the collapse of the USSR, the exact number of victims remains unknown. Even today, new mass graves are still being discovered. The Great Purges resulted in the execution of over three-quarters of a million people, and enabled Stalin to position himself as the unique inheritor of Lenin. He was able to put in positions of responsibility those faithful to him no matter how incompetent they were. Strangely, very few outcries came from the West to denounce the crimes committed during the Great Purges. On the contrary, panicked by the rise of barbaric fascism and recognizing their complete inability to block its course, many intellectuals – including the most gifted – considered the only solution to be a blind confidence in Stalin and his party, the sole defenders of democracy.[1] Historians confirm that from September 1936 until November 1938 under the direction of Nikolai Yezhov's NKVD, many citizens, from party dignitaries to ordinary civilians, became the victims of repression. The objective was to meet established quotas of counter-revolutionaries to be eliminated.[2]

Jacques tried to understand why the destiny of the young secret agent had been less final than that of the executed dignitaries. Like the time he was arrested in Poland as a communist student, the young Soviet military spy insisted that he occupied the lowest rung on the ladder. That is how he explained why he had not been executed. His shock and pain were no less acute. For him, the cause had died. He was a communist, and here he was in a communist prison – a member of the Communist International, a secret intelligence agent of the Red Army of the Soviet Union. And here he was in a Soviet prison. Instead of saying to him after a certain time, "Excuse us, comrade. We've made a mistake. You are a courageous revolutionary," they let him wallow in what Jacques calls with bitterness that "bloody sewer."

> In the beginning, I thought that if Stalin "knew," I would be rehabilitated with all the other innocent people. Then I finally realized that NO: Stalin knew. I heard Russians who were older than me who said: "Oh, if Lenin were still alive this would not have happened!" I believed that too. However, after a certain period of time, I understood that if Lenin had been alive, everything would have been the same. That was the problem. We had a wonderful project, just great. But it was unfeasible, a dream. From the time we understood that it was a dream, a utopia that was impossible to put into practice, we could not accept that fact. We then had to spread terror among the people before they started to demand a reckoning. One's own citizens were persecuted who were unlucky witnesses and who knew that the beautiful vision was only an illusion.
>
> I insist – even if I am repeating myself – that there was an evolution. In the beginning, everyone believed. That is why the punishments were not severe and one could still breathe the air. But as the project eventually transformed into a mirage, rather than saying, "Comrades, we are on the wrong track; let's stop and change course," we continued to advance and make others advance through terror towards the abyss. The objective of the Great Purges consisted in explaining to the public that the beautiful dream was not being realized because of these scapegoats. The purges were also meant to intimidate the population so that it did not ask questions.

Let us not forget that among the differences between fascism and Marxism-Leninism was the fact that communists (Soviets and others) persecuted their own citizens, while the Nazis, in spite of purges carried out within their own party, eliminated mainly those they considered alien – minorities, like Jews and gypsies. That is why Jews and gypsies were victims par excellence. No Jews wanted Nazism. It was the same for Russian peasants who refused the collective farms and were arrested for that reason and executed. They were also victims. They also refused communism. If I hadn't been a communist I would not have found myself in the Gulag. Because I was, I went there willingly.

I believe that when you are as committed as I was, with all your heart, then you should be able to judge. If you can't understand that we were trying to create an unrealizable utopia and that such a commitment could only lead to crime and lying, then you shouldn't pretend to be a hero. I compromised myself in the pursuit of that utopia. I was guilty. I paid the price. Here in the West, I have met leftists with whom I have discussed a lot. At first, they were quite interested in my experience and in what I had to say, but then quickly they avoided meeting me because, in fact, I represented a living witness to their hypocrisy. Despite everything, they preferred to continue to believe in communism and to believe in Santa Claus. And they were content to think that everything was the fault of Stalin. We are all the same, me and the others. We like dreams. We like to believe in Santa Claus, especially when it costs nothing. But I had to pay the price.

All of these considerations were still far from the mind of young Jacques when he waited in his first transit cell in the Lubianka prison (with his fancy suit, his suede shoes and felt hat) to be transferred to the "dog house." All the innocent former fifty-eighters [political prisoners or those sentenced for so-called counter-revolutionary activity] speak about the trauma of being arrested, that fracture of one's entire being, which propelled some of the weakest into madness. It was a storm that pushed the present into the past and transformed what was unthinkable into probability, and then into reality. At that time, the stupefaction, the fear, and the concern for the woman he left behind during this shattering of all his reasons for living must have occupied Jacques's thoughts. Above all, he was preparing to prove the mistake, to vindicate himself, to show his total innocence point by point. At the same time, despite the brutality of the shock, he had not changed from the man he was the day before. He remained a good communist, convinced that in the USSR people were not arrested for nothing and that his prison companions, unlike him, must have all been enemies of the people.

From that moment, however, the first seeds of doubt were planted in his mind. He was also overcome by an ineffable force that those of us who are the privileged on earth know only from hearsay: that mysterious determination to survive.

# PART 2

# During

By some ideological sleight-of-hand, the vision of the horrors of the Nazi camps served to mask the realities of the Soviet camps.

Hannah Arendt

# 9 From the Dog House to the Train Station

Every free citizen is a defendant without knowing it.

Jacques Rossi

The unanimous opinion of those who have gone through the experience of arrest is that the first twenty-four hours are a time of interior chaos where the newly indicted prisoner cannot understand what is happening. At the same time, a ray of hope shines before his clouded eyes, convincing him that his arrest can only be a mistake that will be quickly cleared up.

From the moment the first door (with no doorknob but with a Judas window) closed behind Jacques, a vast field of research opened up for his perpetually curious mind. Mentally, he started to write *The Gulag Handbook*. For this linguist it was the word that inspired the text. He was guided by precise observation based on practice and, if needed, on mental research. The first of these words was the key that opened that universe, which until then Jacques, like so many of his fellow prisoners, did not know existed: *Gulag*. Jacques was still convinced that Soviet prisons were only for people who were "truly" guilty, and he was entering the first circle of that hell whose importance and perversity he did not yet see. I read in *The Gulag Handbook* his entry on the term *Gulag*, which was written after his release. Here is the essence of that entire passage:

> From 1930, the term GULAG was the Russian acronym for the Main Administration of Corrective Labour Camps and referred to the concentration camps of the OGPU (the Russian acronym for the All-Union State Political Administration). At the same time, the camps

were renamed from "concentration camps" to "corrective labour camps," and touted as camps where prisoners were rehabilitated through labour. The first directors of the Gulag, Genrikh Yagoda and Matvei Berman, were both shot as "enemies of the people" during the Great Purges. The prisoners of the Gulag, or *zeks*, built the first grand construction projects of Soviet socialism. Jacques indicates in *The Gulag Handbook* that the word *zek* emerged from the official acronym *z-k*, meaning "a prisoner on the canal." It originally referred to inmates who worked on the notorious White Sea–Baltic Sea canal project of 1931–33. The absence of machines would be compensated for by the physical strength of hundreds of thousands of hungry and poorly dressed *zeks*. There was pride in re-educating the habitual criminals and the so-called counter-revolutionaries and transforming them into enthusiasts for the building of socialism.

On 10 July 1934 a joint decree of the USSR Central Executive Committee and the Council of People's Commissars created a joint General Directorate for corrective-labour camps and corrective-labour colonies. For the first time, all Soviet camps and places of detention came under one administration. "The Gulag" generally referred to the Soviet forced labour camp system until 1953 when, after the death of Stalin, the camps were gradually dismantled. Like Solzhenitsyn, Jacques sometimes speaks of the "little zone" of the Gulag and the "big zone" of the Soviet Union, a metaphor that underscores the fundamental imprisonment of Soviet life.

During the night following his arrest, Jacques was transferred to the basement of the main Lubianka Prison. The place was used as a dumping ground for those who were arrested during the night until the administration could put them into cells or transfer them to another prison. In Gulag slang used by generations of prisoners, this place of transit was called *the doghouse,* where the prisoners were crowded together but rarely stayed more than twenty-four hours. Access was through an interior courtyard down several steps. "Everything was organized like a script. As prisoners were arrested, they went through that room that looked like a customs office. Around ten or eleven in the morning of the next day, the prisoners were sent elsewhere and the doghouse was ready for another batch of newcomers." When he arrived in the holding room, which was quite small, Jacques found two men on metal camp beds covered with boards. Then every hour a new arrival entered and the cell filled up during the night.

Was it the memory of the civil war? As if they already knew the customs of imprisonment, some of them lay down head to foot alongside one another. It is true that some of these men who were in their forties could have had memories of that period. Those who arrived later slept on the floor. In the morning the room was completely full. There was one person who was panicking and who spoke only to complain. The others were very calm. Russians, in general, know their country. In *The Gulag Handbook*, I mention the proverbs that since tsarist times have expressed Russian and Soviet fatalism towards the world of prisons and the law. For example: "Jail and poverty are always hung on your nose." That was under the tsars. Or "Find the man, the code will do the rest," a Soviet paraphrase of an older dictum: "A rope can be found if there's a neck to put it on."[1] Among the Soviet detainees, not a single one asked the slightest question. They simply formed groups according to their regions or their professions.

I spoke about Soviet agriculture with a civil servant and specialist. I was just a communist patriot curious to know the real situation, without suspecting that it differed from propaganda. In fact, everything he told me I could have read in *Pravda*. He was older than I was. I was twenty-eight, and he was forty. He knew from experience that everything that did not correspond to the party program could not be spoken aloud. As for my other fellow detainees, they were Muscovites from different groups: civil servants, workers, a merchant who probably did some illegal trading, a young immigrant, and a high-level officer. For the first time, I met a cross-section of the Soviet population that I had not encountered during my stays in Moscow between missions.

From this pre-imprisonment population Jacques remembers a young Polish Jew and an admiral whose stripes had been ripped off, though Jacques could see where they had been on his coat. The young Pole whined and complained constantly: "I was a communist in Poland!"

This was normal for someone who knew he was a good communist. He must have been in the so-called fascist prisons of Pilsudski, because the CP had let him go to Russia to let him lend a hand to the building of socialism, and now he found himself in a situation that was just as difficult! The poor fool! The admiral was fearless. The next day, when we were dispatched to other cells, I heard his name: Kireev. He had been the commander of the Pacific Fleet.[2] He was completely in control of himself even though he knew what to expect.

Jacques tried to console the young Pole, who was very unhappy. At the same time, he admired the stoicism of the admiral, who accepted his fate without talking about it to strangers.

> When in a difficult situation, energy should not be wasted taking pity on oneself and one's fate, as this weakens a person. I understood the despair of that young man. He was probably a secret agent, without important responsibilities. But he was really too weak. One cannot appear to be weak when in the clutches of the NKVD! As for the admiral, I read afterwards in a book on the purges that he had been shot. He probably was not tortured too much. The only possible consolation!
>
> This situation made me think of a story I used to read as a child. Several people spoke about their misfortunes and compared them. One had lost his wife. They had left for America and she died on the boat. Another had perished in a fire. They had all experienced terrible misfortunes. Then little Olav, who was five, arrived crying loudly. For the first time, he had realized his dream of owning a clay whistle. And someone had broken it! Finally, it was Olav who received the prize for having the most important misfortune. Well, the young Polish communist who found himself in the Soviet prison resembled little Olav.

The Soviet admiral and the Polish communist symbolized two sides of the misfortune that was also Jacques's, even though he was trying to distance himself through observation of the others and through different forms of empathy.

> I worked a good ten years in the underground. I was really surprised to find myself where I was. But it wasn't a worldwide catastrophe. I remained an idiotic communist. I considered all the others in the doghouse to be "enemies of the people." Or common criminal offenders. An Armenian dancer started to talk with a Russian, and from snatches of the conversation I thought I overheard a story about the black market. It made me feel clean, as if I had gotten lost here by mistake. I convinced myself that things would soon be cleared up for me. I knew how the investigator could clear me of all suspicion. I tried to distance myself, to detach and observe the spectacle as a rather interesting experience. Of course, I was not at all aware that it was to become the experience of a lifetime.
>
> When in the morning the prisoners were given tea with a lump of sugar and cigarettes, Jacques, who did not smoke, gave his cigarettes

to the young Pole, who seemed the most miserable of his companions. The Polish communist and the Soviet admiral – one a reflection of himself and the other an ideal type. "I had known for a long time that I was not the centre of the universe." Jacques chose to be concerned with himself as little as possible, and this is the advice he gave *a posteriori* to that pitiful Polish communist: to take interest in others rather than lament one's own fate. That is one of the reasons he was able to survive.

Later in the morning, the doghouse discharged its batch of accused. Jacques and his fellow inmates were led through shiny, clean, completely silent hallways into a courtyard where five or six steps led down to a basement. At the end of the small staircase, the prisoners only had to walk a few steps. The exit seemed like a dark hole because it led directly to the open door of a small truck that took them away. Jacques recognized this kind of delivery truck that he had often seen on the streets of the Soviet capital. The trucks were painted in bright colours and had signs in big letters in Russian, French, English, and German, referring to bread or meat, so that everyone would know that nothing was lacking in Moscow. Sympathetic foreign correspondents were impressed by these trucks that criss-crossed the city bringing food to the people. The arrests were usually made at night. Because these trucks had become so numerous during the day, they were camouflaged as delivery trucks. At the end of *The First Circle*, Solzhenitsyn wrote about this perverse practice that had tricked so many. Jacques observed them long before that famous novel was written. "I remember 1937. Being in the bread truck rather than in the meat truck improved my morale. The situation was not particularly pleasant, but this detail distracted me." The innocent small truck was, in fact, an armoured paddy wagon for transporting prisoners, and they were called the "Black Marias."

> We were made to climb one by one into the back of the vehicle. Between the back door and the first partition there were seats on the right and on the left that would be occupied by the accompanying soldiers. We then went through a very narrow door and a kind of small hall onto which opened some kind of cages, three on each side. I was made to enter one of them where there was just enough room for one seated person, with his knees bent tightly. Once I was in the compartment the door was closed. I could not see the other prisoners who were one by one closed in their boxes. I heard the five doors slam shut one after the other. I learned later that those who were isolated like I was in a cage were considered the most dangerous. This strict

separation was intended to conceal from the victims themselves the mass nature of these arrests.

The others got into the larger compartment in the centre of the vehicle, just behind the accompanying soldiers and the driver. In the larger compartment, where fifteen or so people were packed like sardines, or in the cages, there were no windows and no light either, only air vents. Of course, we were terrorized. No one made a sound. When one was a new prisoner, he did not try to scream. We were dying of fear, that's all. On several occasions I was put into this kind of vehicle. I made a very detailed drawing of it in *The Gulag Handbook*.[3] The common criminal offenders or the thugs did not restrain themselves. They yelled: "Ivan, are you there?"

What could the guard do? He knocked on the door. He threatened them. The real criminals usually seemed more courageous than the others. Most of us were having our first experience. We were crushed by fear. And so silence reigned. Our silence was proof that we were all "politicals," that is to say, people who had committed no crime. As for me, in order to control my fear, I tried to observe and to understand what was happening.

Later Jacques would discover that these Black Marias, also called Black Ravens, first appeared in Moscow in 1927.[4] They were the first trucks weighing a ton and a half, built after the civil war by the automobile factory AMO. The interiors went through several transformations until their final design at the beginning of the thirties. When Jacques was arrested, these vehicles were sometimes decorated as delivery trucks, sometimes painted a very dark green. At the same time as the Great Purges, there appeared enormous Black Marias weighing five tons painted in dark colours that were only used at night. They took entire families, "enemies of the people," often with book collections, as prisoners' books were typically used as evidence against them.

The Marias drove off. In the box with no air where he was squashed without being able to move, Jacques could not yet recite the poem "Requiem" by Anna Akhmatova that he would learn later:

And innocent Russia writhed
Under bloody boots
And under the tires of the Black Marias

He was too busy trying to figure out where he was, to determine his destination.

Nothing could be seen. It was completely dark. No opening, no hole that allowed one to see outside. When the vehicle stopped, the squeaking of a metal door could be heard. After a while it was closed. We waited. The vehicle moved, turning. And we waited again, which was prophetic of the life of those in the Gulag. As soon as we were not at the worksite or in the prison, whether it was in transit or moving or going somewhere, it was always wait and wait again. Then very quickly, climb in, go down, run, "go quickly!" and then wait again. Finally the vehicle turned again. We waited. We heard the sound of boots around the vehicle. Some orders that we did not really understand. We waited again.

And after a long time, I heard the door of the armoured vehicle open. We were led out – first, those of us who had been in the cages, the isolated ones, emerged one after the other so that we could not see one another. Then the travellers in the compartment were let out. We were led one by one just like when we got into the vehicle. We went directly into the hall of the prison, where the guards suddenly pushed us: Quickly, quickly, quickly! And each one of us was rushed individually into a room that in Gulag slang, since tsarist times, was called *the station* and locked in a box the size of a closet.

Jacques was then in the triage station, a kind of admissions hall for the Burtyka prison, the first building on the left after the entrance where the Black Maria had brutally dumped him. It was an enormous room with boxes lined up against the walls. Very quickly he was locked in what was called in Soviet prisons *a closet*.[5]

There was barely room to put your rear end on a bench. You couldn't stretch out your arms without touching the door. Tiny, with no toilet. I stayed there a certain time, about two hours. And then a guard holding a paper in his hand opened the door and asked me my name. I told him and he looked at the paper. Then he made me get out of the closet and sat me on a bench behind a table where there was another guard with a register. He asked me again my name, my birthdate, and asked me other questions, especially about my nationality, that is to say my ethnic origins, in my case French. He methodically filled in all the lines.

Once he was registered, Jacques was led to an individual shower by the guard, who continued to hold the paper with his photo. It was his first contact with the "sad shower of prisons."

The shower worked this way: the prisoner entered the shower and got undressed. The first question was always what to do with one's clothes because there was no place to put them. Usually they were soaked when one left the shower. As soon as the door was closed, the guard went to work. He was the one who controlled the water: sometimes boiling hot, sometimes freezing cold. A Scottish shower, it was not! But when we screamed because the water was boiling hot, the guard rarely continued with the hot water.

I want to emphasize that the guards, for the most part, were not sadistic, even though during their required political training, the commissars had told them that they were dealing with terrible "enemies of the people." The guards witnessed scenes that were terribly cruel. They knew that the people who were taking showers would probably be tortured during the interrogation, that all of them would be condemned, that a great many of them would be executed. Because there were no exceptions. None of those who were guarded by them would get out free. Or perhaps one in a million. As for the executions, they were carried out in the same prison. Often it was the same guards that supervised the showers who shot the bullet into the neck of the condemned. In a world where executions were so common, there was no professional executioner. Every guard had his turn. My guard, the one who had controlled the hot water, could have been the executioner of my neighbour or me. However, he did not go beyond his orders.

The shower lasted several minutes. The soap was almost black, a piece of stinky clay the size of a small box of matches. Quick, quick. He didn't have time to rinse, nor to dry himself; in any case there was no towel. Anyone who managed to find their clothes more or less dry was lucky. A Westerner, who was more naive than even Jacques, asked why there were no towels. His answer: "This is not a sanatorium!"

The sanatorium. Quite a wild luxury for a Soviet citizen! Not everybody could go there, but everybody dreamed of going there! There was no point in asking whether the guards could be a bit compassionate at times, as this was impossible. Any charitable gesture from a guard could mean death for him. The guard himself was watched twenty-four hours a day. And he knew it. The slightest expression of pity or solidarity and he was finished. Even if he was not mean, he would never run the risk of compromising himself for a prisoner.

Jacques got out of the shower soaked, still convinced that he was getting to the end of his odyssey, that everything would be okay because the communist system was just. Then they searched him for the second time in twenty-four hours.

> The search took place in a large room where we were completely naked. The rules, I learned afterwards, stipulated that the person conducting the search had to be the same sex as the person being searched. This rule was not always observed, but there was no excessive voyeurism. The guards slid a gloved finger in the vagina of women. Men were made to squat down and spread their buttocks. Every place where one could hide even the smallest thing was carefully inspected – hair, beard, mouth, tongue, and armpits.

A surprising drawing by Jacques shows with precise lines the malicious inspection of the anus of a respectable bearded fifty-year-old. The "counter-revolutionary" aims his rear end at the penetrating gaze of a guard, whose lowered head has a cap decorated with the red star. The points of the red star, symbol of the empire, are projected symbolically towards the hole that modesty usually hides. Like *Tintin in the Land of the Soviets*, reviewed and corrected by an authentic *zek*, sometimes the atmosphere of popular comic books existed in Jacques's adventures. Jacques was a fatalist in the Gulag. For example, in a small cartoon called "A Story of Siberia," which was found among his sketches, there was a bird that had happily fallen into cow dung and was pulled out from that shit, unluckily, by a cat. From this edifying story the author drew several conclusions: In Siberia before acting you must think; he who shits on your head is not necessarily your enemy; if you are in deep shit there is really nothing to be happy about; he who gets you out of the shit is not necessarily your friend.

At the moment, the new prisoner did not have the heart to draw. Dressed again, he found his things. He still had his camel hair coat and his suitcase trunk, the suitcase of the pseudo–South American on his Spanish holiday. The guard ordered him to take a clean shirt and a toothbrush. Then: "Hands behind your back!"

> When he proposed that I take a shirt and a toothbrush, I refused because I was sure that there had been a mistake and that I was going to leave. What good was it to take those things if I was going to be freed the next day? I said no, that they were of no use.

I refused to believe it. I asked Jacques to repeat the story. How could he have let himself be so abused? Unless he wanted to be defiant in order to ward off his doubts. He told me that in the days that followed he could not understand why the mistake had still not been corrected.

He crossed a courtyard. Jacques remembered, "There were trees. I liked that. For nearly forty-eight hours I had not seen the sky!" He was led to another group of buildings where another guard awaited him.

Again a door opened. It was his first cell. There he was, installed without knowing it, in a system that would try in vain to break him over the course of twenty-four years. Like in the Black Maria that he had recently left, there was no opening, no way out, no trial that would permit him to avoid this common destiny. The man had been found, and now the system would do the rest.

# 10  We Don't Torture Foreigners

> Nothing is ever equal, by and large, in life, and this is all the more true in camp.
> Aleksandr Solzhenitsyn, *The Gulag Archipelago*

When the door of the cell opened, Jacques, with his hands behind his back, had no possessions except the suit and the suede shoes he was wearing the morning before, on the day of his arrest. He was still so sure that he would be freed. His heart seemed to stop beating and he could not breathe as he stood by the door. His incredulous eyes discovered a cell about six by twelve yards with wooden beds one above the other along the walls on the left and on the right. When he entered the cell it was almost empty. There were about ten men, although it was designed for twenty-five prisoners. It would fill up during the day. Two days later, it contained one hundred and fifty prisoners.

> The door closed. I was in the cell in a state of shock unable to move, like a statue. I was in front of those I considered "enemies of the people," denounced every day in *Pravda*. My enemies. What struck me initially? It was how exhausted they appeared, how worn out their skin and their clothes were. It was the first time in my life that I had seen how human skin could become prematurely worn out and grey. Two men left the group and came towards me. They were yellow, thin, with several-day-old beards, their clothes in rags, their pants tucked into their socks. Later, I would understand why. I was dressed like a European. At the time, that was evident: Soviets and Westerners recognized each other immediately because of their clothes.
>
> One of them looked at me with an envious sigh and he said something strange:

"Oh, a foreigner. It seems they do not torture foreigners!"

Shocked, I said to him: "What do you mean?" It required great restraint for me not to hit him in the face. Talk to me about torture, a communist in a communist prison! My first reaction was to hit him in the face, but I had some experience – in capitalist prisons, of course – and I knew prison manners: you don't fight when you arrive in a cell.

In addition, I was embarrassed to be wearing elegant clothes among these modest Soviet citizens. The suit I was wearing was my work outfit that wouldn't attract the attention of capitalist authorities, the same ones that we communists were going to destroy. In my heart, of course, I was for the Russian proletariat and I would have preferred a thousand times more to work in a Soviet factory in order to build the wonderful future. The party had decided otherwise. I respected party discipline, and now this creep, this "enemy of the people," had come with anti-Soviet propaganda inside this prison. I was really disgusted! In any case, I controlled myself.

The first hours of adaptation in this Soviet cell were among the hardest of an ordeal that would last twenty years. The men were squeezed onto the planks like sardines. Jacques calculated that each one had less than a square yard of living space. They had to lie down one next to the other on their sides. There was no room to lie on one's back.

Jacques's neighbour on the plank bed, a fifty-year-old, started a conversation. In another life he had been an engineer, largely working under the tsars. This aroused Jacques's curiosity, and he began to ask him a lot of questions. "Before the revolution, like many people who lived well, he must have been a party sympathizer, in order to have a clear conscience." The engineer alluded to torture, the torture *here and now* in the Butyrka prison.

> I was a little bit more prepared to hear that than on the first day. I listened, but I was still incredulous:
> "It's not possible. It's impossible."
> "You don't believe it? You still have things to learn in the Soviet Union!"
> Some days later we were led out for a walk, always two by two, my bed neighbour the engineer and me. Leaving the cell, while we were walking in a hallway, I heard a cry for the first time, the terrible screaming of a person being tortured. That wail penetrated my ears. It upset my guts. I almost vomited. Then my engineer companion whispered in my ear:
> "Did you hear that?"

> And I, with my communist pride and foolishness, responded: "No! I didn't hear anything."
>
> This shows how stupid one can be. Like all the French intellectuals who did not want to see or hear about Zinoviev or Kamenev or Piatakov or Serebriakov or Bukharin or even Krestinsky, who nevertheless retracted the confession wrung from him during the Moscow trial. Nor, later, Kravchenko and so many others. I, who had only had several hours of experience in the Gulag, I remained headstrong and stupidly stubborn. When you insist that the truth is not what it appears, that it is what you really want it to be, then you move away from the truth into blindness, into the destruction of yourself and others. Later, after many years in the Gulag, I would recognize my blindness. But you leftist intellectuals – you benefitted from that luxury and the protection of a capitalist state that never locked you up for crimes you did not commit. In fact, I did the same stupid things as you did, but I paid for them. You didn't have to pay.

What could I say when Jacques spoke this way? That some of us were, indeed, honoured for less dangerous commitments, that we had not paid the price for our irresponsibility, that we had been lucky, that I am still not proud of my former good intentions. I decided to remain silent and listen to this voice that must not have changed since the Great Purges, a voice that resonated with me.

> You must understand: what interests me is not being right. It is getting closer to the truth, even if this involves a gradual recognition of my own errors. Getting closer to the truth, that is to say, distinguishing what is true from what is false. That is what inspires me, what I am passionate about. Not being right!

Jacques started, then, to listen to his fellow prisoners, some of them elderly, who had participated in the Civil War, old Bolsheviks from before 1917 who participated in the first Russian Revolution, that of 1905. It was 1937, thirty-two years after the first revolution and twenty years after the second one. And some of these men (not many) were eighty years old.

> When I spoke with them about the revolution, they mentioned names that I had never heard of in my studies of the history of the Soviet communist party. In fact, the names that I considered to be the most important according to my official readings, they did not

mention at all. Obviously I didn't suspect yet that history had been truncated and falsified. Always the *tufta*, the cheating! But I was starting to get worried. How was it possible? Either the people who had risked their lives for the revolution were ill-informed about what really happened or something had actually eluded me. Of course, I rejected with indignation the idea of any kind of deception. But I was troubled. It was a first sign, one of the first seeds of doubt.

I started to think about another experience that I had never really thought about before. When I came to Moscow in 1929, I went to see friends of mine, old revolutionaries who lived in a dacha. I chatted with their neighbours, dyed-in-the-wool Russians who had never travelled or participated in the revolution. One of the neighbours, an old man, had no government position. He might have been about sixty. He had been an accountant under the tsars and continued to work in his profession. He trusted me because I was French. I would learn that later. I was curious about interesting details, so I asked him where he was in October 1917. He answered that he had been in Petrograd. After I asked him a lot of other questions, I learned that he had never heard of Stalin. This contemporary of the revolution only knew two names: Lenin and Trotsky. If I had revealed during my interrogations that Ivan Petrovitch had never heard of Stalin during the revolution, he would have certainly ended up in the Gulag too. The last editions of *The History of the Communist Party of the Soviet Union* did not mention [Stalin's diminished role] because that wonderful history continued to evolve *ad majorem Stalini gloriam*.

This is how the first hours, weeks, and months progressed, and eventually such moments did end. Despite the monotony of prison, life went on. Jacques got used to it. He changed. From the time he arrived completely soaked after his first shower in the Butyrka cell, he constantly recalled the final experiences that preceded his being locked in the cell. While completing the suspect's questionnaire, he had to fill out the reason for his arrest. When he asked why he had been arrested, he was told: "You will know tomorrow!"

He waited for *tomorrow*. He wanted to know why he was there and to clear up this misunderstanding, the obvious mistake that had placed him among these "enemies of the people." He had dedicated his life to fighting against those same enemies.

Tomorrow came. He was still waiting for his interrogation. At every moment he was ready. Each time the Judas window was opened to call up one of his companions, he was prepared. But he was not called, neither that day nor the following days. Nonetheless, it remained so clear to him that there had been a misunderstanding.

> In the end, it was incomprehensible. I had to come back urgently from Spain. The clandestine line of communication that was so important for the cause had been sabotaged. Not to mention my young comrade, whom I had abandoned because there were no instructions for her. All that to lock me up with enemies of Marxism-Leninism!

The rights of the accused in Stalin's prisons were practically non-existent. Any contact with the outside world, visits, correspondence, books, newspapers, pencils and paper were tightly controlled and often depended on the permission of the investigating commissar. What was one to do during those unending hours of waiting, interrupted only by the distribution of a little food, going to the toilets, and taking walks outside? His neighbour on the plank bed spoke to him and, moreover, compromised himself by talking about torture. Other prisoners talked to him also, trying to help him with their experience and their knowledge of the system. Jacques was surprised.

> Many of them trusted me. It was surprising and I would appreciate this even more later because in prison there was no confiding in others. Any confidence, any information could be used to fabricate accusations. Under the communist regime, everything that you said or didn't say could be exploited and used against you. Now I realize how dangerous it was for those Soviets to confide in me.
> Finally, much later, after Butyrka, I asked them the question:
> "Why did you take such risks by telling me all that?"
> Two or three of them gave me exactly the same answer with different words. It was not in the same prison. One was a peasant and the other an intellectual. But the message was the same:
> "You are a foreigner. You are not a product of this horrible Soviet system. You were not used to this corruption. You are a normal human being like we were under the tsars. So we can trust you."
> In the Soviet Union, this perversion began in 1917–1918, with the birth of the new regime. I saw it with my own eyes. I heard children whose first words were "Lenin" or "Stalin." They were shown pictures of mother and father. And they said "Lenin, Stalin." And how proud the mothers and fathers were!
> What differentiated the Soviet camp system from other systems of detention in the world was not only its immense and unimaginable size, but the deadly living conditions. It was necessary to lie endlessly

to save your life, always lying, wearing a mask for years and years and never being able to say what you thought. In Soviet Russia, "free" citizens were also obliged to lie.[1]

To explain the strange confidence that people had in him, Jacques said: "One of my fellow inmates in the Gulag admitted to me much later that he confided all that to me in the vague hope that I might testify, if by some miracle I got out." He, Jacques the foreigner, Jacques the Frenchman, as he would be called all those years in the Gulag, he who had not dared to make friends when he worked for the Comintern, discovered that people liked him, that his fellow inmates were less suspicious of him than of the other prisoners. And contrary to the spy service, where he had to avoid contacts, he was now free to be close to others and to listen to them carefully. It was one of the rare freedoms that was left to him. In his first cell in Butyrka, he was the one who was initially suspicious of all those "enemies of the people." However, the stories that they told him resembled his story. They had been arrested during the most ordinary situations of their daily life. *Apparatchiks* had been summoned to Moscow and were arrested when they got off the train or between two stations, somewhere on the road, or when they got to the office, where they found NKVD agents who asked them to follow them: "This comrade is going to take you to meet another comrade." In the morning, they left their family as usual, took the train, and then disappeared.

It was always the most surprising circumstance for the person, who suspected nothing. Someone left the house for a few minutes to buy cigarettes, and never came back. Thus, once they landed in the Butyrka cell, they worried about their wives and the children they left behind. Typically, the families knew that such arrests might happen. They lived in the Soviet Union, after all. In the big cities they could get information and ask whether a person had been arrested. But a woman hesitated to draw attention to a husband or son whom they believed was above all suspicion. In Moscow there was a system that consisted of going to an office of the NKVD. At the window, the wife or family member would give the name of the person they were looking for and hold out fifty rubles, the authorized amount. The bureaucrat examined the registry, answered "no." He did not see the name on the list. Or if he accepted the fifty rubles the family understood that the person was a prisoner somewhere. Then they had to go from one prison to another, offering fifty rubles each time.

My cell mates dreaded the thought of their wives or mothers going from one place to another looking for them.

All these stories helped pass the time in that Gulag cell where Jacques awaited his first interrogation. He would spend time in many different cells. In each one there would be men and still more men. Some cells he would just pass through, in others he would stay for weeks and months. He would forget their shape, their dimensions, and their odour, but that first cell in Butyrka where he met his peers and experienced an intense period of training he would recall more than sixty years later as if it were yesterday.

The Butyrka or Butyrki, his first prison in the communist penitentiary system, was the detention centre for those awaiting sentencing. It was a prison of the NKVD-MVD of the USSR, one of the largest in Moscow. There were the former barracks for the cavalry regiment of the Butyrki of Catherine the Great, transformed into a prison and then modernized at the end of the nineteenth century. The prison was enlarged during the Soviet period and consisted of twenty two-storey buildings with individual cells, in addition to large rooms with twenty-five beds that during the time of the Great Purges held as many as 170 prisoners when the total prison population reached about 20,000. In 1993, after having been in numerous prisons, Jacques revisited the one where he lost his innocence. He would learn from the director that there were still 6,000 prisoners in buildings built for 3,000.

But we are still at the end of the sinister year 1937, and Jacques was just starting the apprenticeship that would lead him to write *The Gulag Handbook*. He was still waiting for the first meeting of the judicial inquiry. Since that first confrontation with his fellow prisoner, who was jealous because Jacques had escaped torture, he had seen men leave and come back after their interrogation. They were broken, bloody, beaten black and blue, half dead. Every night the door of the cell would open and close upon these haggard individuals whose suffering was worse than could be imagined. He could not continue to close his eyes and ears. He awaited his turn. The "tomorrow" that was promised was postponed day after day. He would wait for two months. Finally, Jacques the Frenchman was summoned to appear before the commissar-interrogator.

# 11 Confess, Filthy Fascist!

If the intellectuals in the plays of Chekhov who spent all their time guessing what would happen in twenty, thirty or forty years had been told that in forty years interrogation by torture would be practiced in Russia; that prisoners would have their skulls squeezed within iron rings; that human beings would be lowered into acid baths; that they would be trussed up naked to be eaten by ants and bedbugs; that ramrods heated over primus stoves would be thrust up their anal canals (the "secret brand"); that a man's genitals would be slowly crushed beneath the toe of a jackboot; and that in the luckiest possible circumstances, prisoners would be tortured by being kept from sleeping for a week, by thirst, and by being beaten to a bloody pulp, not one of Chekhov's plays would have gotten to its end, because all the heroes would have gone off to insane asylums.

Aleksandr Solzhenitsyn, *The Gulag Archipelago*

Jacques was arrested, he says, at the end of December 1937. He claimed that the mass use of torture began during the night of 17–18 August 1937. "I was told that on the morning of August 18 most of the accused in the Butyrka prison came back beaten from their night interrogations. Apparently, that night the same thing happened everywhere in the Soviet Union." Jacques was fearless and was still holding onto the notion that this was perhaps the result of sabotage by the NKVD. He thought that it was unthinkable there could be torture in the country of Lenin and Stalin. He waited day after day, hour after hour for the guard to announce the first letter of his last name. The guard did it softly, and all those who had the same first letter of their surname had to identify themselves one after the other to the guard, who then, according to what was on his list, asked them their first name, the name of their father, and their birthdate.

If everything corresponded, the man was taken away. Later, Jacques learned a little more about this strange custom. Some sixty days after his arrest, the name of Jacques Robertovitch was called: "Get ready to go out."

> I was quite sure that I was going to be freed. In my case, this procedure surprised me. I firmly believed that an officer would be waiting for me behind the door to offer me his apology. The inquiry commissar or interrogator – I prefer this title to that of "examining magistrate" used by French and Russian translators, which implies a separation of power that does not exist in communist countries – was waiting for me, seated behind his desk in a khaki uniform and boots. It was the first time I was given a real chair with wheels. Later, during interrogations, I was on a stool fastened to the floor in a corner far from the desk.
>
> When I presented myself to the inquiry commissar, he asked me the typical question, one that I would fear later. The question surprised me:
>
> "Do you know why you are here?"
>
> "But this is a mistake …"
>
> "You have to reveal to us your counter-revolutionary activities. We have been informed. We concluded that you were too dangerous to remain free. Be truthful. It is to your advantage to be truthful. You must confess your crimes."
>
> These short sentences were not uttered all at the same time but spread out among my periods of silence and declarations of innocence. Then I began to worry. I knew to what extent these tactics were used. Since we were arrested for no reason, a reason for the arrest had to be invented. The new prisoners often asked the old prisoners in the Gulag the reason why they had been put in prison. Among the answers: "because of the Americans." This was a reference to the Soviet citizens who had been liberated at the end of the Second World War by the Americans, or "because of the English." Other reasons included: "For chatting," "for one word," "because of the bastard" (a denunciation), "because of laziness," "because of betrayal by my husband." You could be arrested because of a glass of water given to an inmate or for a "tone of voice." One legend recounted that in the twenties an old lady who was waiting in line for bread had read out loud *Science for the Workers* in a voice judged "equivocal." If someone answered "for nothing," fellow prisoners knew to respond with indignation and a Gulag joke: "How long? Ten years? Liar! For nothing you get twenty-five years. If you got ten years it was because you did something."

Jacques ignored what he would later describe so well. He was Candide in the jails of the Marxist-Leninist Inquisition. He tried to understand his "crime." Under such circumstances, the brain goes a hundred miles an hour! Hadn't he refrained from denouncing his radio transmitter co-worker who begged him not to go back to Moscow? "Of course, I bawled her out, but I should have denounced her. It was an unacceptable and undisciplined counter-revolutionary act!" But how could this private scene have come to the attention of the interrogator?

> Everything was known. I believed in the all-powerful NKVD. At the same time, I *confessed* nothing because I already had some prison experience. Of course, it was my first time in a Soviet prison, but I had enough good judgment to apply what I had learned in other jails to this Russian jail. So, there was no way I could confess to them what I believed at the time was the reason for my arrest.
>
> Then I thought about another possible explanation. Among members of the Comintern, we sometimes told disrespectful jokes, and a comrade said to me one day: "You know how they finish off those who have told too many jokes? They end up digging the canal from the Baltic to the White Sea!"
>
> One or two years earlier, I had gone to the movies in Moscow with some Italian comrades. Near the exit we saw an enormous armchair, a bit apart from the other narrow wooden seats. Suddenly looking at this out-of-proportion armchair, one of the comrades said in Italian: "This is the seat of government." We all laughed. This enormous seat was suitable for an enormous rear end. The cult of rear ends and personality. We were all good communists, but we laughed anyway. I laughed like the others. And thinking about it, I thought that maybe that was the reason I was arrested. Perhaps one of the comrades had told that story to someone else. Perhaps he had spoken about the attitude of one of us who had not reacted as a good communist should have. A spectator in the movie theatre could have understood Italian and written a denunciation in fear that he himself might be denounced. But again, and for the same reasons, I did not communicate any reason for my arrest.
>
> At the same time, I wanted to help my interrogator. I stupidly believed that he was looking for the truth, not for a lie. Finally, I did not cooperate by talking about those trifles. He was the one who finally said:
>
> "You are a Polish-French spy."
>
> Me?! A double accusation because of dual nationality. I was so astounded that, despite the horror of the situation, I nearly laughed

in his face. I felt almost relieved. How could he suspect that I would be guilty of such a crime? He was making fun of me. It could only be a bad joke in bad taste. Accusing me of being a French spy when just a few weeks ago I was risking my life in Spain for the Red Army. Really, I had to make every effort not to burst out laughing! Such an obvious error could be easily corrected. I asked him to telephone such and such, a comrade, my important bosses. But he did not seem at all interested.

"We have found information. Only your sincere confession will help you to get a lighter sentence." And he insisted. He repeated that the accused were all the same, that they tried to trick, to dissemble, to give him false information. I was no exception. In fact, I acted no differently than the others. Later, I read hundreds of accounts of political prisoners. All answered the same way. And the first question was always the same: "Do you know why you are here?"

After that first meeting, Jacques was accompanied back to his cell. One can only imagine his state of mind. He was becoming conscious now that although, in his eyes, he was different from the others, he would not be treated differently. Several days passed before the letter *R* was called again, and he was again called to appear before the interrogator. Gradually, the interrogations worsened. Jacques continued to deny everything. He was always put on a stool in the corner, seated with his knees close together and his hands on his knees with instructions to sit up straight. Suddenly, during the interrogation, the commissar ordered him to stand up. He stood up with his hands behind his back.

"Don't sway back and forth!"

This order to stand up with no time limit was known in Gulag slang as *the conveyor*, from the Russian word that refers to factory work. He stood for two hours, five hours, eight hours, ten hours, twenty-four hours without a break. Yet in the beginning, the length of time he had to stand did not increase progressively. After an interrogation where he had to stand, there was another interrogation where he was seated.

The first time, he accused me of being a spy. The second time of being a counter-revolutionary. And then the third and fourth times he started to insult me. The most common Russian swear word, translated literally in English, is "I fucked your mommy." I found it comical that he used the formal "you" in that expression instead of the informal "you" together with the word "mommy." I could also hear what was being shouted in the nearby offices.

"Confess, prostitute. Come on, confess!"
And a woman's voice answered:
"But I am not a prostitute!"
"Okay, then, confess, honest woman! If you are honest, confess!"

Jacques's resistance did not weaken. Nor did the strength of his convictions. "During the first interrogations with the commissar, I could hear hitting in the next office, and the muffled noise of people falling. I could hear loud cries and screams. I said to myself: it must be a recording, a montage to intimidate me. I did not want to hear it. For a long time, I clung to that idea." Returning from a conveyor that lasted the entire night, the interrogated prisoner would find a bowl of cold soup that his companions in misery had kept for him. One was not permitted to go back to bed after the wake-up call at six in the morning. He would have to wait to sleep. He would be watched constantly by the guard through the Judas window until the following evening, that was, if the conveyor did not start again during the day or did not continue for another night.

If the guard had an ounce of compassion, there was always an informer who would go and tell on him to the security officer, who would quickly summon the guard: "You see, poor guy, the price to be paid for being too nice with these bastards. That 'enemy of the people' who you let sleep, he was the one who turned you in."

The longest conveyor that Jacques had to endure lasted ten days, with one-hour breaks in the morning. There were five or six tormentors, one after the other. Then they started to hit him, sometimes gently, sometimes brutally. Finally, the machine went full speed. He was in the eye of the hurricane. He would evoke this vision of Medusa with precision and sobriety in the narrative *Fragments of Lives: Chronicles of the Gulag*, in one of the episodes where he is both the narrator and the protagonist:

"Confess! Confess! You dirty fascist! Pile of shit! You scumbag!" It's daytime and another tormentor has taken over.
"Confess! Confess! You dirty fascist!"
I've been here over twenty-four hours, standing with my hands behind my back. Is it the result of stress? I feel neither fatigue nor hunger. After forty-eight hours the interrogator summons a guard, signs a slip, and hands it to him. The guard takes me out. As we go by a desk, a sergeant takes the signed paper that my guard hands him, writes something in a big register book, and covers the page with a large metal jacket. A narrow slit in the sheet allows me to see only the line that concerns me, hiding the rest of the page.

"Sign here!" says the sergeant, giving me a pencil.

I see my name, the date and time. Five forty-three. It was the same procedure when I arrived two days ago.

.....

"Confess, you dirty fascist, confess!" "I have nothing to confess," I say from time to time. Each time this unleashes a new outburst of anger from the interrogator. They interrogate me in shifts of five to six hours each. I remain standing, hands behind my back, for five days and six nights in a row. By then I'm not really aware of what's going on around me. The Klieg light disappears. I'm walking ... Then I'm being led down the hallways ... Have I signed the sergeant's big book? ... The door opens ... How good it feels to be back in my cell!

They come back and fetch me just a few moments later. This time it isn't the usual route. Where are they taking me? Never mind, as long as it's not to the interrogator's office! They lead me down the basement, past some cellars, through a door. A barren windowless room with a plain light bulb shining down on a concrete slab floor. There are several dark and damp blotches, a faucet, and a full pail of water. A corporal and two soldiers are standing with their backs against the wall. They wipe sweat from their forehead. The corporal glances at the slip of paper that my guard hands him. He sticks it onto a protruding nail with quite a few others on it already. Without a word they start to beat me. I don't know how I end up on the concrete floor. Blur ... I open my eyes. I look up and see one of the men with an empty pail in his hand. I realize that I've just been splashed. They stand me back up and start to beat me again. They punch me and kick me with their boots. Before I faint again I see the insignia of the Communist Youth League on the corporal's lapel: the profile of Lenin on a red banner. The same Lenin for whom I risked my life in Spain.[1]

Jacques does not speak about torture apart from this episode, and he describes it with his signature, striking detachment.

Yes, that happened the first or the second time that I was taken into the basement where they tortured. I fell on the floor, and falling on the floor was particularly painful and humiliating because the sphincters loosen. And it was just before I lost consciousness that I saw the Komsomol badge that reminded me of my affinity with my torturers. Later, much later, when I thought about that scene, I focused mainly on those young peasants who beat me up and on the brainwashing that they had gone through to get to that point of beating the innocent and of insulting them.

To be able to do that, they must have had a kind of training, courses where "their brains were shit on" as we said in the Gulag, and where they were prepared to beat up those "bastards," those "enemies of the people." I know from prison or camp guards that these young peasants were often soldiers who, after being demobilized, chose to work as guards rather than return to the collective farm. They ended up in those sinister places to perform the work of brutes.

When he arrived at the Butyrka, Jacques was the only foreigner. Others arrived later, mainly Germans and Poles but many more, including an Afghan, the only one he ever met. In this absurd universe it would be tempting to evoke a distorted sociocultural determinism. The triage station deposited numerous engineers who were accused of sabotage, theatre actors who were accused of terrorism (the backstage of theatres was a good place to meet party leaders), stamp collectors who, of course, were guilty of spying, and students known for their love of throwing bombs. Cosmopolitan Jews were particularly suspicious. You just had to be named "Moshe" and have an elderly aunt who had made the mistake of emigrating to the United States.

"Even later, I met in Krasnoyarsk a group of four or five students from Leningrad who had been jailed because they were interested in lyrical poetry and did not glorify the greatness of factory builders. They were imprisoned for five or eight years. Russia may have lost a new Mayakovsky." I asked Jacques the usual question about his resistance to torture. Had he confessed by telling any lie to finally be left in peace?

> I was lucky. At the moment when I was about to say just about anything because the pain was too great, I fainted. Here is an example of my luck: during one of the beatings, one of the torturers hit me badly on the plexus. I could not breathe. I was suffocating. My mouth was open. I was trying desperately to breathe and I could not. Meanwhile, he was getting ready to hit me again, just next to the plexus. I saw it coming, so I had this great idea to scream, as if I were dying, and to point to where I wasn't hurt too much. My torturer was tricked. He started to hit the place that supposedly had caused me to scream. That hurt me, of course, but at least it was not the plexus. I told this story to a former member of the Comintern whom I met in prison, a good communist like me, but who had not been beaten too much. He reacted with indignation: "But you fooled the Soviet authorities! Aren't you ashamed?"

# 12 On Interrogations

> At times he was surprised that he was able to stand it. But he knew that lay opinion set far too narrow limits to men's capacity of physical resistance; that it had no idea of their astonishing elasticity. He had heard of cases of prisoners who had been kept from sleeping for fifteen to twenty days, and who had stood it.
>
> Arthur Koestler, *Darkness at Noon*

> It must be agreed that in the art of obtaining confessions enormous progress has been made since the reign of Nicolas I and that the successive chiefs of the Cheka, the OGPU or the KGB had nevertheless more knowledge than Count Orlov, the general commander of the third division of His Imperial Majesty.
>
> Claude Roy

In order perhaps to improve morale, the commissar-interrogators during the Great Purges liked to tell the following story to the accused: "During my training I was locked in an office where there was only one table. The leg of a chair was put in my hand and I was told: 'You cannot leave here until you have gotten a complete confession from this table.'" The narrator of this story, a model servant of the Soviet state, managed nevertheless to break the chair leg when he hit the table with it. The interrogator was an important person in Jacques's life and in the lives of millions of other accused individuals.

> Between 1917 and 1991, the commissar-interrogator, an employee of the police (political or not), was responsible for obtaining information about individuals, arresting the suspects, investigating the case, formulating the accusation, and presenting the case for a decision, either in court or in a special political commission. The regular suspension of

the law against torture kept the interrogator from officially breaking the law when he resorted to torture. Millions of condemned people, many whose confessions had been obtained through torture, were rehabilitated after the Twentieth Party Congress. The interrogators who tortured them were not punished. A good interrogator was not the one who discovered the truth but the one who produced the information that was demanded beforehand by the secret police.

The commissars who did the interrogations at night received special bonuses. As we have seen, the accused was brought back to his cell at five in the morning after a difficult interrogation that lasted the entire night. He was not allowed to rest or close his eyes until bedtime the following evening: "I still remember well my comrades who were silent the entire day and didn't even touch the morning bread, the semolina at noon, or the evening soup. During periods of constant interrogation we lost weight rapidly. We were just waifs."

As for the sleep deprivation that Jacques suffered for five days and six nights in a row, this was a common practice, which many victims have described. The combination of standing for a long time, thirst, the strong lights, and fear of the unknown destabilized and undermined one's will power and reasoning. Sleep deprivation, which leads to a loss of identity for even the strongest individual, had several advantages for the system. It left no traces and it cost nothing. The victim could not complain because he was never touched. The hitting left no marks either, as it was done with rubber bludgeons, mallets, and bags of sand. It resulted in sharp pain especially on the bones or the tibia when it was done with kicks from boots.

The interrogator was a communist who either wilfully or by force "distanced himself from his human reactions." Jacques underscored the intense competition that existed among the commissars, as these auxiliary zealots of the system also lived in terror.

As it happened, I grew close to a comrade in prison who had been a commissar. He revealed to me the things that he was not supposed to know about. I learned that the commissar who interrogated me had a boss and that boss said to him every day:

"So, Ivan Petrovich, you have a comrade, an interrogator in another bureau who managed to obtain the confessions of one hundred 'enemies of the people.' And miserable you, during the same time, you only have forty!"

Thus the unhappy Ivan had to try harder to get those sixty confessions, otherwise he would be sent where those victims came from and he himself would become the forty-first to have to confess. One of my fellow accused, a Polish engineer who worked in a factory near Moscow, had a particularly sadistic interrogator who had him questioned for days and nights. Suddenly, the hell stopped and he benefitted from a week of respite during which he was called into the office of a "new commissar." The latter told him that his predecessor, an agent of Hitler, had been unmasked. The engineer was relieved and began to dream about being freed. The opposite happened. The new commissar, with a tic in his right eye and a steel tooth, used even more savage methods to obtain a confession from the accused, this time concerning his complicity with the former commissar. Hearing this description of the second torturer, a prisoner who had just arrived, a tall ungainly person, asked the engineer whether the second inquisitor had a scar on his chin, for he himself had arrested the man with the scar and the steel tooth the day before. We all wondered when the person who had arrested the ungainly person would arrive in our cell. In the Gulag, change was constant and even an inquiry commissar was never sure where he would be the next day.

And that is what was called, in their own idiom, "the liquidation of the liquidators." In Gulag language, those interrogations that were considered the most difficult were referred to as "robust investigations" or "intense investigations." The expression used to describe beatings during questioning was "turning the accused into a lump of hamburger." The Soviets employed classic psychological methods such as blackmail – telling prisoners "We are going to arrest your wife," "We are going to lock up your daughter with thugs!" – as well as intimidation, total isolation, the complete absence of information about one's case, and the impossibility of consulting a lawyer.

Blackmail put a lot of pressure on the prisoner. It led some to accuse themselves or accuse innocent people. Blackmailing someone was called "finding one's keys." When you have lost your keys and you want to get back inside your house, you look at an old key ring and try to find the key that will open the door. The police got to know the keys – the weaknesses in all of us – and remembered them for the times when they had to "unlock" another prisoner.

These psychological techniques were used during the entire Soviet period. From the middle of the sixties under Brezhnev, while Andropov was head of the KGB, "special psychological methods" were used more and more frequently, and used especially against dissidents. Interrogators were often well trained and, in critical cases, a doctor would decide whether an interrogation could continue. The person responsible for the interrogation made the decision. The death certificate of an arrested person who died under torture routinely included "heart attack" as the cause of death.

Jacques insists that the commissar-interrogators were not inherently cruel. Rather, he considered them zealous bureaucrats who were unable to act independently.

> After a certain amount of time, when the commissar failed to exact the necessary confession, he would ask his boss, the head of the department, whether he could "use the methods." The superior would put his signature on a small innocuous card indicating that the "methods" had been approved. There was no question, as in the case of the Nazis, of killing just anybody for the sake of it. In fact, during my twenty years of imprisonment, I can count on both hands the number of officials who took pleasure in making us suffer. Nonetheless, that did not inhibit this enormous system of human oppression from functioning to the fullest.

During the initial years of the Soviet regime, there were no established schedules for the investigation of a case. Eventually, time limits were established for investigations, but they could always be prolonged. During the Great Purges, investigations typically lasted five to seven months. In certain cases, the Presidium of the Central Executive Committee of the USSR forced investigations to speed up. The accused were then judged and executed within ten days after their arrest. But there were cases in which investigations lasted two or three years. Solzhenitsyn made clear that "the time allotted for investigation was not used to unravel the crime but, in ninety-five cases out of a hundred, to exhaust, wear down, weaken, and render helpless the defendant, so that he would want it to end at any cost."[1]

Jacques confirmed and elaborated upon Solzhenitsyn's assertion.

> As far as the ethics, legality, or humanity of such practices were concerned, the method was clear. Whatever served the interests of the Soviet state was ethical, legal, and humane. According to Marxism-Leninism, ethics and legality could only be "class" concepts, "socialist" ideas. Lenin had written: "For us morality depends upon the interests of the proletarian class struggle." "The struggle for strengthening communism is the basis for communist morality." Lenin also declared that "the communist party was the avant-garde of the proletariat." This avant-garde was supervised by the Central

Committee, which itself was directed by the Politburo. Thus it was a very small group of individuals that, in fact, alone decided what was legal and democratic.

In the history of the Soviet Union, the notion of legality without any qualification was only mentioned during a very short period of time, during the brief thaw that followed the death of Stalin. But very soon legality once again became "socialist." If so ordered by the party, Soviet authorities disregarded their own rules and laws. Nothing was considered illegal if it had been ordered by the party. Thus victims' complaints could never be taken into account. The KGB chief declared in a speech in 1961: "Soviet laws are the most humane in the world, but their humanism must only apply to honest workers. As for other 'elements,' the law must be strict for them because they are our 'enemies.'"

Humanity, however, was not completely absent from the cell of the accused where Jacques was schooled between two interrogations, during the painful wait for the end of the investigation.

I was taken back to my cell around five in the morning where, if I had wanted to, I could eat cold soup left over from the previous evening. I did not eat because I was too upset, too anxious. I lay down on the boards. My companions gathered around me, took off my shoes, and massaged my legs. There was always a comrade with a little money who had bought sugar at the camp store and who shared a lump to nourish me. It was solidarity. Luckily, my feet did not hurt too much, unlike some of my fellow accused whom the guards had to drag behind them because they had ulcers on their feet. Usually, the most resistant were those who held important positions. The others gave in quickly. I can still see them, those who broke down – a young student, a doctor, a captain.

Jacques, the foreigner, apparently was not ostracized during that initial period when almost all the men felt bewilderment and deception more than fear. They felt a horrible sense of betrayal, as well as shame for their own countrymen. "I remember the distorted and battered face of Karlik, one of my fellow inmates who was not treated gently by the interrogating commissar. Returning from one of these terrible interrogations, he pointed at me while his desperate compatriots looked on and he said that I, Jacques the Frenchman, did not suffer as much because it was not my country."

Karlik's remark – and those of others – remained in Jacques's consciousness and changed him in ways that later enabled him to survive and to resist. Of course, he was still a good communist, but he wasn't a Soviet citizen. This new dissociation would progressively lead him to embrace his national and cultural identity. It was because he was Jacques, a Frenchman, that he would not give in to despair. It was because he rapidly became Jacques the Frenchman, with no comma, that he would fight to get out and go home. When all his reasons for living no longer existed, he discovered Leontine again, his French mother, who watched over him and nourished his pugnacious and defensive strength. Her presence, which took the form of faith, slowly displaced his other faith, the faith in communism. It remained with him not only during the twenty-four years spent in the clutches of the NKVD-MVD-KGB but also right up to his return to France in 1985, nearly forty-eight years after the Great Purges.

Jacques remained in his cell in the detention prison of the Butyrka prison, waiting anxiously, fearing that the guard would announce, once again, the first letter of his name. An atmosphere of panic reigned in the cell of the sixty accused men as the time for the interrogations approached. "A discreet murmur could be heard in the cell, then dead silence when the face of the guard appeared in the Judas window. He whispered the letter so quietly that a young man had to turn towards us and repeat it more loudly." All these rituals were organized by the administration for good reasons. If the guard or "dragger" spoke softly, it was so he could not be heard in other cells or, in case he was at the wrong cell, he would not say the name of someone who was not there and thereby communicate some information. The accused could not know the identities of those in the other cells because such information might assist them in their defence.

Once they were condemned, the answers to questions such as name, surname, article of the criminal code, length of sentence, and the end date of one's sentence were all used by the guards to determine the relative danger of each inmate. A person condemned for involuntary homicide was considered more dangerous than a petty thief, but less dangerous than one condemned for premeditated murder. The most dangerous and pernicious was the so-called political prisoner or basement dweller. In addition, someone whose sentence was about to end was considered less dangerous than someone who still had many years left to serve.

When the door of the cell closed and the prisoners were outside, the guard started asking questions again and checked that they had the same names as those on the sheet he was holding. Two other guards twisted the prisoners' arms. "Forward! The prisoner, scared to death, walked between the two guards without asking where, because he knew only too well where he was going." Jacques experienced this ordeal only about fifteen times, during this tumult when he was dragged without respite to the interrogation and into the basements of hell. If he never confessed to imaginary crimes, as others had done, it was not only because he was more defiant but also because he was the least important person in his intelligence agency. They persisted less with him because the others in his group had already been arrested and condemned. "If you were beaten long enough, you finally broke down." It was easy to break a man, to make him say what you wanted him to say and to make him accuse his best friends. Some held out longer than others. But there are physical laws that limit a person's capacity to resist.

I also saw people give up even before they were tortured. In Butyrka, I remember an accused prisoner whose interrogator had threatened to transfer him to the Lefortovo prison, which at that time had a reputation for inflicting special torture and for the horror of its "coolers" [punishment cells]. He must have broken down because after several days he came back from a long interrogation very calm and relaxed and afterwards he was never transferred.

In addition, the cells were filled with informers whose job was to push – in Russian, the word for this kind of informer is translated literally as *pusher* – the accused "to confess" everything he knew: "You will be tortured … Your wife and children will be beaten … They will be sent to Siberia … So confess! … You will save your family!" VIPs were placed in cells for two people. Sometimes the other so-called prisoner was actually a commissar disguised as a prisoner. The "pusher" tried everything to destabilize and convince the real prisoner to confess.

There was also a phenomenon that in Russian was called "the tail." This included everyone who was arrested following someone else's arrest. It was like the tail of a comet. It's initially thick and bright, but then it fades and spreads out like a fan before disappearing. The brighter the comet, the longer the tail. Those who were arrested first were the people who had occupied important positions, who had relationships with important bosses. Their information led to the "unmasking" of others, that is to say, it was used to invent crimes for others. I was at the end of the tail, the last on the list, a subordinate. I interested them less. I was not executed and I was beaten less than the others.

Once again, Jacques considers himself very lucky, or perhaps this remark merely disguised that vague feeling of guilt that haunted so many survivors.

# 13 Everyday Life at the Butyrka Prison

I could never have imagined, for instance, how terrible and agonizing it would be never once for a single minute to be alone for the ten years of my imprisonment.

Fyodor Dostoyevsky, *Memoirs from the House of the Dead*

Every ten days, prisoners had the right to draw up complaints that they could send to the judicial services of the state and the party, and every ten days the chief guard asked us who wanted to make a request. We raised our hands in silence and shortly afterwards we were brought, according to the rules, purple ink, pens, and the precise number of quarter-sheets of paper that were the size of post cards. The prisoners carefully tried to disprove the accusations against them and to raise questions about the methods used to extort their confessions. I believed for a long time that these complaints went right into the trash, but I eventually learned that passages from them were often used to fabricate additional charges.

Like so many others, Jacques fervently insisted upon his innocence in a number of petitions, but they led to nothing. He still did not know that he would remain in the Butyrka detention centre for a year and a half. Compared with what had preceded and what would follow, his memories of it are not too bad. "After a certain time, the interrogations stopped completely. I felt fine in prison when I was not interrogated: no fear, no physical pain, and no beatings."

Jacques later learned that although it seemed meagre, the food ration of a prison inmate who did not work included four ounces more bread and half an ounce more sugar than that of a labour camp prisoner who refused to work. Eventually, he experienced some calm because he no longer had an interrogator. His lengthy detention in that prison afforded Jacques considerable advantages.

For example, each time one inmate left and another arrived, the other prisoners took great interest in the newcomers. Imagine a cell measuring six yards by twelve yards packed full of prisoners. The newcomer got the worst spot in the cell, usually on the floor, under the beds, or near the door where the toilet bucket was. Privileged and envied was the prisoner who could sleep far from those odours, on one of the camp beds near the window. That is why departures were carefully watched. As soon as the privileged one left the cell with his belongings, there was a discussion. And it was then that a key person intervened, the inmate responsible for the cell:

> "Who wants the free place?"
> Several hands went up.
> "Length of detention?"

Length of detention referred to the time since one's arrest, and conferred rights on the more senior occupants of the cell. As his stay grew longer and other prisoners changed cells, eventually Jacques emerged as the prisoner who had been in the cell the longest. "Practically, at least, during my stay in Butyrka, there was never any conflict. It's true there was no record book. Since they were transferred from one cell to another in groups, the others could confirm that, yes, Petrov had been arrested in the month of September 1937 and Jacques in the month of December. The months passed and I became the veteran of the cell."

The person who distributed these advantages and who presided over the group decisions in the cell was called in Russian a *starosta*, an elder, a person responsible for the cell. When Jacques arrived at the Butyrka prison in 1937, the *starosta* was elected by a show of hands. And then, during a routine visit by the administration in 1938, the situation changed.

> Usually the cells were visited once every ten days or so. That day as usual, the administrative officer came in. Everybody stood up. Total silence. The officer asked us if we had any questions, and these questions typically concerned technical or domestic matters. Inmates would say, for example, "we don't have rags to clean the floor" or "we haven't seen the guard who distributes the food we buy in ten days." Those who had money on their account could buy extra food every ten days. We didn't talk about our cases because we knew it was useless.

That day, before asking the usual question, the officer asked us if we had a *starosta*. That person identified himself:

"It's me, Sidorov, Ivan Petrovitch!"

Without even looking at him the officer glanced at us quickly, pointed his finger at someone by chance and said:

"It's you who will be the *starosta*."

"At your command!" answered the designated prisoner.

It was a person who had previously been in the military and who always wore his uniform. His service stripes had been ripped off accordingly. In a place where the accused were deemed counter-revolutionaries even before any trial, the democratic election of the *starosta* could only be viewed as a threatening anti-communist conspiracy. We understood that such a scandalous thing could not be tolerated in a Soviet prison.

Historically, the *starosta* had existed in tsarist prisons, where he was elected among fellow prisoners by a show of hands. At that time, he represented all the cells because during the day the cells were open and the prisoners could freely communicate with one another. In Soviet prisons, very quickly such free communication between the cells was forbidden and the doors were closed twenty-four hours a day. Thus each cell had a *starosta*. From the thirties on, the election of the *starosta* had to be approved by the administration. When the administration deemed it necessary, it would dismiss the *starosta* and order a new election. From the time of the Great Purges, the *starosta* was no longer elected in all Soviet prisons, but was appointed by the administration. Later, the position of *starosta* was eliminated and replaced by just someone responsible for the cell.

There were usually no important people in the common cell with Jacques.

Sometimes, there were exceptions. Nogtev, the [first] director of the Solovetsky camp, spent twenty-four hours with us in our cell. That happened due to an administrative error. My companions in that big cell had been arrested, like me, for the first time. They did not know a lot about Soviet national security and, at that time in their detention, they did not hesitate to speak openly about the circumstances of their arrest or the brutality of their interrogations. A man who had held political responsibilities knew how to hold his tongue. The first violinist of the Moscow opera could be a master as far as music was concerned or back-stage intrigues, but he nonetheless failed to understand that he was being watched constantly.

No matter what cell Jacques was in at Butyrka or his place within that cell, the daily routine never changed, and was only interrupted by announcements. The inmates got up at six o'clock, went to the latrines, and had *kasha* soup at noon and at five. "The Butyrka was the only prison where the sorghum *kasha* was different every day of God's week. Since there was no fat in it, it was like eating wood. The buckwheat soup was too thin, but sometimes there was also lentil and pea soup. After the meal, we did the dishes and let them dry at the table."

The next routine of the day and the most trying concerned the expedition to the toilets. All the administration's energy was focused on keeping prisoners from communicating with one another when they were at the toilets. "One day, for example, the officer on duty devised a plan 'to trick the adversary.' Cell 74 would be the first to go to the toilets but the next one would be not 75 or 73 but 60, so that prisoners could not know when it would be their turn. Thus they would be denied the ability to possibly leave a message at the toilets. What care, what manoeuvres to complicate communication and spread confusion!"

Prisoners had to wait so that the order in which they went to the toilets satisfied the twisted fantasy of a petty boss. Whether they liked it or not, they had to make their intestines wait. In those rooms where the prisoners tried to wash by sprinkling themselves with water, Jacques discovered why his companions had the bottom of their trousers tucked into their socks.

> At that time, trousers were quite wide and while bathing they got wet. To avoid getting the bottom of the trousers wet, inmates tucked them into their socks and their shoes got wet instead. This is how I eventually ruined my elegant suede shoes.
>
> Once every ten days we were taken to the showers, where we met a guard with a grey smock over his uniform who acted as the barber. He had clippers to shave us. That is why we were all so poorly shaven. While we were accused (not yet sentenced!) we were permitted to keep our own clothes and wear our hair as we wished. As long as we were not sentenced, our heads were not routinely shaved. If you stayed for a long time in detention, as I did, you quickly grew a mop of hair.
>
> Such was our dilemma: our hair represented a symbol of freedom and most of us clung to that. If we asked the barber to cut our hair, he shaved our heads. There was no other cut. However, we discovered a solution. Since the trip to the latrines twice a day took a long time (there were ten toilets for a cell of sixty), the hairy ones who finished

going to the toilet went into a corner of the cell that could not be seen through the Judas window and their comrades burned their hair with matches. I remember a former worker for the Comintern who was a real artist. We used a comb as long as it was fireproof. We worked with great care, but there were accidents. Nonetheless, we held onto our hair of free men. We all had no idea what awaited us.

I waited impatiently for the trip to the toilets. It was the only place where one could breathe fresh air. With a window that was always open, the atmosphere was different from the crowded cell. By my calculation, we were living in six by twelve yards, with up to one hundred twenty people who every day ate that black Russian bread which made you fart. It was the kind of bread that was very heavy and stuck in your hand like clay when you squeezed it. It had irrepressible effects. Also, since smoking was permitted and Russians were chain smokers, the air in the cell quickly became unbearable. So the toilets were wonderful because the windows were always open there, letting in fresh air.

The accused men's time was spent doing practical things like repairing their clothes.

When you live on wooden planks, your clothing gets worn out very quickly. We had to mend them with multicoloured pieces of cloth. Two needles were allowed in the cell and they were noted on documents. If, by some misfortune, one of them went missing, we were searched and if the needle was not found there was collective punishment. Concerning our clothing, I remember that I had red pajamas left over from my wardrobe as a secret agent. During each celebration in October [on the anniversary of the revolution] they were confiscated just in case I, the dangerous "political prisoner," would have dared to wave a red flag in honour of the revolution. And each October I had to file an official request to get my pajamas back.

To breathe a bit of fresh air, we went for walks. We had permission to walk if we were not being punished for something, but the procedure was even more complicated than going to the toilets. Theoretically, the walk lasted between ten and fifteen minutes. The time was measured by an hourglass in the guard's sentry box. We could never see the hourglass because there were too many of us. We calculated that there were about twenty thousand accused during the Great Purges in the Butyrka prison. And because there weren't enough courtyards, we even took our walks at night. Everyone in the cell was woken up. The door was opened and:

"Get up. Get ready for the walk!"

Then everybody woke up suddenly, those on the ground, those in the *metro*, and those in the *airplanes*.[1] At Butyrka we walked in circles two by two, our hands behind our backs in small courtyards about seventeen yards long and nine yards wide. There were several dozen of us. It was like being at the bottom of a well. Talking was forbidden. A guard watched from above and in case of an infraction we returned immediately to the cell. One time during the day I saw a pigeon flying above us: he couldn't be arrested. Sometimes also a tiny piece of grass managed to grow in a crack in the asphalt. Each time it was like a present for me. Comrades told me that at the Lubianka prison, which was the tallest building in Moscow, the walk took place on the fenced-in roof.

In the overcrowded cells, we installed these airplanes when the curfew alarm sounded. They measured two and a half feet by a little more than six feet and were between two rows of camp bunks attached to opposite walls, allowing more people to lie down. The first prisoners lay down on the ground under the camp bunks and in the passageways. When there were too many people, we had to lie on our sides and if one of us turned over, the whole row also had to turn over.

Then we placed the airplanes above the ground and the prisoners slept there on their mattresses, head to foot, their heads against the feet of those who slept on the camp bunks. Their heads were against the wall as if in a coffin. Above them the "aviators" stretched out. When one of those who was sleeping on the ground had to go to the night latrine or was ordered to an interrogation, one of the airplanes had to be lifted. The person had to carefully place his pack of clothes and shoes on the airplane and then disturb two or three men. If the person was called by the feared commissar, he had to get dressed next to the bucket by the door after having stepped over the heads and feet of several sleeping men. Many of my fellow inmates had nightmares and woke us up abruptly with terrible screams. If we were kind, we would gently touch the sleeping person or shake him so he would stop.

Some nights, the prisoners were disturbed in their dreams by an order from the guard through the Judas window:

"Everybody with your packs!"

This order could mean two things: either a search or the "reorganization of the cell," a Russian military term that meant spreading out the inmates in order to break up potential groups.

Between eighty to one hundred twenty of us were crowded into a well-guarded space, nicknamed "the dry bath" because it looked like a bathhouse, completely tiled and clean, with a plaque attached to the floor by a frame of thin columns, and unmovable benches attached to the walls. The guards wore grey smocks and the prisoners were naked with their packs. We stood one behind the other. The guard would say:

"The shirt!"

We would give him the shirt and he would touch all the seams. The same thing happened for each article of clothing. I hated to put my bare feet on the floor, so when he asked for my shoes, I would only give him one. I would stand on one foot while he examined it, to make sure that no rigid object was hidden inside. He would throw the shoe back at me. I would put it on and give him the other one.

These searches at Butyrka preceded others that were dispersed throughout Jacques's incarceration. Only once, in Siberia after fifteen years in the Gulag, did a guard give him the order to put both feet on the ground. "I was really angry with him because that search took place in the latrines, since there was no other room. I had to put both of my feet on a floor soaked with urine. I understood then that the Siberian guard had always lived in conditions like that and he thought I was making a big to-do about nothing." The cell was also searched from top to bottom, between the boards and between the airplanes. The smallest cracks were inspected.

At Butyrka, it was almost impossible to hide anything. But later in Siberia, I found a small piece of tin that I rubbed against the cement to sharpen into a blade. I willingly lent it to my fellow prisoners, but none of them ever knew where or how I hid it. We made all kinds of objects with the stuff at hand. For example, we made glue from potatoes. At Butyrka there was a very ingenious Cossack colonel who was skilled with his hands. While he was tinkering, he would tell us stories about horses. But punishment was severe. For even the smallest blade, it was ten days in the cooler.

Later in the camps, Jacques recalled the time he spent in Butyrka, once the interrogations stopped, as almost a wonderful experience. This was due to the human qualities of most of the other political prisoners or thirty-seveners (those arrested as "enemies of the people" during the Great Purges in 1937), the relative absence of the so-called thieves-in-law or the criminal recidivists, along with a kind of camaraderie among the detainees, that eased the harshness of prison life. Jacques, the inmate who still had his hair and held out hope deep in his heart that he would be cleared of all charges, turned towards his companions in misery. He formed lasting bonds with them that sustained him during his deportation.

# 14 The Story of a Blind Man and Coffee with Milk

> The Gulag is not a perversion of the system, but the system itself.
>
> Jacques Rossi

After some time, the length of Jacques's stay conferred upon him certain advantages, that of choosing, for example, a library book. The distribution of the books was handled by the person responsible for the cell. Once a month the guard opened the door with a pile of books in his arms and said, "Take the books!" The two strongest inmates placed them on the table. Another prisoner, the one "responsible for culture," read each title. Hands were raised. Once again, it came down to seniority. Jacques was getting further and further away from the day of his arrest and had been there the longest. So he was the one who was first to choose his book.

> The prisoner "responsible for culture" was someone who was himself cultured. There were professors and very educated engineers. So when he said, for example, Balzac, *The Human Comedy*, volume 2, he often gave a short summary, a description of the book. It was moving to see all those hands raise to ask for books. But, of course, there were too many of us. There were more prisoners than books!

The library at Butyrka was well stocked because it was systematically enhanced by the books of persons arrested. People were brought into prison with their books. Entire private libraries were added to the already excellent collection of the old prison. Nicely bound, typically devoid of any sign of the private owner, the books were marked with the stamps and seal of the prison, which depersonalized them. What a surprise, then, what a feeling the day one discovered in a book the signature of Zinoviev or of Bukharin, signatures that had escaped the careful eye of the censor. Thus traces of those executed after the Moscow Show Trials were still fresh.

The books remained in the cell between four and six weeks, and they were often exchanged. When one of the inmates finished reading a book, he would put it on the table.

"Who wants to read this?"

"I do."

"Length of detention?"

"Ten months."

And then the ten months became twelve months, fourteen months, and sixteen months.

Among other books, Jacques read John Galsworthy's *The Forsyte Saga* in Russian translation. Books in foreign languages practically did not exist. Russian translations were accepted by Soviet publishing companies, but they included an introduction that painstakingly described a proper Marxist reading of the text.

> Everything that was published by the Soviet publishing companies was considered legal from the point of view of the NKVD. However, in the thirties there was a publishing company in Moscow called Academia (the name was written in Latin script) that published foreign authors in Russian, such as Shakespeare, Balzac, Dante, Cervantes, and Goethe, as well as non-Soviet Russian classics like Tolstoy. Invariably, the text included a foreword of ten or so pages in which someone explained how these unenlightened writers had ignored social justice. Thus the censor would allow such books to be published. For the most part, we only got Soviet publications of little value and full of propaganda. At Butyrka I came upon French or German books once or twice. However, around 1956, following the Twentieth Party Congress, in a high-security prison, I met German and Japanese officers who were lent books in foreign languages.
>
> Everyone wanted to read or at least have a book to leaf through, except perhaps several old illiterate peasants. Between the official distributions, of course, we exchanged books. At a date decided by the administration, the guard told us through the Judas window that the books had to be collected. And for those who hadn't finished their books – too bad. The inmates piled the books up on the table and when the guard looking through the Judas window was sure that the books were all on the table, he opened the door and said politely:
>
> "Bring out the books!"
>
> And we piled them up outside the door.

It was strictly forbidden to make any markings in the books. Since the inmates had no pencils they could only underline or leave a mark with a fingernail or a match. The librarian was responsible for examining the books, and each time he found a mark, he stamped the page with the library stamp and indicated the cell from which the book came. So the entire cell was held responsible for the markings. If there were several stamps for one cell, all the inmates of that cell were punished and deprived of books until the guilty person came forward and admitted what he had done. It was much easier for the administration to punish collectively by eliminating the books or the walks, but in any case, we changed cells often and the punishment did not last forever. The perverse result of the system was that a marked book with a lot of stamps indicated right away juicy passages. In general, they were passages where the underlined words referred to our situation even indirectly, like in works by Russian or foreign authors of the nineteenth century. When we were in prison, we were sensitive to these allusions. They were small pleasures for us.

Many interesting things happened to Jacques's reading companions in the detention cells at the height of the Great Purges. In one of the cells, as was typical, there were *apparatchiks* of the party and the state, military personnel, engineers, students, diplomats, a stamp collector, Esperantists, a deaf-mute, some foreign communists like himself, and an old Bolshevik who had taken part in the revolutions of 1905 and 1917. In *Fragments of Lives*, Jacques drew some of their portraits, evoked some of the dramas, and condensed and transformed through fiction where the absurd rivaled the tragic.

One of them was the Baltic inmate K.D., who had formerly taken part in dirty deeds. K.D. was next to Jacques in the bunk. He was obliging and accommodating. K.D. had earlier been a minor officer in the tsar's army and a member of a Bolshevik cell. He then worked in the first division of the Cheka, and was assigned to Lenin's security guard regiment. Jacques wrote:

> Sometimes he would reminisce about Lenin. He talks about him with much affection and admiration. I am surprised to see another side of Lenin, quite different than the one conveyed by the official propaganda. He is no longer a Bolshevik icon glued to his veneer, but rather a god of Olympus with many faults and shortcomings. K.D.'s message is also unconventional: he doesn't use any clichés, always refers to "the October coup" whereas for many years it has been renamed "The Great October Revolution of the Proletariat."[1]

Another prisoner at Butyrka was Nikifor Prozorov. He had been a peasant in a collective farm near Moscow, and was thirty years old. Nikifor saw a want ad in the papers asking for a cabinetmaker at an address on Herzen street in Moscow, and decided to try his luck. Once on the street, he couldn't find the street number and asked a policeman, who offered politely to drive him there. The trip ended in a cell at Butyrka, where the unlucky Nikifor learned from his comrades that the address was that of the embassy of Japan. Nikifor Prozorov was condemned to eight years in a corrective-labour camp for spying for Japan.

Siegfried, a young Jewish cardiologist from Vienna, had taken advantage of Stalin's generous hospitality extended to Nazi victims before the Nazi-Soviet non-aggression pact. He wanted to express his gratitude to the Soviet Union, so he worked devotedly in a Moscow hospital. There he discovered rampant anti-Semitism, and decided to leave the USSR with his wife Esther and little Rebecca who had just been born in Moscow, and move to the United States, where he had family. After much effort, many procedures, and many contacts, the family finally found itself on a train for Riga in Latvia, from where they were supposed to embark for New York. However, after several thorough verifications of their passports and their luggage at the border, an officer asked Siegfried to follow him "just for a minute." Siegfried was condemned to ten years for being a spy for Nazi Germany.

Another fellow prisoner, Latsis, was a proletarian from Riga, a Bolshevik from the very beginning who had participated in the assault on the Winter Palace in Petrograd. He had a good career serving the party and in the early thirties became director of a department at the national Soviet petroleum company. He would be condemned to eight years for so-called counter-revolutionary sabotage and would come across Jacques again much later in the camps. Jacques also talked about a Hungarian comrade who had been a member of the Red Guard during the civil war. "He married a Russian woman and was not interested in politics. In prison, he kept his Tyrolean hat and his little bushy mustache. He took a liking to me and sometimes invited me to share the biscuits, butter, and black bread that he could buy with the money orders that he received."

In Butyrka, Jacques, who had only his one ruble and 167 kopeks, was considered poor, but he discovered a network of social help, the kind that Varlam Shalamov wrote about in his *Kolyma Tales*. Those inmates who had money were obliged to donate ten per cent of what they bought at the camp shop to the "committee for the poor."

This practice recalled a policy that the Bolsheviks instituted in the countryside in 1918, but [that] had been largely abandoned during the period of forced collectivization. It was, however, seared in the memories of the thirty-seveners, the former party activists who introduced a similar practice of sharing in the prisons. Eventually, the authorities banned the practice, but prisoners tried to replace it with an informal system. The "rich" were asked to help the poor, despite the fact that the rules forbade this and the cells were filled with informers. I only remember one prisoner who refused to participate. He was an accountant arrested during the purges who thought that if he was helping the "political prisoners" (he did not realize that he was one himself) then he would be committing a counter-revolutionary act. He became our whipping boy, and he had to be careful to avoid the vengeance of his fellow inmates!

The main attraction in the life of an inmate at Butyrka was placing an order at the camp shop every ten days. The list of available products was given to the cell. All those who could do so prepared their orders. The orders were grouped together by three or four usually privileged, strong prisoners. You can imagine a cell with about a hundred men, each one buying two or four pounds of bread, at forty-five kopeks a pound, without counting the extra bread for the privileged. Upon their return everything was placed on the table and the committee started the distribution. I had the right to receive a small piece of bread or some sugar when my fellow inmates received their purchases. For a while my neighbour in bed, an old man who suffered from stomach problems, could buy white bread. And so he gave me his share of black bread. Other privileged prisoners gave away their soup. Since I was young, I had an enormous appetite and I devoured everything.

Friendships that emerged were often interrupted by the transfer of inmates to another cell. These systematic transfers were intended to keep prisoners from forming relationships. In the eyes of Soviet authorities, friendship ties among prisoners could only signal the creation of counter-revolutionary groups whose sole purpose was to overthrow Soviet power.

It was at Butyrka that Jacques discovered what he would consider a quintessential element of the Soviet system – *tufta*, that is, cheating or making false claims. "Lying is like blood circulating. One's old title is replaced with 'prisoner,' and the term 'political prisoner' is replaced with 'enemy of the people.' That's all that is needed, and it happened at all levels." As a result of transfers from one cell to another, Jacques was surprised on several occasions to meet men who had participated in the infamous population census of 1937, a census that was later denounced and officially abandoned by Stalin, its lead statisticians executed. Why?

Because it reported a sharp population loss in the millions, while the Soviet leader insisted that the population was growing due to the exceptional development of the country. Stalin ordered a re-do of the census. More haphazard and less honest, the 1939 census somehow erased the excess deaths evident in the 1937 census. This is an example of *tufta*.

The word *tufta* appeared in the twenties in the vocabulary of the criminal recidivists. It comes from the acronym "TFT" (*tiazhelyi fizicheskii trud*) meaning heavy physical labour. The term was later "translated" by prisoners as *tekhnika fiktivnogo uchota truda*, that is, "a technique for falsely calculating work." This idea, Jacques insisted, was fundamental to understanding the essence of the system and the Soviet economy. The ideals of Marxism-Leninism were not realistic. Yet since Stalin decided that the utopia would become a reality, the whole country had to resort to *tufta*, that is, to widespread falsification, in order to validate the lies of the party.[2] One of Jacques's fellow inmates, who had been arrested by the Nazis, then liberated by the Red Army, then arrested again by the Soviets, explained: "The Gestapo tortured me so that I would tell the truth, the NKVD so that I would lie."

How can you enable people in the West to understand a system where the citizen is a mere instrument serving the state, and not the other way around?

> In order to illustrate the opacity of relationships in the communist world for those who have always lived under a system of democratic legality, I'd like to tell the story of the blind man. The blind man was sitting in a cafe with a friend of his who could see. The one who could see ordered coffee and asked his blind friend:
> 
> "Do you want coffee too?"
> 
> "Of course," says the blind man, smelling the coffee. "It smells so good."
> 
> "Do you want black coffee or coffee with milk?"
> 
> "Milk, what is milk?"
> 
> "Milk, it's a liquid."
> 
> The blind man knows what a liquid is and he makes the gesture of opening a faucet. The man with sight notes: "It's a liquid but a white liquid."
> 
> "What is white?"
> 
> The man who can see starts to get tired.
> 
> "A swan is white."
> 
> "What is a swan?"
> 
> "A swan is a bird with a bent neck."
> 
> "Bent, I don't know what that is."

The man puts his hand on the blind man's elbow and he squeezes it, then he bends it.

"Now it is bent!"

And the blind man exclaims loudly:

"Very good, coffee with milk please!"

When "Soviet" was spoken, we thought we understood what that meant, but we didn't understand anything. By the way, what is milk?

Intellectual and cultural activities were not lacking at the Butyrka detention prison. There was no shortage of highly qualified people for organizing the cell, either. "We exchanged our experiences of life abroad. I told the stories of French novels. I talked about my trips by describing the cities, the monuments, and the museums. Someone else spoke about the book he had just read, being careful to present it from an official Marxist-Leninist point of view. No one wanted to risk an additional sentence. That's why there were few volunteers for philosophy. It was too dangerous."

With new arrivals, news from the outside came into the cells of Butyrka. The same scenario repeated with each newcomer: He was recognized by his shaved face, his clothes in good condition that contrasted with the torn and mended clothing of those who had been arrested long before. He had a normal haircut. Above all, he brought recent news, so the group would gather around him to listen. There was still war in Spain and most of the detainees were good communists. They were worried about the fate of the Republicans that the USSR supported and knew the geography without a map, by heart. The newcomer announced right away: "Teruel has just fallen!" Everyone knew the city. The so-called enemies of the people worried because the Spanish communists and the Republicans were their brothers. Another one announced the Comintern's dissolution of the Polish communist party. There were many Poles in the cell. Their party had been totally decimated by all the arrests. Each Pole asked him about the reasons for the dissolution, but they were very respectful and careful not to express any criticism of the party's decision.

There were important trials during those years. In March 1938, the third Moscow show trial took place, the one concerning the "Anti-Soviet Bloc of Rightists and Trotskyists." The names of Nikolai Bukharin, Alexsi Rykov, Christian Rakovsky, Nikolai Krestinsky, and Genrikh Yagoda were discussed in the cell, in addition to other rumours. It was said that twenty-one of the accused were executed and that Krestinsky was the only one to change his deposition, extorted through torture by the famous Andrei Vyshinsky. Others said that the presiding judge had immediately suspended the session, after which Krestinsky confirmed his initial deposition.

These men, some of them tortured every night, could only speak about their most intimate fears in whispers. Teruel had fallen. There was no longer an independent communist party in Poland. Bukharin had been broken. And Jacques, what would become of him? Months, years passed. Jacques the Frenchman still awaited trial. He did not know that his verdict would be announced with no trial at all. Didn't he suspect that a bit? After Zinoviev and Kamenev, after Piatakov and Serebriakov, and now Bukharin and Krestinsky? But no. Despite his lack of certainty after one year and four months of detention, Jacques was still fully convinced that his innocence would be recognized by Soviet judges. However, he was no longer alone. Gradually he realized that his fellow inmates were not "enemies of the people" either, for the most part, and that they too were no more guilty than he was. He awaited justice not only for himself, but also for his comrades.

# 15 The Verdict: Now We're Going to Put into Practice Marxist-Leninist Theory

> The impossible is impossible ... But the OSO is here.
> Popular Russian saying from the mid-thirties

On 7 April 1939, exactly sixteen months after he was arrested, Jacques was condemned to eight years in the Gulag by the OSO (*osoboe soveshchanie*), the Special Council of the People's Commissariat of Internal Affairs (NKVD), an extrajudicial branch of the NKVD that handed down sentences in absentia. Six hundred other sentences were handed down the same day, during the same session. They all had the identical number [Article 58] on their official report. Jacques would leave with the same convoy as his six hundred fellow inmates, eastward towards Siberia.

During his months of detention in the Butyrka prison cell, Jacques had had time to get used to his imprisonment. He was aware of the various accusations against his fellow inmates. One by one they returned to the cell, after being informed of their sentences.

> Some of them came back in silence, their faces inscrutable. We asked them no questions. Others were so upset by the stupidity, the banality, and the falseness of the motives for their condemnation that they exploded. There were more than sixty of us steeping in the stinky atmosphere created by the motives given. We said amongst ourselves: "This is a catastrophe in the history of socialism. It is probably a conspiracy of the political police. How come the Central Committee cannot stop them?"

Jacques remembers a dignified school director after the last interrogation and review of his file. The most serious denunciation against him was from a colleague who testified: "When he read news in the press concerning the successes of socialism, he was not happy." Thus the school director was sentenced to ten years. But Jacques the Frenchman was stubborn. "There were times when I realized that it was all over for me too, that I was not going to get out of this mess. I could not believe it. I would say to myself – this is too stupid, it can't be serious, it's impossible, surely I am going to be freed. You cling to something, you have to cling to something." Jacques believed for some time that attempts had been made to free him. Could it have been his superior who wanted the best for him and who removed all traces of his mission in Spain from his file?

> My detention had been much longer than normal. The typical stay in prison detention lasted only two to eight months. Well-known personalities might stay longer, while accusations were fabricated to justify execution. But that wasn't my case. For months on end I was neither interrogated nor tortured. So I had reason to believe that I would be freed. Much later, when I left the Gulag and I read studies about the period, I realized that it was possible that superior officers may have considered releasing me. And then, perhaps, they forgot about me, and my file remained in the clutches of a bureaucracy that never forgets. Once condemned, I was taken away with no chance of returning!

Jacques waited more than sixteen months in the Butyrka prison before his time finally came. The inquiry, or rather the caricature of an inquiry, was considered complete. There was no trial, no court decision, only the interrogations, the beatings, the torture, and the long wait. One day Jacques was taken to see an official who seated him at a table and let him read his file. Reading one's file was a legal requirement, but it was only a formality. Testimony was usually falsified anyway. What purpose did it serve to have resisted torture only to discover in the end that the investigator had invented the testimony? Jacques did not have to face that situation, however. But he did have access to other testimonies from people who were responsible for "unmasking" him.

> There were two testimonies from people that I knew vaguely. One was a Russian woman who worked in the Comintern. I knew her husband, and I saw them from time to time. They invited me for dinner to their home once or twice. The other was a Russian man from the international espionage service. The content of their testimony was very formulaic: "He is the son of bourgeois parents. He speaks many foreign languages and that is suspicious" or "I am not sure that his father's first name is correct." Later, another Gulag prisoner

helped me to understand that these people were often threatened and terrorized, that they said the minimum of what they thought they had to say in order to avoid prison themselves.

In addition to these testimonies, there was that of one of Jacques's superiors. Could it have been the one Adam had said was displeased with him? We'll call this superior Boris. According to Boris, this secret agent coming from a powerful, well-placed family, speaking several languages, seemed highly suspicious. Years later in Siberia, a zealous official named Pavlov wanted to take advantage of Boris's denunciation and tried to get Jacques to denounce Boris.

Once Jacques had looked over his unenlightening file, the NKVD official read him the verdict of the OSO. It was an extract from the official record of the session. Jacques, like Solzhenitsyn several years later, was asked to read the document that described his fate. The NKVD official demanded that he sign. Jacques refused. "It doesn't matter," the official replied. "The supervisor will sign for you." So Jacques signed. If he had not signed, the official would simply have written "Was informed of the OSO decision" and the supervisor would have confirmed that by signing himself.

The form or extract of the official report was no larger than a postcard. It contained a printed heading, "special meeting of the NKVD." Below it on the left was written "hearing" and on the right "decision." Below the heading "hearing" were typed Jacques's first name, surname, date of birth, and nationality, that is to say, his French ethnic identity. His party membership was also noted, plus his place of employment and his position. Jacques had never been a member of the Soviet communist party. His transfer from the Polish communist party to the Soviet communist party would have been logical, but it was never even initiated. Since 1934, the party purges and purification of party documents carried out by the NKVD had resulted in the suspension of most transfers from a fraternal communist party to the great Soviet communist party. Under "decision" the motive and the length of the sentence were noted: "spying for France and Poland." Jacques was thus condemned to be deported to "a corrective-labour camp for eight years under Article 58." He reflected on the absurdity of the fabricated charges against him.

In the Gulag, I met a man who thought he was being smart by "admitting" that he had been a spy for Nicaragua. He thought the authorities would understand that this was ridiculous and they would let him go. However, that tiny country on the other side of the planet, despite its exoticism, did not really interest the interrogator. Nicaragua interested no one who was high up in the party. So my comrade was beaten again so that he would "confess" that he was a spy for the Japanese! This was politically correct at the time.

After reading his sentence, Jacques acknowledged it and reacted strongly. He was, he says, "stunned" but still incredulous. The misunderstanding had not been noted. It was unfortunate, but he believed this only delayed the moment when his innocence would be recognized. At the same time, the dream of seeing the communist utopia become a reality was being deferred. In the same way, the moment when he would experience being declared innocent by the system continued to be delayed, until that time when he finally realized the enormity of the deceit. But when this ardent revolutionary learned that the revolution itself was condemning him, that moment of realization was still far away. Even when being notified of the verdict, he still remained hopeful that his innocence would be recognized. Well versed in the techniques of detachment, Jacques could also convince himself that he was being carried away by a cataclysmic upheaval that went far beyond himself.

It was very late when he was led back to his cell after learning of his sentence. The cell was full of dozens of men who had all been condemned without trial under the same protocol.

Article 58 for everybody. For me, section 6, spying. Section 7 was counter-revolutionary sabotage, and section 8 terrorism. Most of them had gotten eight years like me. Very few had five years. Only one person in a convoy of six hundred men who left for the East got three years. We knew that because of the roll call that we had to answer all the time, repeating like a prayer, the length of our sentences, with "eight years" at the end like an amen.

The next day, all the condemned in the cell were taken by groups of five or six to another building. There they discovered a crowd of people like themselves, the six hundred thirty-seveners, all condemned on that day. They were among the millions of victims of the Great Purges, a campaign of mass violence that resulted in the execution of nearly eight hundred thousand people.

Then the bureaucratic routine began. They were given their possessions. Jacques was still wearing the same western suit, formerly chic but now inappropriate and in pitiful condition. The suede shoes were in pieces because they got soaked when Jacques washed himself. The water had cracked the leather. "They were not at all suitable for the Gulag. I have to find the company that made them. I would not sue them, but I would give them friendly instructions so they could prevent damage to their shoes in this kind of situation." Jacques still had his Parisian felt hat, which a very young fellow inmate wanted to buy. Jacques gave it to him as a present.

> At that time during the transfer from Butyrka to the camps, inmates who had no clothes could buy old clothes from the administration. I gave my Parisian hat away because a cell comrade laughingly told me that where I was going it would be really out of place. He gave me a dark blue cap with yellow edging that he had bought at the camp store. It was a bad gift, for it turned out later that it was the old style of police *shapkas*. But the gift giver, a foreigner, did not know that.

Jacques got rid of his secret agent's bulky trunk, but he kept the winter camel hair coat that was more appropriate for where he was going. One of his companions, a German communist, said ironically: "We already took classes in Marxist-Leninist theory. Now we're going to practise it." Jacques did not really like the joke. But he had changed since his arrest. He continued to believe that his own innocence would be recognized, but he also came to see the innocence of his companions in misery.

> I still thought that this craziness would stop and we all would be freed. The German comrade was a proletarian. Workers have a better feeling for reality than dangerous intellectuals. I looked at him sternly. The "practice" work was, I knew as well as the others, cutting down trees, extracting ore from mines, building railroads in the most horrible region on the planet. To be rehabilitated, prisoners were forced to do "socially useful labour" that no one else would ever choose to do. I knew this, but I thought it only applied to others.

After sixteen months at Butyrka, Jacques finally saw the door of the prison open, not to freedom but to what another prisoner called the Archipelago: that collection of islands of camps and prisons dispersed across the vast Soviet territory. He would, though he did not yet know it, travel through this Archipelago for two decades. The Black Maria that took the condemned to the station did not look at all like the one that had taken the accused from the Interior Ministry to the Lubianka. This one was not disguised as a delivery truck. It was just dark green. It did not have camouflage markings on it like the first one had – no bread and no meat either. It could be clearly seen that this armoured paddy wagon equipped with cells transported prisoners.

> None of the vehicles with cells inside were camouflaged. Prior to my arrest, I had seen enormous Black Marias at night weighing five tons. I learned later that they were for transporting families. In some cases everything was taken, even the furniture. When there was no *babushka*, aunt, or someone else to take care of the children, they were also taken. The police knew what they would find before they arrived at the home and, in certain cases, a female member of the NKVD came to take care of the children during the transfer. Children could be sent to the Gulag if they were fifteen or older. Thus at fifteen, they could be transported to the Gulag legally as sons and daughters of "enemies of the people." Younger children were immediately transferred to orphanages. To protect them, their names were changed. The son of Beria, for example, was given a new name after his father's arrest in 1953. Because of such practices, it's a miracle that some families were later reunited.

From then on, Jacques, like his companions in misery, was no longer an ordinary citizen who was called *comrade*. He was now a *zek*. During roll call, he would answer with his last name, first name, patronymic, date of birth, and sentence – Article 58 Section 6. He would list the crimes and counter-revolutionary misdemeanors that he was accused of, and his term of eight years. ROSSI JACQUES ROBERTOVITCH; OCTOBER 10, 1909; ARTICLE 58; SECTION 6; EIGHT YEARS. "A dead *zek* is worth more than a sick *zek*." Thus went a saying that circulated during the Great Purges. It would require strength and resistance for Jacques the Frenchman to prove this saying wrong.

# 16  Destination Unknown

Centuries pass, villages flame
are stunned by war and civil war.
My country, you are still the same,
Tragic, beautiful as before

                    Poem by Alexander Blok, quoted from memory
                                            by Jacques Rossi

They travelled in the suffocating humidity of summer, in the penetrating icy cold of winter, without air, without water, nourished by a piece of black bread and a small salted herring that made them even more thirsty for hours and days. Jacques was one of the hundreds of thousands who travelled during the spring of 1939 across unending country, in rail cars that had been designed by Pyotr Stolypin, minister of internal affairs and prime minister under Tsar Nicholas II. These were railcars designed to take peasants, newly freed from serfdom, into the Siberian interior in order to help colonize the vast Russian empire. They were cattle cars, transformed so one half was for animals and luggage and the other half for families.

The communist regime continued this practice, but in its own way. The Stolypin railcars had become quite dilapidated since the time of the tsars. There were bars on the windows, and in the space where, sixty years before, four peasants had a reasonable living space, now the Soviet authorities piled in up to thirty prisoners. Jacques was pushed into one of the convoys located on a side track far from the central station, so that no one could see the *zek*s being loaded onto the train. Loading and unloading the condemned took place far from travellers, under the unique supervision of the switchmen and the railroad men, who never talked to anyone about what they had seen there. Jacques and his companions were thrown into those railcars as soon as they left the Black Marias.

Imagine the young Jacques entering the Stolypin railcar. He had not changed clothes since his arrest, but he was wearing a strange cap, a police cap whose origin he did not know. His suit had stood up quite well after having rubbed against the boards of Butyrka for a year and a half. The suede shoes were in very bad shape. Jacques had carefully kept his dark-brown London camel hair coat that would make many people envious or curious in his place of destination. "In the transit prison I met three Inuit who wondered what kind of fur it was made of. They touched the cloth, spread the hairs apart, and touched the synthetic lining. They believed they had discovered an extraordinary animal. They had learned a lesson: that's why they were in prison, to broaden their horizons!" Jacques kept the comfortable English coat until his first month in the prison at Dudinka. In the fall he hid it under a plank, and someone stole it. Later, Jacques saw his coat on a free man who had bought it from a thief. Men and goods in the Gulag seemed to regularly disappear and reappear.

As for the wonderful trunk with the yellow corners that was supposed to have gone with him on his mission, Jacques asked the Gulag administration to send it to a friend, Valentina S. "We had the right to send our things to someone close to us, but with no accompanying letter. Why lug that suitcase with me with the stickers of Europe's grand hotels?"

It was a very heavy trunk with all his clothes. Valentina would understand what had happened and she would sell the clothes. "I did the right thing. In my convoy there was an American with a beautiful leather suitcase which the supervisors confiscated during a search, when we arrived at the fifth or sixth transit prison. They thought that he had hidden a razor and blades in the suitcase. During transit, the inmates could have no rigid objects."

At first Jacques thought only that the gift would please Valentina. The suitcase contained beautiful suits made to order in England. She could sell them for a good price. Jacques remained so convinced that his innocence would be recognized, that he did not consider the trouble he was creating for her. However, he thought about the potential danger for Julita, his Spanish fiancée to whom he sent nothing. "Julita was more in danger because she was a foreigner. To protect her I wanted to prove that we no longer had a relationship. Later I was so relieved to learn that she had left the USSR!" But when Jacques finally understood this Machiavellian system, he regretted having exposed Valentina to danger. As soon as he could, about ten years later, he asked a comrade who had been freed from the Gulag to find out about the young woman's fate and to express his apology to her. Valentina was extraordinarily lucky to have had no problems, but she complained to Jacques's messenger that the sender's status had poisoned the gift. Overcome by suspicion, Jacques often wondered whether the luck that saved Valentina was not, in fact, an indication that she had been an informer.

Along the two walls of each compartment there were four levels of boards. There were twenty-eight people, Jacques and his companions, in nine square yards of space. All had to lie down with their heads towards the bars of the hallway. Through the bars the guards were supposed to identify all the heads.

The inmates spent the whole trip lying down because there wasn't enough space to stand up in the railcar. In the seating area, a board linked the seats on the left to the seats on the right. In the sleeper cabins or compartments another board was placed, then two more, thus creating four levels, not counting the floor below. The first people to enter were put on the benches. It was impossible to stand because the boards were too close to each other. It was also impossible to sit down for the same reasons. "When you were at the top, it was horrible because it was very hot and there was no air. Under this arrangement, up to thirty inmates could be crowded into a compartment normally designed for eight seated passengers on four beds."

The prisoners were given their rations before departure or during the trip. The rations consisted of one and a half pounds of black bread and a salted fish each day for each man. The accompanying soldiers were supposed to give them water to drink, but they had to go get the water in the stations during stops. A bucket of three gallons was barely enough for a compartment, and the distribution took a long time because the guards had only one cup. Seven compartments of thirty men meant two hundred and ten thirsty men. It was easier to watch over one cup than several, so the smallest quantity of water possible was handed out. Sometimes the inmates in the Stolypin travelled ten days in a row without staying in a transit prison. Typically, the passengers in these railcars travelling to far-away places were disembarked at transit prisons, and did not stay more than three days in a row in their railcars.

At one end of the Stolypin railcar, also called the *vagonzak*, there were the toilets for the escorting soldiers and, at the other end, those for the inmates. Given the crowded conditions, the inmates were only taken to the toilets once a day instead of the statutory twice a day. The guard took each inmate separately, closed the door of the compartment behind him, and made the prisoner use the toilet that had no doors. Women were treated the same way. They were also policed by male guards.

> The guard had to be able to see what was happening at every moment. You had to be quick because hundreds of people were waiting. We ran, we crouched down and quickly, quickly, quickly. We could not wash our hands! No soap, no towels. The inmate went back to his compartment cell and climbed over bodies with his dirty shoes. The filth would drip down for the rest of the trip.
> Amidst this confusion and panic, I saw men who had managed to find a piece of paper and who wrote: "I am alive ... en route to the camps." They would fold the paper in the shape of a triangle to make a kind of envelope. They wrote the address of their family on it and, tricking the supervisor, managed to slip it into the hole of the toilet. Incredibly, despite the pervasiveness of Stalinist terror, road men and railway men often retrieved these letters and took the risk of delivering them to their addressee. They did not put stamps on them. Letters lacking stamps in Russia were typically paid for by the recipient. Later, in the camps, I learned and could not believe that almost all of those letters that went through the latrines arrived at their proper destination, and that the senders even received answers. Usually we did not know where we were being transported. But when the escort soldiers handed over the prisoners to the guards of the transit prison, the prisoners sometimes managed to peek at their files and see the address of their final destination. They then communicated this precious information to their families. Later when I was in Norilsk, I managed to send a letter to Julita, "advising" her to go see her brother, which was a way of asking her to leave the Soviet Union. I was so happy to receive an answer that reassured me. Julita finally managed to escape arrest and was able to leave the country. This was not the case for many Spanish Republicans.

In the first Stolypin, Jacques travelled only with other political prisoners, all condemned by the OSO on the same day, under the same protocol.

> In the railcars we were all former inmates from Butyrka. All ardent communists. This situation created ties that would last, a kind of clan, like the Gulag Mayflower. Almost all of us had suffered terrible interrogations. Together we had waited in vain for our trials. And suddenly we were going to a completely unknown destination. Most of us had been condemned for the first time. The labour camps! We

did not know a lot about them, except that they were for the enemies of communism and that's what the enemies deserved. But hope springs eternal. In the camps perhaps we could request a review. We would be outdoors. We would be participating in building communism. Many regretted that their professional training had been wasted during the months in prison in Moscow. There was almost a wind of hope.

So much candour is confusing. But Jacques insisted that many of his comrades, like himself, continued to believe. He returned again to his comparison between the Stolypin convoys and the decks of the boats that took immigrants to the New World. Of course, despite the risk, some men protested: "It is not really rational. How can the Central Committee ignore how we are being treated?" But the confidence that they had in the party, the habit of obeying and, for some, the denial concerning their fate led many to accept their plight. That state of mind was especially common among first-time offenders, that is to say, most of them.

What did they know about what awaited them? The majority had been arrested in the Great Purges, unexpectedly and unpredictably. It was unthinkable for us and for all communists in the West. We wanted to believe in the imminent realization of our beautiful communist dream. Seeing so many of us stuffed into these convoys made us suffer beyond our personal misfortune of being prisoners. It made us suffer for the communist dream in general. It became obvious to us that the situation was serious and went beyond individual dramas. It was perhaps unavoidable because communism was a project that was going to transform the world. We would repeat the Russian proverb: "When trees are chopped, the chips fly." But we had to accept the evidence that it was not only the chips, but the trees and even the entire forest. A little more than ten years later, the French communist Marie-Claude Vaillant-Couturier claimed that the Gulag was by far the most humane system in the world for re-educating delinquents. Of course, she had never been there! I choose Marie-Claude Vaillant-Couturier, among others, because I was told she was honest.[1] How many thinkers in the Latin Quarter obstinately kept their eyes closed while our eyes were being opened?

Until they confronted their misfortune clearly for themselves, the good communists who occupied the Stolypin cars did not really want to listen to the few former Gulag members who were among them and who were returning for a second or third time. "They 'knew' and could have communicated their knowledge to us, but we thought that they were exaggerating. We refused any damaging truth about our beautiful utopia."

Jacques clearly remembers a certain Rosenberg, a Jewish Pole who had studied in France. "He was returning to the camps where he had already spent ten years. A new case was fabricated against him. Perhaps to have him shot? He must have suspected that, since his unusual stories revealed the cruelty of life in the camps. But we turned a deaf ear."

All these political prisoners lacked experience. Labelled "enemies of the people," they were confined all together in the first Stolypin railcar. The human relationships among this group of new travellers remained more akin to those of Moscow than to those of the camps in Siberia or in the Arctic. They had not yet been in contact with the "thieves-in-law." After the first transit prison, this tight-knit group began to disperse. The men were mixed with others and sent in all directions. They separated but would occasionally meet again. Their destinies were suddenly moving in different directions in a train station in the middle of nowhere. Whenever they would meet again, they immediately felt the connection of their Mayflower experience at Burtyrka. Ordinary criminal offenders came on board the train as well as the professional criminals or *urkas,* who could be brutal and unscrupulous. "The smallest possession would be stolen. I still had my French suit and a vest and they were later stolen. They beat you. They spit on you. They peed on you. And you could do nothing about it."

Grigory Dimitrievitch, another character in Jacques's Gulag chronicle *Fragments of Lives*, was not part of the same convoy as Jacques the Frenchman. Jacques would meet him much later, in 1953 in the central Alexandrovsk prison in eastern Siberia. Grigory was arrested during the sinister year of 1937, and made the long trip with thousands of other prisoners in cattle cars.

> This former longshoreman of Odessa, a Bolshevik since 1917 who believed in Lenin and in Stalin like his mother had believed in God, had courageously resisted his interrogator. For that his ribs were fractured, his teeth were broken, and he was sentenced to fifteen years' hard labour for counter-revolutionary crimes. During the long trek towards the east in cattle cars he told me that he convinced himself that the party had decided to send experienced militants to Asia in order to thwart a plot hatched by the Japanese imperialists. In order to really trick the enemy's secret police, the party had decided to disguise their faithful members as "enemies of the people," and to treat them as if they were enemies.

At the time when Grigory told Jacques this story, he had become an invalid with no teeth but he was still a "believer." From Moscow to Krasnoyarsk the trip seemed unending. Along the way, they stopped at transit prisons where the deported often stayed for many days, even months, without knowing why. Sometimes their file was just put aside. Sometimes it was lost. "In that case, the comrades left and we panicked because we stayed behind. I experienced that after my first convoy. In the beginning, I was always with the same companions, which reassured me a little." It was in that convoy that Jacques met Oleg P., the son of an elite family from Saint Petersburg whose father was of Swedish origin.

> I think that his father or his grandfather had been a well-known geographer under the old regime. He was born in Russia and spoke perfect Russian but he pretended he could not pronounce the *r*, in order to sound like a refined Westerner. We never used the familiar "you" form, but he had good manners and I felt close to him. And then one day when we arrived in a transit prison he left in another convoy. I met him again much later in a camp. He was the one who fabricated a new case against me when I had finished my eight years.

At first, Jacques could not believe that Oleg P. had betrayed him. He had not experienced detention long enough to understand the pervasiveness of the informers' network. He missed his early companions and others that he would never see again, as he ventured deeper and deeper into the depths of the Archipelago.

At the time of the Great Purges, the Stolypin railcars were typically attached to regular long-distance trains. The prisoners' car was positioned first after the locomotive, thus hiding them from ordinary travellers. If there were curious passengers on the platform, the escort soldiers made them move away quickly. In any case Soviet citizens, even though they were kept in total ignorance of what was happening, knew from experience and instinct not to approach a window with bars. The Soviet Union, Jacques used to say, could not be separated from the Gulag any more than from its own shadow. Like many other inmates, he considered the entire country a kind of Gulag, so the freed prisoner went simply from the little Gulag to the big Gulag. The terror that reigned among the population that resulted from all these transfers of "enemies of the people" was part of a system of widespread oppression that was fueled by rumours and whispered half-truths in addition to blatant official lies. In this colossal undertaking of misinformation everything concerning the Gulag must have seemed mysterious and terrifying. Those who left the Gulag had to swear in writing that they would reveal nothing about it, or they would risk returning to the camps.

The trip in the Stolypin lasted so long that it was in itself a period of Jacques's life. Solzhenitsyn states that during that time in the railcar his ideas changed, his character changed. According to Solzhenitsyn, what "distinguishes Stolypin passengers from the rest of the train is that they do not know where their train is going and at what station they will disembark: after all, they don't have tickets, and they don't read the route signs on the cars."[2] The inmates tried very hard to learn their destination. Sometimes the position of the sun helped them to determine whether they were going north or east. Solzhenitsyn wrote:

> If it is summertime, the station loudspeakers can be heard: "Moscow to Ufa departing from Track 3. Moscow to Tashkent still loading at Platform 1 …" That means it's the Kazan Station, and those who know the geography of the Archipelago are now explaining to their comrades that Vorkuta and Pechora are out: *they* leave from the Yaroslavl Station; and the Kirov and Gorky camps are out too. They never send people from Moscow to Byelorussia, the Ukraine, or the Caucasus anyway. They have no room there even for their own. Let's listen some more: the Ufa train has left, and ours hasn't moved. The Tashkent train has started, and we're still here. "Moscow to Novosibirsk departing. All those seeing passengers off, disembark … All passengers show their tickets …" We have started. Our train! Nothing so far. The middle Volga area is still open, and the South Urals. And Kazakhstan with the Dzhezkazgan copper mines. And Taishet, with its factory for creosoting railroad ties (where, they say, creosote penetrates the skin and bones and its vapors fill the lungs – and that is death). All Siberia is still open to us – all the way to Sovetskaya Gavan. Kolyma too. And Norilsk.[3]

Norilsk, that was it. That was the word that a comrade saw during a roll call on one of the envelopes that the escort soldiers was carrying. Norilsk, final destination. Their fate was sealed. Jacques would be deported north of the Arctic Circle to Norilsk. But they hadn't arrived there yet. One's destination could be known, but that didn't mean that a prisoner was going to get there. The transit prisons represented stages in a hidden itinerary, where the intersections sent inmates in many directions, somewhere and nowhere.

# 17  Transit: May Your Memory Be Your Only Travel Bag!

Do not be the one who gets cheated. But more important, do not be the one who cheats.

Jacques Rossi

The arrival scenario in the transit prisons was almost always the same: the prison staff came to the train station when the trains arrived. The escort supervisor prepared the files and others checked to make sure that those were the prisoners who were assigned to their prison, because there were all kinds of mistakes. Sometimes prisoners had to wait for the next prison. Sometimes the prisoners were supposed to have gotten off at the preceding station.

> In that case the administrator of the local prison complained because he didn't want any prisoners who were not officially assigned to him. He already had too many prisoners and not enough space. Our fate depended upon how well the administrator and the escort supervisor got along. If they were good pals, then the prison accepted the prisoners who were not assigned to that prison. Otherwise they argued. And we waited.

> After the prison administrator had checked all the files, the inmates were taken off the train. They had to squat down on the platform to prevent any attempts at escaping or rebelling while the guards were chasing the rubberneckers away. Then they got into the armoured paddy wagons.

> In the provinces the Black Marias were not disguised. I never saw either "bread" or "meat" written on them. In small towns it was useless to go to any trouble. For other procedures it was the same

as at Butyrka: interminable waiting in the courtyard of the prison, formalities, body searches and showers. No photographs were taken of us because they already had photos of us. They checked, though, in any case, to see if the photo was really a photo of us. Then we were divided into already crowded cells.

Every three or four days the prisoners who were travelling in the Stolypin railcars were taken off the train and disinfected. The medical-sanitation department of the Gulag was well organized. Its goal was to keep this incredible source of manpower in shape for working to build the Soviet industrial empire.[1]

This system of oppression and exploitation had at least three objectives. The first one, that I have already mentioned, was to find scapegoats for the utopia that was not being realized and whose realization was quickly fading away. The second was to frighten the population so that it remained docile. The third was to make the mass of prisoners work. As soon as workers were needed somewhere, a group was dispatched to that camp.

The official data were always manipulated by the camp directors. If they did not obtain from prisoners the amount of work required, they minimized their responsibility by falsifying the numbers. The production output required was always unrealistic. In the transit prisons, where thousands of prisoners came together from the four corners of the Soviet prison empire, I met minor officials who knew the real data – for example, the numbers concerning the rations of distributed bread. I am sure that their numbers were greater than the official statistics given by the camp directors. After the dissolution of the USSR, those statistics were discovered in archives. Once more, it was the *tufta*. The prison directors cheated like everybody else in order not to be blamed for their poor performance.

In the transit prisons the prisoners of a convoy were divided up according to "colours," that is to say, the newly arrived prisoners were separated according to the following categories:

*So-called honest thieves*, *bitches* (crooks having broken underworld law), *muzhiks* (inmates not belonging to any group but who knew the laws of the thieves' world), and *pigeons* (individuals who did not belong to the thieves' world, and who were preyed upon).[2] They were separated in order to avoid brawls between "enemy colours" and to ensure the optimal use of the manpower. "Colour" indicated one's rank in the prison social hierarchy. At the top of the pyramid were the "coloured" and the "mixed coloured." Among the "coloured" certain professions or crimes automatically determined one's social position. The bank burglar had a higher position than a pickpocket, for example. At the bottom of the ladder were the "crumb collectors," the "misers," "the shit eaters," and "the garbage collectors."

Sometimes the separation of these different groups was not respected, and this only led to more terror. In a cell where he hadn't noticed them at first, Jacques met a group of criminals and managed to get their attention by telling them about his life in Paris. "They were perhaps not the meanest ones. Who knows? You needed to keep your brain working to survive in the Gulag. And you needed luck, too."

His first real conversation with a criminal recidivist took place in the Sverdlovsk transit prison. Preferring always to see the glass half full, Jacques's sense of humour often made him more optimistic. He remembers, however, his surprise when years later he went back through those same transit prisons going west and a guard wanted to put him with the hardened criminals.

> In 1955, several months before the Twentieth Party Congress, when the police received instructions to act a bit more civilized, a guard asked me whether I would agree to be in a cell with the recidivists. I couldn't believe it. It was like suddenly I was being invited into a four-star palace. It was as if he had said to me, "Would you tolerate, dear sir, being put among those people?" Normally they didn't give a damn about our opinions!

Very quickly, after the first thefts by the thieves in the Stolypin railcars, Jacques no longer possessed any objects of value, except for the famous camel hair coat. His condition recalled Solzhenitsyn's memorable lines: "Own only what you can carry with you: know languages, know countries, know people. Let your memory be your travel bag. Use your memory! Use your memory! It is those bitter seeds alone which might sprout and grow someday."[3]

According to Jacques's *Gulag Handbook*, many of the transit prisons were former tsarist prisons, but the Soviet regime also built new ones. The most well known on the road east were Kirov, Sverdlovsk, Novosibirsk, Omsk, and Krasnoyarsk. Jacques also mentioned the Viatka transit prison in *Fragments of Lives*. Usually the identity of those who arrived was verified according to the information on the envelope of their file, but that envelope was not opened. The inmates were then searched, led to the showers, and sent to different cells. In some of these transit prisons the prisoners were placed in small groups in tiny spaces that were like closets before being sent to the cells.

I have forgotten the name of the prison where we were closed up in a closet. It was a small group of ten or twelve "Article 58" inmates, that is to say, political prisoners. Among us there was a small boy who seemed to be eight years old at most and who didn't know how to speak correctly yet. He was laughing, telling jokes. He thought that our sad faces were very funny. Our tiny space was separated from the hallway by a partition that was about eight feet high. It did not intimidate the little boy. He climbed over the partition, let himself drop down on the other side, released the outside lock, and triumphantly opened the door, yelling like a guard:
"Everybody with their pack!"
We didn't move, frightened to death at the idea that we had illegally opened the door. A guard who passed by slapped the kid and insulted us. What kind of adults were we who had not been able to control a little kid!

However, in these temporary prisons the discipline was quite relaxed. The administration knew that they would not be able to punish the prisoners by sending them to the cooler before they left. At the same time, liaisons with women were not as rare as elsewhere, especially as prisoners moved farther from Moscow.

One time, when I was being taken to my cell, I could see a women's cell through an open door and this was completely forbidden by the rules. Because it was very hot and the women were very crowded in the cell, they were naked, except for their bras, because some of them were embarrassed to have sagging breasts. What a sight, all those naked bodies and their bras grey with filth. There were also the young women parading around with their naked breasts that didn't need any support and the other women were shouting at them that they were showing off. As for me, I heard a lot of jeers as I passed.
"Hey guy, come here, come on, we'll party. Any kind of wood warms us up!"
I must say that this commotion made an impression on me. In the Gulag there were all kinds of rumours concerning the Yaia camp, one of the first camps for women, a camp mainly for common criminal offenders that had opened in the beginning of the thirties on the Yaia river near the Trans-Siberian railway line, about one hundred ten

miles east of Novosibirsk. In 1951, Yaia would become a camp for men. In the women's camp there had been, it was said, gang rape committed by the women prisoners, raping male prisoners whom the administration had assigned there for specific tasks, like transporting the water kegs. The kegs were placed on carts that were pulled by oxen. The man was thrown down, masturbated, and as the women got on top of him they inserted his penis with a handkerchief over it so that the erection continued. Of course, the raped man ended up in the hospital. I never saw this scene with my own eyes, but men spoke about it with great detail and a kind of holy terror.

Jacques evokes those transit prisons with fondness, as places of human connection, as crossroads and places of learning. They were communication centres, always in flux with a continual flow of people coming and going, departing for unknown destinies and destinations. "It was really there, in the transit prisons, that I came up with the idea for my project *The Gulag Handbook*, given all the information that was circulating and the unique stories that came from all parts of the Gulag empire." News from the outside world filtered in. On 24 August 1939, a non-aggression treaty was signed between Stalin's USSR and Hitler's Germany and a rumour concerning it reached the prisoners.

> For my Soviet fellow inmates, this pact was a tragedy and you could see it on their faces. Some were completely silent. They did not dare express their disappointment for fear of receiving another sentence. For me, a militant anti-fascist, it was also a terrible, an unbearable disappointment. I was convinced that Soviet strength should be able to annihilate Hitler. So I searched for far-fetched justifications. I convinced myself that this treaty was comrade Stalin's trick to demolish Hitler. I don't remember whether it was in the transit prison or later that I learned this terrible news, but the impact was the same.

All those stories, all the men who appeared and disappeared, all the dramas and the indescribable chaos – Jacques would write about these and more in a systematic fashion in his *Gulag Handbook*. The keen eye of the former Beaux Arts student observed all this. He listened, at first incredulously and then attentively. Until then he had only studied ideas, but now he observed human beings who suffered in both body and spirit. Earlier he had fought for justice. Now he was in contact with human beings who were being crucified by the injustice that men like himself had paradoxically caused in their fight for that same elusive justice. He observed. He listened. "Our conscience is an infallible judge, provided we do not kill it," wrote Balzac.[4] Jacques's conscience, which had only been stifled, would come back very slowly because his convictions were so deeply rooted, with forward and backward movements proportional to the amount of truth a man can bear at any one time without dying. But it is obvious that the seeds planted during the trauma of being arrested, during the inquiry, and during the condemnation and then the progressive discovery of the number and variety of his companions' misery: those seeds started to germinate in the great upheaval of the transit prisons. Those growing seeds would disrupt Jacques's conscience. In that lucid mind, forever shaken by the undercurrent of the Gulag, the fallout from that disruption remained with him.

Jacques still has memories of his fellow inmates, sometimes vague memories, sometimes precise memories. He remembers the arrival in prisons, the newcomers who usually looked for people like them, from their "country." They asked, "Are there any people here from Moscow? Are there any people from Belarus? Are there Ukrainians?" In the continual flow of transit, where men were loaded and unloaded like packages, sent away and sent back, Jacques's memory of one of them is very precise and ingrained. It is of Szmul Szwarc, a young Polish Jew who had fled to Russia to escape the Nazis.

> What struck me were his large brown eyes. They were at the same time so sad and so surprised. He must have been about eighteen. He seemed lost in this courtyard where there was a gathering of all kinds of people. It had suddenly become a very crowded place, and then shortly after curfew the administration brought even more people in. Everybody had managed more or less to find a spot, swearing, bumping into people left and right. And he was still there, standing, his hat on crooked. What a strange creature! He intrigued me.
> "Where are you from?" I asked.
> He turned his eyes towards me. "From Warsaw."
> "*Mówisz po polsku*? Do you speak Polish?"
> "Yes."
> I learned that his father was a hatmaker in the Jewish quarter of Warsaw. The pact between fascist Germany and communist Russia allowed Hitler to begin the Second World War. Shortly before, his family had to flee from Hitler's army. When they reached Russia, the family was quickly separated and sent to different camps. He did not know where his father was or his mother or his two sisters and his little brother.
> My new acquaintance, Szmul Szwarc, was only at the beginning of his suffering, but mine had been going on for quite a while. I

was about ten years older than he was. Because I had experience, I managed to find a place for him to sleep.

During the short time they spent together in the transit prison, Jacques the older brother would initiate Szmul Szwarc into the universe that he knew much better than the young Pole. Soon they were sent away in different convoys. But chance would assign them to different parts of the Norilsk camp. When Jacques was, for the first time, sent to the punishment cell or "the cooler," Szmul tried to send him his own bread ration. It was stolen along the way, but a witness to the fate of this gift told Jacques the story several months later. He still cannot believe it. "It was incredible for this young man to offer me his own bread ration, being so naive as to think that the person to whom he gave that precious ration would give it to me! Sixty years have gone by, and even today, I am still thankful to Szmul for that gesture of enormous generosity."

The punishment ration for a prisoner in the cooler was typically only three hundred grams of bread, and often less. It was a starvation ration, and well below the standard ration for prisoners who fulfilled their production quotas. The time spent in a transit prison depended upon the efficiency of the administration and the availability of transportation. It varied between several hours and several months. As for the itinerary he followed during that first transfer, it remains very vague for Jacques. First there was Kirov, Sverdlovsk, Novosibirsk, and then Omsk. It is estimated that all the *zek*s visited at least four or five transit prisons in the course of their confinement, but for many, like Jacques, there were many more.

> About a dozen in all. I remember mostly the showers that in fact were not showers but baths with small wooden or metal basins to wash and rinse in and faucets with hot and cold water.
>
> It so happened that in 1955 during my return to the West, I found myself in that same prison in Omsk where I had been during my transfer from Moscow to the East at the beginning of my career as a member of the Gulag. And there in the showers I met four young men, probably common criminals who had the date 1939 tattooed on their arms. It was their date of birth. They were sixteen. But for me, it was a measure of the time that had passed since my beginnings as an "enemy of the people." Between my trip to the East and my return to the West, these four boys had been born and had grown up to adulthood. They were handsome, strong, blond, quite nice, not at all

the criminal type. But the Gulag would take care of that. Their ages corresponded to the length of my captivity.

In Jacques's memory years later, his movements back and forth through similar transit prisons had become confused. Jacques had no watch and no hourglass in the Gulag, but he had several points of reference like this one. Later, after Norilsk, he was sent to a high-security prison in eastern Siberia. While having his hair cut by the prisoner-barber, he was surprised that the grey hairs falling on the floor were his own. Since entering prison, he had never had the opportunity to look at himself in a mirror. Hair that had become grey and four strapping young men born just after the beginning of his ordeal – these were the hands on an invisible clock. They marked for him several stages in the passage of time that prison seemed to halt.

Within the Gulag empire, one had to surrender to time. Like everywhere, there was a rhythm that permitted those who knew how to adapt not to let themselves give up, in spite of everything, and even to count backwards and to see how much of their sentence remained. The transit prison was a progressive initiation ritual before the brutality of the camps. The time spent in transfer was perhaps not useless. It marked a slow descent into hell – first the Stolypin railcars, then the transfer prisons, and finally the transit camp and the boat that led to his destination, the House of the Dead.

# 18  An Operatic Voice on the Yenisei

The Northern Dvina, the Ob and the Yenisei know when they began to haul prisoners in barges – during the liquidation of the "kulaks." These rivers flowed straight north, and their barges were potbellied and capacious ... The journey in such a barge was no longer prisoner transport, but simply death on the installment plan.

Aleksandr Solzhenitsyn, *The Gulag Archipelago*

I remember the old northern legend of how God created the taiga when he was still a child. There were few colors, but they were childishly fresh and vivid, and their subjects were simple. Later, when God grew up and became an adult, he learned to cut out complicated patterns from his pages and created many bright birds. God grew bored with his former child's world and he threw snow on his forest creation and went south forever. Thus went the legend.

Varlam Shalamov, *Kolyma Tales*

Leaving Sverdlovsk, the inmates all got off at Krasnoyarsk, all of them except Jacques and four of his companions. For some unknown reason, they had been refused by the administration of the camp and boarded a Stolypin railcar again bound for the terminus, Irkutsk. "So then we continued eastward without being able to see the famous Lake Baikal. But in Irkutsk, the guards didn't want us either, and so we travelled the twenty-five hundred miles or so back to Krasnoyarsk. In all, that was about five thousand useless miles."

Jacques's last transit prison on that long voyage to penal servitude was Krasnoyarsk along the Yenisei river where Dudinka, the Norilsk harbour, was located, and twelve hundred miles north on the Trans-Siberian railroad. At the time, Krasnoyarsk was a city of three hundred thousand inhabitants. Today there are more than a million. Jacques and his companions of the first convoy, which lost some prisoners and acquired others, would stay about ten days in the transit prison.

The difference between a transit prison and a transit camp was that some transit prisons were still run by the police. Under Stalin, forced labour occurred in the transit camps but not the transit prisons. The transit camps were often integrated into larger camp complexes. The camp in Krasnoyarsk along the Yenisei river was an enclosed compound surrounded by barbed wire. It included several prisoner barracks and was part of the vast camp system of Norilsk. As mentioned above, the term "Gulag" is derived from the acronym GULAG, referring to the Main Administration of Corrective Labour Camps and Colonies. The camps were omnipresent in the Soviet Union, as the tentacles of the Gulag reached everywhere.

It was that sense of separation that made Solzhenitsyn's metaphor of the "Archipelago" so apt and precise. We were as isolated as we would have been on an island in the middle of the ocean. Two people within the same camp might never meet for years. Fifteen years after I left the Gulag, I met a Polish engineer. We discovered that we had spent years in Norilsk, one mile from one another, but our paths had never crossed.

At Krasnoyarsk, the prisoners for the first time walked to the transit prison and to the transit camp in the same city. "We were carefully guarded. There was a line of about a hundred of us. We walked on the peripheral streets of the city." For the first time in months, Jacques walked in a place that was not a prison. Some free people watched him and his companions walk by, in groups of five surrounded by armed guards. The Siberian towns were built out of wood, with scattered small three-storey buildings. Very quickly the prisoners were in the outskirts and old women from another era watched the unending lines of prisoners from the doorsteps of their huts.

In the line next to me there was a general. He had just had his boots stolen in the transit camp. He was walking barefoot, being very careful where he put his feet in that muddy road, wearing his elegant military overcoat whose stripes had been ripped off when he was arrested. The old women in front of their huts looked at us with intensity, not saying anything. Under the tsars the situation had been similar, but there were fewer prisoners. Then, the villagers gave bread and tobacco to the prisoners and showed them signs of compassion, but the Soviet regime had forbidden all signs of compassion. So the old women, who had perhaps a son or a husband in the same situation, said nothing. But their eyes spoke for them. There was not one hostile gesture, despite the fact that they were bombarded throughout the day and night with propaganda concerning all the "enemies of the people" who were responsible for their bleak future. Since it was during the day, the men were at work. There were only women and children watching.

I was pleased about the change, and the fact that I now lived in part of a real city, and one that was so exotic to me. I looked with curiosity at the slightly primitive homes and the general filth. There was something inherent in the landscape that I could not explain: the greyness and the dirt. I spent years of my youth in Norilsk, and I have always loved films about the Arctic. But when I saw a documentary film, I knew right away whether it was in the Canadian, American, or the Soviet Arctic. In the Soviet Arctic there was always that filth. If there was a reindeer harness, there were ten knots instead of one. If there was a sled, it was all patched up. If there were men, their clothing was terrible. In the Gulag Archipelago, the Arctic was one of the most feared regions. I knew Siberia and the Arctic a little. The Siberian prison seemed like a pleasant stay in the country compared to the Arctic!

For the first time in the two years since his arrest, Jacques was not in a prison. Now, he was outdoors in what appeared to be a camp surrounded by barbed wire and watch towers. It was a kind of empty field on the outskirts of the town not far from the banks of the river. This was not yet a real camp but a transit camp. For the first time, he saw barracks crowded with thousands and thousands of people.

When we arrived, the guards shouted at us to go into the barracks. We had to run very quickly. I already knew that you had to be first to get a good place. What was the best spot? It was in a corner because you could defend yourself better there.
    A thug appeared shouting: "Are there human beings here?"
    We were fifty-eighters and for him we were not humans.
    I was the quickest because I wasn't weighed down. I got rid of my suitcase when we left Moscow. The others had their packs with whatever they were able to receive from their families: clothing or food. I possessed almost nothing. I wasn't burdened. I was only thirty years old and still quite strong. I ran quickly to the corner spot and was the first to get there.

Meanwhile a thug arrived and said to me: "Get out of here!"

He pulled me by the foot and threw me on the ground. I was a newcomer and I kicked him several times with my other foot. He was very surprised. In the Gulag, the criminal recidivists were used to being considered the undisputed masters that no "pigeon" would ever dare resist. As a rule, the criminals helped each other out, but for the pigeons it was every man for himself. My attacker realized immediately that I was a pigeon and that he had acted appropriately. However, my unexpected resistance surprised him and, surprisingly, he left me alone. In the meantime, my comrades had arrived to help me, and we secured that spot.

Jacques would stay two or three weeks in the transit camp of Krasnoyarsk.

What impressed me the most there was the posted notice detailing the food rations in Norilsk, our "promised land" that awaited us twelve hundred miles to the north. Propaganda for a work camp – as if we were free labourers who tried to be hired there! As if we had had the possibility of choosing our employer! Later, I carefully studied those rations. They appeared in my *Gulag Handbook* after other sources had confirmed them. At the time, I did not think about that yet. But I was impressed by the extreme precision and the Soviet term *grammatura* that stipulated the food portions in grams per person. I did not know at the time I was carefully examining those precise ration tables that I had before my eyes a top-secret document. In fact, during the tsar's reign, such rations were public information. But the ration schedules of the Gulag were in principle highly classified.

It was spring in the Krasnoyarsk camp and the snow had melted. There was still snow in Norilsk, much further north. Little by little, the prisoners left the camp. Two barges transporting prisoners had left recently, and Jacques was among those who remained in the camp, awaiting another departure. During the day, he leisurely studied his companions in misery. Those who had been there a long time appeared tanned by the wind. Around their eyes there were crow's feet, white lines created by wincing in the bright sunlight. Their skin that experienced third-degree frostbite had permanent markings from the cold. Their clothes were as damaged and worn out as their faces.

In the Krasnoyarsk transit camp, the atmosphere was more relaxed than in the prisons. There was no established bedtime. Prisoners could go to sleep when they wanted to. Only the distribution of meals took place at fixed times. Boiled water for tea and the bread ration were distributed between seven and eight in the morning. Lunch at noon consisted of a very liquid soup and porridge. Dinner was around five in the evening, just soup. "In the transit camps I never saw any dishes. Some resourceful prisoners had managed to obtain old tin cans. Others had their soup poured into their caps. During the day we did not work." Having been closed up indoors for two years, Jacques savoured the fresh air. The inmates took walks. They told their stories and exchanged news.

> We had been isolated for so long and all of a sudden we were with other people. We were like people at a spa in Vichy or in another resort. We went for strolls. We talked about ourselves and about others. People told anecdotes and jokes. I still had my beautiful English camel hair coat. A young friend borrowed it from me supposedly because he was cold. But in fact it was to show off.

But Krasnoyarsk would be only temporary. The Yenisei river awaited its cargo of convicts on their way to the work sites of the Far North. Jacques and his companions had to undergo a final body search, the kind he described in detail in his *Gulag Handbook*. This body search was performed by guards in grey smocks that hid their uniforms and drew attention to their caps with the red Soviet star. The leather suitcase of one inmate was confiscated along with a pile of forbidden objects. "This Finnish-American had come from the Ford factories in Chicago to help the Russians build their first automobile factory in Nizhni-Novgorod. He was nicely thanked for his effort!" Like the other rivers, the Yenisei had started to transport barges of prisoners at the beginning of Stalin's forced collectivization drive. For deported kulaks, the unending voyage on the water represented less a transfer than a form of extermination. The Yenisei is about twelve hundred miles long and flows towards the north until Dudinka, which is on the sixty-ninth parallel.

> These caravans of large barges were towed by a paddleboat that usually carried free passengers, that is, official personnel and staff of the camps along with their families. These individuals were probably unaware that there were hundreds of human beings crammed into the holds of the barges behind them. Upon arrival the passengers disembarked first, long before the dark holds were opened, long before the guards with their dogs on leashes and with their rifles and machine guns arrived.

Jacques's convoy consisted of two barges with a total of about two to three thousand people. Jacques and his companions first climbed from the riverside to the deck of the boat on the gangway. Then in groups of ten, so as to be more easily controlled, the prisoners were led down a wooden stairway to the hold under the supervision of armed soldiers, ready to shoot. Transferring the men to the hold took a long time. The space had to be filled with human beings to its maximum capacity. Prisoners did not even have room to sit.

One thing struck me. The spectacle I had before me reminded me of the old engravings of slave trader boats transporting slaves that I had seen in books or in museums during my other life – "before." Yes, there was no mistaking it. The fleet of the Gulag resembled that of the slave trade in the eighteenth century. There was only one difference. We were not chained, which allowed us during the weeks of the voyage to go to relieve ourselves in the latrine bucket. Our unlucky predecessors arrived "safely" soiled by their own excrement. I believe that, confronted with this fact, even the most adamant anti-communist would not be able to deny the obvious superiority of Marxist-Leninist slavery! However, the bucket of drinking water was placed next to the latrine bucket, and the latter was always filled to the rim with a stinking sludge. I decided not to eat or drink so that I would not have to go near that stink. We had been given bread and those eternal herrings for the first day. Food was distributed every morning. I did not swallow anything. Then my comrades, those in my convoy from Moscow, from our Mayflower, who were starting to form a kind of family, tried to convince me to reconsider. No one knew how long this ordeal might last. It was imprudent not to eat.

They finally convinced me and I started to eat again. From time to time, I had to repeat the torment of going to the stinking bucket. There was no seat. We squatted above it like a bird on its two legs and we stayed squatting even to pee because otherwise it was too high. Above all you had to keep your balance because there was nothing to hold onto and you could easily fall over at any moment. If you fell forward that was all right. The men did not typically help each other in such situations. The women showed greater solidarity during such private moments.

They had been on the barge for more than twenty-four hours and still hadn't moved. The day after they got on the barge, bread was distributed once more. But more time was needed before the moorings were cast off and suddenly the barge began to move. From the hold the riverside could not be seen. Usually the voyage lasted between seven and thirteen days; their voyage would last seventeen days. To fill the bucket with drinking water, the guards gave a prisoner a wooden bucket. On the deck he would lower the bucket into the river, pull it up filled with water, and hand it to another prisoner. There were two or three prisoners on the staircase, and the last one would empty the bucket into the drinking water bucket.

> The one who was on the deck was very lucky. He could breathe the fresh air, see the sky, the landscape of the taiga, the forest with fir trees and larches and rare birch trees. Further on in the North there would only be the tundra. Taiga or tundra, the landscape was monotonous. Yet in spite of that, every time the lucky one came back down from the deck into the darkness of the hold, he was asked to describe what he had seen.

The latrine bucket was emptied in a similar fashion, with an identical wooden bucket:

> Since the two buckets were side by side, some drops of filthy liquid from that bucket did indeed fall into the drinking water bucket. The result was that after three days everybody without exception had dysentery. However, there were two staircases. Why did they absolutely have to put the two buckets one next to the other? It was probably not intentional. This was another enigma of Soviet reality that I could not understand! I have already said it: I encountered very few examples of pure sadism, like those that the escapees of Nazi camps speak about. The first concern of camp officials was simply to apply the rules. Without thinking. In communist Russia, it was the system that was criminal first of all, not necessarily the men. In the cell of the Alexandrovsk central prison where I would be imprisoned years later, there was a sheet of ice on the wall that stayed there from October until April. I had a knitted wool sweater, but the rules forbid me from having it in my cell. I had to give it to the clothing depository. I was condemned to twenty-five years there that I, fortunately, did not finish thanks to Stalin's death. My nice woolen sweater stayed in the depository while I froze to death. That is institutional sadism. It wasn't an individual that punished me but a system and its absurd rules.
> In that crowd of men, closed in the barge, there were of course some thugs. And with the mob it was always the same scenario: fighting,

hitting, and playing cards. What was the most difficult in that closed space was that the thieves continued to steal. Under such conditions, it was surprising that there weren't more deaths. Faced with such a terrible ordeal, there is an incredible capacity in human beings to mobilize their inner psychological and spiritual energy, and to accept their fate. Unlike the coddled human beings in civilized societies or in countries governed by the rule of law, the Russian constantly confronts ordeals that would have destroyed other human beings. This resilience still impresses me. Later in winter, I discovered that when they took us to the baths and we had to leave the baths naked with a temperature of 5 degrees Fahrenheit and run to get our clothes, no one caught colds.

He had become really tough, that fragile child who couldn't go to school for fear he would get sick. He overcame dysentery, exhaustion, the cold, the lack of fresh air, hunger, and the fear of what awaited him at the end of the infernal voyage. The seventeen days went by. The two barges with their holds filled completely with "human material," an expression that Jacques says was used by both the Nazis and the Soviets, slowly descended the Yenisei river. Suddenly on one of those days, a voice was raised deep in the hold. Not to protest. But to sing.

Where did that amazing strength come from after months of misery and humiliation? Among us there was an opera singer, a bass voice that resonated in the depths of the hold as if in a cavern! One of us was singing and his song gave us back our dignity. When he began we were all spellbound, without exception – the thugs, the escort soldiers, and all the inmates, whose average IQ was quite high. I think it was an aria from *Boris Godunov*. It was wonderful! I didn't know if he was standing up or if he had managed to sit with his back bent forward at the place where the bunk ended. Perhaps he was even lying down!

I remember that the soldiers who were guarding the hatchway leaned down so that they could hear better, and when the singing stopped, one of them asked with great admiration, "Where did he learn to sing?"

We answered him proudly: "He was a singer at the Leningrad Opera."

The soldier could not believe it. Then all the escort soldiers wanted to see the singer in person. The singer came to greet them at the hatchway, which was not covered, so you could see the sky.

In addition, you could see the soldier's knees, proof that we were being carefully guarded. The singer was very pleased with all this attention. It was obviously a new situation for him: usually artists look at their public from above on the stage even if there are boxes and an orchestra. He was looking at his audience from below. The soldiers were several yards above him. From the hatchway there was a slight ray of light that came from the observation area of the soldiers. We were all in the hold in obscurity. I can still see his face, that was quite ungrateful looking upward, towards those soldiers who appeared small to us and who from their superior position manifested their admiration for him.

The singer came back to his bunk quickly because the soldiers were afraid to continue speaking to him. Like everybody, they were afraid. They had a supervisor who watched them, and that supervisor also had a supervisor above him who was just as afraid. And so on and so on. In this universe, everybody trembled. In any case, a young guard called down to another prisoner who was not far from the hatchway and whispered softly: "Here! Give this ration of bread to the singer."

The escort police, like the prison guards, were often draftees who had finished their military service, and signed a contract with the penitentiary administration in order to avoid returning to the collective farm, where the conditions were not much better than those of the Gulag prisoners. Later, many of my fellow inmates in the Gulag would confirm this to me: there was no big difference between the prison and the collective farm. I admire that young guard who took such a risk because of his love for art.

Afterwards, there was a surprising event. One night, one of the young soldiers fell asleep during his watch and his rifle fell down into the hold with us. This incident could have become a political affair, perhaps ending with the death penalty. The prisoner who caught the rifle was a thug. He took the gun and, with great care, looked to see that all was quiet on the deck and that no one was looking. He then gave the rifle back to the soldier. As a result, during the rest of the voyage, packages of tobacco and pieces of bread were thrown down from above into the hold with no precise destination.

The barges loaded with the men finally arrived at their destination – the Dudinka harbour on the Yenisei, the access route to Norilsk.

The barge had stopped. We could feel it. We could hear the water lapping at the sides of the boat, but the boat was not moving. We were led off in groups of ten. The escort soldiers, who knew that they were being watched, had become more brutal with us. The charm of the singer was no longer apparent. I went out on the deck with my nine companions to see the sky, which had clouds that looked like long, stretched-out wire. I felt very cold in the fading evening light. It was *the end of the world*. As far as the eye could see there was the tundra, empty with no end to it, nothing but greyness. Not a tree nor a bush, just from place to place the moss of lichens. On the riverside where the barges had moored I saw some wooden cabins sunken into the ground with men as grey as the sky and guards carrying rifles with bayonets. Above me there was that cloud formation with cloud after cloud in parallel lines like the train convoys that rolled along and finally merged with one another and blended into the horizon. These parallel lines that converged seemed to represent the end of the world. I have never been able to explain that strange astronomical phenomenon. But I will always remember how it impressed me when I got off the barge. It was really the end of our world. There was nothing beyond.

# 19  Dudinka: The End of the World

> We believe that we have revealed, or recognized, that there is no inherent difference between the "normal" system of man's exploitation and that of the camps. That the camps are simply a sharpened image of the more-or-less hidden hell in which most people still live.
>
> Robert Antelme, The Human Race

It was spring 1939, and Jacques the Frenchman and his two thousand fellow prisoners had arrived at their destination beyond the Arctic Circle – one of the camp sections of Norilsk in the Dudinka region. This was a relatively new camp, as Jacques would later learn, since it had been in existence for only three years. His keen eyes could discern that prisoners had not inhabited the place for very long.

> The people standing along the bank of the Dudinka port looked at the prisoners passing by with both indifference and curiosity. It wasn't every day that they saw two to three thousand men arrive at the same time. This occurred only every summer! And these "newcomers" lent a bit of colour to the monotony of the landscape. We had to squat in groups of five, so as not to attempt escape. It must be said that escape was not easy for someone squatting and surrounded by soldiers with rifles. One would first have to stand up, and any movement would have attracted the attention of the entire escort.

The local guard grouped prisoners in such a way as to separate the most dangerous criminals from the others, and thus expressed what Jacques and his companions had already observed. Along with the hunger, the cold, and the hard work, the difficulty of cohabitation with serious criminals represented one of the worst ordeals of camp life.

The guards had a distinct ability to select those criminals who were to be placed in separate barracks. "However, following the orders of the political commissar and consistent with Soviet policies of repression, the political prisoners of Article 58 often found themselves in barracks designated for serious criminals. We were elated when we avoided those barracks!" Over the course of the last few decades, the public has become sadly familiar with the structure of the camps, how they were divided into sectors or compounds, surrounded by barbed wire with watch towers at the four corners.

> The surrounding wall of a compound consisted of wooden poles two and a half metres to eight metres high. When *zeks* worked outside the camp, the guards marked the space with four stones or four sticks. Any prisoner who went outside that symbolic boundary could be beaten. The watch towers were located at each corner of a compound, just outside the compound, so they remained inaccessible. A watch dog ran around the enclosure attached by a ring on a wire.

Newcomers passed through these structures and were eventually led into one of the barracks within the camp zone.

> In the evenings, we were not given bread but hot soup that would have been very welcome if there had been bowls into which it could be poured. Sadly, there were no bowls. So we managed as best we could. If you were lucky enough to have a cap, the soup was poured into it. If not, you had your hands. In general, the portion was eight ounces. Of course, your two hands together were not big enough. So we took what we could and lapped that up as quickly as possible. That's what I did. I only had my hands. However, some of my comrades had been smarter and had picked up empty tin cans when we were in the Krasnoyarsk transit camp. The cans were very dirty and had sharp zigzag edges, but they could hold more soup. The best, however, was a cap, especially if it was stiff and filthy. Before the liquid could drain through the material, it was in someone's stomach.

Like one's first day in a prison cell, a prisoner's first day in a camp seemed interminable. The mind had to be open, to be prepared to receive so many new orders, new work, and new cruelties. There was a certain hope raised by the departure, even by the voyage, as terrible as it had been. But that hope had disappeared. What remained was the nagging question: What will become of me?

The next day, we had the medical commission visit. We all lined up bare chested, one after the other, and we were called by our names in alphabetical order. The medical commission asked our name, our year of birth, the article of the penal code under which we were sentenced, and the length of our sentence. We all stood there before the doctors in their white coats. The medical examination was quite rudimentary. Sometimes we were asked: "Do you have a serious illness?" But, in fact, the answer was of no importance. We were treated like livestock rather than human beings. A doctor listened to my heart and mumbled some words in Latin to a scribe behind a table who wrote it in my file. Then another member of the medical commission asked me, "Do you have a profession, a specialty?"

Given his experience, Jacques profoundly understood that in the Gulag being a linguist, philosopher, or art historian meant nothing. Nearly all professions led one directly into heavy physical labour, with no possibility of a lighter job.

Each one of us thought carefully about what to say. A comrade who was an astronomer decided to say that he was a shoemaker because he reasoned, rightly so, that astronomy would not be useful to him in a camp. We knew that forced labour or what was called the "general work" of the camp was the most difficult – felling trees, construction, making embankments, and building railroads. This astronomer, who was an intelligent and practical man and did not live in the clouds, believed that as a shoemaker he might be able to work in a workshop. I said that I was a painter because I had been a student at the Beaux Arts. Of course, I did not say anything about my knowledge of languages or linguistics. I knew that was dangerous. My artistic talents did not impress them very much at the time. But later, with my pencil, I managed to earn a bit of bread.

At some point, bowls arrived, though not enough. We had bowls but no spoons. No detail in this universe of camps was unimportant. Spoons might appear minor but they were a major concern for inmates no less than the administration. The latter feared that if the spoon was made of steel, a dangerous material, the security of the Soviet system could be in danger. Therefore spoons had to be made of aluminum or wood. For the prisoner, the precious spoon posed a problem too because utensils and bowls were in constant danger of being stolen.

When we finally managed to obtain a bowl and a spoon, camp officials watched us carefully. A spoon, certainly, could be put in a pocket. But a bowl? It couldn't be taken with the prisoner to work, so it had to be hidden somewhere. Of course, according to official camp rules, prisoners were supposed to be given a bowl and a spoon. However, both were in extremely short supply. In the Soviet system, there was never a lack of barbed wire or bullets for the guards' rifles. But bowls and spoons, yes.

Jacques finally managed to get a spoon in exchange for a portrait he drew of a common criminal offender. The spoon probably had been stolen. There were two kinds of barracks: those that had two levels of bunk beds with wooden planks and those that had continuous bi-level bed boards. The barracks were built with the cheapest materials available, usually concrete, and they were largely one-storey structures. Typically, the walls were constructed of two boards. The gap between them was filled with sawdust and cinders, and then the boards were plastered. Roofs were covered with sheet metal, covered by a double layer of latex or another material. It was common for prisoners to be housed in buildings that they had just built themselves, and where they installed temporary sleeping boards.

A hall that served as an entrance area separated the two parts of the barracks. Each had a stove and only one light bulb and housed between sixty-four and one hundred and twenty inmates. At the entrance, there was one light bulb, simple sinks, and two buckets of drinking water that we used sometimes as a tub. Usually the person responsible for the barracks was in charge of cleaning and overseeing each section of the barracks. This, however, did not stop thefts.

The new arrivals were surprised when they first entered the camp barracks, which were so different from the prison cells they were used to. After two days, prisoners were divided into groups of fifteen. The supervisor pointed to a man who looked energetic, and said – you will be the team leader! "Then under careful guard, we went off to clean the garbage that was along the riverside. There was no pier. They had to prepare the riverside for the arrival of other barges." Jacques and his companions had probably been in the second group of barges to arrive that spring.

At the time of their arrival, there were still blocks of ice floating on the Yenisei river. Jacques did not see the ice thaw on the river until the following year. He learned that when the Yenisei was frozen, from October on, a railroad line was built from one side to the other. The thick layer of ice – two to three yards thick – was as solid as steel. Construction started on the right side of the river where the supply buildings were located. In order to maintain one side of the river free for the arrival of boats, wood was transported to the left side of the river until the winter. After the first cold snaps of the winter the *zek*s built that railroad line that permitted the transportation of wood on flatcars pulled by locomotives. In May, when the ice began to melt, the tracks were quickly dismantled so that they would not be carried off by the rising water.

> Iron was very costly, so we reused the rails. And, yes, I helped build the railroad line on the layer of ice on the Yenisei – but not only there. The railroad line of Dudinka-Norilsk fifty miles to the east on the tundra ground had already been built when I arrived, but I built others because the work site was enormous. Local transport had been operating on very narrow railroad tracks.
> 
> The layers of logs stored on the left side of the river had to be moved, and the deepest layers of logs were completely frozen. Since we couldn't remove those logs with dynamite, we had to dislodge them with pickaxes and picks. The logs were as heavy as boulders. We had to transport them and pile them up on the flatbed railcars or else on sleds pulled by tractors.
> 
> I viewed the railroad as a beast that swallowed my sweat and blood, an executioner that killed me slowly. In the spring, we dismantled the railroad tracks, which left brownish marks on the ice. When the thaw came and the ice melted I watched as my torturer, the ice, broke up and dispersed. Later, around June and July, enormous ice flows came rushing down the river. When pushed from behind, the sheets of ice piled up one on top of the other and floated down the river. This time of year, the sun remained in the sky for twenty-four hours and melted nooks and crannies in the ice blocks, and when the ice blocks bumped into one another, those massive sheets of ice would break apart and give off a tinkling sound like little bells. This pleased and fascinated me, but most of my fellow inmates did not share my interest.
> 
> Once we saw a giant sheet of ice twenty-two yards long blocked by other icebergs downstream. It was heading straight for the watchtower of our compound. The soldier on guard in the tower, his rifle in hand, could no longer keep his eyes on the compound. Terrified, he watched the sheet of ice coming straight for him. When it was about three yards away, the guard ran down the ladder of the tower, rifle in hand. The ice scraped against the tower before breaking

it up completely like a box of matches. In one sense, we were pleased. It was the revenge of the ice for our slave labour. Alas, the next day we were sent to rebuild the watch tower.

The unloading of the logs took place in a traditional manner.

We unloaded the logs and took them to the embankment. We placed them onto a very long chain with hooks that lifted the logs high into the air and dumped them down, with fits and starts. Below we took the logs and rolled them onto the flatbed railcars of the train. There were six of us in our team: the astronomer Kozyrev, a professor at the Military Academy, a professor of dialectical materialism, two other people, and me. With great difficulty, we rolled the logs to the railroad line while Fritz, the gypsy, worked on a horse that the administration had given him. We did exactly the same work, Fritz with his horse on one side of the river, and the six of us on the other side. The logs were wider at one end, which meant that they did not roll in a straight line. Fritz managed that well. He attached the horse's straps to one end of the log and then he easily straightened out the other end. He was much more efficient than we were. Nikolai Alexandrovitch Kozyrev and I sighed. What good was all our knowledge when faced with a horse? It was a lesson in humility!

Let us return to that first day in what would become the city of Norilsk, a special day in the life of the *zek* Jacques Robertovitch Rossi in Dudinka at the seventieth parallel north. Following a two-year prison odyssey, he woke, for the first time, in camp barracks to a routine that would repeat with mild variation for about ten years, regardless of the season or the industrial sector of the camp.

> Even before we were awake the orderly for the barracks brought us our coats, our shoes, and our socks, that is to say, strips of clothing that the Russians wrapped around their feet. We went quickly to the pile of rags to find ours. There were disputes among the prisoners, and hitting. We went to wash up in the sinks in the entrance area, a kind of small room with a door that opened to the outside. It was almost as cold in there as it was outside, and the water was frozen from October until the middle of May. Every ten days we could take a bath before which our heads and pubic hair were shaved. Meanwhile, the orderly came out with two buckets of boiled water for breakfast, and then with our precious bread, sticky and sour. The rations weighed exactly one to two pounds, and half of it was water. The distribution of the bread was followed by the distribution of soup or porridge, usually millet.

Then we got ready for forced labour. We pulled a quilted cap down on our heads, attached the earmuffs, and put a rag tightly around our necks. Finally we put on our coats, which we buttoned carefully. We put string tightly around our waists, our wrists, and our ankles. We had to be prepared to go out and work for ten to twelve hours in cold temperatures that sometimes reached minus 40 Fahrenheit. The orderly for the barracks stayed inside the barracks watching over our meagre possessions. His share of work outside had to be done by us, and that was tricky. At precisely six o'clock in the morning the *zeks* trotted out with fatigue and a sense of resignation. At the door the armed escort and the dogs waited to take them to the worksite where they would add their stone to the edifice of communism.

Look, don't lose hope, this will only last for ten years! Looking back, it seemed that these words of Solzhenitsyn's rang true, like a prediction, and resonated with Jacques and so many others.

# 20 The Polar Night

> Alas for the dreamer: the moment of consciousness that accompanies the awakening is the acutest of sufferings. But it does not often happen to us, and they are not long dreams. We are only tired beasts.
>
> Primo Levi, *Survival in Auschwitz*

In the résumé that Jacques submitted in 1982 in the hope of teaching French classes at Georgetown University, he included his "career" as a *zek*. He described his roughly ten years in the Norilsk labour camps, north of the Arctic Circle, as follows: "Inmate of Soviet camps and prisons (more than 50). I experienced all facets of work and on-the-job education. During this period I learned how to be a miner, dock worker, cargo loader and unloader, digger, railway and highway builder. I also was a draftsman, decorator, and tutor in basic English to free Russian engineers working for the Gulag; letter and legal inquiries scribe for my insufficiently literate Gulag comrades, and translator, interpreter, mediator for inmates who did not speak Russian but knew German, French, English, Chinese, Hindi, and others." It was a professional and ordinary résumé of an entirely unordinary life trajectory. With the details of his work added, this real work and "on-the-job education" appeared neither professional nor ordinary.

"Step to the left! Step to the right! The escort will fire without warning! Understood?" "Understood!" we respond altogether, in a monotone, without thinking. That's the warning from the escort guard after he's counted us a number of times when exiting the camp. We have heard this formula a thousand times, acknowledged by our response, "Understood," like an "amen." We call it "the prayer" – a most unusual one because we have seen some of our fellow inmates shot for stepping out.

The escort now orders us to march off to work. There are more than four kilometres ahead of us. It is the end of May. The Arctic sun no longer goes down. Twenty-four hours a day its warm rays lick the snow accumulated from eight months of winter. However, the ever-frozen ground – permafrost – miles deep, remains impervious. The tundra turns into an ocean of mud. With every step, we must make an effort to remove our legs from the sucking mud. We keep on slipping, falling, getting up again, and we have to mind our pathetic army boots. We are exhausted from years of malnourishment and the relentlessness of hard labour exceeding our physical strength. Our legs are numb from the accumulated fatigue.

….

We finally see the worksite. We are completely exhausted and need to get our tools from the hut – pickaxes, iron crowbars, shovels, etc. Some of my fellow inmates look for a specific shovel or pickaxe. They have experience. They know which tools are the easiest to handle. How? Well, "You ain't at university! You've got to think!"

Once we have our tools we march off to the worksite. We need to dig foundations. The ground is hard as cement. Where it has been hit with iron crowbars and pickaxes it has turned into mud thanks to the spring sun. Those who dig at the end of the pit trudge through deep mud mixed with rocks and pebbles. Some shovel out the mud, which others load onto wheelbarrows, which are then taken to the dump. Once they are emptied, they are brought back, and so on. We have set up tracks by putting together wooden planks – to be able to push the wheelbarrows, we prevent the wheel from sliding onto the rough and muddy terrain. Accidents can be a major issue for the brigade because they cause a decrease in output, which inevitably affects the bread ration. Unlike worksites anywhere else in the world, the Gulag does not hire professional or skilled workers but uses only those sent by the state police. Amongst us there is a barber, a professor who specialized in Marxist philosophy, two officers, three peasants, a young delinquent, three Communist apparatchiks, one singer from the Novosibirsk Opera, and a few manual workers (railwaymen, miners, etc.). Some are more efficient than others, and they are the ones who can secure the rations. They are the same ones who inflict psychological and sometimes physical abuse on the "weaker ones," i.e., those recognized as physically incapable. Such abuse, when it lasts years, is as trying as the material conditions of the camp. Yet its effects on you are evidence that the Gulag has not yet completely crushed you.[1]

Although Jacques did not speak about it, he was one of those who endured that terrible pressure for a long time. It is obvious that the precious child of a gentle mother, the son of a rich father, the European student at the Beaux Arts and at the School of Oriental Languages, and even the secret agent who put his life in danger without complaining, was ill prepared for life in the Gulag. "This is not a university; you have to think." Jacques often heard this saying, and he repeated it because this unusual saying resonated with him. The clumsiness of this educated man made him the target of jokes. His fellow inmates were even hostile towards him, and he became their scapegoat.

Here's an example. When two of us carried a rail or a tree trunk, great care had to be taken when it fell to the ground. If the person who was behind let go of his end too soon, even if it was just a fraction of a second, the sudden motion of the other end could break the jaw of the person who was in the front or, in any case, injure him seriously. Because of my inexperience and my exhaustion, I sometimes dropped my end of the tree trunk as soon as we arrived at our destination. I wasn't careful enough and my brigade comrade would be in terrible pain and furious, and think that I had done it on purpose. In any case, whether it was seen to be premeditated or not, my clumsiness led to hostility and hatred among my fellow prisoners, which more or less persisted. It lasted until my comrades finally understood that I was simply incapable of performing these tasks correctly.

Another example involved taking care of the fire at night in the barracks. When it was my turn, I tried very hard. I kept myself from sleeping in order to take care of it as best I could. As the awkward former son of a rich father and in spite of all my efforts, in the morning the stove was cold. Imagine the justified anger of all the comrades, who really bawled me out, convinced that this was another manifestation of my arrogance and my condescension towards them. I was angry with myself. I am still angry with myself because of my incompetence and my stupidity. I realized that any attempt to explain myself to them would have been useless. So I said nothing. However, it happened that one of the men had woken up during the night and had seen me trying to poke the fire. He really couldn't understand my attitude and so, rather than defending me, he said: "I did see Jacques busy around the stove, so why doesn't he want to explain the problem to us?"

Luckily there were about a hundred of us in the barracks so it was my turn only every one hundred days! And there were two summer months. It was really difficult for my comrades to admit that someone who was educated, who spoke many languages, and who could draft requests in correct Russian when he was asked was not capable of keeping a fire burning in the barracks or handling heavy loads at a worksite without injuring others. After a while they finally realized that my lack of practical sense did not mean that I was malicious, but just clumsy. Meanwhile, I was transferred to another worksite and to other barracks, so I had to start all over.

Today every time I walk around a city in the developed world and I see public works, it's music to my ears, like Mozart, Beethoven – those pneumatic picks, those sophisticated machines, and those gentlemen workers with their work helmets and their hands protected with work gloves, comfortably clothed and with rubber boots. When they want to dig a hole, they just press a button and a machine digs the hole. We worked with our hands in the mud because once we had managed, after a superhuman effort, to get through the frozen ground that was like cement, the ice melted and we were wallowing in mud. Our only machines were the weak and meagre muscles of men who were malnourished, poorly clothed, poorly treated, and lacking everything. So when I meet workers in the street who are well fed and well equipped I think about my fellow prisoners and also my comrades who continue to slave away in Russia, where the work conditions have not changed much and are not so different from the Gulag.

The work day was interminable. When we returned we barely had the strength to drag ourselves to the fence and to the barbed wire. The guard at the entrance opened the door and counted us to see whether all who had left twelve hours before were still there. With no escort we walked back to our barracks. Sometimes I collapsed on my sleeping board and slept without waiting for the evening soup that a comrade brought to us in buckets. Then my peasant comrade would try to wake me up: "You have to go eat!"

Jacques's contribution to building communism was not limited to digging in the frozen ground. The camp expanded its activities to include the metallurgical complex of Norilsk. That region was very rich in nickel, copper, cobalt, and coal. These minerals had to be extracted. Then the raw materials had to be refined before sending them to "the continent." That is how prisoners in the Gulag referred to the Russian mainland, as if they were separated by an ocean.

The mines had at least one advantage: the temperature never went below 10 degrees Fahrenheit. However, there were numerous accidents because the galleries were poorly supported and there was no effort to make them safer because the only thing that counted was the production rate. I never felt that horrible fear of going underground that was felt by some of my comrades.

The nickel of far-away Norilsk was important for the production of steel. So the *zek*s were working for the war effort. Factories that did not exist yet had to be built. Housing had to be constructed for the workers, the engineers, and the supervisors. The buildings were often made of wood because there was a lot of it in the region. But cement was used as well. Jacques also built roads, unloaded coal barges on the Yenisei, and loaded tree trunks on flatcars after having pulled them out of the ice and rolled them in the snow. "With a temperature of minus 31 degrees Fahrenheit, Arkhil and I carried nine yard-long boards. He was behind and I was in front. That did not stop us from talking. He talked to me about Georgia and I talked to him about France. When the foreman heard about our talking, he separated us!"

Jacques is reserved and discreet. It took him more than fifty years to write a short text about hunger in the Gulag. He did not talk about it in *The Gulag Handbook* except in quotes from Dostoyevsky. He did not include it in the first *Fragments of Life*. He did not talk about it during our interviews. Hunger was the essential element of collective misery in the camps, a daily privation, a shared suffering that touched everyone without exception, a continuous torture. Jacques finally wrote about it in *Fragments of Lives* as if he could exorcize it once and for all, for his companions in misery:

> The folds of my empty stomach lining are contracting and rubbing against each other. Not the slightest bit of food to keep them apart. It is as if they want to devour each other. I am not sure if that's what's happening but that's how it feels. It is a nagging pain that only sleep can relieve. In the Gulag there is a saying, "The prisoner's sleep is sacred. It is good for his nerves and gives him a sense of not being hungry."
>
> I am hungry. I have been for years. I know perfectly well that it's never going to change. Never. Hunger torments one's mind as one's stomach. I feel I'm losing my grip. Confused memories emerge from the distant past, of the free world before I arrived in the Soviet Union, before my arrival in the Gulag ... memories of determined fights for social justice, liberty, and so on. We are five or six young devoted activists talking about how to change the world. Everyone quotes Marx, Engels, Lenin. The world revolution is just around the corner.

It is inevitable. We are sitting at a table with some leftovers of dinner: scraps of white bread (!) hardly touched, chicken drumsticks with some meat left on them, glasses with drops of wine at the bottom. I strive not to think about this crazy mirage. In no way should one allow such "gastronomic masturbation," an expression used in the Gulag to describe our gastronomic souvenirs. Its consequence is to weaken the resistance of the starving convict that the almighty political police of the almighty communist dictatorship is already determined to break. Let us not make it easy for them!

*I am now strolling along the Champs Elysées. The weather is nice. I pass some beautiful shop windows, cafés, bars, I see happy people sitting around ... No! Not again! This time I am taking a walk in the Louvre. The Winged Victory of Samothrace, the Venus de Milo, the divine Joconda, and nearby the Flemish paintings with Rubens and his exuberant representations of human flesh, some still lifes with heaps of delicious enticing food ... Oh no! To hell with those souvenirs! There is no escape. Even if I were to swallow my six hundred grams of rye bread in one gulp – the daily ration of an inmate – hunger remains.*[2]

If a *zek* worked more, he received more food. But the extra food did not compensate for the energy expended. So there was this Gulag saying: "It is not the small ration that kills. It is the big one." Theoretically, in certain camps and at certain times in the Gulag's history, the extra work was compensated. But Jacques believed it wasn't worth it: "At Norilsk around 1940, I could earn twenty-seven rubles per month by working very hard. At that time a package of tobacco cost two hundred rubles. So it was better to work less and eat less." In addition to exhaustion from work and hunger, there was, in those polar regions, the unbearable suffering from the cold.

When it was minus 40 degrees Fahrenheit we could feel each additional half a degree on our skin and we felt our skin freezing to our bones. At minus 58 degrees Fahrenheit it was difficult to unstick your eyelids. Each breath was like a knife piercing your lungs. The lowest temperature that I remember was minus 70 degrees Fahrenheit. That happened only once [during my camp experience, but the cold lasted] two nights in a row. We only had string to tighten the ends of our sleeves around our wrists and the ends of our trousers around our ankles. We also put string around our waists like a belt. We pulled down our caps over our ears and we wrapped rags around our necks and over our faces. Because it was freezing, when you breathed a layer of ice formed. Of course we had nothing that resembled a handkerchief. We tried all the time to blow off the drop that formed at the end of our noses, and some prisoners left their noses exposed with the risk that they would freeze. Our fingers were so stiff that we couldn't button our pants and coat after having relieved ourselves.

The guards, who were protected by their sheepskin coats and felt-lined boots, made us light fires around which they constantly warmed themselves. We could only warm ourselves by the fire five minutes each hour. But we had to be very careful because all our clothes were made of cotton and were very flammable: underwear, jacket, quilted pants, socks, coat, and cap.

The fifty-eighters were attacked constantly by the criminal recidivists. Jacques, like the other prisoners, was attacked.

I was attacked several times, for robbery and other reasons. During the first months at Norilsk, I worked with metal hooks and iron bars that helped us to move the logs. A guy, whom I had immediately identified as a thug, came up to me and called me a bastard. He said that, looking me straight in the eyes. At that time I wasn't afraid yet. Later I understood that even if you were shaking you could not show that you were afraid. After a long time, my attacker quieted down. He said, "If you were a hunting dog, a policeman, you would have the eyes of a dog. But you have human eyes."

Later I understood that he thought I was a cop because the cap that I had been given in Butyrka was a policeman's cap. Despite their appearances, the thugs were very perceptive. They did not make mistakes.

It was also in Dudinka that, because of a thief, Jacques experienced the cooler or punishment cell for the first time.

The thugs had beaten me up. People knew and talked about it and my work slowed down. According to a Soviet rule, anyone who contributed to interrupting work, whether they were responsible or not, was sent to the cooler. It was the first time for me, but it would not be my last. That was when the young Szmul Szwarc, without my knowledge, gave me his ration of bread. You were sent to the cooler for the slightest reason: not greeting the supervisor correctly, being late at roll call, being late to go to bed or to get up, or for having kept a random object in the barracks. As for the cell, it was always cold, humid, and dark. The cement floor was always damp. Above the door there was one light bulb surrounded by metallic mesh. A dusty and smelly bucket served as the toilet. One of my cooler cells had a tank filled with frozen water under the floor. So the temperature there was always freezing. I could only take three steps in each direction or remain standing in the middle to avoid feeling the dampness.

The wake-up call was at 5 a.m. and the curfew at 11 p.m. During the day, I could only have my underwear. In the evening the guard gave me my "bed," which consisted of three planks attached to transverse boards. I put this "bed" on the ground. I put on my clothes and I fell down on my planks. I remember having been woken up by the bitter cold several times during the night. I tried to warm myself by getting up and walking a bit. But each time from behind the Judas window the guard yelled at me to go back to "bed." It was forbidden to get up before five in the morning.

There were punishment cells or "coolers" everywhere – in each prison, in each penitentiary institution, in the boats and trains that transported the prisoners. According to estimates made by prisoners, between the middle of the thirties and the death of Stalin, about 10 per cent of all prisoners were in coolers. Was being in the cooler the worst experience Jacques had in the Gulag?

The worst? What does that mean, the worst? There was no worst. There was always worse than the worst. The person who says, "There is nothing worse than" is a happy man whose easy life has made him ignore that there are no limits to the worst. Having the luck to ignore the worst does not mean that it doesn't exist. I will tell you an anecdote from the Gulag. The places for torture were usually situated in cellars in the basement. It was said that a prisoner who had been taken to the cellar to be tortured thought he had arrived in the last circle of hell. The door closed and suddenly he heard someone knocking below him. Because there was always something further down below.

Like most Gulag survivors, Jacques understood that those who experienced the worst of the worst are not able to tell us about it. Where did the limits begin and where did they end? Solzhenitsyn recognized that the fate of the poet and writer Varlam Shalamov, a "goner" at Kolyma, was worse than his own fate. "Shalamov's camp experience was more bitter and longer than mine, and I acknowledge with esteem that it fell to him rather than to me to plumb those depths of beastliness and despair to which the whole camp way of life was dragging us all down."³ However, Shalamov and Solzhenitsyn were both, like Jacques, survivors. That is to say, they were not among those who knew the worst. Yet they carried their responsibility to be the trustees of the collective "worst," the sum of the misfortune experienced by all of them. They felt it was their mission to testify for them all.

As the years passed, Jacques managed to integrate the reality of life in the camps into his very being, to the point where his memory of life before became confused and blurred.

> I had been a prisoner for perhaps six years when I had a dream. I was building a road with difficulty with a pickaxe when I saw my stepfather in one of his elegant suits. He was standing on a small hill as if he were supervising the work. I woke up suddenly with that last image which I still could see with precision. I was stupefied. I couldn't believe that I had ever known such a person. I believed that I had never lived anywhere else except in the Gulag.

It was in this context of forced labour, solitary confinement, hunger, cold and, finally, the irreparable loss of his reason for living – that is, his faith in the communist system – that Jacques managed to survive. In the words of Alain Parrau, "Surviving is, of course, without doubt luck, but it is luck which leaves you with a wound that will not heal because you have come out of a disaster with no name. The wound is not because you are guilty or ashamed to have escaped the fate of so many, but it is the memory of the misfortune of all of them, the misfortune without limits. It is that memory deep in the consciousness of one person."⁴

# 21 Surviving

The person who survived in such circumstances will always keep the dregs of that "life" in his soul, like something shameful and infamous. "Why am I not dead?" That is the ultimate question ... And in reality, why am I still alive, me, while all the others are dead? ... It is worse than death: the disappearance of life while one is still alive.

Andrei Sinyavsky

Why did I survive? Because I was very stubborn.

Jacques Rossi

The summary of the reasons for survival given *a posteriori* are numerous. Jacques goes over them again tirelessly with a touch of disillusionment, as if it were continuously necessary to explain the inexplicable.

> I was in good health. I was not really badly beaten. I didn't have any family so I could not be blackmailed with that. I had been trained in the strict techniques of clandestine operations. I was always curious about others and I wanted to understand what was happening to us. In addition, I had read and I had studied. In short, I was lucky. I was never forced to play dirty tricks on others. I met several human beings. In short, I had guts ... and France.

If the *why* of his survival embarrasses Jacques, you can't get him to stop talking about the *how*, and about the thousand and one times he almost died in the Gulag.

> I never saw shooting outside of the space marked by the four corner sticks placed in the ground by the guard. But stepping over the line meant certain death. I saw a man brought down while he

was defecating. He didn't want to do it within the tight limits of the overpopulated space. He went slightly outside it. He fell dead into his own shit. Another time we were being taken to our worksite on a path strewn with bags of flour. They were soaked because the barge that was transporting them sunk, and the precious food had been fished out of the water. The bags were being dried in the fresh air because humidity had cracked them open. Lumps of flour that looked like crushed plaster were falling out of the bags. We were very, very hungry. Suddenly two very young men from our group got out of line and threw themselves on the bags of flour. Without hesitation, the guard with his very powerful military rifle shot them. The same bullet went through the spine of one and through the skull of the other. Both of them fell in a puddle. When we came back after our eleven and a half hours of work, the puddle was still bloody red.

Jacques indicates that it is difficult to estimate mortality in the camps. Many factors intervened. He found himself in one of the most dangerous situations. He was a new *zek* in the camp and he came from detention prisons where he had spent one and a half years. There the hygienic conditions were better. At Butyrka, the water was boiled. The camp had just been built, and everything was not yet working. The newcomers dropped like flies from dysentery that spread quickly because of the shared latrines. As for other nuisances, lice and bedbugs were quite common in the Soviet camps. If labour competition was one of the basic means for building the "new Soviet man," hygiene competition proved similarly important.

> Camp section number one decided to compete with camp section number two in getting rid of the bedbugs, and pledged in writing to undertake a certain number of sanitary efforts during the year. If we couldn't spread out the efforts over time, we undertook several projects in the same week. That meant burning sulfur in the barracks and sleeping outside three or four nights in a row on the frozen ground. At night the sun was low and mosquitoes and gnats joyfully bit us everywhere. At least we got rid of the bedbugs for a while.

Fundamentally, survival in the camps depended on each person's cleverness and ability to circumvent the rules of "rehabilitation through labour" – avoiding tasks that were too difficult, finding lighter jobs, bartering a talent or a skill for a bit of butter or sugar. Jacques used his talents as an artist to acquire additional bread. Someone else used the material of the shoe shop where he worked, to make house slippers for the girlfriend of a thug, in exchange for soup.

If you were a slacker, you created problems for your brigade because it meant more work for your comrades. However, I never hesitated to pretend to work when it was individualized labour or to exploit the system whenever I could. I took scraps of paper off cement bags and when I managed to get a pencil, I made drawings that amused my comrades.

One day we were unloading cases from the barges on a conveyor belt that was working so poorly we had to carry the enormous cases on our backs. It started to rain on the riverbank, so there was less supervision. A few of us found shelter in the electrician's cabin. Suddenly one of our important supervisors, who was greatly feared, came into our shelter. I had the instinct to calmly take out my notebook and turn the pages while looking at the clock at the moment the conveyor belt stopped. The supervisor thought I was an employee doing his work and I avoided punishment.

Slacking off was just another form of *tufta*, cheating or fudging that could lead to a charge of wilful sabotage. "With the enormous stone blocks that we went to get in the quarries, instead of building the platforms that we were supposed to build, I built structures with nothing inside them. I worked very hard before placing the cornerstone. I put forth a useless and pointless artistic effort, but I was so happy to be cheating the system." The hardened criminals in the Gulag were highly skilled when it came to refusing to work. They were called *blatnoi*, or the thieves-in-law. When they were part of a work team or labour brigade, they let the other prisoners do the hard work of reaching the mandated production quotas. There was no way to get them to do their part. They took advantage of the women and helped themselves to the food with impunity. The average *zek* also tried to avoid heavy physical labour, in a much more roundabout way, but no less stubbornly, because he knew well that heavy labour could kill you even before it depleted you.

I had several work accidents, but I was lucky because I never died. Once we were building unloading docks on a river with enormous wooden cases made from hollowed-out tree trunks that we filled with rocks so that they would sink in the water and serve as a support. It was work that we did at night in the month of May when the water was very deep. When the water level went down, the unloading docks would be ready for the boats. The night was very cold, but it was light outside, as if it were the middle of the day. All of a sudden I slipped on a tree trunk and I fell into the water. Luckily, a comrade, an Uzbek inmate, managed at the point of death to hold onto another piece of wood and to stretch out his hand to me. No one stopped working and I continued my work completely soaked and frozen.

Sickness, mutilations (voluntary or not), and work accidents landed you in the infirmary, where the main person who determined life or death, as he wished, was the doctor. The infirmary, a barracks that was thirty-three yards long, had actual beds instead of sleeping boards. There was a hallway in the middle between the rooms on the right and the rooms on the left, and some of these rooms were isolation rooms, used in the case of infectious diseases. It was one of the rare places where, with enormous caution, inmates could make love. That, however, was not why Jacques was envious.

When I went for the first time to visit my Ukrainian friend Petro who had fallen from a log and been broken into pieces, I remember thinking, "How lucky he is! I would like to be in his situation!" Not only because he had special food, but because a nurse helped him urinate since he could not walk.

Whether the doctor was a free man or an inmate, his attitude was the same. Contrary to Solzhenitsyn's experience in the Gulag, I met some compassionate doctors among the bastards. Several years later, in the Alexandrovsk prison, I met a blind inmate. A Mongolian doctor from the Irkutsk region had examined him and had given him a diagnosis. This was against all the rules that stipulated that no information should be given to the prisoners concerning their health. The doctor told him that an operation could restore his eyesight. The blind man did not realize that his numerous requests to be transferred to a prison where he could be operated on would cause problems for the Mongolian doctor. He finally received a notice from the administration that I read to him. It stated that "after careful examination it has been determined that the sentence and place of imprisonment would not be changed!" As for the Mongolian doctor, he was severely reprimanded. That is how he was thanked for being humane.

One of the distinctive features of the *zek*s was their health.

Every six months we had a medical examination and we were classified according to our physical condition. TFT was the first category, in other words: "Fit for heavy physical labour." There were three invalid categories, but only the first exempted the prisoner from work. With one hand you could work, with no hands you couldn't. I once met an inmate who had cut off his second hand.

For centuries, the best way for prisoners to avoid total exhaustion in the Russian tradition of penal servitude was to seek refuge in a hospital. Dostoyevsky wrote about this. Jacques described it as well.

I often went to the doctor to be excused from work. Typically, I was well received and I could slack off a bit. I did this until I realized that by taking advantage of slacking off I was encroaching on the rights of my fellow prisoners who really needed to be excused from work. The number of exemptions a doctor could grant was limited. It was true that until 1943 those quotas were often not respected. All these rules and regulations varied according to the year and the camp. Special camps were, of course, much tougher. According to a Gulag proverb: "When you carry your head under your arm, then you'll be exempted from work."

Just as some doctors could be charitable, Jacques also met among the brutish guards some individuals who maintained a bit of humanity.

In 1941–1942, one of the guards who accompanied us to work had fun playing with the breech of his gun and he tickled our buttocks with his machine gun. In contrast, another guard, a Tatar, put his gun in his boot so as to not frighten us. At the Alexandrovsk prison where I was serving my second sentence, there was a female guard who was known for her brutality. But one day I saw her pick up a wounded swallow in the courtyard. She was warming it in her hands and whispering words of tenderness to the bird, words we could not imagine her ever saying.

According to regulations, the *zek*s were supposed to be given one day of rest every ten days. In the Arctic, in winter, there were often blizzards, severe storms of the Far North marked by strong winds and heavy snowfall. When the camp weather service predicted a blizzard, the guards would refuse to work, to accompany the inmates to the worksite. They could only supervise the inmates if there was minimal visibility. It was the same in the summer when the wind blew very strongly, so strongly that even without snow, men were flattened to the ground. On such days, the director of the weather service would forbid outside work.

In those cases we stayed in the barracks. The day we didn't work replaced our rest day. If the blizzard or the windstorm lasted for three consecutive days, we were given no rest days for a month. Not a single one. When it blew for six days, a very rare event, we had to work for two months straight, without a rest day.

The days when we did not work, we stayed in bed later, of course. Our bodies were completely exhausted. When we finally woke up and became conscious, we could read. The available selection was very basic, with mainly works of propaganda. But sometimes there was a book by Chekhov or Tolstoy. Pages were missing from these books because they had been read so often. There were also bits of newspapers with which the smokers made their cigarettes; they could buy tobacco at the camp shop. The person in charge of the camp propaganda service, called the "Cultural-Education Department," was often a common criminal offender, who would come and read to us from scraps of torn newspapers. On good days, he even left us a *Pravda* to read before the pages were rolled into cigarettes.

In addition to those wonderful moments of grace when Jacques had several minutes to read parts of a newspaper, there was the view of the Arctic's stunning landscapes.

During very cold nights when the sky was completely clear, there was aurora borealis, like a multicoloured veil – a pallet of dark blue, of sea green fading into green, of flamboyant red fading into rose – which was floating across the immensity of the firmament, as if a giant were sprinkling evanescent and changing colours from his bucket. Usually from the depth of their exhaustion after more than twelve hours of work, my comrades did not make the effort to contemplate the aurora borealis. But I was overcome and imbued with the beauty that tore me away from my restorative sleep. Yet I knew that this incredible beauty announced greater cold and more suffering. In the summer it was never night. The low sun cast violet light. Even the greyness of the tundra was glistening.

Concerning obligatory chastity, it did not seem, unlike the absence of food, to have bothered the *zek*s. Far from it! The issue seemed scarcely relevant and even incongruous, in a universe where sexuality was a luxury. It was most often reserved for the criminal recidivists or the thugs of the Gulag. They monopolized the most desirable women sent to the Gulag.

When young men arrived at the camp, of course, they asked right away:
"How are we going to manage to have sex?"
And the old timers would answer:
"Rather than you having sex, instead, it will be you who will be had. Very simply, in a few months, you will not want to do it."
It's true that we were so completely crushed by hunger and by the work that usually our instrument stopped working. But sometimes it did.

According to regulations, sexual relations between inmates and also between inmates and free people were forbidden, and *zek*s who were caught in the act were sent to the cooler. If lasting romantic ties had formed, those involved were separated and the inmate who was the easiest to replace was transferred elsewhere. The phenomenon of the "camp wife," a female inmate who lived with a male inmate, existed mainly among the thugs. But there were women, condemned under Article 58 (professors, lawyers, and doctors) who by necessity became the "camp wives" of thieves and delinquents.

The intellectual or the innocent woman who had been condemned for nothing managed to survive by being with a tough guy, with a thug, but if her protector was transferred to another camp, she found herself without protection, and she had to find another protector.

For women, the camps were really much harder than the prisons, not only because of the work, but because when there weren't enough female guards, the women were guarded by men. There was a Gulag saying that ten thousand quarts of water replaced one ounce of meat! In some transit camps body searches took place outdoors. Theoretically the men were kept at a distance, but there were always some little thugs who got an eyeful. And the women had to endure their appraisal and their jokes. Some female prisoners who were common criminals were very insolent, and they would respond to them in a similar manner. It was extremely humiliating for other women who found themselves in that situation for the first time.

In general, the Gulag was a school of perversion for the young women who had the misfortune of being locked up there.

I saw with my own eyes the daughter of a party secretary, who had been raised in luxury, who had landed in the Dudinka camp. Her father got into trouble so the family was punished too. She was fifteen years old, with an angelic face, very charming, and with the manners of a well-brought-up child. Two years later I saw her again. She had changed completely – thin and ugly, with a cigarette in hand, strutting around like a prostitute.

And then there was gang rape. Jacques told the story of a young Polish woman, a graduate of Warsaw's Polytechnic Institute, who had been arrested after the Warsaw insurrection against the Nazis, in which she had participated. This beautiful Polish woman was found by her friends abandoned at the bottom of a well, the victim of a gang rape organized by the administration.

The good Soviet people called that "being run over by the tramway" or even "submitting to the *kolkhoz*," or "submitting to the choir." I knew, however, a young woman who had managed to refuse all of them. The men whom she had rejected finally created a kind of organization for her protection based on the principle that "since I didn't sleep with her, neither can you."

As for homosexuality, Jacques says that he never heard anyone talk about it.

From the time I was there until the end of the fifties, it was rare. I remember a modest Armenian merchant who was arrested for homosexuality, a misdemeanor that was punished by five or six years in prison for the first time, five to ten years for the second time. Since we had to repeat the article of the penal code under which we had been condemned at each roll call, no one could ignore his misdemeanour. Traditionally, Russians have denigrated homosexuals and spread rumours that in the Caucasus and Central Asian cultures there were more homosexuals. From the sixties on, according to the memoirs and stories of *zek*s of that time, homosexuals were less discreet. But I had already left the Gulag by then.

The chapter that I called "The Cigarette Butt" in *Fragments of Lives* was about the time when I surprised a couple that was having sex in the latrines. The scene revealed to me, more than any book, the human deprivation that resulted from so-called rehabilitation in the Gulag camps. And this re-education was the result of an enormous sociopolitical experiment to create "a New Man." Consequently, it was not only the Gulag that was in question, but the entire Soviet system of which the Gulag was its most concrete expression. Slowly, I began to realize that we (either myself or the majority of the other prisoners) were not victims of a judicial error or of the system's imperfection. In the struggle for survival, I started to become aware of the fact that the so-called New Man was none other than that abomination, that human pile of rags, that was created, developed, and cloned by the Gulag. I realized that the Gulag was part of the Soviet communist system that we had accepted as a model and for which, in the past, I had been ready to give my life a thousand times over.

What explains Jacques's longevity in the Gulag and for years after was not only the will to survive, which he shared with many others, but his particular traits of character.

# 22 Yes, I Am a Communist and You Are Too; Only Between Us There Is Barbed Wire

> In camp it is the work that kills, and anyone who praises it is either a scoundrel or a fool.
>
> Varlam Shalamov, *Kolyma Tales*

Essentially, if Jacques persevered until the end it is because he knew how to overcome his weaknesses. It is also because he had several strengths.

> I was aware that I was only a small atom in the mass. I did not focus on myself, and I was highly motivated to know and to understand rather than to pity myself. And then I knew how to draw! Very quickly I met several engineers who were tops in their fields and we became friends during our transfer to Norilsk. They managed to get assigned to the planning department. Some of them had influence even if they were inmates. A research department head could say that he needed someone to draw like Jacques the Frenchman. I drew portraits. In the beginning I drew my comrades, who wanted to send their portraits to their wives or their mothers. Then my work became known. The worksite supervisors wanted their portraits too, which was good publicity for me. Even the officials at the worksite, who could easily have had photographs taken of themselves, preferred my drawings. It happened that instead of digging the frozen ground with a pickaxe or unloading logs from the flatcars or even working in the mines, I was invited to a small cabin office where I made portraits with a pencil. This pleasure happened only rarely. Of course, the drawings had to resemble the person. A portrait of Stalin by Picasso in the Gulag and it would be the cooler for sure!

Such privileges did not last long. One night they came to get Jacques in his barracks to take him to a police officer whose office was outside the compound. Jacques was escorted by his guard and presented at the sentry booth. The doorman made him enter and took him to the security officer:

"Here's the prisoner you wanted."

He was asked to sit in the waiting room, where he waited for a long time. It was in the middle of the night and Jacques was thinking about the next day's work, about the wake-up call at five and about the hunger he felt when he was not sleeping.

Finally, the political officer opened the door and led me into his office. He started a general conversation by talking about the magic of the aurora borealis. It was like we were in a cafe! That lasted about ten or fifteen minutes. Then all of a sudden:

"So what's happening in the barracks?"

I was taken aback:

"Nothing. Right now everyone is sleeping. And I was awakened in the middle of a deep sleep!"

"Don't worry. You'll go back and sleep." And then suddenly: "When you were in western Europe in 1935, your boss was a certain Boris."

When I was sentenced, I was able to read Boris's deposition in my file. He had been a fighter during the revolution and the civil war and at the very beginning of the Great Purges, around 1936. After working with me for two years, he told the authorities that I was suspicious because I was the son of a bourgeois family and I spoke several languages. Adam had already warned me at that time about Boris. It was when we were together, Adam and I, on the Neufchatel lake. Later, Boris's declarations were used to complete my meagre file. And now he had also been arrested and Moscow was asking this lowly bureaucrat in a faraway region, deep in his Arctic region, for a deposition that would permit my former boss to be accused. Searching though documents, they realized that the Frenchman had seen Boris's deposition against him in his file. So they thought that he must bear a grudge against Boris and that it would not be difficult to encourage me to have Boris condemned.

I answered the officer, whose name was Pavlov, a name I did not forget – Vassily Kondratievitch Pavlov – that Boris was a bastard, certainly, because he had wrongly slandered me, but that I had no knowledge of any counter-revolutionary activities on his part.

Naturally, Pavlov was insistent. He encouraged me openly to take advantage of this opportunity, but he never took the risk of advising me to take revenge by giving false testimony. I stuck to my version, which was the truth. Boris had played a nasty trick on me, but at the time he was my boss and I trusted him.

That being said, I was not cooperating with Vassily Pavlov's plans. For that modest guard of the slaves at Dudinka, I was ruining a wonderful opportunity for his advancement. Because of my stubbornness he saw that the opportunity was fading away, the opportunity to put together a superb deposition that would send an important officer of the Red Army to the firing squad.

Seeing that I was being uncooperative, Pavlov suddenly changed the subject. "So what do you talk about in the barracks?"

I tried to concentrate: "Yesterday we talked about Boris Godunov." (That was true. The bass singer from the Leningrad Opera had gone off to another worksite, but two engineers in my barracks had talked about operas before going to bed.)

"And in addition to that?" He pretended to not understand that I was making fun of him. Naively, I was playing games with him, which I really should not have done. Finally, he got to the point. He wanted to know what we talked about. He wanted me to be an informer. And knowing my weaknesses, he said: "Are you a communist?" (He knew that I was a communist).

"Yes, I am a communist. And you are too. Except between us there is barbed wire."

"But I have nothing to do with that. I did not sentence you. You were certainly sentenced by mistake and I am sure that you are going to be freed."

"When I'm freed, we will both be communists. At present, there is a communist behind barbed wire and another one outside."

From that moment on and during the five years that Pavlov stayed in the camp, every time that I found work that was less tiring, Pavlov learned about it through his informers who were everywhere. And every time, I was sent back to heavy physical labour. There were, however, people who tried to help me. I remember that comrade who was part of our Mayflower, our first convoy from the Butyrka prison. He was responsible for unloading coal from barges. Without my having asked him anything, he had me come to his cabin so that I could draw up forms for him. He had to prepare reports on forms that did not exist. Paper and pencils did not exist either. We had to manage with birch bark or plywood. It was nice and warm in his cabin. After two days Pavlov discovered my cushy job and I was sent to another brigade, on a worksite that loaded tree trunks onto flatcars.

Another time, I was sent to a work site far from the camp, where I knew no one. The head supervisor was a Korean who had been condemned for smuggling. When he met each new labour brigade, he examined the men with a piercing stare, like a herd that was being evaluated at the slaughter house.

"Jacques, come into my office! They say that Pavlov wants you dead!"

That brave Tsoi, who was even a member of the former noble world of mobsters, with its traditions of honour, put me in charge of keeping the stove burning in the hut. But that good fortune did not last long either.

Yet another time, an engineer comrade who was in the central zone of Norilsk requested that I be his industrial artist. He asked the general who was in charge of all the operations. From Dudinka, Pavlov, the commissar, himself answered that this was not possible because I was in the hospital. In fact, my hospital was heavy labour, where I had been killing myself. The rumour finally spread. I was known as the sacrificial victim of Pavlov's persecutions.

Jacques' story confirms Solzhenitsyn's analysis of the techniques used to convince a potential informer who is usually hesitant in the beginning. Technique number one is to tell the prisoners, "You are a good Soviet citizen." In Jacques's case, it was, "You are a good communist." Technique number two involved exemption from heavy physical labour, a better place in the compound, an extra ration of gruel, some money, a lightening of the sentence because of easier jobs like the ones that Jacques was unable to maintain. Technique number three was similar – the threat of losing one's cushy job and being forced back into heavy physical labour. Technique number four involved blackmail, especially in the case of family (being told "your wife and children will be sent to the camps"), but such blackmail could not be used against Jacques. The commissar Pavlov also used the prisoner's desire for vengeance against the one who denounced him. An eye for an eye.

But Jacques refused. Was this the result of a character trait or a personal choice? Was there no particular reason? Later, when he developed the passage on informers for his *Gulag Handbook*, he gave an indirect answer to the question concerning his motivation. There, he demonstrated that informing was praised as a civic virtue by the Soviet regime and that the informer was considered to be a hero. On this subject Pavlik Morozov's story is enlightening. He was the son of a peasant who denounced his own father as a *kulak* during the forced collectivization drive of 1929–32. For betraying his father, he was beaten to death by outraged villagers. But the Stalinist regime elevated Pavlik Morozov to the rank of national hero. Many "Pioneer Palaces" are named after him.

> Under the tsars, the use of informers and instigators was not uncommon, but such activity was generally scorned by the public. Later, Lenin's political police organized a network of informers who infiltrated organizations everywhere. I remember the newspaper *Pravda* from December 20, 1937, which affirmed that "the most noble and sacred duty" of the Soviet people was "to collaborate with the security organizations of the State." A law in 1934 condemned the family of a militant who had fled abroad and who had not been denounced by his family. Such a family could get a ten-year sentence.
>
> In the camps it was the security officer who recruited informers. In fact, he studied each inmate and gathered as much information as possible about him in order to blackmail him effectively. Certain inmates volunteered to be informers in order to have more bread or tobacco or because they sought vengeance. An informer had to sign a document with a code name that was placed in a strong box. He had to submit reports to intermediaries or slip them into a mailbox. In exchange for his services, he received payment in the form of being assigned to a job where he could steal some food. The most sought-after designation was that a prisoner was "committed to the path of rehabilitation." When the informer became too well known and therefore ineffective, the security officer transferred him to the compound of the camp housing the very inmates he had betrayed. If the latter were criminals, his head was chopped off with an axe and thrown into the garbage.

Prisoners did not typically become informers because they were motivated by genuine political zeal. Rather, the weaknesses of certain men were exploited through blackmail. Once the first betrayal had taken place, it was nearly impossible for the inmate to stop. The ideological principle that dictated that the interests of the Soviet state always superseded those of the individual ensured that one's informing would continue.

Such details concerning the universe of informers help to explain more convincingly Jacques's reaction to Pavlov's proposal. A certain self-satisfaction on Jacques's part was justified. First of all, contrary to most of the *zek*s, Jacques the Frenchman had not received a Soviet education. It was too late to inject the informer virus into a man with such solid ethical values, which had only strengthened his blind faith in a communist utopia, one that was not rooted in reality. He was a man who observed carefully and keenly, and who understood that the life of a camp informer was full of uncertainty and most often resulted in a violent death. Of course, denunciations were obtained through torture or the blackmail of family members. But Jacques insists that he was not tortured. NKVD officials did not risk submitting an inmate to torture for his "personal" good, but only for the good of the Soviet state. Moreover, his character was important to his survival, as was the image he had of himself.

His refusal to allow his soul to be corrupted also strengthened his ability to carry on.

In any case, the price to be paid was not negligible. During the five years that Pavlov reigned over that section of the Norilsk camp, Jacques gave up any hope of having a lighter work assignment, which would have allowed him to escape exhaustive hard labour. He ultimately had to wait for the departure of his persecutor in order to occasionally take up his pencil once more. He even worked for a while in a workshop for fashion drawings. The French were being honoured! This workshop was for engineers, chemists, and other specialists who were not prisoners.

> In 1943, the fashion workshop where I worked had the honour of being visited by a vice-admiral. The woman in charge of the workshop, the wife of a big shot, was trying to charm the guest. Suddenly, I recognized the vice admiral. It was Robert Pavlovich whom I had met and spent time with in Moscow "before," at the home of an old revolutionary who was one of my friends. At that time both of them spoke loudly and were pleased to share their Parisian memories during the twenties and thirties. I never tried to find out which of the three agencies they worked for because I thought that all three of us worked for the worldwide revolution.
>
> Meanwhile, the woman in charge continued to charm the admiral: "Please show me the tie that you prefer! Our artist will reproduce the tie of your choice." She then turned to me: "Jacques Robertovich, please draw this tie!"
>
> The vice-admiral then looked at me and I looked at him, as if we were seeing each other for the first time. I was happy to learn that a good friend of mine had avoided the Great Purges!

Jacques also used his former talent as a man of the theatre. When he was a young enthusiastic communist, as noted above, he helped educate workers by staging plays and scenes from plays.

> The "free" [non-prisoner] camp personnel had a theatre in which prisoners performed, in the old tsarist tradition of having inmates

put on plays or having serfs play the roles of property owners. Dostoyevsky wrote about this. Soviet Marxism-Leninism had not completely eradicated the old customs. There were two kinds of *zek* theatres. In my camp section, the actors were not excused from hard labour. They were required to both work and act. However, the truly professional actors were officially recognized as theatre actors for the entire camp. This was not really according to the rules because all the political prisoners had to be re-educated through the hardest physical labour. The head of the camp, who was responsible not only for discipline but above all for fulfilling the economic plan, understood that theatre improved the morale of the troops and contributed to their efficiency in building the factories.

Theoretically, two different types of theatre existed for the same public. The "Kultura," as the Russians called it, was propaganda theatre that was supposed to motivate inmates to exhaust themselves in work that would build a glorious future. Why did almost everybody know how to read in the Soviet Union? In order to blindly swallow propaganda. Among the actors, there were excellent ones from the Bolshoi and the Kirov theatres in Moscow who were serving ten-to-fifteen-year sentences and who were happy to practise their profession. They were happy even under such conditions, even if they were acting for the officers who exploited them. It was better than digging in the frozen ground. It was the same thing for the numerous singers whom I had discovered during my baptism to song in the barge on the Yenisei river. Sometimes I made the sets for this theatre when we had the necessary materials. After Pavlov's departure, I also worked as a set decorator at the theatre for free audiences.

Sometimes the inmate-actors wrote humorous scenes that made fun of their free audience. This was after the Second World War. The Soviet economy was still doing poorly, so our playwright *zek* created a sketch in which a free engineer – similar to those in the audience – beat his chicken who did not lay fresh eggs, but only egg powder. This scene took place off stage, of course, because obviously we had no chickens, so an actor made the cackling sound. The angry character then jumped back onto the stage and complained that his chicken would only lay powder and that the war had been over for three years and officially the economy had been rebuilt. At other times, the actors acted out only one scene from a classical play because we did not have the means to produce the entire play.

All those engineers and managers in the audience lived comfortably in new buildings in the town of Norilsk. Jacques and his companions were able to make these buildings emerge from the frozen ground of Siberia in the course of a few years of back-breaking work.

When I arrived, Norilsk was a mere dot in the tundra. There was no town. It was the inmates of the Gulag who built the town entirely with their hands. The plans were designed there. There were two Armenian architects, Masmarian and Kotchatrian. After obtaining their degrees, these two promising artists had been sent to Italy to study architecture. When they came back to the Soviet Union in 1937, the police were waiting for them. Weren't they coming back from abroad where it was well known that everybody was recruited to spy? It was thanks to their work and that of other architects, as well as tens of thousands of other prisoners, that the town of Norilsk was built. When I returned in 1996, I found a city of about 250,000 inhabitants.

Perhaps someday we will honour the builders of those cities and factories who, like the slaves of ancient times, built the pyramids, the last residences of their masters and exploiters. In the meantime, some have asked: If the *zek*s had been freed, who would have built those cities, who would have cut down the trees, who would have dug with their hands in the frozen soil of the faraway Arctic? Had Jacques continued to be a good communist, he would certainly have understood that the *zek*s were essential. Except that Jacques had stopped being a communist.

# 23 How Jacques the Frenchman Ceased to Be a Communist

> The *Gulag Handbook*, *Fragments of Lives*, and the book I am now writing with you – they are meant to undo all the bullshit that I created when I pushed people to become communists.
>
> Jacques Rossi

Jacques does not answer the question: "*When* did you cease being a communist?" He prefers to describe *how* he ceased to be a communist. In faith, as in love, there is a beginning phase when things crystalize, as Stendhal described so well. Yet, at the end, there is also a kind of decrystallization before we cease to believe or to love. Jacques's disenchantment took time, a long time. But he refuses to give a date.

> No, I cannot identify a precise moment. I have asked myself this question thousands of times. It would have been great to be able to say, "on that day," once and for all. Perhaps some people have been able to say that as though they had been struck by lightning or by grace. But not me! I was so profoundly convinced that only Marxist-Leninism would lead to social justice! Sometimes indignation smothered me when I was faced with the spectacle I witnessed. I always tried to convince myself that the arrests and the camps were a perversion of a noble project by corrupt people. And that Stalin ignored what was going on. I hung onto the slightest details, the smallest signs and rumours. The churches had been reopened! The collective farms were going to be closed! So many predictions, perhaps announcing that Marxism-Leninism was going to triumph over the gangsters who were perverting it. Alas!
>
> Everything was getting worse and worse. I had setbacks. I had them for a long time. But I still maintained hope that my case would

be reviewed. Between my arrest and Stalin's death, I wrote more than twenty petitions. After Stalin's death, of course, I started agitating even more. But no. I do not know when I understood that the process was irreversible, that this bloody cesspool in which I lived was part of the communism that I had wished for so intensely.

Solzhenitsyn wrote about the "right-thinking inmates" who unconditionally believed in Soviet power. They were often the Gulag inmates who had been arrested for no reason. Solzhenitsyn tried to talk to them, using the same examples and arguments, but he finally rose up against the "right-thinking inmates." With a similar frame of mind and perhaps for a longer period of time than Solzhenitsyn (who was younger that he), Jacques remained faithful to his belief system. Contrary to those who refused to have their vision of the world affected by their Gulag experience, the Frenchman evolved: "Should we change our ideas as Marxists because we find ourselves in prison by mistake?" His terrible experience slowly chipped away at his belief, and finally his convictions simply faded away.

For Jacques was not a Soviet man. He did not share the attitude that consisted of "submitting to a tyrant," which Claude Roy described so well concerning Dostoyevsky and the "two pillars of the Russian tradition," that is: "the art of getting the victim to not only stretch out his neck for the axe or the nape of his neck for the revolver but before dying to also glorify the one condemning him."[1] Jacques was still a communist, but less and less blind.

The works from the Age of Enlightenment that he so enjoyed when he was an adolescent in his father's library had left their mark on him. Despite having read works by Lenin, he was still influenced by the works of the Enlightenment: their encyclopedic approach, Voltaire's irrepressible laughter in the service of individual freedom and tolerance, Rousseau's egalitarian and moral rigour and his concern for truth, and Diderot's systematic destruction of conventional wisdom – the exemplars of critical thinking. And what if the worst was hidden by the very same skills that were supposed to eradicate it?

In the beginning there was my mother, my language, and my French culture. However, I did not feel French or Polish or Russian. I felt like a citizen of communism. And then I changed like animals that lose their skin, their feathers, or their carapace. This casting off took a long time. And that casting off left me vulnerable, especially in the environment of the camp. So I tried to remain blind for as long as possible until the blinders fell from my eyes!

During this long process there were many stages that transformed this fervent communist internationalist who worked in espionage for the Red Army, this unconditional apostle of class warfare and social justice, into an aggressive adversary of the Marxist-Leninist system. Jacques was predisposed to evolve in stages and make discoveries because of his sensitivity. For example, the discovery concerning the peasants who survived forced collectivization upset him. First, he felt compassion and indignation, and then shame for having refused to open his eyes when something could have been done.

I met Nikanor in 1940. He was in his ninth year of prison, while I was in my third. An old Russian peasant whose parents had been serfs, he had been a witness to the revolutions of 1905 and 1917. With the monotonous voice of a commentator, he spoke about the death of his twin great-grandsons. In 1931, they were born in a cattle car. The first of the twins died two or three hours after birth. The other one survived until the next morning. The train was taking hundreds of peasants and their families, who were labeled *kulaks*, to an unknown destination. Entire families – from the newly born to the very elderly – were loaded onto railcars after their village was surrounded by armed soldiers. They had to give their land, their buildings, their herds, their furniture, almost all their possessions to the collective farm.

While I was listening to the fatalistic lament of Nikanor in 1940, a memory of the Comintern came back to me. It was during a clandestine mission in a city in western Europe. At that time the capitalist bourgeois press was full of sensationalized articles concerning forced collectivization in the USSR. I had rejected with indignation such "abject slander concerning the first worker and peasant nation in the world." In the same way that public opinion worldwide refused to believe the first news of the Nazi death camps in 1943, I refused to believe the disgrace committed against Russian peasants. For this reason, I consider myself complicit in this disgraceful act and carry the guilt with me even to this day.

For Jacques "the communist" who believed that he was serving peasants and workers, the discovery of the reality of forced collectivization produced intellectual and human trauma. It was perhaps the most painful torment in that slow process of demystification. For it was no longer simply a question of him and his peers, intellectuals or militants who came from a detested class and who criticized themselves for their inflated egos and the remains of their petty bourgeois individualism. It was the sons and grandsons of serfs destroyed through a process of extermination that resembled methods the Nazis would later use.

A long passage in *The Gulag Handbook* pays homage to these peasants. They were exemplary victims of a system that devoured its own children. The party carried out dekulakization between 1929 and 1932 with secret instructions and no published governmental decree. It was implemented by OGPU troops and battalions of armed party militants recruited from the cities and assisted by local "committees of the poor" that often had accounts to settle. The rich peasants were identified as so-called *kulak*s. In the non-Russian territories of the Soviet Union, dekulakization could be even more brutal. Local communists had to demonstrate their devotion to the communist party by showing that Soviet interests were more important than the interests of their own countrymen. Surprise was the technique that was used. "Committees of the poor" were organized; villages were surrounded at the last minute and farms were invaded by armed soldiers. The families of peasants who were declared *kulaks* were taken away in trucks, then in railcars intended for animals. The long journey to an unknown destination could last several weeks. It was a horrible ordeal that preceded the Nazi deportations and ended thousands of miles deep within the Soviet interior.

There, by truck or on foot, the survivors were taken further north, far from any inhabited areas. They were contained in restricted areas where they worked as "special settlers," with rudimentary equipment furnished by the OGPU. Those who had fled or who had managed to escape dekulakization were hunted down throughout Russia and sent to the camps. The severity of the conditions along with the absence of medical treatment accounted for the very high mortality. The exact number remains unknown, but it is estimated that millions were either shot or perished in the course of deportation and settlement. The forced collectivization drive permitted the party leadership to use methods of mass repression. Later, those methods would be employed again. This dark period in Soviet history took place at the time when the young Jacques worked for the Comintern and had access to the free press. When he later learned what had actually occurred, Jacques had to confront his own errors and his own wish to ignore what was happening.

Other events that were taking place while he was in the Gulag would also play a role in his evolution. On 22 June 1941 Nazi Germany attacked the Soviet Union, violating the Nazi-Soviet pact of 1939.

I was in Norilsk in the Dudinka camp. Every morning before going to work we listened to the official radio, which was the only radio station in the Soviet Union. That day we heard nothing. There was a total blackout that lasted for three days. But once we got to the worksite we heard the news about the war from the free workers.

My fellow inmates who were Soviet citizens were devastated. It was as if something worse than the horrible fate of each one of them had come crashing down on the entire country. I understood their reaction and thought about the consequences of this event for France and occupied Europe.

The great majority of my comrades were very worried. They were less worried about their families than they were about the cause. Their reaction illustrated the difference between the USSR and "civilized" countries that considered families to be more important. Free peoples see the state as an instrument to serve them. By contrast, some of my comrades had the mentality of former Bolsheviks. For them, citizens were there to serve the state. Many of them were prepared to die for a state that had oppressed them so greatly. As for me, my casting off was still not complete, and I believed that I was still not a patriot of any country. However, I started to be worried about the whole world.

After the signing of the Nazi-Soviet pact and the beginning of the war, Soviet propaganda had spoken of the success of early German advances with much sympathy, while denigrating first the Polish and then the French, British, and other allies. That part of the war had been particularly painful for me. I was the only French citizen in that part of Norilsk, so I was often attacked and ridiculed by some of the thugs as well as members of the administrative staff. I emphasize – some of them.

Following the breaking of the Nazi-Soviet pact, we received news concerning the progress of Hitler's troops. The Russian front was withdrawing and the Germans were advancing to Leningrad and were at the doorstep of Moscow, Voronezh, and on the Volga near the foothills of the Caucasus. In our camp, the pressure diminished. We were treated better. At least that was what happened in the Norilsk camp. Other Gulag prisoners in other camps did not have the same experience. I had the impression that the administration had calculated that if Hitler won it would be necessary to take better care of the fifty-eighters who might rise up. (Theoretically all those prisoners were considered to be logical allies of Hitler, although the penitentiary administrators knew very well that the majority of the inmates were as loyal Soviet citizens as they were.)

Hope was reborn. The symbols changed. For example, some new and incredible scenes could be seen in photos: peasants who were crossing themselves to bless soldiers who were leaving for the front. And then the churches were reopened. An unimaginable event! Not only the fact that it was happening, but that it was being shown in the newspapers and talked about on the radio. For us, this meant that the government was radically changing its practices. Priests were even offered freedom on the condition that they return to their parishes in the same churches that had since been transformed into warehouses. And these were the same churches from which they had been driven. People, especially peasants, began to believe that a change in direction had begun. Perhaps Soviet power had become aware of its errors and perhaps the collective farms would be disbanded. So there was hope again.

Then there was the siege of Stalingrad in 1942–1943. At that time, we had a lot of official news. Of course, I was pleased to hear about the Russians pushing back the Nazi troops, but worried that the vise of the Gulag would be tightened around us. In fact, the regime became even stricter from that time on. The security officers and members of the political control agency were very afraid that they would be sent to the front like the guards. Many guards had already been sent and had died at the front. So they started to invent thousands of fake Hitlerian plots, condemning men once again. It was to show that they were essential and that they had to remain at their jobs. In the widespread panic that existed, accusations of having instigated conspiracies serving the enemy increased and no one was safe. But the Red Army's advance pleased everyone. During the entire war and until victory, the inmates, especially the peasants, experienced a kind of euphoria. We were waiting to be freed or at least expecting our sentences to be reduced.

And then, once again, disillusion returned. The war ended and the Gulag regime became more and more brutal, applying laws that were more and more ferocious. In 1948, three years after victory, the Moscow authorities realized that the local authorities did not always respect the instructions that stipulated that political inmates had to be used exclusively in heavy physical labour. (The supervisors, who got bonuses and decorations according to their productivity, could not without difficulty do without specialists, who were mainly political prisoners.) A new system of "special camps" was created. They were very strict. The barracks had locked windows with bars and the hardest labour was assigned to those who were suspected, often wrongly, of having had contacts with the enemy. On their worksites the foremen were sworn in and the brigade leaders were common criminal offenders whose food rations depended on the productivity of the brigade.

They came from everywhere, these so-called "traitors to the motherland," just like the "enemies of the people" in 1937. It was the beginning of another wave of arrests. Among them there were many ex-Soviet prisoners of war who had returned from Nazi camps. They were sent to the camps to test their loyalty. Although the authorities knew that their propaganda was false, they felt obliged to consider as suspicious anyone who had spent time abroad, far from the Soviet secret police.

And they all ended up in the Gulag. In the Gulag, there was Dimitri Petrovitch, a Russian soldier, taken as a prisoner of war by the Germans. He had escaped and joined the Red Army so that he could fight again. He was constantly being told: "But how did you manage to escape? Confess! The Germans let you come back to spy on us! Confess!"

In the Gulag, there was the old Pelaguia Petrovna. She had given a thirsty young German soldier some water from her bucket. A witness to the scene denounced her. She was sentenced to twenty years. In the Gulag, there was the young Alexandra Benoît, the descendant of a French painter who lived in St Petersburg in the nineteenth century. Faced with the advance of the German troops, she refused to abandon the young children in the daycare centre in Leningrad where she worked as a volunteer. She ended up in Norilsk, where I met her. She remained dignified, but she would have to face the worst hard labour and the worst challenges.

At the end of the war, Jacques was almost at the end of his sentence. He had been sentenced for eight years in 1937. Did the change in his beliefs lead to anxiety concerning his liberation? The commotion created in the camps by the Second World War distracted Gulag inmates from what had been their unique experience: death as a result of heavy physical labour. However, the real masters of the Gulag were not the guards or the bureaucrats, who suffered perpetually from uncertainty. According to Jacques, the real masters were the hardened criminals who terrorized others. The system's redistribution of power to the fiercest criminal recidivists undermined any illusions about the process of rehabilitation. Jacques and his comrades had wanted to fight against the profiteers and the wrongdoers, against a society ruled by the law of the jungle of free markets and dictators. They believed that between the strong and the weak, it was freedom that was oppressive. Only a just system would truly liberate people. Order in the Gulag depended upon arbitrariness and the blind tyranny of a handful of criminals without faith or law. They ruled over unprotected common people, peasants, workers, and intellectuals, with brutality. It was the last *coup de grace* for the utopia.

# 24 The Friends of the People

The thief steals, all the others slave away.

Gulag saying

The intellectual convict is crushed by the camps. Everything he valued is ground into the dust ... The criminal world, the habitual criminals ... are mainly responsible for this corruption of the human soul.

Varlam Shalamov, Kolyma Tales

The horrible event of the "cow" is well known to readers of Rossi's *Fragments of Lives*. Jacques told the story of an expedition in the tundra. There was a team of six *zek*s, two escort soldiers and three engineer-topographers. In the infinite whiteness, the members of the team saw a grey spot that turned out to be a man, an inmate who was frozen solid in the snow. The scarf of the dead man covered two incisions in his neck at the location of the arteries. His jacket covered two wounds near his kidneys. The dead man was a "cow," a term that referred to a person whose blood and kidneys had been swallowed by his companions, usually thugs who, during a work evasion, had nothing left to eat. Jacques recognized him as a prisoner who was fifteen years old and who had just arrived at the camp. He had offered to give Jacques his scarf that his mother had knitted for him.

Jacques had already written about this story, but he added several details during our meetings. The victim had his throat slit with a knife. The escort soldier found marks on the neck of the young man. The thugs, after having drunk the blood from the arteries, made two incisions to remove the kidneys. In the camps and in the prisons, those who ate the "cows" were called cannibals, but they did not brag about their cannibalism, which was a practice even the mobster world did not approve of, although it sanctioned other horrible bloody crimes. In the beginning, the young victims were very proud to have been selected by the kings of crime. The latter pushed their cynicism to the point where they even asked the victim to carry the salt they would use. In case they found an unexpected source of food, the "cow" would be saved. This is what happened to another inmate who told Jacques his story. He had been recaptured afterwards, and it was only later that he realized what he had escaped from.

The phenomenon existed even under the tsars when a certain V. Vassiliev, who had escaped from a labour camp with another inmate, ate the flesh of his companion before being captured. The practice became so common during the Soviet regime that it gave birth to a series of Gulag slang words. These terms do not, it should be noted, appear in Russian slang dictionaries published in the nineteenth century and in the beginning of the twentieth century, but they appear in *The Gulag Handbook* by Jacques Rossi. This is why Jacques was proud of a scholarly reference in a Russian publication: "The Dahl dictionary (the Russian Webster) lists about a dozen prison terms. Rossi's dictionary lists 45 official terms and 41 slang terms."[1]

Even more than in *The Gulag Handbook*, the stories that Jacques told me reveal his ambivalence concerning the criminals. Of course, he was aware of the cruelty of their world. He observed it with the curiosity of an ethnographer. His relationships with the world of serious delinquency are as mixed as his emotional feelings about it. Didn't he captivate them by telling them the story of *The Count of Monte-Cristo* and others about inmates and escapees, all in order to please them? In exchange for his drawings, didn't he get protection whose effectiveness he would never forget and even describe with enthusiasm?

The thug he called Grishka-the-Pox was pleased with the portrait that Jacques drew in pencil on a piece of a cement bag. And the court of this crime boss could not stop praising this "masterpiece," which very faithfully depicted the original. The thug Ivan the Eye Poker even talked directly to the portrait, saying how handsome and how virile he was. Jacques was proud of this recognition, which came together with two pounds of bread and protection that was more solid than life insurance in the camp. The thug's territory was sacred, and as long as Grishka-the-Pox lived, Jacques knew that he would be protected from the extortions of the mob. But the thugs usually had a short life.

Jacques drew a distinction between the "ordinary criminal offenders" who were petty thieves and minor delinquents and the serious criminal recidivists. He often talked about the first group with compassion, the kind he typically reserved for the fifty-eighters and for "the enemies of the people" condemned for fabricated counter-revolutionary crimes. Concerning the second group, Jacques often spoke of them with strong emotions. He painted lively portraits of them.

Soviet jargon referred to the serious criminals as "friends of the people," the opposite of "enemies of the people," or as the "socially close" as opposed to the "socially alien," so-called counter-revolutionaries. As the expression indicates, the "socially close" were paradoxically considered closer to the communist social ideal than the alleged "enemies of the people," who were considered to be irredeemable. The rehabilitative element of the corrective-labour camps focused on the criminal offenders, who, unlike the political prisoners, were considered capable of being rehabilitated through labour in the camps.

One of the peculiarities of the Gulag universe that many survivors describe concerns the ways in which the privileged crime bosses of the Gulag, "the socially close," could with impunity and with the blessing of the prison administration exploit, oppress, and enslave the "socially alien" as they wished. Margarete Buber-Neumann, Aleksandr Solzhenitsyn, Varlam Shalamov, Jacques Rossi, and many others speak of an upside-down world, a genuine hell. Hardened criminal recidivists, both men and women, reigned not only over the lowly bread thieves but also over the university professors from Kazan, the important German communist intellectuals, the officers of the Red Army, poets, intellectual Troskyists, and secret agents of the Red Army or the Comintern who had been purged in 1937. Thus, in practice, the hardened criminals, who were officially considered to be socially nearer to the Soviet model of humankind, became the masters of the Gulag. According to Jacques, they felt more at home there than outside the barbed wire. For them, time "outside" between two stays in the Gulag was like a vacation at the end of which the serious criminals were content to return home to the Gulag.

Aleksandr Solzhenitsyn was a twice-commissioned officer in the Soviet army, decorated two times, a brilliant student of mathematics as well as philosophy, and someone who emerged naturally as a member of the Soviet elite. He did not have strong enough words to characterize these outlaws who had become inmates. Given the shortage of camp guards and the NKVD's inclination to trust the criminal over the political prisoner, this population of inmates often became the *de facto* bosses and the masters over honest citizens who had been sentenced for no reason. Solzhenitsyn could not hide his indignation, when faced with this reversal of values that placed criminals above honest working people of their own country. The camp system effectively encouraged criminal recidivists to abuse other inmates, but the rise in work-refusers and "violations of camp discipline" in the late Stalin period proved that this social hierarchy was untenable.

Nonetheless, for years, the most hardened criminals were very proud to be members of a dominating caste in the Gulag whose class interests were the same as those of Soviet power. Solzhenitsyn attacked their "contemptuous attitude of hostility" towards the other inmates, encouraged by an administration that considered them to be prodigious children of the system and gave them unlimited power everywhere in the Gulag, in the prisons and in the camps. The alleged "enemies of the people" according to Article 58 were supposed to perform heavy physical labour regardless of their physical condition. If they didn't work, their sentence could be lengthened for "counter-revolutionary sabotage." At the same time the "socially near" ate well and sometimes with impunity refused to tire themselves out for a prison that was already depriving them of their freedom. Solzhenitsyn observed that at no time in history were there examples of such absolute power granted to hardened criminals over a country's population that had been reduced to slavery.

For his part, Jacques observed with interest the customs of this strange tribe that exercised over him the power of life and death. Above all, Jacques the linguist listened to them and delighted in their strange jargon, in the expressions and sayings that formed a kind of language inaccessible to anyone who had not known the particular culture of the Gulag nation from the inside. Jacques the polyglot became familiar with this new language. With his excellent memory and his closely guarded notes, he was able to transmit this language to the world outside the Gulag, once he returned to the world of paper and typewriters. Thus he had the idea for *The Gulag Handbook*, which he initially conceived as a dictionary of Gulag terms largely invented and inspired by criminals.

The documentation that he gathered concerning the history of the Gulag and the evolution of its laws and customs enabled him to offer a different window on the camps, distinct from the works of Solzhenitsyn and other chroniclers of the Gulag. Like Shalamov and other authors, Jacques drew a distinction between the "honest thieves" who conformed to the traditions and laws of their environment, and the traitors, the so-called bitches who, encouraged by the administration or Soviet power, violated those sacred values. The "honest thief" or the "thief-in-law" showed little regard for those who were not "real" thieves like he was, for the other criminals, the so-called pigeons, or for the penal authorities. He was bound by duty to express solidarity with his peers. He did not collaborate with the authorities. He did not attack women with children in public. He didn't touch the bread ration of another inmate (the ration was not bread obtained in exchange for something or bread that was stolen) even if it belonged to a pigeon.

Any infraction of the thieves' unwritten law was judged by a "tribunal of honour," which was made up of criminals who condemned others and gave no opportunity for appeal. The sentence was either exclusion from the group or decapitation. The decapitated head had to be presented to the judges. Becoming "a real thief" in the Gulag involved a rite of passage that might include killing an informer, or bitch.

In an attempt to weaken these organized traditions of solidarity among the "honour" bandits, the camp administration, since the early years of Soviet power, tried to disrupt the network of the real thieves and to use corruption to diminish their ties of solidarity. The number of bitches, or traitors, increased greatly, leading to gang wars between criminals. The Soviet Union's entry into the Second World War made this situation worse. Following Hitler's attack against the Soviet Union, many thieves were drafted. Some of them even became officers because of their courage in battle. When they returned, the typical thugs accused them of having collaborated with the state and started a ruthless battle against them. During this postwar "Bitches War" in the Gulag, the camp administration took advantage of the savage rivalry by putting the warring factions in the same barracks so that they would kill each other. In the same manner, the authorities used the thugs to eliminate certain political inmates.

Jacques witnessed one of these bloody events to settle scores. He would talk about it much later. Sacha, a thug from one gang, had been sent as a scout to the barracks of his adversary. He was thrown by the group onto a hot stove, where he was roasted alive to the music of a balalaika while two hundred pigeons pretended to sleep. They were obeying one of the most important local rules for survival: see nothing, hear nothing, say nothing.

The criminal Tolia, who was swindled while sharing some loot, became the informer of his former comrades. In the beginning, he benefitted from some small privileges in return for the service he rendered to the authorities. Very quickly, however, his role was discovered by his comrades. Tolia could no longer be used by the commissar. The latter sent Tolia to that part of the camp where the inmates that he had squealed on were quartered. The next day the chopped-off head of Tolia was on the floor near the latrines.

The criminal Tooth-Gap had had enough of being beaten by the inmates on duty every time he had to leave for the camp worksite. He dreamed of being in a detention facility where one didn't have to work and where inmates had more bread than was given to work-refusers in the camps. So he resorted to the simplest method. He murdered the first inmate to come along, his neighbour in the barracks.

Jacques indicates that these criminals were also tough on themselves and did not hesitate to resort to drastic action when necessary. The criminal Jorka, upon orders of the captain, was about to be transferred to another place far from his easy job in the bakery. He was surrounded by escort guards and was being sent elsewhere. He lowered his pants, sat on the ground, took a nail out of his pocket, and pushed it into his scrotum. Jorka was not transferred.

As for the criminal Sergey, he had two stumps where his hands had been. He told his story to Jacques with great detachment. He chopped off the first hand to escape heavy physical labour, and the second hand because he was forced to carry water. He put that hand under a circular saw. However, self-mutilation was considered an act of sabotage in the Gulag, so this criminal found himself demoted to the category of political prisoners, the fifty-eighters. This explains why some hardened criminals shared barracks with political prisoners.

In a story from *Kolyma Tales* titled "On Parole," Varlam Shalamov describes a game between criminals. The loser of the game had bet a sweater that was knitted by the wife of Garkunov, one of the inmates. Garkunov had to be killed to give up the sweater. Jacques described similar habits.

> The criminals were inveterate card players and made fun of Gulag rules that forbade card playing. They made cards with whatever they could find. For example, they made glue from cooked potatoes and glued cigarette papers together. Using bits of shoe leather, they wrote on them. These cards were about two and a half inches by one and a half inches. These card games would not have concerned the other inmates unless there was a bet involved too. When a criminal lost everything playing cards and no longer had anything left, he would bet something that did not belong to him. He could bet the shoes of a "pigeon" who didn't know anything about the game. He could also bet on the fifth person, that is to say, he would promise to choke to death the fifth person who entered the barracks. If the fifth was a guard, the criminal risked the death penalty. If the fifth was only an inmate, he could get three to five more years in the Gulag. If the criminal bet on the twenty-eighth waiting in the soup line, he knew that he was only risking the life of an inmate and therefore he knew that his own life was not in danger. The criminals also bet on women. The most virtuous, the virgins, and those who had a strong protector

were obviously the ones most sought after. A criminal who did not pay his game debts risked greatly. He was "excluded" from the clan. In the barracks I saw this kind of execution in the presence of about ten inmates holding their breath. The criminal, with a blow of an axe, cut off the head of the person who had "betted" and threw it at the feet of the winner.

It appears that mainly criminal offenders attempted escape. They employed traditional methods and got their hands on special weapons. But what about the others?

There were attempts by all groups of prisoners because everywhere there were people who were fearless. Even among the thirty-seveners. There were stories of escapes during the twenties, in the beginning of the thirties, from the famous Solovki camp on the White Sea in the north of Russia. But I witnessed only one escape. Ivan Petrov was an accountant who had been sentenced to ten years for stealing. He was a common criminal offender and did not belong to the world of the hardened criminals. He came from Krasnoyarsk, and arrived one spring, like we had, after the thaw, when the Yenisei could be navigated. I met him then. In the autumn he managed to make the trip in the other direction, probably hidden in the hold of a barge with the complicity of a sailor who was guilty of murder and whom Petrov was blackmailing.

In Krasnoyarsk, which he knew very well, he went straight to his home, or rather, because his wife had left, to the home of his children. He stole their food ration coupons, which he exchanged for an internal passport with a legal stamp and the name "Boris Kuznetsov" from Odessa in the Ukraine, as far as possible from Krasnoyarsk. He fled to the east, thousands of miles away, and landed in Khabarovsk in the far east. There the administration of the region accepted and stamped his ID and gave him lodging. Very soon he found a position as an accountant in a cooperative for artisans.

Everything would have continued to go well except that three years later while drinking beer, another person at the table talked about an incident, a passionate crime that had taken place in the city of Odessa. And since everybody observed everybody, there was an informer who noticed that Boris Kuznetsov's memory seemed a bit weak concerning the geographic details of his native city. The informer contacted the local political police, who called the police in Odessa. After being beaten, the Ukrainian accountant Boris Kuznetsov finally admitted that he was none other than the *zek* Ivan

Petrov. It was by chance that I met him again in Norilsk – there were sixty thousand prisoners there – and he told me his story. Normally an escapee who was caught by his own guards could be beaten to death and his cadaver displayed at the entrance to the camp. He had only been sentenced to an extra ten years in addition to his first sentence. Twenty years in all. We could say that he had been lucky!

Escaping was called "the green prosecutor" or the "white prosecutor" by the inmates, depending on whether it took place in the summer or in the winter. It was a permanent temptation for them but remained more a fantasy than a real possibility. In a desperate world where the work was tantamount to a slow suicide, where slacking off was difficult and dangerous, where death always came too soon, escaping remained, despite the risks, the most obvious means of altering one's destiny. That was the choice made by Slavomir Rawicz and many others.[2]

As for Jacques, at least in the beginning, he did not think about escaping from the camp. His first concern was to be declared innocent by the system itself. He remembers, however, having met a certain Krautman in 1935, an old Bolshevik who told him that he had thought of escaping after he was arrested by the Cheka. He refused to admit that he worked as a secret agent. Jacques thought again about the idea of escaping during his "liberation" period when he was under house arrest. The first thing he did was to order a small box of cookies from an inmate, supposedly for the films in the photo workshop where he worked.[3] That didn't prevent him from being accused of having invented a fantastic project of escaping "into thin air." It may have been easier for the hardened criminals rather than for the political offenders or fifty-eighters to successfully escape the Gulag.

# 25  Continuing in Spite of Oneself

The generation of new prison terms, like the growing of a snake's rings, is a form of Archipelago life. As long as our camps thrived and our exile lasted, this black threat hovered over the heads of the convicted: to be given a new term before they had finished the first one.

Aleksandr Solzhenitsyn, *The Gulag Archipelago*

It was the end of 1945. The eight-year sentence to which Jacques had been condemned was about to be completed. He was arrested in December 1937 and even if the verdict was pronounced in 1939, the years in prison detention counted. Was Jacques delighted with the prospect of his release? Not really. For, like everybody else, he had heard about the infamous order that banned the release of certain prisoners until the end of the war. This enabled the administration to continue to detain certain categories of prisoners until further notice.

> This law took effect on 22 June 1941, the day that Hitler's army attacked the Soviet Union. It was a decision of the OSO [the Special Council of the NKVD] according to which the majority of individuals sentenced for counter-revolutionary crimes would continue to be imprisoned "awaiting special orders." The details of these orders remained secret, but it was assumed that their imprisonment would last until the end of the war.

So on the night before the last day of his sentence, Jacques was informed that he would remain in prison as a result of this infamous order. Jacques asked to read the text, and this request surprised, even amused, the commander of the camp section. Of the two or three thousand *zek*s he commanded, the Frenchman was the only one who asked to read the text:

"What kind of an idea is that, wanting to read the text! I have never heard of that. And in any case, I won't let you go until I have explicit orders to do so. Written orders. I don't understand what the problem is." Jacques's companions in misery didn't understand the problem either. As Soviet citizens they did not understand the problem:

"Now that we are at war against the most terrible enemy that humanity has ever known, it is normal for the Soviet government to do everything to protect itself from a fifth column."

"But you, who are talking to me, you are not an enemy of the Soviet regime!"

"Of course not, only the government does not know that!"

The "new order" condemned Jacques to nearly eighteen additional months of imprisonment. The order was lifted two years after the victory over the Nazis, on 15 April 1947 according to a release certificate. One day, with no explanation, Jacques was freed but – and there was always a but – he was not allowed to leave the territory. Simply stated, the *zek* became a "free" citizen, that is to say, he could leave the barbed wire behind, but he could not travel too far away.

> So there I was, transferred from the little Gulag to the big Gulag that was the Soviet Union. But contrary to the majority of the inhabitants of this big Gulag, I had to stay in the neighbourhood of the small Gulag. Every fifteen days I had to check in with the police. If one didn't, the authorities would start a search and the "fugitive" risked being handed another sentence.
>
> My release! I had waited for it for so long that I couldn't feel in my gut that it was real. At the time of the so-called liberation I had a kind of hallucination. I saw myself ten years before in 1937 with my felt hat, my dozens of ties, my comfortable camel hair coat, and my great suitcase trunk covered with stickers, starting my voyage in a sleeping car. And then I looked at myself. I was unrecognizable, in a railway cattle car with a kind of garbage bag and my *zek* rags, and then, with a strong kick to the rear end, I landed down on the side of the tracks. This liberation was not a return to my former state of being, but a definite downfall. That is how I felt about my "liberation." In fact, my life had not changed a lot. I did the same work, but I was quite well paid in rubles and not in bread.

The work certificates that Jacques obtained after a request dated 3 May 1960 indicated that he worked in Norilsk from 25 August 1947 until 22 June 1948 as a translator-engineer, from 22 June 1948 until 29 September 1948 as a geologist-technician, and from 29 September 1948 until 20 March 1949 as a photographer.

I worked in the Office of Scientific Information, writing reports based on magazine articles that concerned mine work and the extraction of nickel, particularly in Canada where in the Arctic regions the climatic and geological conditions resembled those of Norilsk. Then after a certain amount of time, I was fired for no reason. Since I still had the mentality of an inmate, I did not even try to get an explanation.

I found another job in a photography workshop in the office of Gorstroi [municipal construction]. I lived on Ordzhonikidze street in a very simple Norilsk hotel that I had helped to build, just like many other buildings in the town, during the time I was in the little Gulag. The hotel personnel, above all the women, were almost all former inmates. Some of them were elite intellectuals. There were also real "free" people. In the Soviet Union life was not easy, and in the Arctic it was even more difficult. Nevertheless, the salaries were better than on the "continent" that attracted ordinary citizens.[1]

In this environment, most of the workers, engineers, and researchers were former inmates. We lived near the barbed wire. There was only one cafeteria-restaurant, which also served as a club for the free engineers. We all met there for our meals. The first time I went to eat there, someone I did not know, but obviously a former *zek*, came right up to me and shook my hand without saying anything. I must say that I was touched by this gesture of kindness.

We have several testimonies concerning Jacques from that period, although details of the Frenchman's biography remain quite sketchy. Pavel Vladimirovitch Tseburkin, who knew him in section 2 of the camp, indicated that as soon as he was freed, Jacques received a new five-year sentence. According to a certain S. Shcheglov, the cause for his new arrest was an article about Norilsk, published by a Canadian magazine, *The Mining Journal*, to which Jacques is believed to have contributed. Perhaps that was the reason why he was fired from the Office of Scientific Information. These testimonies give us a general impression of how the man and his legacy were perceived by Soviet citizens around him. Here is the portrait drawn by Sergey Alexandrovitch Snegov, whose memories of Norilsk were recorded, according to Shcheglov, at the end of the forties and the beginning of the fifties: "Jacques was a charming man, slender and intelligent. He liked to talk and he was without a doubt the most handsome man I ever saw in Norilsk. We had a good relationship. He often came to see me. Just looking at him made women swoon. He was not only physically handsome, but he was also by nature a real man. He was a professional spy."[2] In that period, Jacques's state of mind was sombre, filled with uncertainty:

I was waiting. I felt that it was not the end of my ordeal, that at any time I could find myself once again behind the barbed wire. I don't know how, but I felt that I was being watched. When the trap finally caught me, I was not really surprised. But in order to stage the arrest, the KGB used another Frenchman, and that was an unpleasant surprise. He was the only Frenchman that I ever knew in the Gulag.

Jacques was not suspicious of this other Frenchman, François P. Neither was he suspicious of his old companion from the first convoy, the Russian-Swede Oleg P., who also had been arrested in 1937 when he was studying at an engineering school. He, too, was arrested for spying at the same time as Jacques. However, at the end of their sentences, while Jacques was kept "awaiting special instructions," Oleg was freed. As an engineer, Oleg was obliged to stay in the Norilsk region where he worked as a "free" wage labourer. He was the foreman of a worksite and he supervised the construction of a factory. It was there that he met the *zek* François P., who was working as an inmate. To these two names, a third must be added, that of Alexis G., another "friend" whose task as an informer consisted of translating from French into Russian the correspondence between Jacques, François P., and the commissar Arseniev, who invented the whole affair, hoping that he would get credit for it from the proper authorities.

One day, when Jacques was finally a "free" wage labourer and working outside the barbed wire, he received, via his old friend Oleg P., a message scribbled in French and signed by a certain François P. We have already seen that in 1948, three years after the celebrated victory over Nazism, Soviet authorities established a new system of camps for forced labour. François P. was in one of those "special camps." During a visit to that work place, Oleg P. saw François P., who asked him to put him in contact with his compatriot Jacques Rossi, as he had heard about him.

> I was very moved to receive his first letter. It was written in real French, with Latin characters. And they were written in the French style! There were some spelling errors, like *buerre* [butter] spelled with only one *r*, but they were common spelling mistakes for French people with little education. François P. told me his story. He was a real French patriot. He had fought for France against Hitler's army while I was blindly building with difficulty a totalitarian empire, a criminal project that would turn into imperialist Grand Russia. François P. had been arrested, or rather kidnapped, by the Soviets in Paris in 1945 and was sentenced to twenty-five years.

No one could have been more sympathetic to me than a French victim of the same system that had oppressed me and so many others, especially at that time, when my faith in the communist ideal was waning. Our correspondence lasted several weeks. I sent him what I could – tobacco, some sugar and butter. I sent him special foodstuffs, words of encouragement and consolation. He asked me for a lemon for a "chemical experiment," and I managed to get one for him. Another time he told me that he was going to "organize something" and that he needed a syringe. I was suspicious of that. I sent him rich foods, sausages and other special foods, but not the syringe. I don't remember exactly what I wrote about in my letters. Above all, I tried to reassure him and to give him hope. Oleg secretly gave this correspondence to Alexis G., who translated it into Russian for the commissar. It still remains in the archives of Krasnoyarsk in Siberia.

I had the pleasure of meeting François P. when he was accompanied by guards for some unknown reason to the photography workshop. I worked there from the time I was fired with no explanation from the Office of Scientific Information. For the first time in years, I spoke French with a French person. How naive I was! Speaking a foreign language was a misdemeanour. I should have understood that all of this was a set-up. How could I have believed that in the Soviet context what was happening was nothing other than manipulation? To Soviet authorities I simply *had* to know, personally, the man with whom I would be accused of orchestrating a plot.

Oleg P., being a good intermediary, brought me a detailed secret map of the Norilsk region and suggested I take a photo of it to send to the French ambassador. The idea was to attract the attention of France to the miserable fate of this citizen, a good patriot and former resister of the Nazi occupation, who had been sentenced to twenty-five years in the Gulag in the toughest special camps. Oleg P. convinced me that the photo of the map would let the French better situate the location of the Norilsk region because they didn't have the slightest idea where it was. He had to go to Moscow on a mission, and he would take advantage of that trip to take my letter on behalf of François P. and the photo to the French consulate. According to Oleg P. this would help the French locate François P. Later in my file, I found three copies of the photo. They were going to be used to implicate the British and American consulates, as well.

The web had been carefully spun, and all the parts were in place for me to get ensnared. Oleg P. developed the photo that I had taken, and he gave it back to me. Several days later the same Oleg P. set up a meeting with me in his hotel. I was to bring the letter and the photo of the map. Oleg was in a hurry. He was leaving for Moscow the next day. As a former clandestine trained in the practices of secret agents, I had prepared a book for him so that he didn't have to carry the documents in his pocket. Following my former habits, I slid my letter and the photo under the book cover and carefully glued it back together. I arrived there at the meeting carrying that "explosive" material – aware of the risk, but wanting to help my compatriot.

It was March 1949, late in the afternoon. I remember that it was already dark when I arrived at the meeting. Before I even entered the hotel, the commissar Arseniev was waiting to nab me with the proof of my misdemeanour. And then there I was at the police station in Arseniev's office. Of course, he was delighted, but he played along, as if he hadn't pulled all the strings of this masquerade in order to imprison me again – and for such a long time that had it not been for the death of Stalin and the events that followed, I would still be imprisoned.

Of course, they didn't need all this evidence to condemn me again, because – as I have already indicated – the mere suspicion of a suspicion was sufficient. Basically, Arseniev wanted to be seen by the higher-ups as a super-cop. They could have gotten any inmate, after a beating and a promise of freedom a year ahead of schedule, to denounce me. But Arseniev was a kind of zealous artist who was bored in that faraway Arctic province. The affair was not commonplace. There were not many French people in the Arctic streets of Norilsk, nor in the barracks of the special camps. And, for once, they had caught not one but two. Plus Captain Arseniev knew very well that this feat of "revealing an international plot" would remain in his file like a title of glory even if everybody knew that basically it was a lot of rubbish. He had played his role perfectly. He looked at the book I was carrying very seriously as if he ignored what it contained.

Then he said to his assistant, "Scissors!"

The assistant searched in a drawer and found only an old notched razor blade, which Arseniev used to cut the book. He did it so slowly and so solemnly, like in a bad detective movie, that I would have laughed if I hadn't been in the role of the victim. But I realized I had been manipulated by Oleg and by Alexis, my old Mayflower comrades. I was conned by François, my compatriot, who supposedly had been ready to die for France. All of it had been orchestrated by Arseniev, who was silently laughing his head off, but literally, it could have been my head coming off.

A single photo – one piece of damaging evidence for the Soviets – and a letter to a foreign ambassador. What could be better? What irony. Jacques was so careful. He was so secretive. He, who had spent his first years in the Gulag being suspicious of everything, was now facing terrible charges of spying based on authentic documents that he himself had given to his informers. He was accused of having instigated a plan for himself, his compatriot François P., and a few others to escape by airplane in the middle of the tundra. And he had planned it with the complicity of the French ambassador, the British ambassador, and the American ambassador, no less! The formal testimony of François P. lent credibility to this version, which was supported by the translation of the correspondence. However, in that correspondence, Jacques never talked about any kind of escape plan. "Of course, I had never suggested an escape plan, which would have been impossible for [François P.], a western European who was ignorant of the Soviet world as well as the world of the Arctic. As an old hand in the Gulag, I knew that. That is why in my letter to François P. I tried to help boost his morale. There was enough in this letter to have me condemned."

This second sentence for Jacques the Frenchman was related to his first in 1939. The first was not as serious because there were no documents. And it was no longer 1937, but rather the end of the forties, the time of another wave of purges. Jacques's new sentence took place at a time of mass arrests, when many people who had been sentenced in the late 1930s were being re-arrested on new charges. Millions of *zeks* were returning to prisons and camps with sentences of ten, fifteen, even twenty years, much longer than the sentences of a decade earlier. In the case of this second sentence, as in the first, Jacques was not "tried" in a regular civilian court but by the OSO, that is, a Special Council of the NKVD.

> During the purge of 1947–1949, this practice of renewing sentences began. Shortly before the end of prisoners' sentences, certain categories of political prisoners became subject to new judicial procedures that often merely repeated the original accusations in order to prove that the first arrest had not been in error. The NKVD never made mistakes! The commissar-investigator recorded the complaints of the accused, who was not made to confess his "crimes" through torture, as these affairs were not tried in courts but by the OSO, which always condemned the person in absentia.

Jacques spent a good deal of time in the detention prison of Norilsk, where he was immediately sent. He reflected upon that patiently hatched scheme that turned him into a kind of permanent member of the Gulag. First, there was Oleg P., the informer, who had been freed so easily. There were no excuses for Oleg, but he did have an old mother whom he loved dearly and whose health depended on medicine that the police could easily have kept her from obtaining. Alexis G. the former inmate, who had come on the same convoy as Jacques and Oleg, was formerly a journalist for *Izvestia*. He had travelled extensively and had lived in Paris. As a former inmate who was freed, like Oleg, without permission to go home, his fate also hung by a thread and depended on the political police. As for François P.:

> After having participated in that fake scheme that landed me twenty-five more years, he was transferred to another camp where he was known as an informer. I learned that during the filming of a television show about the French in the Gulag. It was filmed by Bernard Germe, another Frenchman whose misfortune was to be with the occupying troops in Vienna in 1945. Bernard had gone to see his girlfriend in a place where he shouldn't have been. And he was sent off to the Gulag without even knowing why. Concerning François P.'s arrest, I can only hazard a guess. What appears certain is that he had been arrested on foreign soil and that was the reason he was freed before I was. He must have been involved in the black market either in Germany or in Austria, which was then occupied by the Russians. He might even have been in France because at the end of the war the Soviet repatriating commissions were looking for displaced persons. In any case, Arseniev used him with the precise intention of catching me. Arseniev must have assumed that after the catastrophe of having lost my faith in communism, I would have sought solace in French patriotism. François P. was a loser and it was easy for Arseniev to use him against me. Several of François's comrades were condemned because of him. They had supposedly given him advice about how to structure an "important affair" that would implicate three ambassadors of the free world!

In 1993, the whole affair was officially reviewed at Jacques's request. He received a document from the military court of Russia stating that the decision taken by the OSO in 1949 concerning Jacques Rossi, François P., and four other men – an Estonian, a Ukrainian, and two Russians – was annulled because there had been "no crime." Another document in the file was a copy of the 1949 indictment. It stated that François P., who was tried in 1948 by the OSO and sentenced to twenty-five years, was serving his sentence at the time of the indictment in an NKVD camp.

Continuing in Spite of Oneself   223

Jacques's hostility towards François P. lasted longer than other equally legitimate feelings of resentment. It was because François's betrayal had transgressed certain sacred values that Jacques honoured to an extreme. For him, these values replaced the communist ideal and represented a source of survival and resistance. Jacques had been betrayed by François, a Frenchman whom he once wanted to save. However, this betrayal did not have the effect of damaging the carapace, more cultural than national, that Jacques was constructing for himself and that would enable him to distance himself from his communist identity. The man François had only been the instrument of a system whose perversity Jacques himself had denounced, a system that during these dark years multiplied its instructions to apply more sentences, to double the length of sentences, and to control its enslaved manpower through a reign of terror. Life was uncertain, and the *zek*s who were finishing their sentences lived in constant fear of another sentence.

This time, however, Jacques refused to let himself be pushed around like he was ten years earlier when he arrived at the Lubianka detention centre convinced that he was going to be the exception. Now that his eyes were wide open, he would pursue other means to vindicate himself. The "preliminary investigation" this second time did not follow the same rules as the first one. Arseniev started by sending Jacques to the detention centre in Norilsk, which had been built by the inmates themselves. His situation there was worse than in the camp. The bread rations were very meagre, and there were no outside walks. Detained in solitary confinement, he could only wait.

Weeks, months, a year went by. Arseniev's investigation continued, and the accused was often escorted to the interrogator by a guard. The rest of the time Jacques was alone in his cell. He didn't work. He didn't have any books. He was afraid that he would go crazy.

In the morning, I sat cross-legged facing the window, and with my finger I traced the Chinese characters of the dynasties. For each dynasty, I tried to remember the major political and cultural events. And when I did remember, I traced with my finger on the boards the names of painters, poets, the important battles, everything that my memory could recall. I occupied myself this way until the noontime soup was distributed. Then I ate the soup very slowly with great concentration, in order to make it last. Then I sat cross-legged with my back to the window, for a change, and I waited until five or six o'clock by reciting poems, in all the languages that I knew. French, of course, but also Polish, Spanish, Italian, German, English, Russian, Persian. Although I didn't know novels by heart, I still remembered sentences, paragraphs. Today I would not be able to do that. But I don't want to return to a Russian prison. I am so much better in a housing complex in the Paris suburbs!

It was in the Norilsk detention prison that Jacques spoke with an entertainer and flatulist (*un pétomane*) who gave him some comforting information:

> He was a former gang member, an inmate in the camps, and a stove setter by profession. That was a much sought-after profession in the Arctic, where there were a lot of stoves. He was housed in the detention prison so that he could take care of the heat in the police officers' apartments. The wife of the main supervisor of the prison was a good woman who paid him by feeding him pounds of green peas in return for taking very good care of her stove. I was alone in a cell that was divided in two by a partition. My bed was placed on a metal platform that went from one wall to the other. During the night I was awakened by a concert of deafening farts. It was the stove setter, the eater of green peas who had gone to bed in the other part of my cell. I started to knock on the partition according to a basic system of taps, used in prisons. The Russian alphabet has thirty-two letters. We divided them into five lines. For example, one tap for the first line, followed by another tap for A, two for B, and so on. The other person answered me, and one thing led to another, and every night we had a short conversation that helped me in my isolation. Of course, we spoke about our fellow inmates: "And so and so, did you meet him? In what camp? In what prison?"
>
> It was then that he told me that in June 1941 he shared a cell with a prisoner whose name I knew. According to my farting stove setter, that man had been treated brutally by the interrogator because he refused to testify against – Jacques Rossi. I must say that after the betrayal of François P. and other "friends" of mine, this news astounded me. When I met the guy, he did not appear friendly, but now I was learning what he had done for me. There was no doubt about it, you met all kinds in the Gulag!

One night, after months of solitude, Jacques's sleep was disrupted by three thugs who came into his cell. The three large men, after having him move from the top bed to the lower bed, ate all his bread. Jacques said nothing. His years in the Gulag had taught him the truth of an old Russian saying: "Don't sue someone richer than you and don't pick a fight with someone stronger than you." During the night, the guard came to get Jacques in his cell, to escort him once again to the interrogator.

I sat facing the commissar, very straight, my thighs tight one against the other and my hands on my knees, according to the rules, on a stool in the farthest corner of the office. The commissar started with a polite statement concerning the fact that I had been locked in solitary confinement in my cell for months, but now I was fortunate to be getting company – none other than the notorious cannibals who didn't hesitate to eat human flesh. After this introduction he started the interrogation. What had been my strategy in sending secret information to the governments of foreign powers, who were my accomplices? When? How? Why? It was a very tough interrogation. When I was with the captain, my cell was searched by officials and a book by Engels was found that the cannibals had managed to hide while they were pretending to shake out my quilted trousers. When I returned, half dead, to my cell I had almost forgotten the presence of my fellow inmates. To my surprise they gave me water and sugar. The strongest of the three told me that they had been promised three ounces of tobacco if they beat up the particularly stubborn inmate. Such selflessness warmed my heart.

This was the way of life, at least in the Gulag. Jacques had been betrayed by close friends and by a compatriot, while a comrade he hardly knew chose to endure a beating rather than denounce him. And strong cannibals refused to beat him up. In any case, Arseniev persisted, and he was not lacking in motivation or imagination. He didn't seem to notice either that Jacques's situation appeared increasingly unusual, even for the Gulag. According to regulations, the inquiry was to be finished within two or three months, at most. Jacques should have been informed that the inquiry concerning his case was finished. He should have appeared before a sham court or should have been informed by the OSO about the length of his sentence. Instead, months passed and nothing happened.

Exasperated by the painful wait, he began to wish that he could go "back home," that is to say, to the labour camp. He had become like the criminal recidivists for whom the Gulag was home, their *home sweet home*, the only fixed point in their lives where they felt themselves really at home. "I had almost the same frame of mind as the criminals. I finally understood that I would never get out of the Gulag, that henceforth, it was going to be my world. I wanted to go 'back home,' to the labour camp. Thus in order to learn what fate had in store for me, I decided to go on a hunger strike."

# 26 The Rebel: The First Hunger Strike

In the beginning the Bolsheviks did not consider hunger strikes to be "counter-revolutionary acts against the Soviet regime." They did not forbid them until the end of the twenties. The Great Purges filled up the prisons and the camps with crowds of Soviet citizens who never had the idea of going on a hunger strike. In the sixties, hunger strikes reappeared with the dissidents. However, for many years they were not punished.

Jacques Rossi

A documentary showed that the handful of French citizens who survived the Gulag all knew how to resist, each one in his own way. Bernard Germe, the soldier in occupied Austria who was arrested by the Soviets while he was visiting his girlfriend, rebelled by refusing to work in the mines. As a result, he spent most of his sentence in the punishment cell or cooler. Liliane, from the French military mission that worked to repatriate prisoners, was arrested at a Red Army post in Germany. She got pregnant, then decided to produce a scar near the baby's eye so that she would recognize her offspring one day and get the child back. Jacques went on hunger strikes, well before the time of the dissidents. His first hunger strike occurred in the detention prison in Norilsk after his short time as a "free" person.

Jacques knew very well what the regulations were concerning hunger strikes because he was informed by a former fellow inmate, a doctor who worked supervising prisons. Every morning the prisoner was given his bread ration. If he refused to eat it within three days, he was taken to the infirmary, where a nurse would put a tube into his mouth or his anus. If he resisted, the guards would be there to force him. The liquid was poured in through a funnel. Typically, the liquid consisted of a cup of milk with butter and sugar. If there was no milk, it was replaced by water. If there was no sugar, it was not replenished, and so on. Arseniev refused to abide by this regulation for Jacques, and had no respect for the legality of Jacques's protest.

> As soon as I declared that I was going on a hunger strike, I was taken to the cooler. There was no light, which surprised me because normally a prisoner had to be visible through the Judas window day and night. During the day, I walked all the time. There was nothing in the cell except a smelly bucket. To rest, I squatted so as not to sit on the humid and stinking ground and so as not to lean against the cold and dripping walls.
> At eleven in the evening, the guard gave me a panel of three boards nailed together, which I placed on the ground. I laid down on it, and the cold penetrated deep into my bones. I heard the sirens of the Norilsk factories, which wailed at seven o'clock, at noon, at seven p.m., and at midnight. Those sirens gave me an indication of the passage of time. In the morning, bread was brought to me and I always refused it.
> Arseniev, however, refused to have me force-fed after three days, in conformity with the regulations. This would risk triggering an investigation if I died, which clearly did not bother him. After eleven days I drafted an official request that I immediately be informed of the verdict, given that a year had passed since my "investigation" concluded. Then Arseniev called me to his office. I was so weak that I couldn't climb the stairs to get there and a guard had to hold me up. Arseniev was crazy with anger because my request was addressed to his superior and not to him. Obviously, it was not his superior but he who had decided not to force-feed me, without the permission of his superior. He had violated the regulations. In the Soviet Union, arbitrariness was inherent in the system. However, a single individual was not allowed to commit arbitrary acts on his own initiative, only with instructions from his superiors. He finally told me not to worry about my request, and he said that the decision would be communicated to me. And so, I had a reason to end my hunger strike without losing face.
> Arseniev realized at that moment that it would not be easy to make me give in. I was returned to the cooler, but very quickly I was taken back to my former cell. I had the impression that I had come home following a lengthy voyage. I remember the very strong mouldy smell when for the first time I unbuttoned my jacket after eleven days and eleven nights in the cooler. Oh! It was so good to be home. At soup time the guard opened the grating. Without saying anything,

the criminal offender in charge of distributing the food poured a lot of thick wheat porridge into my bowl. The guard let him do it. They both knew that I hadn't eaten during my hunger strike and that I must be starving. They took a risk. I still have not forgotten that.

Many long weeks went by before Jacques was sent, this time by plane, to the KGB detention prison in Krasnoyarsk.

They chartered a plane, and I boarded with my hands handcuffed behind my back. I knew the two escort soldiers because I had done their portraits in the labour camp. Several civil servants, an accountant, and a colonel were waiting in the plane. The colonel lit a cigarette and offered me one, which I refused. The position of my arms made me very uncomfortable. It was in the winter and I was wearing quilted clothing. So I complained, and the soldiers explained to me nicely that the prisoner had the right to remain with his hands behind his back for six hours without complaining. I still remember that expression: "You have the right." A *zek* had no rights! Finally, they released the handcuffs behind my back and attached them to my hands in front. The trip was long – it was twelve hundred miles between Norilsk and Krasnoyarsk. When I arrived, a car was waiting for me, not an armoured paddy wagon.

Krasnoyarsk was a large city along the Tran-Siberian railway that Jacques had already been through on the way out. However, this time he was not in a transit prison with its lax regimen.

I left Norilsk and the Arctic where the conditions were notoriously bad. Norilsk was in the provinces, whereas Krasnoyarsk was the capital of an enormous region that spread out over three thousand miles from north to south. Going south was rather reassuring! It was in Krasnoyarsk that I saw a sparrow for the first time in years; a tiny free bird that cared nothing about the KGB came and landed on my hand.

At the Krasnoyarsk detention prison the regime was the same as in other prisons – cells with two metal beds, a regime in which prisoners had to wake up at six, go to bed at midnight, and walk outside between nine and noon. But Jacques was soon disappointed. He realized that the investigation was not closed, although the sentence had probably been decided a long time ago. If they were making him wait, it was probably because they hoped to extort other denunciations from him in return for a shorter sentence. Of course, he had to "cooperate."

First, they called me in, with no brutality, and asked me if I knew Rada Z. Rada, the Polish-Ukrainian with whom my friend Zenon and I had fled Poland and crossed over into Czechoslovakia some twenty years earlier. I thought for a minute. If I said that I did not know her, and they had proof that I did, then they would suspect I had reasons to hide this connection, and they would persist. So I said that I met her in the underground communist movement in Poland in the twenties, but had not seen her since. I was called in several times and asked the same question. And every time I gave the same answer.

Several weeks later they asked me a different question:

"Do you know Tou Tian-cheng?"

Tou Tian-cheng was a good friend of mine. When I arrived at the Norilsk camp in 1939 he had already been there for two years. He was political commissar in the famous army of General Ma in the twenties in China. At that time in the Chinese civil war, several armies were fighting against one another, and he was stationed in the northwest region of China. The ups and downs of the conflict forced him and his companions to seek refuge in the Soviet Union. There they were imprisoned and forced to work cutting timber. Every now and then, prisoners would be arrested for alleged political crimes. Thus Tou Tian-cheng became a political prisoner. At that time, his Russian was worse than my Chinese, but I helped him to understand or be understood. In time we became friends. He was well educated and knew Chinese literature. Then during my detention in Norilsk, Tou Tian-cheng was released. He was still a Chinese national and he wanted to go back to his country, which was then ruled by Chiang Kai-shek.

I knew his story. I had advised him to communicate with his brother, who lived in Manchuria, by sending him a postcard. That way, the censors would know he had nothing to hide. By chance I remembered the name of the street in Moscow where the Chinese Embassy was located, and I gave him the address. The card did not escape notice. Soviet authorities pretended that the message was coded and that Tou Tian-cheng was trying to get in contact with the Chinese secret police. At the time that I was transferred to the detention prison at Krasnoyarsk, Tou Tian-cheng lived there as a free man. The authorities had now organized a confrontation between him and me. They were trying to persuade him not to leave for China and that I was a dreadful spy, already sentenced to twenty-five years, although I did not know it yet. Clearly, it was very unfortunate for anyone to have me as an acquaintance.

The terms of this confrontation were also scripted according to an inescapable ritual. The individuals involved in the confrontation were informed that they could be sentenced to two years if they refused to testify or if they gave false testimony. Even if they didn't speak Russian, they could only use the language of the investigation or a language understood by the interpreter. First, the accused was led into a room and seated with his back to the door. Then the witness who was supposed to make the accusation was brought in and seated as far as possible from the accused. The accused could not look left or right, he had to keep his head straight, his knees one against the other, and his hands on his knees. If the witness was also a prisoner, he had to obey the same rules.

The confrontation was very difficult for both of us. I was not happy to see Tou Tian-cheng morally crushed. He looked like a beaten dog. He seemed humble, almost servile, his hands on his knees, in compliance with instructions. The Soviets were trying to prove that he never had a brother and that the name on the postcard was actually a code. I stuck to the truth, that is, that I had advised him to write to his brother. Tou's position was ambiguous. On the one hand, he admitted that he had a brother and that he had written to him. On the other hand, he said that he had no desire to visit him. He had met and married a Soviet-Chinese woman, and he wanted to stay in the Soviet Union and start a family. He gave the impression that I had forced him to go and see his brother. For Soviet authorities, the brother's name could only be a code for the Chinese secret police. I had the impression that he had been "worked over" by the authorities, who hated having foreigners in their country – people who might, at any time, have legal cause to contact their consulates. They wanted him to give up his Chinese citizenship. An encounter with a spy would condemn him to a long sentence and only make his situation worse. The meeting lasted only ten minutes. I never saw him again and I don't know what became of him.

At Krasnoyarsk, Jacques was subjected to two commissar-interrogators. The old lieutenant colonel Ostrologov spoke Russian incorrectly. He had a poor education but the political enthusiasm of the early Bolsheviks. Jacques thought that he must have participated in the Civil War of 1918–21. During the interrogation, this commissar stated: "When I see a postcard being sent to China, it interests me because I am in charge of security."

The other interrogator, Captain Denissenko, most certainly had a "certificate" (the Russian equivalent of a high school diploma). I could feel that in our conversations. For they were conversations, not threats, as in what I experienced with Arseniev. After a while, he realized that I wasn't going to make any grand denunciations concerning Rada. I hadn't seen her in decades and she may have even died. As for the Tou Tian-cheng affair, nothing extraordinary had come out of it either. So I said to him, as I said to Arseniev: "This situation I'm in is completely illegal. You have dragged me from prison to prison and I still don't know whether I've been sentenced or not."

He started to leaf through my file and took out a page. He spoke with a neutral but kind tone, and said to me in a detached way:

"Actually, you have been sentenced to twenty-five years for spying for France, Great Britain, and the United States." (In 1939, I was accused of spying for France and for Poland, which had since become communist and an ally). "By 1973, you will have completed your sentence."

The sentence had officially started on an earlier date, some eighteen months prior, as it was already the end of 1950. It had been declared "in absentia" based on a decision of the OSO. The document specifying the verdict had been sent not to the accused but to the prison director: "Inform prisoner so and so that he has been sentenced to twenty-five years without parole for spying for France, Great Britain, and the United States." Twenty-five years! I must say that I was devastated. First, it was eight years. Then "new rules" were applied. Then it was release without the right to live beyond the barbed wire. And now I had twenty-five years! A kind of interminable detention. If you are in hell, you think you know how deep it is. Suddenly you are made to see that there is no bottom.

Jacques, however, was not one to be discouraged.

I said to myself, once again, that I am a Frenchman and will never allow myself to be crushed. I realized then that when I was serving my Marxist-Leninist ideals, I was really only advancing Russian imperialism. I have many dear friends who are Russian. I was (and remain) an internationalist who collaborated at the time in order to defeat global capitalism. For me, a passport was a document of no importance. Nonetheless, I was French, and I felt French in my bones. I would have done anything to save that Frenchman [François P.], and my comrades understood that. How many times did I hear them say: "We trust you because you are not a product of the Soviet system."

For me, this failure to create a "New Man," as the Soviets conceived him, is illustrated perfectly by the terrible events at Katyn. Fifteen thousand Polish officers and others fleeing Hitler's army surrendered to the Soviets, and they were assassinated on Stalin's orders. Poland was divided between the German Nazis and the Russian communists. In my *Gulag Handbook*, I mentioned Stalin's report to Beria where he asserted that the prisoners simply wanted to be freed, as if this were a crime. Therefore, they had to be massacred – all of them. Stalin signed the report with his important signature. For a long time, it was the Germans who were held responsible for that terrible massacre.

Shortly after Denissenko "confided" in him concerning his fate, Jacques was once again transferred to another prison. He was sent to the big Irkutsk prison several thousand miles to the east where he would spend several weeks without interrogation. That did not surprise him since he knew that he had already been sentenced long before and for a long time.

Irkutsk is a city made of wood that I only know in photos. When you take the train to Vladivostok you go around the southern part of Lake Baikal, which is said to be incredibly beautiful. But I was not lucky enough to observe that beauty. Although I was not far away, I was quickly sent to the high-security prison in Alexandrovsk some forty-five miles north of Irkutsk.

Around 1951, at the time Jacques was transferred to the high-security prison in Alexandrovsk, he was about forty-two years old. He had already been imprisoned for fourteen years in the Archipelago, where he came to know many of its islands and detours, pretrial prisons, transit camps, and the different parts of the forced labour camps. He was not without challenges in this concentration camp world. He insists on his disillusion concerning the communist ideal. The betrayal of some of his comrades was also a challenge, he adds. However, these were among the least of his misfortunes. Ahead of him lay the spectre of twenty-three more years of additional detention. How could he be certain that he would not be given additional sentences, if he managed to survive this one?

In the meantime, history continued to march on. Stalin died within two years. Beria's execution would come before the Twentieth Party Congress. And later: the collapse of an empire. There would be one prison after the other, one hunger strike after the other. But the day would come when millions of destinies would once again change.

# 27  In the Central Prison of Alexandrovsk

As the documents recently brought to light from the Gulag archives show, the beginning of the fifties was marked by both the peak of the concentration camp system and by an unprecedented crisis in the system. There had never been so many inmates in the labor camps and special settlers in the "colonies."

Nicolas Werth

Jacques officially started serving his second sentence around 1951, in the high-security prison of Alexandrovsk. He was supposed to remain until 1974. His personal belongings had followed him from the pretrial prison of Norilsk via that of Krasnoyarsk. In his meagre luggage there were a number of sketches and drawings that he had done in the labour camp, which he managed to save from the clutches of prison officials.

> In the camp I drew as soon as I could. I did portraits and many caricatures, or rather what I called "character drawings" where I slightly accentuated a character. I usually used the wrapping paper of cement bags with which I made small notebooks. I used them as sketch notebooks. We were searched regularly and my notebooks were confiscated. But I managed to hide and hold onto a few of them. I found several of these drawings when I was in Alexandrovsk. After Stalin's death, I was much freer to make new drawings.
> 
> Suddenly, we were permitted to have paper and pencils and we could even order paint and brushes for watercolours. In the high-security prison, I did portraits of my comrades in the cell. They had very different ethnic backgrounds, but they all possessed the same melancholic resignation that was typical of prisoners. When I left Alexandrovsk I had a good collection, which was partially stolen during one of our transfers. In the transit prisons, there was a kind

of consignment system. You left your belongings there when you arrived and you received a receipt in exchange. But it was poorly supervised. Because of my box of drawings, my bag appeared larger than the others. A thief must have wanted to take things from it. He must have been disappointed, and he probably threw the box away. Or perhaps my portraits were cut into small pieces to make playing cards. There only remained some small drawings that followed me afterwards to Vladimir and then to Bykovo.

The central prison of Alexandrovsk, a former distillery during the time of Catherine the Great, was situated in the village of Alexandrovsk near Lake Baikal. It was an old tsarist prison built of bricks with walls that were six feet wide. It was used at that time as a stopping place for prisoners who were being taken to Sakhalin Island, and who already back then sang the Russian prisoners' chant: "In the central prison of Alexandrovsk, a prisoner hung himself …"

In the Russian and Soviet tradition, prisons were considered worse than labour camps, given their isolation. In prisons you could not see the sky. I actually preferred prisons to camps, because, first of all, there was no forced labour, although that has since changed, and, second, in prison you could read. At Alexandrovsk, there were books. Of course, it was unreadable socialist realist literature, but there were also books published in the twenties or thirties that were interesting. Among them, I remember the memoirs of Felix Dzerzhinsky, a prisoner under the tsars in the same prison. In Alexandrovsk, you could walk around freely in your own cell. Some prisoners gave classes in Marxism-Leninism. But it was forbidden for one to know who was in the neighbouring cell. Shortly after Stalin's death we could even subscribe to a newspaper. Until then we could only read the local rag, but it was by reading the paper that we confirmed what we already knew. Yes, there was a war in Korea.

Officially, there was no war in Korea. The Soviet press did not mention it. This was another state secret, although the prisoners of Alexandrovsk were better informed than average Soviet citizens. Why? Because one of the newly arrived inmates had worked on the railways.

He was an old white-bearded man who must have been in his fifties or sixties. In order to get to our prison he must have been in many transit prisons, made a long voyage, and met other prisoners who were former railway men. Now, railway men were like a race apart, with exceptional solidarity. From his railway comrades that he had met in the convoys, our companion had learned that strange freight was being sent to the east. It was probably military freight. The material was covered with tarpaulins and guarded by young men in civilian clothing who were in small watchtowers on small platforms on the cattle cars. The perceptive employees of the railroads had deduced that they were military units being sent to the east, to Korea. So thanks to our new companion at Alexandrovsk, we learned what was really happening.

In the first months following his arrival at the central prison of Alexandrovsk, a wonderful misunderstanding resulted in Jacques's being placed in the same cell as a Japanese prisoner. The authorities wanted to punish him by distancing Jacques from Soviet inmates, but instead they put him into a much more cultured world. In any case, that is how he viewed it at the time.

I had absolutely no idea which cell I was being sent to. With my escort guard I found myself in front of a grey door, like the others all along the corridor. I remember that the door had the number "48" painted in black. The guard of the corridor looked at the document that the other guard displayed for him with indifference. He opened the enormous padlocks one after the other, put a big key in the lock, turned it twice, pulled the door open, and made me enter the cell, closing the door immediately behind me.

I was pushed into a cell that was very big and in which silence reigned. I saw about thirty faces that were turned towards me all at once. Asians. Most of them were sitting cross-legged on their beds, all of them dressed like me in awful striped pajamas, all of them as skinny as I was, having been served only prison rations for a long time. Something new and strange struck me immediately about these men: the dignity in their expressions. There was no trace of that starved jackal expression so common among the dying starving men of the Gulag. They were Japanese. These officers of the Imperial army were Soviet prisoners of war. When I saw these prisoners, I had the impression of a breath of fresh air and of a calm and serene sunrise. I wrote about that in a story. They were entirely different from the pure and authentic Russian communists whom I had believed in, yet who had subjected me to all these hardships.

Jacques learned he had been placed with Japanese POWs by the camp racists, in their view to humiliate and to punish him. The POWs' courtesy, integrity, and cleanliness was markedly different from "the filthy dirt" of the camps and the injustice, provocations, arrogance, and perversion that governed life in the prison Archipelago. "Fortunately, the Soviets had decided not to mix the Japanese with other Gulag inmates. This saved them from having their souls corrupted, which was very difficult to escape in that Gulag universe. What saved me during that period between 1949 and 1956 was that I met up again by chance with my Japanese companions during transfers from one prison to another."

Japanese was one language that Jacques did not speak. But he could have discussions in English with Prince Fumitaka Konoe, son of the ex-prime minister. Above all, among all the Japanese in that cell, he met Misao Naito, who remains to this day more than just a friend, but truly a chosen brother.[1] With Misao, Jacques sometimes spoke Russian, sometimes Chinese, and sometimes English. Neither one of them imagined that a half-century later, in 2000, Misao would publish under the pen name Gohsuke Uchimura a book with the evocative title "The Russian Revolution Which Has Gone through My Body," a book inspired by discussions he had with Jacques. The author wrote: "In this book, like a powerful undercurrent, the reader will discover a dialogue between Jacques Rossi and Gohsuke Uchimura during five or six years in the Gulag. It also reveals the exchange between two cultures, French and Japanese in the twentieth century, with Russia as an intermediary. I hope that in the future some people will be able to follow the flow of this undercurrent."[2]

This was a time when German and Japanese inmates had permission to correspond with their families abroad. Soviet diplomacy was trying to stop West Germany and Japan from getting closer to the West. Misao shared with Jacques the letters from his wife Hamako. They contained news from the free world, and they reflected the warmth of Misao's family. Slowly, despite the constraints of censorship, Hamako slipped messages for her husband's friend into the letters. Jacques, who had for so many years lost any contact with the world of his youth, saw a door opening and "fresh air coming from the free world blew through the walls of the prison." It was paradoxical that through the Japanese and Misao, in particular, he grew closer to his homeland. What separated him from France was less the distance of seventy-five hundred miles than the customs of the Archipelago. Since their time in the camps, Misao and his family have become Jacques's family. Manami and Rurika, Misao's daughters, call him "Uncle Jacques," and since meeting Jacques in 1982, I have heard him speak of Misao as his Japanese brother.

However, the fact that he was made to frequently change cells often deprived Jacques of this exceptional company. The lack of privacy in the other cells with thirty to forty people was unbearable.

Never alone, not even in the latrines. You grew to hate even inoffensive men, after seeing them hold their spoon in the same way when the soup was delivered or always wiping themselves in the same way with that infamous toilet paper that I described in *The Gulag Handbook*. In fact, in the high-security prisons, at the entrance to the toilets, the guard gave each prisoner a sheet of coarse wrapping paper, three-and-a-quarter by three-and-a-quarter inches. During the Great Purges of '37 the guards took back all the sheets at the exit of the toilets, wearing rubber gloves. They tossed the used pieces on one side of the door and the unused ones on another side. This way the inmates could not keep the paper and use it for a clandestine counter-revolutionary project.

In the same way, hearing my fellow inmates singing for hours while they were thinking between two chess game moves drove me crazy. Then there were fights, which broke out over nothing – over soap, for example. The Russians could not accept the fact that some washed their own bowls with soap. Usually you washed it with hot water. But we didn't have hot water. Most of the non-Russians, the Baltic prisoners, the Germans and me, those of us who came from the West, we washed our dishes with soap and rinsed them. Certain Russians couldn't stand that.

Then there was the window. Should it be left opened or closed? It was a dilemma. There were two kinds of prisoners – those who wanted to die from the cold and those who wanted to die from asphyxiation. There were the "pro-window" inmates who wanted to open the window and the "anti-window" inmates who wanted to keep it closed. Most of the Russians were for closing the window. Like most of the foreign inmates, I was one hundred percent in favour of the open window. Even more so because some prisoners smoked, which made the air impossible to breathe. Officially, tobacco was part of the rations, but in reality, it was never distributed. In the labour camps it was used to encourage productivity. In prison, it simply disappeared after the sinister year of 1937. But the prisoners who received money orders could buy some tobacco.

Nevertheless, Jacques described a certain intellectual atmosphere in the Alexandrovsk cells.

You met really interesting people there. I remember a German diplomat, the Ukrainian patriots who fought in the Ukrainian Liberation Army not only against the Soviets but also against the Germans and the Poles, a Cossack lieutenant who told wonderful stories about horses, and a metallurgist who offered genuine instruction on various ways of making steel. There was also a kind of druid, bald with a long beard. He came from an old family of millers in the south of Ukraine and had been a Soviet civil servant who oversaw the cultivation and sale of wheat. He had served the regime, yet he had been sentenced to twenty-five years. He could talk about wheat the ways that others spoke about the adventures of Marco Polo. In certain ways, as inmates, we were freer and more eclectic in our conversations than the prison officials. They included a small group of lieutenants, captains with an operative, a commander, and a major who only met to spy on each other and get drunk on vodka. They had to be careful to ensure each statement they uttered was in conformity with what was in that day's *Pravda*, while hoping the newspaper would not change its message the next day.

The regulations concerning correspondence and censorship were extremely detailed. In letters that were sent to inmates, anything that was considered "unnecessary" was crossed out with India ink by the censor and then stamped "approved." But the mail sent out by the inmates had no markings from the censors. If the censor detected the smallest "non-essential" detail, he would confiscate the letter without informing the inmate. The mail sent by penitentiary institutions did not have the stamp of the institution and, therefore, could not be identified. An ordinary criminal offender who once worked as a censor told Jacques about the instructions he received. The goal was to make sure that inmates would not develop emotions that would harm their productivity. For example, in letters coming from the outside, all information concerning the high cost of living, catastrophes, and other bad events was deleted or crossed out.[3]

After the Japanese and the Germans, the right of correspondence was extended to include other foreign citizens. It did not apply to Jacques, who was not considered a foreigner by Soviet authorities. Since he had no family in the Soviet Union for all those years he never could receive or send mail. In the high-security prisons, inmates had to follow a complex series of rules in order to read their mail. They were taken from their group cells and locked in individual cells. Although Jacques did not receive any mail, he was nevertheless taken secretly with his comrades to the isolation cells. In *Fragments of Lives*, he described with humour how this mail ritual enabled the security officer to have a personal meeting with each prisoner. It happened that on one of these occasions the security officer asked Jacques to describe the Louvre statue of the Pompeii couple who were surprised while making love by the eruption of the volcano. At the end of the story, he described the security officer's confused reaction when a guard arrived unexpectedly. In the Gulag, even a man as powerful as a security officer was afraid of being caught off-guard by a subordinate, in a moment of erotic-aesthetic curiosity.

On 5 March 1953 Joseph Vissarionovitch Dzhugashvili, also known as Stalin, died in the Kremlin of a cerebral hemorrhage. Since the twenties, this God had been showered with different titles – official and unofficial – quoted hundreds of times on every radio program, in every newspaper, and in scores of languages. Now the immortal, the "genius Stalin," "the father of us all," "the wise Leader," "the humane, good Stalin," "the Lenin of today," "the best friend," depending on the occasion, of gunners, minors, children, collective farmers, pilots, tank drivers, and oppressed peoples around the world, had taken his last breath. In addition, his dark double "the boot polisher," the "beast," "the godfather," "the black ass," "the mustached devil" died at the same time. That very day, in the central prison of Alexandrovsk, Jacques was in the cooler, "arbitrarily," he said. "I don't even remember why I was there."

When he returned to his regular cell five days later, he heard the news from his three German-Austrian fellow inmates who had the right to read newspapers. Although the news was shocking, nothing was made of it. It had no immediate impact on the bureaucratic routine in the prison. Stalin's death? A day like every other in the Gulag. Followed by other similar days. Jacques tried to remember who was the guard on duty in the cooler on 5 March, but he could not recall any change in the guard's behaviour.

> My German-Austrian fellow inmates and I were surprised. We said, "The machine is running well! The big chief dies and not a grain of sand in the mechanism." Later, when I was in communist Poland, I heard friends tell me that in the Polish political prisons on the day of Stalin's death and in the days following, they had to stand at attention for hours without the slightest idea of why. No news filtered into those prisons at all. "Our place" was nothing like that. But slowly and, nonetheless, rather rapidly, especially after Beria's arrest, prison discipline became more relaxed. For example, we

started to talk out loud in the cell. We dared to go to the window, climb up to it, and look out at the courtyard, at our fellow inmates taking their walk. It was like the capitalist prisons! What freedom! I must say, though, that the noise bothered me after so many years of prison silence.

Thus the early beginnings of liberation had started with commotion, although we would hesitate to call this the resumption of free speech. Jacques experienced this chatter of freedom with regret, as just another nuisance. It appears that changes to the prison order initially struck him as odd, as if something were missing. Amidst that confused rumour which rose from the cells and disturbed his ascetic interior, was Jacques not aware that perhaps he had reached the depths of hell? Of his own hell. And that he was about to start the climb up out of it.

## 28 The Beginning of the End

> There is no nation in the world that is not represented in the Gulag.
>
> Gulag saying

Stalin was dead. And for a short time one man occupied the scene. It was the man who since the Great Purges had been referred to in official propaganda as simply "L.P. Beria, fellow soldier and Stalin's personal friend."

At the end of the summer of 1938, Beria was appointed assistant to Yezhov, chief of the People's Commissariat for Internal Affairs (NKVD). He succeeded Yezhov following the former chief's arrest, and became commissar in December of that same year. Beria directed the NKVD and eventually led the entire state security apparatus. He used torture, police provocation, and the fabrication of evidence to generate false accusations no less methodically than his predecessor. However, following the death of Stalin in March 1953, Beria's power was short lived. As early as 4 April, a high-level communiqué from the Interior Ministry declared that the Doctors' Plot, also known as the plot of the "White Shirts," represented a provocation designed by the former Minister of State Security. This "plot" was made public on 13 January 1953 while Stalin was still alive. The explosive memo was followed by the amnesty of a million prisoners. This relaxation of terror, however, was not enough to save Beria, despite the fact that he was greatly feared by other members of Stalin's entourage. The death of Stalin did not immediately affect "political" prisoners, those condemned for various so-called counter-revolutionary activities. These political prisoners were excluded from the amnesty, but the large amnesty of criminal offenders in March 1953 represented an early sign of another era.

For Jacques, that era was marked by at least one fundamental change. He could now occasionally get pencils and even ink while in detention. It was then that he started to take notes and compose rough drafts of what would one day become his celebrated *Gulag Handbook*.

> Shortly before Stalin's death we were given the necessary material to make lists of the inmates in each cell and to verify whether they corresponded to the lists of the administration. We were lent precious pens, some inkwells with the famous purple ink, and pieces of paper the size of postcards. After the death of Stalin, the noose was loosened a little: we could then write to whomever we wished. I wrote on little scraps of paper and I managed to keep them hidden. I am not bragging, but I was very good at hiding them during searches in all the most intimate parts of my body. I will not reveal my strategies, which could be used against other potential inmates using the same strategies as I. Sadly, prison life has not ended simply because I left the Gulag! I even managed to conceal those tiny notes when I was searched in Moscow at the police station after I left the French embassy.

Thus Jacques the Frenchman very quickly took advantage of the post-Stalin era. Despite his instincts and his experience of the Soviet system, he did not lose sight of the West. The new KGB officer, a certain Tshuva, seemed more good-natured than his predecessor. Each month every inmate individually met this officer for the security search and the distribution of mail. Of course, Jacques did not receive any mail, for the reasons we have mentioned. But this time he was gutsy and he asked if he could have permission to write to his family – in Italy. Why Italy? Because he remembered the address of friends that he said were his family – parents, children, brothers, and sisters. His other family members didn't count. Tshuva did not seem surprised that Jacques remembered an Italian address more easily than a French one. He was interested in Europe, and he knew that people could move around easily there without bureaucratic obstacles. "It was the first time that an inmate had asked him permission to send mail abroad. He knew that the Japanese and the Germans had permission to use Red Cross postcards. This practice had become institutionalized as a result of the Politburo's calculations. Since some foreigners could write, why couldn't others? So I left my letter with him, as the censorship regulations required." After several weeks, Jacques was called to commander Tshuva's office. Tshuva had him read the official instructions that had come directly from Moscow. It read, "Please inform the inmate that under no condition can he send mail abroad because he is a citizen of the Soviet Union."

I was completely astonished, I must say. I never asked for Soviet citizenship. Not that I wouldn't have done it in the thirties when I was a minor agent working for the Comintern. If I had been asked I would have obeyed. The only problem was that I had never been asked. At that time, it was not necessary for me. During my stays in the Soviet Union, I was always lodged in a dacha of the security police, outside of civilian police jurisdiction. Each time I was given a document certifying that I could come and go freely. This document was my unique ID during my stays in the USSR between two missions abroad. The question of eventual Soviet citizenship was never raised. Suddenly, after more than thirteen years in the Gulag – where all I did was dream about returning to my own country, France – I was now calmly informed that I was really and truly a Soviet citizen! I lost all self-control. I was beside myself. I started to scream! "I have no need for your shitty Soviet citizenship! You can stick it up your a—!"

Strangely, commander Tshuva remained calm. He had me escorted back to the isolation cell where I was before going to his office. And all along the hallway I continued to shout, "Your shitty Soviet citizenship. I don't give a damn about it!"

The strangest thing about this story is that after this frenzy and the noisy anti-Soviet clamour that was heard in all the cells, Jacques, the same person who had been punished for offences a thousand times less serious than this one, was not even reprimanded. "Remember that this was after the death of Stalin ... The KGB feared that the Politburo would compel them to ease the pressure. Tshuva was a bit corpulent and a good guy. He was approaching the end of his career."

Meanwhile, history was being made. One faction of Stalin's old entourage viewed Beria as its most dangerous competitor because he was the most powerful. They managed to arrest him and have him imprisoned in July 1953. He was then executed, but only in December would the public be informed of the fictitious secret trial. This trial had supposedly revealed that Beria was guilty of violations of socialist legality. Despite this new political execution, as François Furet explained, "The logic of de-Stalinization, however, when combined with that of the succession, propelled them forward ... It was inevitable that the critique of Stalin, implicit in the measures of March and April, would be taken up, like an anxious interrogation, by the hundreds of thousands of prisoners released from the Gulag that summer. The rehabilitation of the 'White Shirts' automatically brought calls for the rehabilitation of the countless former enemies of the people who had been arbitrarily condemned or summarily executed. Having glimpsed freedom, how could the millions of *zeks* languishing in labor camps have remained there passively?"[1]

At that time, an ex-lieutenant of the Red Army arrived at the Alexandrovsk prison. He had been a member of the strike committee at Norilsk. "Some uprisings had started after the so-called Beria or Voroshilov amnesty, an amnesty that did not apply to political prisoners or serious criminal recidivists. According to this inmate, the uprising at Norilsk was triggered by a guard who shot his gun inside the prison. That was against the rules. I could only listen to this man with respect, for he had the courage to rebel. I was only an indirect witness to these problems, which existed before a certain relaxation of the system." In his own way, though, Jacques continued the spirit of the uprisings. For the second time during his stay in the Gulag, he began a hunger strike. "Why? To protest the Soviet citizenship that they wanted to stick on me. And then to ask to be freed because my arrest was phony. I had always proclaimed my innocence. And now Beria was being recognized as a bandit, the same man who was one of the main masterminds behind those false arrests. So I undertook a hunger strike to denounce one of Beria's extortions, the one against me, one person among millions of others."

This time, unlike during his first hunger strike, he was force-fed after the third day, according to regulations. "Of course, the prisoner could hold his jaws tightly together to keep the liquid from being swallowed. In that case, they used a very simple technique. They separated the jaws with a hard object that was very painful. However, if the prisoner accepted the tube without resisting and especially if he held the tube between moistened lips so no air passed through, he suffered a bit less." The director of the prison reacted very quickly this time. He called the hunger striker to his office and tried to persuade him to stop the hunger strike that posed a danger to his health. After so many years of detention, Jacques was certainly not in good physical shape! But things were now about to change. Jacques persisted in submitting his request. He no longer knew whether it was the twentieth or the thirtieth time. In the course of his sixteen years in the Gulag, he had written many times requesting a review of his trial, which had been a formality, and the cancelation of the two unfounded accusations against him.

> I understood that Beria's arrest was just the settling of scores between bandits. The chief bandit had died, and his associates wanted to take his place. The other bandits of the Politburo were afraid of [Beria]

and decided to get rid of him. I had sufficient experience with the world of crooks and understood the system. But the director of the prison was not a bad guy. "Things are going to change," he would say. Of course, if he had instructions to cut off my head, he would have done it, to demonstrate his good discipline. But he would not have done it on his own. He still had an ounce of humanity, which made him want to convince me to stop my hunger strike. His attempt was disinterested. He was protected. If I died, he would have had to draft the death certificate: the inmate Jacques Robertovitch Rossi died as a result of his own behaviour.

The meeting went on and on for hours. The director agreed to communicate Jacques's request. Then he became impatient and pretended he had to leave. It was after six o'clock in the evening. His family was waiting for him.

It was his way of saying, "I am not going to spend all my time trying to convince you that this is for your own good!" So before he left I made an offer to him.
 "You know that I am on this hunger strike in order to get results, not to die. The only thing that I ask of you is that I be allowed to swallow on my own the ration that they force down my throat with a funnel and a tube. That tube forced down my throat is pure anguish."
 The director thought for a moment and then he made up his mind and called in the chief guard. "Let this prisoner eat the daily ration by himself. He has already been on hunger strikes for political reasons. This is a special case."

And so for several weeks, the prescribed mixture of milk, butter, and sugar (when there was sugar) was served to the prisoner not once but twice a day. And the bowl of food improved, for it was prepared by a member of the staff who wanted to show his solidarity. In spite of his weakened state, Jacques did not give up. He refused to give in, even the night that one of the guards entered secretly and offered him a Siberian specialty, one of those little cabbage pies called *pirozhki* that his wife had made herself.

I was really torn because on the one hand this gesture touched me greatly. This man was taking a serious personal risk, if he had been discovered by the chief guard. But if, on the other hand, it was a kind of provocation, then this would have jeopardized my hunger strike, and I would also end up in the cooler. So I refused to eat the pies. But it cost me dearly. I still regret it when I think of how I must have offended him. Imagine someone who exposes himself to that degree, who whole-heartedly brings you a gift, but you refuse. No, I am not proud of myself when I think about it. But reasonably, what else could I have done?

This was not the first time that Jacques told the story to a friend. The intensity of his regret seems obsessive. He feels bad that he hurt a man of good will who trusted him. The encounter reveals what sometimes brightened the universe of detention – this element of human tenderness that occasionally broke through the darkness of barbarity. It appeared more easily now because the all-powerful system had begun to split up, questioning, as François Furet states, its "two basic passions: fear and faith." Jacques, like so many others, had become a victim of these two passions. Just as the totalitarian system had brought out the worst in people, so the collapse of the system enabled the best in people to find expression. In addition to Tshuva's attitude, the decision of the director of the Alexandrovsk prison, and the gesture of the Siberian guard, there was the initiative of the chief prison doctor.

> A grey-haired doctor who was about fifty came to give me some information – although prisoners had no right to information – about the fact that the Alexandrovsk prison was about to be evacuated. Hydraulic work that was going to be done to build a dam on Lake Baïkal was expected to result in flooding over the entire region. He added that the resulting transfer would be risky for me if I continued my hunger strike because I was in a very weakened state. And then he mentioned that my cause, that is to say, my request, was progressing well, so there was no reason for me to stubbornly continue my fasting.

Jacques gave in to the chief doctor's arguments. In any case, he did not want to die. He simply wanted to give weight to his legitimate request. He started to eat again and spent some time in the hospital, but he underscored that his reasons were not related to his health and the result of his hunger strike. "You can imagine my surprise when, after these events, the guard who came to take me back to my cell took me instead to the cell that I would have most preferred in the Alexandrovsk prison. It was the Japanese cell. I had not been there for a long time. There I found my friends and Misao. Stalin was truly dead." His Japanese friends welcomed him respectfully. They tried to console him: "You see, *Dzhak-san* [*djak*, meaning "Jacques," which they couldn't pronounce, followed by *san*, which is a suffix showing politeness, like "mister" or "madam"), the proof that they do not consider you a Soviet citizen is that they put you in the cell for foreigners!"

We stayed at Alexandrovsk prison for several more months. But we knew that cells were being emptied little by little. Small groups of prisoners were leaving. Mine was one of the last cells to be emptied. We left for the transit prison in Irkutsk. Years later, I learned that the dam project had been abandoned. The prison building remained and was converted into a psychiatric hospital.

His return voyage westward had begun. Once again Jacques passed through several transit prisons and visited a good many of those he had already seen in 1939: Irkutsk, Krasnoyarsk, Novosibirsk, where he met a group of young criminal offenders whose arms had been tattooed with the date 1939. It was their date of birth, as well as the date of Jacques's last visit there. Plus Smirnov, Ekaterinburg, Kirov, and still other prisons that he didn't know.

I have to admit that the atmosphere had changed since 1939. I have already told this story from one of these transit prisons. I was being placed in the middle of a group of criminal offenders, and to my surprise, before taking me to the cell, the guard asked me whether I agreed to be placed among "those people." Obviously, I was returning to the civilized world.

I remember that during the entire trip back I was with foreigners most of the time, Japanese, but also Austrians and Germans who had been arrested by the Soviets during the war. By the way, I do not know whether I have sufficiently underscored the number and the diversity of the foreigners, representing all nationalities with no exception. I met Yugoslavs, Albanians, Englishmen, Austrians, Greeks, Chinese, Koreans, and of course Japanese. I even met a Black American who was a communist and had come to find work and dignity in the Soviet paradise. As a black person – there were practically none in the Soviet Union – he had had the bad luck of being promoted to the position of advisor to the mayor of Moscow. When the mayor was arrested, this man was part of the "tail," that is to say, one of the associates who was arrested for having ties to the boss. That was how he found himself amid the ice of the Archipelago.

Let's return to my fellow inmates who were with me travelling back to the west. These men treated me with a certain condescension, for I was an old communist imprisoned before the war. They were sure that, according to Soviet logic, they would be freed before I was.

The day when, for purely administrative and technical reasons, I had to leave and we were separated, they came to shake my hand with a kind of joy. I could read their thoughts in their eyes – "Good. He's going to serve the rest of his twenty-five years and we will be free!" There was even one inmate who gave me some underwear, a sweater, and other personal things that he thought he would no longer need. Then several weeks later, I was placed in the same prison, in the same cell, with the same inmates. Oh, you should have seen their faces when they saw me arrive!

Jacques laughs, savouring that humorous moment in his story. The trains continued to whistle and there was a succession of prisons and railway cars. The Arctic and Siberia became more distant. The prisoners were getting closer to the Soviet capital. In 1939 the young man who had left Moscow in the Stolypin railway car was not even thirty. Now, at the end of 1955, he was forty-six. His youth had been stolen, as he exhausted himself in forced labour, camp punishment cells, transit prisons, high-security prisons, and the terrible Siberian labour camps.

His fundamental faith in the mirage of social justice had faded after years of deceptions, frustrations, cynicism, and bureaucratic cruelty, and long and useless hunger strikes. More than ever, though, he had remained Jacques the Frenchman. In order to be able to go home, to testify about his experiences that were still not entirely behind him, he was ready to continue fighting. He would fight with all the energy that he had used to survive that frozen earth, that barren Arctic ground where he had sworn he would never be buried. He would once again need that incredible energy that neither his hunger strikes nor the abuses he endured had taken away from him.

# 29 "I *Choose* Samarkand"

On the night of 24–25 February 1956, Nikita Khrushchev gave a reading of his report on Stalin's crimes. That document was transmitted to the secretaries of the foreign delegations participating in the Twentieth Congress ... Thorez and the French Communist Party stuck to the phrase "report attributed to comrade Khrushchev" and defended Stalin's "oeuvre." The report was nonetheless authenticated indirectly by the minutes of the Twentieth Congress itself, which referred to the famous secret meeting of the famous night in February.

François Furet, *The Passing of an Illusion*

According to Nicolas Werth: "In his 'Secret Speech' to the Soviet delegates at the Twentieth Party Congress on 24 February 1956, Khrushchev was extremely selective in his condemnation of Stalinism and did not call into question any of the major decisions taken by the Party since 1917."[1] When the bomb of the Twentieth Party Congress dropped, Jacques was in Vladimir, one hundred fifty-five miles from Moscow in a high-security prison that had formerly been a tsarist prison. It had been enlarged by Soviet authorities in 1937 and then again in 1948. From Alexandrovsk to Vladimir, Jacques travelled a distance of forty-four hundred miles. In the fifties, the Russian trains travelled about six hundred miles in twenty-four hours. Of course, in the Vladimir prison, the large windows of the old building had been partly bricked up and equipped with "muzzles" that kept the prisoners from being able to look out. But there was the radio. Retransmissions of news from Moscow could be heard in the cells. Even if the prisoners did not know all the details of the secret speech, they knew the general content because of radio commentary concerning the minutes of the Congress. Jacques was less surprised by the extraordinary news than the other prisoners. He had waited for this for almost twenty years.

The timid de-Stalinization that had begun after the death of the despot became more official with the Twentieth Party Congress. Khrushchev denounced Stalin's "cult of personality," as well as some of Stalin's crimes and what made them possible – widespread terror and mass arrests by the security police. For Khrushchev, who renounced Stalinist terror but not Soviet dogma, the solution lay in the return to Leninism. Khrushchev's condemnation of Stalin's crimes did not include the effects of Stalinism on the people of the USSR, but only select instances of arrests, torture, deportations, and executions of former communists. Khrushchev focused his attacks on Stalin's Great Purges and the mass arrests of party members following the assassination of Kirov in 1934. The Twentieth Party Congress and the secret speech confirmed that the question of de-Stalinization was at the heart of the succession struggle in the Kremlin. It was at least a partial end of terror, since the heirs had sworn over Beria's corpse that they would no longer kill each other. At the same time, they started to free hundreds of thousands of *zeks*.

Once more, Jacques followed the course of history closely, or perhaps history was following him. As François Furet stated: "The short period between Stalin's death and Khrushchev's secret report, less than three years, shows two quite different faces. On the one hand, everything continued as before, insofar as everything – not only political decisions but all nominations – was initiated by Moscow. On the other hand, since Moscow was no longer Moscow, the entire communist world was adrift, uncertain of the future."[2] Jacques and his friends were brought back to Moscow during that tumultuous period in the history of communism, uncertain of their destiny as well.

As with the old Soviet prisons, the church in Vladimir was used to lodge inmates awaiting transfer. At that time, the high-security prison held numerous German and Japanese prisoners of war, in addition to other foreigners. Did that mean that Jacques was treated like a foreigner? One important fact seemed to confirm his feeling that the system was changing. When he arrived at Vladimir, he was not placed in the same cell as Misao, his Japanese brother. They then submitted a request that they be placed in the same cell. And a miracle occurred! Their wish was granted immediately.

> It was becoming really a four-star place. Usually when you asked for a transfer because the thugs were persecuting you, the officials reacted with delight at your misery – "So much the better if he suffers." But now our request was granted!
>
> Here's another example. There was an Austrian among us. During his transfer his wristwatch was given back to him. It had

been confiscated at the camp where he was detained. According to regulations, objects of value were confiscated during transfers and placed with the file of the owner, in order to be kept safely by the administration during transport. Typically, these objects disappeared. At Vladimir, this Austrian was obviously the only one among us who had a wristwatch and, if only for the pleasure of hearing him answer us with great precision, we constantly asked him: "What time is it? Almost time for soup?"

Of course, all this business did not go unnoticed by our guard behind the Judas window. And very quickly we saw men arrive, wearing grey smocks over their uniforms, in other words, the "chorus" in charge of searches. The regulations usually stipulated that searches were to be conducted without telling prisoners what they were looking for. However, this time they announced what they wanted straight away: "Listen guys! We're here for the watch. If you give it to us right away, we will not bother you."

The Austrian comrade took off his watch and gave it to them.

"Very good. Bye, guys!"

After all those years of extreme rigidity, that joviality seemed like an earthquake. Things were really changing.

De-Stalinization and Khrushchev's secret speech at the Twentieth Party Congress resulted in incredible "luxury" for these members of the Gulag, compared to what they had experienced earlier. Now Jacques was being categorized and treated as he had always wanted to be, as a foreigner. In addition to his Japanese brother who could write to his family, there was a Frenchman, Lucien Goizé, who was an officer in the French army. Goizé had been stationed in Budapest when the country became more liberal under Imre Nagy. Nagy wanted to introduce a more humane form of communism in Hungary. The French officer, caught up in the tumult of the Hungarian revolution, was arrested by the Hungarians first. Later, they transferred him to the Soviets, and it was in Vladimir that he learned of his sentence. "It was quite an event for me to finally meet a Frenchman, the first one after François P., the traitor. And Goizé was someone who had even defended his country! I met him later in Paris and then in the Pyrénées where he settled after his retirement. We got along well, the three of us – Misao, Lucien Goizé, and I! At last, communication with the free world!"

All those foreigners who surrounded Jacques the Frenchman in the Vladimir prison were very interested in a high-level decree that exempted foreigners from serving the rest of their sentences and granted them the right to return to their permanent place of residence.

It was not rehabilitation, nor was it repentance. It was not at all an admission that "we the Soviets, we jailed you for nothing at all." No. It was rather – "Because of our great generosity we have decided that you will not serve the remaining years of your sentence in the Gulag!"

To the best of my knowledge a decree was never published. They just said to me, "You have been released." I had to sign on the back of a small sheet of paper. It was addressed to the director of the prison, asking him to inform the prisoner Jacques Rossi that, in light of the decree of the Supreme Soviet of 16 September 1956, he was exempt from having to serve the remainder of his sentence. Then there was the phrase – you have been freed. Needless to say, no one had to beg me to sign the form.

It was not easy for someone who was once a member of the international communist movement, who had come freely to the USSR before the war and had worked as a Soviet spy, to return to his country of permanent residence. It was easier for a German who was arrested in his own country by the Soviets. Some foreigners left immediately. Misao and the group of Japanese former prisoners were sent to the east to a dacha, and from there they were repatriated to Japan. Fortunately, Jacques had memorized the address of his "Japanese brother" and was thus able to find him years later. The Frenchman and a small group of other inmates in the Vladimir prison were sent in a regular train to a dacha about twenty-five miles from Moscow. They travelled with ordinary passengers but under the control of a very courteous guard. "For me, it was the first time since 1937, almost twenty years earlier, that I was semi-free on the 'continent.' It was an even more extraordinary event for my foreign companions! Some of them had never been *free* in the Soviet Union. They had gone directly from their respective countries into the Gulag."

The dacha where Jacques awaited his proposed repatriation was in Bykovo, on the railroad line that went to Kazan, about forty miles from Moscow. He later learned that it had been the residence of the infamous Yezhov and, later, "none other than Beria." After his defeat in 1944, the field marshal von Paulus was also interned there. "In fact, it was a beautiful two-storey house graced with balconies and verandas and included extensions. Several bedrooms had been converted into a kitchen. The dormitory had real beds with sheets for the inmates, who were mostly men. There were also some women who officially slept in separate rooms."

The dacha was well guarded with a solid wall ten feet high on top of which there was barbed wire that could not be seen from the outside. Guards dressed in civilian clothing were present day and night and could not be seen from the outside either. Jacques found a good library there with many books in German, as well as French and English. The library was probably from von Paulus's time there.

> We were no longer prisoners, but we were not free to move around either. It was the typical Soviet way. The landscape was beautiful around Bykovo with the dachas of rich Muscovites and small houses from the time of the tsars surrounded by lattice fences. They were quite unlike our solid walls. We could stroll under the pines on the paths around our dacha. Many of my foreign companions who left Russia while I awaited repatriation gave me their remaining rubles. This money enabled me to go to the market and to buy some supplies.

The material improvement he experienced at the dacha concerned Jacques less than his impending release. Around him, he saw his comrades, foreigners like himself, sign their papers and finally leave. But he remained in the Bykovo dacha, still waiting.

> Gradually, the KGB contacted the prisoners' countries of origin and drove the different citizens to their consulates. Their administrative situation was clarified and – finally! – they were taken to the train station. I remember Yugoslavs who were repatriated through Austria, which bordered their country. The Germans were transported to the West or East German border, depending on where their residence had been before the war. The Finns were taken to Leningrad and to the Finnish border, where they were met by the authorities of their country.
>
> For me, nothing. I was worried. I knew that time had passed since the Twentieth Party Congress that led to the high-level decrees and to my release. It was October 1956. In the meantime, the KGB was regaining strength and gradually becoming re-Stalinized. The political police of the first "workers' and peasants' state" in the world was programmed to remain the backbone of the state. I had to leave quickly, but I wasn't leaving.

Jacques had, however, established personal contact with the French embassy. He had officially sent a letter during a visit to the market. A merchant there served as an intermediary. Jacques slipped him the letter while the guard had his back turned.

We were allowed to go to the market in small groups of two or three, but with an escort. We could get a little money by selling our clothes or, for those who received parcels, by selling the contents of the parcels. With that money we bought stamps and asked the elderly Jewish men at the market to mail our letters. We could count on them. I never heard that even one of those illegal letters failed to arrive at its destination. Strangely, the censors did not intercept this mail during its trip from the mailbox to the embassy. That does not mean that the letter had not been read by "to whom it may concern." Perhaps this liberalism can be explained by the fact that the regime wanted to prove to the world that it was truly finished with totalitarianism.

Nonetheless, one question could be asked. Why did Jacques feel that he needed to send his letter unofficially while his fellow inmates dealt directly with their respective embassies?

Our cases were very different and I felt that in my gut. They had been arrested as the Red Army "liberated" Europe from Hitler. As I already indicated, some had even been kidnapped by the Soviets in countries liberated by the Allies. Not only had I come on my own free will to work for Russia [Soviet Union] before the war, but my file contained a lot of information about my past in the Gulag: my refusal to be an informer for Pavlov and even to testify against Boris, my former boss in the clandestine service who betrayed me, my second case of alleged spying, and my hunger strikes. In short, it was a terrible file! I was once one of them – a communist agent. I knew too much about their system. Anybody could testify, but I could testify more. I could have written an official letter, but I don't think that it would have been delivered like the others. All of these foreigners that were being repatriated were capitalist enemies.

While awaiting some solution, Jacques wrote, using the same clandestine method, to his old friends in Moscow, an American couple. He had been very close to them prior to his arrest.

After twenty years, I still remembered their address. I didn't hesitate much, as I believed that since the Twentieth Party Congress, contact with me would not put them at risk. It was Emma who came to see me at the dacha. I knew her better than Harry. Like me, Emma had worked for the Comintern – Emma! She was the first person from my life before the Gulag that I saw again. I had so often thought that this meeting would never take place!

There was a small room in the dacha for visitors. We were sitting there, the two of us, when someone came in and interrupted us. The administration was pleased with this new atmosphere of liberalism. That is why I had been permitted to meet Emma. But another, more prudent civil servant realized that the rules only permitted family visits, and this policy had not changed. The administration of the dacha learned that Emma was not a member of my family and that according to the rules, which were well known, I did not have the right to see her. So our meeting did not last long.

It was quite upsetting for me! I thought that she hadn't changed since 1937. She was still exuberant with lively black eyes that shone with intelligence. In the United States she had worked as a lawyer, but she was indignant about the damage caused by capitalism. She became an enthusiastic Marxist-Leninist, and that is how we met each other. Both of us were involved in a clandestine mission in Europe. She was able to stop working for the Comintern to become a professor of English literature in a Moscow language institute. She even managed to bring me some books that did not pass through the inspection.

After her short visit, she wrote me a long letter. She wrote me, among other things, about how she had been petrified to find in her desk drawer American writing paper with the name and watermark of an American company. It was before the Twentieth Party Congress and, at that time, simply possessing paper made in the USA would have been enough to send her and her husband to the Gulag. Emma had good instincts, and during all those years she had become aware of what was happening, unlike her compatriot Walter Duranty, an American newspaper correspondent who tried to share with his readers his unconditional admiration for the regime.

Meanwhile, Jacques thought about preserving his drawings, the ones he managed to save from the camp, the detention prisons, the Alexandrovsk prison, the transit prisons, and finally from Vladimir and Bykovo. He gave them to a young Austrian who was about to be repatriated.

When I went to Vienna in 1964 I looked for him but I could not remember his name. I could only remember the name of one of his friends and compatriots, a certain Dörre, a Viennese merchant, whom I could not find in the phone book. If I had money at that time I would have put an ad in the newspaper, but I didn't have a cent. In the end, out of the numerous drawings and portraits that I did in the

Gulag, I have almost nothing left. I suppose that some of my sketches that were confiscated at the Norilsk camp or elsewhere may have been retained in the archives of the secret police. Those archives must contain the drawings of millions of other fellow prisoners as well as all the literature and the millions of poems written by inmates. Perhaps a museum has been built for all that or will be built in the future. The culture of the Gulag – it could fill an entire universe!

Finally, one day, with no warning at all, the Frenchman was informed that he only needed to complete the final formalities. In the office, the sergeant handed him a paper: "You are freed," he said. "Here is your certification of release."

The release certificate. Jacques remembers it with precision. It hadn't changed in about sixty years. On an official form of the OGPU-NKVD-MVD, the code of the prison was indicated along with the series and the number of the certificate, the first name and surname of the individual, his date and place of birth, nationality and citizenship, the length of his stay in the prison, information concerning the court that had sentenced him and the article under which he had been sentenced. Since 1953, the release certificate stated "Office of the NKVD (MVD)." Instead of information concerning the court, there was the reason for the release, for example, "end of sentence" or "amnesty." The document also included a photograph and an official seal.

Nevertheless, Jacques was still upset.

This release certificate included nothing of significance. My foreign companions didn't need to have one. They were taken directly to the station in order to go home. Finally, I was allegedly released.

Surname, first name, nationality …

There was one last question on the back of the certificate that I had not answered: "Has the former inmate chosen a place of residency?"

"Where do you want to go?"

Since we were twenty-five miles from Moscow, I answered: "Moscow."

"That's not allowed."

"Then, Leningrad."

"That's forbidden, too."

"Odessa?"

"Forbidden."

I must have mentioned ten, fifteen cities that I had at least heard of, but the answer did not change. So very politely, I asked: "To save time, could you please give me the list of authorized cities? The USSR is very big."

"Impossible. That list is secret."

I was stunned. As a former Gulag prisoner, I knew that divulging a state secret meant between ten and fifteen years in prison. I could hardly expect this sergeant to take such a risk, so I continued. I named about fifty places, and all were forbidden. And then suddenly, I had an inspiration. With my training in oriental studies I had always wanted to visit Samarkand, the Marakanda of Alexander, that important stopping place along the Silk Road. Of course, it was three thousand miles to the east, while France was in the opposite direction, but in light of my situation, I said: "Samarkand."

Samarkand was not on the secret list of forbidden cities. The sergeant carefully wrote on the release certificate, "Chose Samarkand."

Together with his release certificate, the authorities gave Jacques the answer from the French consul that he had awaited for months. It had been sent a long time ago, but had been held up by the authorities, probably within the KGB. The letter from the French ambassador, written in the two languages, was brief but said everything that was needed: "We request that you contact the consulate to arrange the repatriation procedure to France."

But on that day, the letter had no effect. Jacques had already chosen Samarkand.

# PART 3

# After

I love military parades. July 14th on the Champs Elysees – an example of discipline that guarantees solidarity. However, I do not like it when people act like sheep. The French take pride in being contemptuous of discipline while continuing to behave like sheep. People cling to illusions despite the Moscow show trials, the famines, the collectivization, Katyn, and Kravchenko. We only see what concerns ME.

Jacques Rossi

# 30 "Sir, You Are Dripping Snow on My Floors!"

All release certificates had the following warning: "This is not an official identification document." It was, however, recognized as such during the individual's entire journey to his destination, on the condition that he not stray from his itinerary and not stop more than three days during transit. Otherwise he risked being arrested as a vagrant and judged accordingly. Upon arrival he had to present himself to the local police and register in order to obtain an identification document.

Jacques Rossi

With his certificate correctly stamped for Central Asia and the letter from the French consul, Jacques received a one-way train ticket, Moscow–Samarkand, with a departure date. The trip would take five days. If the omnipresent police asked for his papers and if he was not on the train for Samarkand on the dates specified on the release certificate, the former prisoner risked returning to the Gulag without trial, this time for the crime of vagrancy, with an automatic sentence of three years.

Upon leaving the dacha, the former inmate had the certificate, the train ticket, the letter from the embassy, and a small amount of money to survive during the six-day journey to his chosen destination. He had to wait forty-eight hours in Moscow for the departure of the train to Samarkand. With these documents and money, he left the dacha – alone. For the first time in almost twenty years, he got on the train without an escort to go into Moscow. The other travellers seemed indifferent towards him. They did not pay any attention to him, as if he were just part of the crowd. Once in Moscow, without hesitating, he followed his steps as before to the place where he had gone with his fiancée just prior to his arrest – to Emma and Harry's. His friends lived in an apartment built under the tsars. It used to be a very chic residence, but now it was a building with communal apartments. He rang the bell. The sound hadn't changed since 1937, but he didn't realize that the number of times the bell was rung corresponded to each family. There were eight families in all, so it was not Emma who opened the door, but an elderly, unkempt woman, dragging her feet in dirty slippers. She looked at him for a minute and then jumped up to hug him.

Although the old neighbour had been angry with the Americans for fifteen years, she recognized this person who came from the cold north and who was still wearing the clothes of a prisoner. Since the Twentieth Party Congress, people felt they could express what they knew.

> She remembered my arrest very clearly. She pushed me into the long hallway crowded with cupboards and assorted furniture. The apartment had eight bedrooms. In the kitchen, there were eight gas stove-rings and in the bathroom eight piles of newspaper cut into pieces hung on eight nails. To get to my friends' bedroom, I had to walk around a closet.
>
> I spent the night with them sleeping on a folding bed, an intense night of rediscovery and sharing. During those twenty years, this couple of old communists had discovered the truth. They had initially been welcomed in university circles during the thirties, but during the war they had suffered the consequences of official xenophobia. I had my Gulag stories, but I quickly understood that my friends, although they had become anti-Stalin, did not want to hear the Gulag details. In their view, any extreme hostility towards the system "played into the hands of the enemy." Of course, if they had given up the idea that Marxism-Leninism was for the good of humanity, they would no longer have had legitimate arguments for their beliefs. I had the painful impression that I was relentlessly trying to break their resolve. Thus began my post-Gulag adaptation. Around five in the morning, while I was still whispering with Emma, Harry, who had to get up at dawn to go to work, told us to "shut up!" It was starting to get cold, so in the morning my friends found me a cap and some leather boots. They couldn't find felt boots. With my beard, already several days old, I did not even look like an average Muscovite, who at that time did not appear especially elegant.

A plan had started to take shape in Jacques's mind ever since he received the consul's letter, and he had a whole day in front of him to carry it out. He knew the address of the French embassy. It was written on the envelope. He decided to go straight there.

In front of the entrance to the embassy there were two robust Soviet policemen who were blocking my passage. Politely one of them asked me: "Where are you going?"

"To the embassy of my country."

"Do you have identification?"

I proudly took out the consul's letter – a note to the attention of Russian authorities asking them to help the bearer of this letter, a French citizen, be repatriated. They examined me. My clothes were clean, but you could see that they came from a prison. My quilted Gulag jacket, although quite new, didn't look like the jacket of a foreigner. To the suspicious policemen, I really didn't look like a French citizen.

"Fine," said one of them, "My comrade will call to see if the ambassador can see you. He may be busy."

The other one left to supposedly call the ambassador but, in reality, he called the closest police station. At the time, there were no cell phones or even walkie-talkies. The first policeman pushed me, politely to be sure, into a small side street along the wall of the embassy, out of sight of any pedestrians. While the other one was calling the "ambassador" he watched me carefully. It was about eleven in the morning.

It was very cold, but I was so nervous that I felt nothing. It was like the interrogations, when I stood up for hours. It was, however, the first time in twenty years – and what years these were! – that I was so close to France.

Suddenly, I had an idea. I looked at the metal fence, which was about seven feet high. I saw a side door and a window on the ground floor. If the door was locked, I decided that I would try to break a windowpane with my head. I was wearing a Russian cap that would protect it. I pretended that I could no longer stand the cold. The policeman saw that I was not wearing the felt boots that were typically worn in the winter. It was after the Twentieth Party Congress, and this decent man had learned that you weren't supposed to treat people badly for no reason. In short, he moved a bit away to see if his colleague was coming.

Immediately I took advantage of that to climb over the fence. And I fell in the snow on the other side – into French territory. Oh God! What emotion! There were about ten yards between the fence and the building. I ran in the virgin snow towards the door. It was not locked. Suddenly I found myself in another world.

There was a small hallway, then a very elegant salon with a nicely waxed parquet floor, a beautiful oriental rug, a sofa, a low table with newspapers in Latin script, well printed on good paper. French magazines, the first I had seen in twenty years. *Le Temps*. No. A new title was written with the familiar style of letters: *Le Monde*. Finally, I saw green plants and above the plants a watering can with an artistically curved spout. Holding the watering can I saw a hand, a small delicate hand with polished nails. Quickly, I looked from the hand to the arm and from the arm to the person, a young woman who screamed when she saw me:

"Sir, you are dripping snow on my floor!"

I was electrified to hear my native language spoken by a French and feminine voice. I got control of myself and answered tit for tat:

"I don't give a damn about your floors. The Russian police are after me."

I had broken into a private apartment of the residence and not in the chancellery. The young woman was the wife of an important diplomat. What I immediately savoured was the wonderful melody of French – real French spoken by a real Frenchwoman. For years in the Gulag, I had only rarely heard French, the awkward French of people who had learned it at school or who had visited francophone countries. I was quite moved. But for the poor woman, I was an alien from another planet.

I quickly recovered my composure: "I would like to see the first secretary!" I didn't dare ask for the ambassador.

She called right away, and the first secretary and the consul Mr M. arrived immediately. They shook my hand amiably. I introduced myself and I was surprised to hear them say:

"You come from the prison in Alexandrovsk."

I was overcome for a moment to discover that for France I was not completely lost. I had not completely disappeared without leaving a trace, the black sheep who had worked for ten years in clandestine operations for a truly diabolical cause, to eliminate capitalism not only in France but throughout the entire world.

The two diplomats started to examine the unresolvable question of how they were going to take me to the chancellery. In fact, the operation was anything but simple. If I went by the hallway, there was a window that faced a building. They were sure that every movement was watched from there. The other possibility was to go through the boiler room where a certain Nicholas worked keeping the boilers going. He was known to be a KGB agent. I was astounded by the way these diplomats let themselves be terrorized by the

Soviets. In no Soviet embassy in the world could one find personnel who weren't diehard Soviets, from the cleaning woman to the driver, all of them following KGB orders. Yet the French let themselves be surrounded by Soviet spies, perhaps because a Nicholas cost less than an employee from France.

Finally, I don't know how, I found myself in the chancellery, in an office, with a secretary at her typewriter: "Surname, first name, date and place of birth?"

And that was the glitch. I didn't have a birth certificate. I knew the family name of my mother and her place of birth. And except for that, I had my release certificate from the Soviets that identified my nationality as French. But nationality for the Soviets meant ethnic identity. Within five or six minutes, I was given a kind of temporary identification card stating that I was a French citizen and that I was returning to France. Then the French diplomats decided to give me two letters. One was for the Soviet authorities so that they would take me to the border. The other was for the French authorities so that they would formalize my status. Since I liked to plan ahead, I had had passport pictures made during a visit to the market. I was able to paste one on the letter addressed to the French authorities. I almost had an official French ID.

The rest of the day we talked. They invited me to lunch and asked me questions about myself and about life in the Gulag. It had been twenty years since I had eaten such exquisite and well-prepared dishes. But I was too nervous to appreciate them. I was very tired after a sleepless night with my friends. I explained to them that I had been a passionate communist. That did not seem to affect them at all. I really felt that they just wanted to help me.

After the consul, the military attaché arrived. When I spoke to him about the Arctic and Norilsk, he insisted that I show him details on a map. No foreigners had permission to go to that region. The French ignored what was going on there. I wanted to enlighten them, to tell them where the mines, the buildings, the offices, and the police were. But he brought a simple school atlas in which that immense region of thousands of miles was represented by just a tiny area. For the second time that day, I was disappointed by my compatriots. The fact remains that in an embassy of such importance, they should have had decent maps of the USSR! As for the consul, he was not interested in the precious coded notes that I had drafted in the Alexandrovsk prison. The content was in French but the letters were Tibetan. They would be useful for me later in Poland when I began *The Gulag Handbook*. I took my notes out of their secret hiding place, but I did not put them back carefully after it appeared that the consul was not at all interested. Because of that I almost lost them during the next body search.

Jacques could have asked, of course, for the official protection of the ambassador instead of risking the possibility of being sent back to the Soviet Gulag. Why didn't he do that? So many others asked for political asylum and remained as refugees on diplomatic territory, such as the Hungarian Roman Catholic cardinal Mindszenty, who spent years in the United States embassy in Budapest.

Frankly, I did not want my return as a loyal French citizen to be a source of embarrassment for the embassy. After all, I was not a prominent person, and I had even fought against the French regime. Having lost my dream, I was now asking them for help. In addition, I was not being heroic by refusing to remain in the embassy. This all occurred after the Twentieth Party Congress, and not before. Someday the Soviets would finally let me go. I did not realize, however, that once again I was naively optimistic. The KGB was becoming stronger again.

It was five o'clock when a small group – comprised of the consul, the interpreter, and four other people – accompanied the fugitive to the door of the embassy. Did they feel uneasy about letting this unexpected visitor leave their protection, the man who had audaciously jumped over the fence and who didn't want to inconvenience them? Before they let him go, a small team of embassy officials, with the help of the interpreter, advised Jacques at length on how to respond to the questions of various Soviet officials. The consul warned Jacques that he probably would be arrested but that because of the letters, he would certainly be let go. He offered to have Jacques escorted to the subway, but Jacques refused. He wanted to leave by himself. So they gave him some rubles and provisions, canned goods that came straight from France with Latin script on the labels.

With this package of food under his arm, Jacques left the territory of his country and entered into the darkness of the Moscow street. There, far from the windows of the embassy and fifty steps beyond the street corner, an unmarked police car slowed down next to him. Without stopping, a door to the car opened and four strong policemen wearing black felt boots and astrakhan hats pushed him quietly and roughly into the car. They grabbed his package. He was put in the back seat between two policemen. The third disappeared. The fourth sat next to the driver and turned around. The three policemen studied Jacques with intense curiosity and with some fear. He was the ex-*zek*, the ex-alien from the free world.

My nose started to run and I started to take my handkerchief out of my pocket. They grabbed my hand to stop me, as if I were going to grab a bomb. They must have been told that I was a dangerous terrorist because they seemed overcome by fear. I wasn't too old at that time. I was only forty-six and I could still frighten people. I then resorted to my old instincts from years at Norilsk where there were no handkerchiefs, and to keep your runny nose from freezing, you blew it. I blew right in front of me. I don't know if the snot landed on the cop in front, but he did not budge. We continued on in silence. I was shivering in my light Gulag jacket, seated between my well-fed and well-dressed uniformed guards. They took me to the closest police station where, following a maze of hallways, I was forced to sit on a narrow wooden couch on the first floor in front of a closed door. It was not the political police. Here they dealt with everyday matters. Numerous pale, yellow-faced Muscovite women were waiting there, and studied me with a kind of resigned sadness that I had never seen elsewhere, not even in Poland.

That lasted a long time, a very long time. They were employing those good old techniques of destabilizing the adversary. After a while I asked whether I could go to the bathroom. That was permitted. So I left my package of fine food from the embassy next to my seat without the guards batting an eye. It could have really hidden a bomb. I went to the toilet accompanied by a guard who watched me do my business. During that embarrassing inspection my guard noticed that I was wearing a kind of old-fashioned belt for the hernia that I had gotten in the camps.

"Are you are an invalid?"

It was the first word I had heard spoken since the gate of the French embassy had closed behind me. An invalid! The idea reassured them a bit and I was flattered because they addressed me using the formal form of "you." I wasn't used to such refinement. Hours went by under their constant surveillance. I tried to lie down on the very narrow bench and to pretend I was sleeping, but I had little desire to sleep. At two in the morning, the door finally opened and I was confronted by a very elegant young bureaucrat with an astrakhan hat. He asked me in French if I spoke Russian because it was easier for him. He also asked me for my papers and I showed him the letters from the embassy. He was extremely polite, using the formal "you" form and calling me "sir." He wanted to explain to me why I had been arrested. Of course, I was French and I had the right to contact my embassy, but I had climbed over the fence, breaking into an embassy that the Soviets were responsible for guarding. That's why they had arrested me. I didn't mention that they hadn't arrested me at the time of my act, but rather six hours later when I left the embassy accompanied by the general consul and with his approval. I only responded by saying that I had to force my way into the embassy because I had been stopped from entering it legally.

He also looked at my train ticket for Samarkand and asked me what I was going to do before my departure the next day. Then he wanted to know what was in my package. I opened the box. He saw the cans but he didn't open a single one. There could have been compromising documents in them. He let me leave with the package, even though he could have sold the cans for a good price on the black market. He didn't discover my notes either, which were not very well hidden. The Twentieth Party Congress had only taken place a short time before. From then on, things became more difficult again. But that same day, after all those adventures, they freed me.

At about three in the morning Jacques was released onto the streets of Moscow. He walked back to Emma and Harry's place. The next day he returned to the police station and managed to talk to a highly placed person, a colonel. The letters from the embassy had given him wings. He was French and he wanted to go home.

At the same time, I was a former Gulag prisoner, and there was no use having any illusions about that. When I was still in the Gulag, I saw how freed prisoners were barred from returning to the interior of the Soviet Union or to important European cities or to the capitals of the so-called republics or forbidden from settling in important cities or industrial areas. But I wanted so much to believe. The colonel was surprised by my story. He asked me where I came from and why I did not have a visa to enter France. I was obliged to show him my certificate of release.

"But ... you chose to go to Samarkand!" He looked at me. He was not mean, just incredulous because he could not believe how stupid I was. "You have to go to Samarkand. Once there, you need to contact the local police. After you present your release certificate, they will give you an ID, and with that ID, you can apply for a visa to leave the USSR. We can't do anything for you because you chose Samarkand. It's the law."

And so, following less than forty-eight hours of suspense and new developments, Jacques the Frenchman, the "freed" *zek*, found himself on a train bound for Central Asia, thousands of miles from Moscow – and even farther from Paris. After having jumped over a fence and broken into the French embassy in the Soviet Union, and having been accused by a young perfumed woman of dripping snow on her well-waxed floors, he had obtained only two letters, a few rubles, and a box of fine food from the French Republic and the diplomats of his homeland. In spite of his feat and in the midst of it all, he was arrested by the Soviet police.

# 31 In Central Asia: The Man Who Came from a Country with No Collective Farms

who knows contentment
thus suffers no shame
and who knows restraint
encounters no trouble
while enjoying a long life

Lao-Tzu, *Tao Te Ching*

Jacques's rail ticket from Moscow to Samarkand had been issued by the camp administration. In every Soviet train, there were always sleeper compartments for the military and the police. Jacques's bunk was on the lower rack. The top bunk was occupied by a military person, a uniformed lieutenant who was going to a new post somewhere in Ashkhabad, much farther than Samarkand. The trip lasted five days and five nights for Jacques, one or two more days for the lieutenant. The two men talked during the long hours.

> First of all, he was the one who talked, while I listened to all his pathetic stories about the Front. At bedtime he put his watch, a very nice watch, on the small table next to my bunk. I had nothing to put there. When I started to talk about myself, I decided to tell him the truth, that I was French, and that I had been imprisoned and then released. He was a decent man. His attitude towards me did not change, but he stopped putting his watch on the small table during the night.
>
> The journey was long. There were a lot of people in the compartments, and Jacques, coming from the Gulag, was hungry for new human interaction. One of the people he met was a female doctor with

Asian features and dark eyes and hair. She was coming back from a convention and was going home to Ashkhabad. She asked him whether he was married and proposed that he come live with her in Turkmenistan where he could teach at the university and she could easily find him a Turkmen wife. But Jacques had "chosen" Samarkand, and for the Soviet authorities there could be no adjustments. The train stopped in the smallest of stations that were just cabins in the middle of the Kazakh steppe. At the stations, the peasants came and sold eggs, chickens, fermented mare's milk, which made one drunk very easily, as well as vegetables, fruit, and white bread. Jacques shared his fine food from the embassy with the Soviet officer.

After five days and five nights, the train finally arrived at the Samarkand station. As in many cities in Central Asia, the station was located quite far from the city centre so that the noise of the locomotives did not disturb the Muslim call to prayer.

There is a time difference of several hours between Moscow and Samarkand. I arrived at dawn. When I got out of the station a bit groggy, I saw a donkey, a striking southern animal for someone who had just spent fifteen years in the Arctic. I even had the pleasure of hearing it bray. It was December, but there was no snow and the trees had not lost their leaves. The women were wearing light caftans. Their chadors were thrown back because they did not cover themselves with their rigid horsehair veils when they were in town. The veils were reserved for the villages. I was grey and dreary compared to the springtime atmosphere – the red, yellow, and blue silks of the feminine clothing, the coloured pants of the men, the older people with their long, brightly coloured quilted caftans and turbans, the beauty of the women as well as the men.

In the standard Soviet bus that travelled to the central square in Registan, or Registana as the Russians pronounced it, I had the pleasure of being squeezed in among these human beings, all the people who were going about their business, who left their homes in the morning and returned home in the evening to their families. I finally arrived at the end of the bus line. It must have been seven or eight in the morning. I leaned on a wall and I admired the superb square with its two mosques and its ancient Koranic school where the ghosts lingered – of former merchants and camel drivers talking in front of their caravans. I thought about Timur-Lang, or Tamerlane as he's called in the West, that prince in the late fourteenth century who continued the work of Genghis Khan and who seemed more present than Stalin in this town of silk. Just next to me, an old man with a white beard, a turban, and a caftan was observing me. He asked me in Russian:

"Do you like it?"

I tried to remember my Persian to respond in his language. He was very surprised because I looked more like a Russian to him than an Uzbek. So he asked me in Persian: "Are you Russian?"

I answered that I was *"farhangui,"* which in Persian means both foreigner and French. But he didn't understand. He wanted to know whether I was German because the war with Germany had even been discussed in Central Asia. So I used the word *"maghrebi,"* which in Persian means the West. I said that so that he could locate France more easily. France – it's west of Germany.

"What is your religion?"

I cheated a little because I did not want him to think that I was Russian Orthodox. I answered "Christian Catholic" rather than simply Christian, but what he really wanted to know was whether there were temples different from mosques and whether people attended them. Then he had another question.

"Are there collective farms where you come from?" I answered no to that question. "Peasants work their own land for themselves."

"Do you live here?"

I had to admit to him that I had just gotten off the train and that I lived nowhere. Right away, he said: "If you don't have a place to live, come to my house."

I discovered that ages-old tradition of hospitality in Central Asia. I was not Russian. I came from a country where people went to church, even if it wasn't a mosque, a country where there were no collective farms. Thus the door of his home was opened wide for me. The patriarch took me to his home, into the part of his home for men, but the rules were not very strict and in the courtyard everybody was together, men and women. They showed me how to come back to the house, and I went off to the police station to acquire the infamous "identification card" that I needed in order to survive and to be repatriated. It was barely nine or ten in the morning. The number and date of that identification card were indispensable for all bureaucratic transactions. However, it was not a passport for external travel, nor was it an internal passport. There were three kinds of identification cards: a regular one, one for foreigners, and one for foreigners with no citizenship. I proudly showed the police the letter from the French ambassador with my photo, without realizing that with this letter I represented a special case. Had I only shown them my certificate of release on which my French citizenship was indicated, they probably would have given me that precious identification card and I could have asked for an exit visa. But that is not what happened. Instead, the bureaucrat consulted with his superiors, who made him tell me that they had no more official forms and that I should come back in five days. After the five days that I had spent on the train, five more days seemed to me like an eternity.

Jacques did not waste a minute. Once he left the police station, he walked around the old neighbourhoods that were the imperial Russian parts of the city. On the front of one of the low houses with barely one floor he saw a sign with the word "typist" written on it.

I went straight into a small waiting room that led to an apartment on one side and to a tiny room on the other side where a fifty-year-old, blue-eyed, grey-haired woman was typing on a very old typewriter. I asked her immediately whether she knew someone who was interested in English, French, German, or Spanish translations. I still looked like a former prisoner. They were easily recognized by Soviet citizens. Within five minutes, that Russian woman knew where I had come from and I learned that her husband, a German from the Volga region, had died in the Gulag.

She tried to help me. She introduced me to one or two Uzbek professors from the University of Samarkand for whom she typed texts. But nothing came of it. Finally, she suggested that I meet the town hall secretary, who was the wife of the representative of the security police, a member of the party committee for the region, and an important person. That woman immediately agreed to meet me. I showed her my French papers and explained that I was going to be repatriated and that I had a brain, two arms, and two legs in a region where there was no unemployment. I wanted to work so that my consul would not have to support me financially. Of course, I noticed that even mentioning the consul made her tremble. For the Soviets, any reference to a consul implied spying. She answered me right away:

"This presents a new situation for us. Come back in three days and we will take care of it."

Before I left, she said: "Do you have enough to live on?"

I had several hundred rubles that the French consul had given me. But since I was a shrewd former Gulag inmate, I said that no, I didn't have anything. She directed me to an office where a comrade gave me a certificate that enabled me to withdraw some money. In fact, I received eight hundred rubles, which was enough to live on for a month.

I then went back to my new friend Abdullah's house, where I would stay. His entire family welcomed me and we shared a meal together. Everyone, men and women, ate together and the conversation was lively. Since my Persian from the Oriental Language School was quite limited, we eventually conversed in Russian. They spoke three languages: Tajik, which was the language of the urban Muslim majority; Uzbek because officially Samarkand was part of Uzbekistan; and Russian. His mother and father were there. My host, Abdullah, looked like an old wise man himself with his wonderful white beard, so well cared for compared to Russian beards. His two sons were also there. They worked as technicians in a research institute. One of his daughters, Habiba, was a student at the University of Samarkand and a party member. For Habiba, being a member of the party meant no more than wearing a red star or carrying a red flag during a celebration. It was a constraint like any other, like not eating pork, for example. Habiba was a beautiful woman who was prolonging her studies at the university so she did not have to enter into the marriage her parents were preparing for her. In general, it was easier for Uzbeks to get their diplomas than for Russians. So the Russians, the Russian doctors for example, were considered better than Uzbek doctors, and this led to a certain discrimination.

Three days later, as planned, Jacques went back to the local town hall. In the interim, the authorities had received information about Jacques, which convinced them to not allow the former *zek* to leave Samarkand. That was easy since all they had to do was refuse to give him the identification card that would clarify his status. Without that paper Jacques was no one with no possibility of moving and no possibility of being repatriated.

He did not have the right to work either. But since they did not want to continue to support him financially, they ignored that part of the law. The Samarkand town hall secretary hired Jacques as a colleague in a scientific research institute.

My work consisted of reading, rather of skimming, scientific English, American, German, and South African publications for this institute. It was a unique institute that studied the raising of astrakhan sheep. There were many astrakhan sheep in that region of the world. The publications came from Moscow, where the articles that were too general were removed because they were considered counter-revolutionary. This meant that the specialized article that was on the backside of the removed page was also cut.

A work certificate that Jacques requested after he left the USSR indicated that he held the position of scientific reader at the Research Institute for Raising Astrakhan Sheep from 17 December 1956 until 30 June 1960. He also taught English to the employees of the institute. In Samarkand, as in the other Soviet republics, the people who held important positions were Russians, like the director of the institute and the laboratory supervisors, the mayor of the town, and all the supervisors of departments and services. In general, they ruled over the Uzbeks. Jacques later learned that the director of the institute met with all the laboratory supervisors to announce the arrival of the Frenchman and to forbid them from asking him questions. Two days later he was officially introduced to them.

In fact, I did not look like a Frenchman with my shaved head with the hair slowly growing back. Since it was hot, I was not wearing my old padded jacket, but I actually looked like someone who had just gotten out of the Gulag. Which is what I was. The polite civilized atmosphere was a change from what I had known for the last twenty years. I leafed through the publications. I called the director of the cytology laboratory. I would inform him of an interesting article in such and such publication. And he would arrive with his note pad. I would just translate into Russian the passages that I understood, with no introduction. After all, he was the specialist. He was supposed to understand the subject. He took notes and then we chatted. It was not back-breaking work!

In fact, I was lucky because the Soviets naively believed that after twenty years in the Gulag, a Frenchman would praise the system if he benefitted from professional advantages. As a result, I was, unjustly, better paid than the others. At that time I met Felitchkin, and his situation was telling. He was of Russian origin and had immigrated to France when he was eight in 1922 with his anti-Soviet parents. Unlike them, he became a fervent communist, a member of the French communist party and, according to what he told me, a journalist for *L'Humanité*. In 1945, he decided to return to the Soviet homeland of his ancestors and to communism. He went back via Berlin. He was not allowed to settle in Odessa, the town he came from, so he was sent to Samarkand. There, the former journalist who wrote in French was given nothing better than a lousy job as a corrector in a Russian newspaper. Felitchkin was a Soviet citizen and I was a foreigner. We were treated very differently.

The Russian researchers insisted that their colleague leave the house of the Tajik patriarch.

The director asked me where I lived. I told him that I lived at my friend Abdullah's home. I told him that I had met him when I arrived and was admiring the main square. Then, like a real colonialist, he gestured in disdain, saying, "Really, you are not going to live with those people!" It was incredible to observe the contemptuous expression on the face of the Russian economist from the institute when he came to get me at Abdullah's home. He looked the house over. The floor consisted of beaten earth and the bedrooms had no doors. The toilet was a hole in the ground in the back of the garden, surrounded by some bushes. You had to say "hum" when you heard a noise so that the approaching person would stay away.

The institute had ample financial resources that enabled it to construct new apartment buildings for its employees. In an unfinished building, a room was prepared for the Frenchman.

Four walls with two windows and a key. It was a special apartment because it consisted of a room and a half. The water was in the courtyard. I was given a bucket and a basin. At my request they built a kind of case with a lid that opened with hinges. When the lid was lowered I had a bed. The administration of the institute gave me a pallet for a mattress, two sheets and a blanket, a small pillow, and a gas camping stove. For electricity they pulled a wire from the closest pole and later, when the house was finished, they forgot to connect me to the building's meter so that I never paid for my electricity.

Thus the Frenchman earned a salary, contrary to the letter of the law. The head of personnel who hired him followed unwritten orders in hiring him, and risked going to the Gulag. But he obeyed the local political authorities. Jacques got used to his new life. Tired of the battle, he finally gave up trying to obtain his identification card from a police station that never received – and would surely never receive – the necessary forms. He established an epistolary relationship with his Japanese brother whose address in Japan he had learned by heart. He spoke openly with his colleagues about where he came from. "After a while I met people who were really nice and I felt that I could have confidence in them." Jacques grew especially close to the head librarian of the scientific library of the institute. An educated Russian woman who spoke perfect French and English, she had been one of the wives of a former Bolshevik who served as the Soviet Union's honorary ambassador to Japan.

When she was young, Mrs Goncharova, whose maiden name was Bloch, had been used to an easy life, much respect and luxury. But in 1937 her brother, a lieutenant in the air force, was arrested. At the same time, she was arrested as his sister and sentenced to eight years in the Gulag. Her former Bolshevik husband immediately renounced his wife who had become a *zeka* in the camps. That was a common reaction, especially for men. I do not have statistics but I think that women were much more faithful and devoted than their partners, who certainly had much more to lose because they had important, powerful positions. The Soviet society that I knew, in spite of the propaganda, was very discriminatory towards women. Women saw their influence diminish after the revolution.

I often went to see Mrs Goncharova in her well-stocked library. From Moscow she received *Pravda* and *Izvestia*. It was not long before Samarkand society referred to us as the former *zek* and the former *zeka*. Through her I met her friend Ekaterina Vassilievna, a female researcher who was about fifty-five. She talked about her grandmother who had been a serf in central Russia. She had been educated in Petersburg-Leningrad. She was anti-clerical and fiercely atheistic, very progressive and pro-revolutionary. She had never been a member of the party.

In fact, I had friends among the Uzbeks and also among the Tajiks and the Russians. People in Samarkand usually worked for the Soviet state, in the fields, on the railway, or in manufacturing factories. But they also had little gardens and sold their own fruit, which allowed them to have small savings. Their life was quite pleasant because they had managed to keep the old customs of traditional Muslim society. They invited me to their celebrations where there were large dishes of rice pilaf cooked with mutton fat. In fact, I could have spent the rest of my life there. I liked the climate, the music, all that oriental culture that I had first known only in books. But I was stubborn. I wanted to return to France and I was being kept from doing that. So I tried everything I could to achieve my goal.

One day an elderly Jewish chemist with whom I was friends gave me some advice. He had a cousin who had married a Polish woman and who had managed, thanks to his wife, to leave the Soviet Union. He advised me to contact the Polish ambassador. Poland was, of course, a communist country, but it was different from the Soviet Union. The Poles knew the repatriation ropes better than the French.

In the beginning, as a former Gulag prisoner, I was terrified by the idea. From experience, I knew what neophyte zeal could be like. I would later learn that in certain ways the Polish communist prisons were even worse than the Soviet Gulag. I knew that in certain non-Russian regions of the Soviet Union collectivization had been even more brutal than in Russia. It was because Armenian, Georgian, Uzbek, and Polish bureaucrats had to do their best so that they were not suspected of complicity with their compatriots. However, because of the impasse in which I found myself, the Poles were my last resort.

Thus Jacques wrote to the Polish ambassador, an illegal letter like the one he had sent from Bykovo to the French consul. He stated that he was a dual national, Polish and French, and gave the names and address of his Polish family. However, Polish diplomacy was not like French diplomacy. It took ten minutes for Mr M. to type a letter, recognizing his fellow citizen without having done any research to confirm it. It would take an entire year for the Polish ambassador to establish that, in fact, Jacques had Polish citizenship and thus could be repatriated to Poland. Just as the elderly chemist had predicted, Jacques's request was eventually granted. Communist Poland had more effectively mastered the system's contradictions.

He was back where he started. Jacques the Frenchman was once more requesting repatriation to his second homeland and was going to become Polish once again. But he required perseverance, the kind that he obtained and cultivated to the highest degree in the school that was the Gulag. In addition, in 1959, the Samarkand KGB commander, the man who had been disdainful of Jacques (and Jacques of him) upon Jacques's arrival in Samarkand, finally gave Jacques his certificate of rehabilitation.

# 32 To Comrade Khrushchev [Stop] I Jacques Rossi [Stop] a Free Citizen [Stop] Am Starting a Hunger Strike [Stop] with No Time Limit and Until Death

> I consider myself lucky to be among the living. I saw death up close six times and, when I look back, four more times.
>
> Jacques Rossi

Some time after his request, Jacques received a telegram with a red heading and white letters: *Governmental Dispatch*. That was the title. "We request that the Polish citizen Franciszek Ksawery H. present himself at the Polish embassy in order to establish the necessary documents for his repatriation." Along with the document there was a money order for six hundred rubles to pay for expenses and the ticket from Samarkand to Moscow. The letter surprised the Frenchman, who had not really expected his situation to turn around.

In principle, without an identification card he did not have permission to travel and certainly not to travel far. In the Samarkand area the police knew him, but elsewhere with no papers he risked returning to the Gulag. Nevertheless, Jacques was not someone who feared taking risks.

> As soon as I received the telegram, I went to see the director of the institute, an important local party boss, and asked him to grant me a ten-day leave of absence so that I could respond to the invitation of the Polish ambassador. At first he was surprised, and asked to see the letter. He tried to dissuade me, but when I stated that Poland was a friendly and sovereign country, he was more cooperative. Not only did he lengthen the leave to fifteen days, but he also gave me a letter stating that I was a colleague at his institute. In case I had a problem, that letter could help me even if I lacked an identification card. In any case, I was so afraid of the Samarkand police that with

my "governmental dispatch" I went to see the famous police officer who had refused for months and years to give me the proper forms concerning my status. He seemed surprised, and he admitted that it was the first time that he had seen a document of this kind. Then he said, "But you are not allowed to leave the city!"

Jacques was worried, but he was stubborn and above all courageous. If the police officer asked the director of the institute for information, he could prohibit him from leaving, using any possible means. For example, he could stage a brawl in the train and detain Jacques as a witness. As a precautionary measure Jacques organized his trip very openly and asked his colleagues, professors and respected researchers, to accompany him to the station and to stay with him until he left.

Once I was in the train compartment, my friends met colleagues from another scientific institute who were going to a convention. This reassured me, for there could be other "potential witnesses." However, I was not completely reassured. I knew too well that in case of an arrest, the police would only need to give the university comrades the following order: "You didn't see anything!" And they wouldn't have seen anything.

After leaving Samarkand, Jacques took advantage of a Soviet policy that enabled people to send telegrams when travelling on a train. The telegraph and post office employees deposited forms in the train stations and then sent them to the correct address. Jacques sent his telegram with information about his arrival – including the number of his car and seat – to the person who had asked him to come to Moscow. He did not include the word "Embassy" because that would have attracted the attention of the censor. As Jacques said, "This was completely useless because the employee had understood everything, but pretended not to." As usual, he knew the address by heart: 30 Alexis Tolstoy Street, Moscow. The strategy worked. When he arrived, he said goodbye to his travel companions. A Polish diplomat was waiting for him just outside his car and spotted him immediately.

I also understood right away that he must have worked for the secret police. What perspicacity! His eyes worked like machines. I learned later that he had occupied an important position as the Warsaw district attorney under Stalin. With de-Stalinization he had been sent as a diplomat to Moscow. Two years later there was re-Stalinization and he had been sent somewhere else in Europe. He took me in an official car straight to the ambassador's office. There I learned that the man who had brought me to Moscow was Z., number two in the embassy, an important person, a delegate of the Central Committee of the Polish communist party in charge of repatriating former members of the Gulag after the Twentieth Party Congress. I had not known him before, but he was around my age, perhaps a bit older than I was, and unlike me had already belonged to the hierarchy of the party before the war. He was a jovial, pleasant man who took his job seriously – his job of monitoring Soviet actions and of resolving potential conflicts.

We spoke. He was close to some of my former comrades who were militants in the party apparatus during the thirties. He expressed a certain nostalgia for our youthful convictions and the way in which everything had evolved. I felt that he respected me. He addressed me using the formal "you," which was the practice among members of the Polish communist party. He was very discreet and asked me no questions, but he did criticize the Soviets who created problems for them and made things difficult. It was quite a surprise for me to observe an obvious distrust between communist comrades of different countries.

They had me sleep at the embassy – which was forbidden for someone with no papers – in the buildings for the Polish staff and their families. I was very moved to be among children babbling in Polish and who said things to me like: "You know, he still wets his pants."

Z. had Jacques meet the Polish consul general, who asked him all sorts of bureaucratic and personal questions about his activities in Poland, the towns he lived in, his Polish family, and the different positions that Marcin H. had occupied during his career. Finally, he recommended that Jacques return to Samarkand and await the verification that needed to be done in Poland so that his Polish passport could be issued. Jacques insisted on coming himself to get his passport when it was ready. The idea that such a precious document could be sent through the Soviet mail system frightened him.

The consul agreed although he remained sceptical. Jacques returned to Central Asia without a problem and waited for news about his passport. However, the Poles had great difficulty convincing Soviet authorities that Jacques was a dual citizen and that he could have a Polish passport. Jacques was tired of waiting. He wrote, he telephoned. He was told to be patient. He waited for almost a year before receiving a letter stating that his Polish passport was ready. In order to make sure this was the case, he decided to once again travel round-trip – under strict surveillance – to the Polish embassy in Moscow in order to obtain the precious document.

Upon returning to Samarkand, he went immediately to the police with his brand-new Polish passport. However, the official stamp of a friendly country did not convince the police officer, nor the bureaucracy above him: "You are not Polish," he insisted. "You are French."

> I begged him to understand. He was not aggressive. No. He did not prohibit me from being Polish. He said he would investigate it – the next day. Here is an example of how even people of bad faith could behave properly. During that period my wallet with my French papers was stolen on a bus and, as was typical, the thief took the money and put the documents back in a mail box. The documents ended up at the police station. And when for the umpteenth time I went to the station to get those missing forms, I was given back my French papers according to the regulations.

The passionate attachment that Jacques had shown for his mother's country turned out to be a double-edged sword. In any case, the communist system for which he had been both a champion and a victim would not let him go. So he decided to resort to more drastic methods.

> I chose my day, a Friday night, because Saturday was the day before Sunday and I calculated that there would be more time to find a solution to the problem. Between Samarkand and Moscow there is a six-hour time difference. It was much later in the capital. Shortly before six o'clock, the time when the post office closed, I went to phone the Polish consul to warn him that I was going to officially protest against the situation in which I found myself. He was very concerned and he warned me: "I strongly advise that you not attempt anything!"
>
> "You advise me to do what you consider fair, but I will do what I consider fair. In any case you have been informed." I forced myself to be careful. It was important that there be a witness in case things turned out badly.
>
> Saturday morning at six o'clock, when the post office opened, I drafted the text of my telegram to Nikita Khrushchev: "I JACQUES ROSSI [STOP] A FREE CITIZEN [STOP] AM STARTING A HUNGER STRIKE [STOP] WITH NO TIME LIMIT AND UNTIL DEATH TO PROTEST AGAINST THE ARBITRARY POSITION OF THE LOCAL AUTHORITIES WHO REFUSE TO GIVE ME AN EXIT VISA." I gave

the text to the telegraphist and while she was reading it I saw her raise her eyebrows and wrinkle her forehead. I said to myself: she is going to call the KGB and have me arrested! But not at all. Once she finished reading it, she looked at me and she said, "Perhaps you would like to pay for the answer!"

"Of course, I will pay for the answer."

With an air of seriousness, she prepared the telegram and gave me my receipt. At six-thirty, I left the post office and went home. I informed one of my colleagues that I would not be going to the institute because I was going on a hunger strike to protest the impossibility of obtaining a legitimate exit visa. I lay down on my pallet and I started my hunger strike. I did not cheat. I swallowed absolutely nothing. I was ready to die.

Jacques kept the receipt of the telegram to Khrushchev. The receipt clearly showed the recipient: "to comrade Khrushchev." It stated also that this "telegram was sent according to procedure 1411." It was signed by the telegraphist Moisseeva. The address of the post office was also specified: Karl Marx Street, Samarkand. The hunger striker followed his plan.

I left the door of my apartment open. The apartment consisted of a room and a half. The building was finished but the rest of the apartment was not yet occupied. Around eleven o'clock I heard steps and attempts to open the doors of the two other rooms. Suddenly there were five people at my bedside, five Komsomol youths, boys and girls, with a big bouquet of red roses wrapped in a newspaper. They said, "Are you the one who is being refused an exit visa to return to your country?"

"Yes, I am."

"We are students at the University of Samarkand. We are shocked by what is happening to you. We think that every man has the sacred right to live in his own country. Please excuse us. We couldn't find a crystal vase so we're giving you the flowers wrapped in the newspaper *Pravda*. What can we do for you?"

"Above all, get out of here. Since there are five of you, this will surely be considered a political demonstration. I thank you. Leave me the flowers and *Pravda*, but don't say anything to anybody."

In fact, I was afraid. But I was also really touched. One of the students was the boyfriend of the telegraphist, and that is how they heard about the telegram. Between six-thirty and eleven o'clock, they had time to organize, but the unfruitful search for a crystal vase had taken time and they were really sorry not to have found one!

I managed to convince them that their presence was dangerous for me. In the afternoon I was visited by the party secretary, a research professor in physiology with whom I had a friendship at work. He tried to convince me not to continue, saying that I was not being reasonable and that he was immediately, upon orders of the director of the institute, going to see the regional secretary to resolve the affair. He came back to see me. According to him the problem was resolved. He was present for the phone call between the regional party secretary and the responsible official in Moscow. My exit visa would be ready in two days, on Tuesday. I no longer had any reason to continue my hunger strike. It was six o'clock. Within a few minutes everyone in the building came to my apartment carrying things to eat. There were dishes everywhere, Uzbek food, Tatar, Tajik, and Russian food – a veritable feast. I was touched and relieved that my fasting only lasted twelve hours.

The following Monday, while awaiting his visa, Jacques returned to work at the institute. Tuesday came and went, then Wednesday, and still no sign of a visa. Wednesday morning he started his hunger strike again. After several hours he had another visit from the same colleague, the party secretary. He assured Jacques once again that he had listened to the conversation between the regional secretary and the responsible official in Moscow. The visa that had been sent was not strictly speaking a paper visa but a telephone instruction to the local police that granted Jacques the right to leave.

I don't know what happened to me then. I lost my voice and I couldn't stand up. I had been on a hunger strike for eleven days in Norilsk without being force-fed and had been able to walk up several flights of stairs to the office of the supervisor. This time, however, after barely four to five hours of fasting, I couldn't stand on my feet.

Two young, strong professors, one a Tajik and the other one Russian, took me under the arms and carried me to the police station. They were with me when my Polish passport was stamped. With the exit visa we triumphantly went back to my building. All the neighbours were waiting for me. It was a real party with those people of Samarkand who were so happy to be able to express their feelings. At that moment I thought about another episode in my long existence: the journey we had made on foot in the mud of Krasnoyarsk watched by the old women on the doorsteps of their huts. Only their eyes spoke, communicating their compassion and their solidarity. In times of terror, the heart cannot express itself. But in Samarkand after the

Twentieth Party Congress, even the intellectuals, who were much more cowardly than the masses, even they were relieved to express their generosity.

Khrushchev never sent a personal answer to Stalin's victim, which would have cost him nothing. The next day Jacques quickly got his third train ticket for Moscow. It was difficult to obtain a seat, since troops and industrial and administrative personnel had priority. During the next three or four days the people of Samarkand came and celebrated and congratulated him and said goodbye. After twenty-four years of a forced stay in the Soviet Union, the only baggage Jacques had was a suitcase and a Persian rug, "security for the future," bought with his savings and which he carried rolled on his shoulder. The day of his departure his friends and colleagues crowded into his place with presents. But, as he said, "my best friends were not there because it was too painful for them to see me go." He put the souvenirs that everyone gave him into a bag that he carried with his other free hand. The whole group left for the station, where Jacques was accompanied like a hero until the train departed and the last hands waving goodbye were no longer visible as the train faded into the Central Asian steppe. The train was travelling westward this time, but it was only slowly bringing the Frenchman closer to the country of his mother.

While the Samarkand-Moscow train moved languidly along, Jacques reflected upon that exceptional moment and the fact that he was about to leave the Soviet Union. The big Gulag and the small Gulag. That "bloody sewer" where he hadn't perished. He reflected on his "luck." He was lucky that he fainted before admitting anything under torture. He was lucky to not have died from exhaustion or not have been eliminated by the criminal recidivists. He was lucky that his third hunger strike had turned out to be so easy, so fruitful at a time between the Twentieth Party Congress and the *refuseniks* of the sixties. Soviet authorities did not know how to deal with those on hunger strikes; Jacques was one of the pioneers. He was lucky to have held on, to have known how to resist when it was necessary, lucky to have preserved his soul – "Because I really care about my soul." Regarding Samarkand, his first stop on the road back to freedom, he maintained the sweetest memory. Although he revisited other places, he never went back to Central Asia.

During the journey he sent a telegram to Adam, his former supervisor in the clandestine services whose whereabouts he had known for several years. Adam. He was the one who chose to return from the United States to Moscow during the Great Purges. He was the one who had warned Jacques about the risks he faced. Jacques had only known for a short time that Adam had been responsible for his early rehabilitation. Adam had been among the first to be freed from prison and was in charge of some files, so Jacques spent several hours with this former comrade in his apartment in Moscow before taking the train to Warsaw. "I immediately bought my ticket for Poland with my passport stamped with the exit visa. As I was walking in Moscow, despite de-Stalinization, I realized that I was constantly being followed. Thanks to my memories of Moscow streets and buildings with several entrances, I managed to lose my tracker, who tried hard not to lose me." It was February 1961 when he took the Moscow–Warsaw train, twenty-four years after the Great Purges. Jacques Rossi was twenty-eight when he crossed the Soviet border the last time. This time he was fifty-two.

> In the compartment I felt very nervous. There was only one other person with me, a communist Italian musician who adored the Soviet Union because a concert series had just been organized for him. He told me at length how he had been well received. He was literally exploding with joy. In a nearby compartment there were other Italians, students or young researchers who had come for a stay in Moscow and of course were enthusiastic about the ongoing de-Stalinization. The next day – the trip lasted fourteen or fifteen hours – we arrived at the border. The train attendant came into our compartment and he suggested to the Italian musician: "You would be better off with your compatriots in the other compartment."
> The Italian immediately obeyed without asking any questions. The attendant picked up his things without waiting for his answer and off they went, leaving me alone in the compartment. I must say that chills were going down my spine. We arrived at Brest-Litovsk. Right away, there was passport control. No problem. They stamped my passport. Then a customs officer and a border guard came into my compartment. They closed the door and pulled the curtain shut. I understood that they were going to do a *shmon*, the infamous prison body search. They had me remove all my clothes except my underpants and they pulled on my underpants to check that I was not hiding anything around my balls. Only my asshole was not inspected, just like at Butyrka. However, they did not unroll my Persian rug, where I could have hidden documents or other forbidden objects. Inside my underpants I had a pocket with my papers, my twelve work certificates, including the one from the Astrakhan Institute, plus another from the military academy of Samarkand where I had taught French to student officers, and above all my

certificate of rehabilitation that the Soviet high court had finally sent to me in Samarkand. Well, all those documents that were much more precious to me because I was going to another communist country, they simply seized them from me unceremoniously. When I started to protest they replied that such forms were not for foreigners and that once I had left the Soviet Union, I could always write to each institution and request the certificates on the correct forms. It was a completely false assertion. Since then I have met other non-Soviets who kept those same papers without a problem. Afterwards, I went through all the trouble in the world in order to obtain copies of those precious documents. Some of them I never got back.

When the customs officer left he told me to get dressed and to tidy up the compartment so as not to attract attention at the Polish border. I didn't do anything. I knew that they would leave the train before the border. I did not even wait for them to jump off. I just put on my pants and I went to get the Italian travellers so that they wouldn't miss out on the spectacle: the compartment was turned upside down; the seats were turned over; the ashtrays were emptied on the floor; all my things, except for the rug, were thrown into the corners. The Italians could not believe it, but they did not dare to say anything. Meanwhile, the train slowed down and the two Russians jumped off. We were arriving at the Polish border.

The Polish police officer who entered the compartment with a very different uniform understood right away. There was a kind of complicity between us. He almost seemed disgusted. He looked at my passport, stamped it, and though he was a communist he saluted me politely and said, "Welcome to Poland."

Did the customs officers and frontier police realize what this standard greeting – "Welcome to Poland" – meant to a man who had returned from hell? With this standard welcome, the fundamental chapter of Jacques Rossi's existence had come to a close. The former prisoner returned home with a very clear objective – to bear witness and to testify.

# 33 Communist Poland: Origins of *The Gulag Handbook*

When it is impossible to describe a new event, feeling or concept for which ordinary human language has no word, a new term is created, borrowed from the language of the legislator of style and taste in the Far North – the criminal world.

Varlam Shalamov, Kolyma Tales

On the platform of the Warsaw train station, Jacques was welcomed by family members that he had been able to contact to announce his arrival. During his time in the clandestine services, prior to his arrest in 1937, he maintained ties with the country of his youth and the place where he first developed his ideological commitment to communism. On his way back to Moscow, after his missions abroad, he stopped in Poland. When he left the Poland of Pilsudski, he was a young communist imprisoned by a right-wing authoritarian regime. He returned to a satellite country of the USSR, a man critical of his former deeply held Marxist-Leninist illusions. What struck Jacques upon his arrival in Poland, though, was the difference in atmosphere as compared with the Soviet Union. After crossing the border, in his initial conversations with Polish travellers on the train for Warsaw, he felt that the atmosphere was less tense, and people were more open and critical, more "Western."

At his friends' home, he was welcomed in triumph. Several days after his arrival, his family that had worked hard for his repatriation had a party in his honour.

> It was more of a reception than a celebration and very European – with little canapés, imported alcohol, gentlemen wearing ties, everybody standing up as in American cocktail parties. People talked

about the theatre, the most recent book with various implicit political references – it was all very intellectual, very Left Bank. Having arrived from the big Gulag – even if I had left the other one, the small Gulag, several years earlier – and listening to all those elegant women chatting, it felt a bit disorienting. At the end of the evening, one of the guests pointed his finger at me and said simply: "You're the one who should have been talking." A drunkard's remark. He did not wait for me to answer, and what could I have said? I was astonished!

The communist Poland that Jacques discovered in the early sixties was quite unlike the Soviet Union. To Jacques, people appeared to be better dressed. Men wore hats and women dressed carefully. The store windows were better stocked. People were more courteous. "In communist Poland, they did not say "comrade" – except in official speeches – but instead used 'sir' and 'madam' and the third-person formal address. Sometimes police officers in the street smiled, which would have been unthinkable in Russia. At work, people did not make anti-Soviet statements, but over coffee they told some [political] jokes."

For work and housing Jacques relied on the repatriation agency that was under the Interior Ministry. He was afraid of being sent to the western region of the country, which had been seized from Germany and which Poland intended to repopulate. Fortunately, he used his connections with former comrades, who managed to find him a job as a translator. He worked in an office that conducted studies on urbanization and industrialization in developing countries that were not wealthy enough to trade with capitalistic countries. Jacques translated from Polish into English, French, and German.

> To give you an idea of the difference in atmosphere: in the beginning, when I worked in that office, we were one on top of the other because the office space was very limited. One of the engineers started to sing a song that was very popular in Poland: "If it rains or if the wind blows, the big pig is welcome here." The big pig was Khrushchev. Everybody laughed and I was deathly afraid. I hid under a desk! And to my great surprise, nothing happened. I had definitely left the Soviet Union!

Given the housing shortage, it was not easy to find an apartment, but at least apartments were not expensive.

A kind of Solomon's rule had been established. Repatriated people could occupy the apartments of people who were leaving definitively.

In general, they were Jews. Any persons who could prove that they had family abroad could leave the country. At the office, I was given an apartment address and I was asked to go and see if I liked it. "If I liked it!" Me – a former Gulag prisoner. I was not accustomed to such treatment. It was a communal apartment with three rooms. I introduced myself to the woman, who immediately said there were no rooms available and closed the door in my face. In fact, she was a widow who lived in one room with her three children. In the second room there was someone else, and the third room was occupied by the person who was leaving. There was only one toilet and one kitchen for everybody. Given the woman's offensive behaviour, I left.

The Housing Office gave me another address. This time it was a studio apartment occupied by an elderly woman. She was going to leave and join her daughter in Australia. The apartment was a bit dreary because the old woman did not take care of anything, but the fact that I could live alone seemed like a dream to me! So I applied for the apartment. I had to wait patiently until the woman left, and things dragged on. After inquiring, I learned that she had purchased her ticket, but that the travel agent needed coaxing because he wanted a bribe and she did not have the money for that. The poor woman had no money and her boat was leaving from Venice for Sydney in three weeks. I decided to take the bull by the horns. Following the advice of a friend, I went to see the travel agent and made him think that I had influential connections in the party and that I could speak about him to someone. He was afraid, and three days later the woman had her ticket and I had my apartment where I unrolled my Persian rug from Samarkand.

When Jacques arrived in Warsaw in 1961, with twenty-four Soviet years inscribed in his mind as well as his gut, he had already begun making plans for the two major projects that would preoccupy him for the rest of his life – his return to France and his testimony. He wanted to bear witness, in any way possible but especially through writing, to the experiences of millions of his fellow Gulag prisoners. His first years in Poland were focused on adapting and rediscovering the Poland of his youth, and recovering from his initial shock. He found himself reconnecting with a world that brought him closer to the world where he really wanted to live. As early as 1961, he began to discreetly work on an idea he had had for a long time. The idea came to him during that unending voyage in the Stolypin railcar when he first came into contact with the world of the criminal recidivists in the transit prisons.

You mustn't forget that I was trained as a linguist. All those criminal offenders were common Russian people who frequently spoke in a very graphic language with amusing and colourful expressions such as: "It's as useful as an alarm clock in a vagina." These expressions made me laugh and they fascinated me so much. Despite the context, I tried right from the start to lock them away in my memory because in the beginning it was impossible to take and keep notes. I used memorization techniques to exercise my memory like you exercise a muscle. I was sure that one day all this material would become useful for me. At that point, I imagined writing a kind of dictionary of Gulag slang.

In time, I realized that the linguistic element included many other issues that were just as important – social, historical, and political questions. Ultimately at issue was the human condition of all prisoners in that system. Moreover, I experienced a horrible sense of disillusionment. I felt that my mistake had been so profound, so serious, that I had the obligation to warn the world so that such mistakes could be avoided. I had kept several drawings and some written notes using Tibetan letters that I had started in Alexandrovsk. They were not discovered during many body searches. They helped me remember details for the three books I would later write.

A "great friend," as Jacques described her, encouraged him to begin work on the book that he had thought about since his arrest. He met her through mutual friends. Her name was Regina G. She was the daughter of Polish landowners and a fervent Catholic. At the time Jacques met her, she was about twenty and he was roughly fifty. Regina G.'s grandfather was arrested just after the invasion of the Red Army on 17 September 1939 and had disappeared. Her father, a Polish nationalist, had to hide during most of the war. He was deported on 9 May 1945, the very day that soldiers celebrated the end of the war in the streets. At the same time, the Soviets took control of the country and crushed all forms of resistance. According to rumours, he was abandoned. He was ill and perhaps had been suffering severely just as his convoy arrived at Novosibirsk. The family never received official word or confirmation of his death. They learned about it only through word of mouth.

Regina remembered with intense emotions the circumstances surrounding her father's arrest and deportation – the frightened families that were grouped together on the platform with their supplies of dry bread that were later confiscated, looking in the distance at the convoy guarded by soldiers and dogs. Her father gestured toward the prisoners who were dying of hunger. Then obeying her mother, little Regina rushed toward the train, towards a soldier who grabbed the loaf of bread, put it on his bayonet, and gave it to her father. The sight of her father sharing the precious bread with other prisoners was the last image the child would have of her father, who never returned from the Gulag.

Jacques had returned from the belly of the beast, apparently intact with clean hands, ready to satisfy the young Polish woman's hunger for knowledge and her desire to participate in his work. They grew close and remained so for the rest of their lives. All Jacques's books were dedicated to Regina. When in March 2001 he felt, mistakenly, that his time had come, he wanted to see Regina one last time and to marry her at the end of his long odyssey.

After their meeting in Warsaw in 1961 they were separated while Regina was studying in England. They met again in Paris in 1964 – accidentally, just in front of Notre-Dame Cathedral – and again in Grenoble and Vienna during Jacques's first trip to the West. Today both of them underscore the longevity, the continuity, and the stability of their relationship. Although she was at first sceptical about the publishing market for books about the Gulag, Regina affirms that the desire to promote Jacques's work remained her preoccupation over her entire life. This explains why, in 1985, she decided to stay in the United States when Jacques chose to settle definitively in France. She participated actively in major events to promote *The Gulag Handbook* – at Georgetown University on 11 December 1987; upon publication of the Russian edition, *Spravochnik po Gulagu,* in London, where she introduced Jacques and read a passage from *The Gulag Handbook*; then at the Frankfort Book Fair in 1989, where Jacques was invited after the book was published in English by Paragon; and finally, in 1992, at a conference in Warsaw where she worked hard to publicize the book.

> I first met Mrs Marie. She had a daughter named Regina who was a student in English literature at Warsaw University. Regina had never been a communist. She always had faith in her Catholic values, which made her a model of courage and strength, in spite of her youth. I was impressed by her intelligence and moral bravery and I grew close to her and her small circle of friends, whom she chose for their ethical principles.

Jacques began preparation for what would become his most important work.

> At first, Gulag expressions were swirling around in my head, but I was still in shock in those early days of my new life. Then one day I

bought my first pair of new shoes. I kept the box, and noticed that the shape of the shoebox was just the right size for holding half a sheet of paper. And that is how I started to collect my notes. When I finished one, I would carefully fold it in half and place it into the box. I wrote down everything that came to mind. For example – *chmon*: the body search. That was a practice that I definitely knew first hand: How was it done? What were the orders? How could you hide something? In high-security prisons and in detention centres you were not allowed to have thread. If we got some thread to mend our clothes we had to return the unused thread along with the needles. If we really wanted to keep some we had to hide it well. Before a body search, I once saw a very important person, a former general, roll thread around the tip of his penis. During some body searches I had been ordered to "open your member!" I had difficulty understanding what it meant to "open" a penis, so the guard made a gesture separating his fingers. You had to pull down the foreskin. I made notes of all these details as they came to mind. However, there were techniques for hiding things that I will never reveal in order not to betray those secrets. (For example, I will never explain how I managed to miraculously keep for months on end a small tin knife one half inch long and a quarter inch wide that came from a piece of tin can that I had sharpened.) The rest appeared with many other details in *The Gulag Handbook* under the listing "body search." I wrote as the details came to mind, in no particular order.

Then came the entry "bread ration." First, the expressions that were used most often came to mind – "the holy bread ration," "the holy crutch," "the bread ration earned by the sweat of your brow," "it is not the small ration that kills you but the big one," "beat the person responsible for the barracks and the bread ration that had disappeared will appear all by itself." Whether it was at night or during the day, I would open the closet, take out the shoebox file, and add a word, two sentences, a paragraph.

Later, I read and studied the memoirs and testimonies of others. For example, I studied what Shalamov wrote in his tale on "the bread ration." At the library of the University of Warsaw, I found a volume on prison rules under the tsars. This work was definitely inaccessible in the Soviet Union because if a curious person tried to draw comparisons with the Gulag, he would have immediately noticed that the tsar's prison rules were much better. It was incredible. But I could establish parallels between the two systems. In the entry "*paika*" or "the daily bread norm" in *The Gulag Handbook* one reads: "The arrestee under Tsarism got a single bread norm – [nearly]

2 pounds (819 grams) per day corresponding almost to two basic daily norms for the Soviet prisoner."[1]

Thus my pile of notes got bigger, so much so that I began to worry. If the Polish police found them, they might not send me to prison, but they would surely confiscate them. I had good friends at the French embassy. In Poland, unlike the Soviet Union, we could have contacts with "capitalists." One of my friends took the risk of sending some of my notes to France through a diplomatic pouch. My notes, of course, were written in Russian because the basic material was the vocabulary and the familiar slang expressions of the Gulag. In my mind I knew that one day they would be translated into French because I was French. It was my language. However, there were ideas that were difficult to translate: "the commissar-interrogator" was not at all an "examining magistrate" as it appeared in some French translations. A commissar-interrogator was a cop, who was not a member of the justice department but of the police. He started by tracking the person he was going to accuse. Then he interrogated him using techniques that are now known, and then he prepared the sentence. He had nothing in common with an examining magistrate. Let us not forget the story about the blind man and the coffee with milk. It was like drafting a description of life on the Riviera for the Inuit. How, for example, would you translate the word "mimosa"? Inuit know a kind of lichen but not mimosas! Later my French friend the jurist Albert Joannon helped me greatly with these translations.

Finally, living alone in a studio apartment in Warsaw and working as a translator helped Jacques to get through his first years in Poland. He kept busy working on the notes that would one day become *The Gulag Handbook*. Finding old friends and family, meeting with others, and being in the company of Regina helped Jacques to rebuild himself internally. He even submitted a request to regain his membership card in the Polish communist party.

# 34 Seeing Paris Again

We like it when everyone knows about our good deeds. The good souls who subscribed to literary tourism in the east before 1980 bragged about what dissidents had told them and anyone else who would listen. In doing that, they betrayed the dissidents. It seemed normal for a Soviet citizen to trust a foreigner whom he considered not to have been perverted by a system that glorified informers. Numerous former Gulag prisoners talked to me. *The Gulag Handbook* benefitted from this.

Jacques Rossi

It was 1964, an important year for the person whom his fellow Gulag inmates called Jacques the Frenchman. That year, he was hired by a special school for translators at the University of Warsaw. A work certificate dated 10 November 1993 indicated that Mr Jacques Rossi, son of Marcin, was hired as a teaching assistant for French language and culture as of 4 September 1964. This new job sent him on an internship in Grenoble as part of a university exchange between France and Poland. It was also in 1964 that the inquiry of the Polish communist party was closed and the affair was shelved. The investigation concerned the two phases of his activities as a revolutionary militant. Jacques was readmitted into the party of his youth, a party that had changed greatly.

For the former Gulag prisoner, the decision to return to the fold of Marxist-Leninism was not automatic. Jacques described it as a security strategy, a way to keep himself and others safe.

> My membership in the communist party was not a matter of belief but a means to an end. By returning to the Polish communist party, I could do something useful for others and for myself.

My primary concern was to avoid any suspicion that could have compromised the production of what would become *The Gulag Handbook*. I also thought that I could finally help others if I acquired some power from inside the party. That is what happened in 1968. Right after I left the Soviet Union, in the beginning of 1960, my dislike of communism was so intense that I could not bear to listen anymore to friends who advised me to rejoin the party. As a former communist, they thought that I would have the trust of other members, and that I would benefit from a certain protection that I could then use to protect others.

Moreover, in a context that was not Russia, I had evolved. It is true that before the war there weren't many party members, a dozen perhaps at the university. However, during the sixties, the number of students and professors who were party members increased to the tens of thousands. It was like the old Bolsheviks from 1905 living in Russia in the twenties. They were like a very exclusive club. Of course, I enjoyed having a certain status. It was very appealing to people that a pioneer of Polish communism, who had spent a long time in the Gulag, wanted to return to the party following his release. All those years in the Gulag inspired more confidence than a political career. By contrast, in the Soviet Union the enthusiasm after the Twentieth Party Congress lasted only a short time, and those who had been rehabilitated kept their distance. Poland was much more liberal. In Polish encyclopedias, one could even find the names of victims who had not been rehabilitated following the Twentieth Party Congress.

At that time, there were two opposing currents within the Polish communist party: the internationalists and the partisans. The internationalists, many of whom were Jewish, had been communists before the war and were devoted to the idea of international communism. Most of them had left Poland during the war due to religious persecution. The partisans were nationalists who at the same time had participated in the anti-Nazi resistance. Of course, I was close to the former, having been an international communist for a long time and having returned from the camps. After 1968, everything changed.

It is important to note that in order to find work, especially a teaching job at a university, Jacques had to prove that he had the requisite degrees. But he had obtained them under aliases. Thus he had to prove that he was a member of the communist party before the war before he could request readmission to the party after the war. Between the two periods, there was no continuity.

It so happened that the minister for higher education had also been a party member before the war. He managed to find in the Moscow archives, among other documents, the diplomas that Jacques had obtained under assumed names when he was a young secret agent. He had those diplomas reissued for Jacques under his real name.

The minister had nothing to gain personally from that. He helped me simply because I was an old member of the Polish communist party and he considered me a victim of Stalinism. I did not share this view. He believed that one had to help a comrade who had suffered, and who could not find work simply because he had earned diplomas under an alias at a time when he was serving the party. I noticed that many of these men who had been idealists in their youth, and who found themselves up to their necks in unpleasant affairs, were very pleased when given the opportunity to do something good and recover a bit of their humanity.

Thus Jacques was able to secure a job at the University of Warsaw.

I taught quite basic classes in civilization. They were year-long classes whose goal was to teach culture to translators who had only studied language. If they were translating a text where there was the word *"charolais"* they had to understand that it referred to cattle. When they translated *"Jarnac"* in the expression *"coup de Jarnac"* they had to know that this referred to history rather than geography.[1] And so on. At my school, I was responsible for the party organization, which had few members. We were only concerned with school management problems. Nothing else.

During this entire period Jacques made many friends. There was, in particular, Ulderio de Silvestri, a young Colombian student at the University of Warsaw who was married to a Pole. He finally moved to Paris, where he remained among Jacques's closest circle of friends. In 1964, Jacques took the first steps towards realizing his dream of over twenty years – to return to France.

First of all, I never said that my primary objective was to leave Poland. This dream is what kept me alive, but I didn't reveal it. As always, my strategy relied on patience, at least for important projects, because in daily life I was easily irritated. As soon as I was hired by the University of Warsaw, I took part in a fifteen-day internship in Grenoble as part of a university exchange, and received a thirty-day visa. This enabled me to spend half of the time in Paris, housed by Polish friends of friends. I used that time to do research on my family.

Why didn't I ask for political asylum in France? For the same reason as several years earlier, when I refused to ask for it at the French embassy in Moscow in 1957. The reason was that I did not want to present myself as the one returning, hat in hand. As long as I stood tall, I was the hero fighting against capitalism. Now that I had been bowed and broken I did not want to ask that same capitalist country to come to my rescue because, over the years, this revolutionary and clandestine agent had changed his views! I finally understood that the capitalism that I still continue to consider far from wonderful was infinitely more humane than our beautiful, noble project. That project logically led to the system that I and thousands upon thousands of my comrades experienced in every respect, with our own flesh and blood, over many years. I said to myself then that if I found my family in France and became a French citizen, I would refuse to rely on the capitalist state that I wanted so much to destroy.

On that occasion, Jacques did not manage to find his French family. But much later, a circle of truly exceptional people – including his friend Albert, his translators, his collaborators, and the founder of the association "Friends of Jacques Rossi" – would take the place of family for him in France. In the coming years, friends and various connections at the French embassy in Poland managed to obtain from the registry office an excerpt from his mother's birth certificate. That's when he would learn, to his surprise, that his mother was born in Bourg-en-Bresse, and was the daughter of a modest craftsman. This contrasted with the environment in which she had lived with Jacques during his childhood. He also learned that his mother's only sister had left just before the war to teach French in Argentina. However, this research concerning his family was secondary to the emotional turmoil that he felt during that first visit to France following his thirty-year absence. And what an absence!

> I could not believe it! I had always imagined all the obstacles that would prevent me from arriving at my destination. I was nervous and tense in my seat on the Polish airplane from Warsaw to Paris. The person sitting next to me, a young man of about thirty, looked at me with a certain condescension. I was in my fifties but I didn't look like a dignitary. He leaned towards me and he asked me whether this was my first visit to France. I replied that I had been there already, but a very long time ago. He asked me how long it had been.
> 
> "Oh, about thirty years!"

"Well, you will not recognize France. I go there every six months and I see changes from one visit to the next."

He wanted to make me see what an important person he was. It was quite uncommon for a Pole to go to France twice a year, except if one were a secret agent. He might also have been an engineer who travelled because of a technical contract or a scientific researcher going to a conference. Anyway, he pretended to know France better than anyone else. I remained modest.

Finally, at the stop in Zurich, Jacques got out of the plane to stretch his legs. He had a few French coins that some old Polish friends had given him. Their last trip to western Europe had been in 1940. He saw delicious food displayed and newspapers from the free world, like *Le Monde*.

I knew that I could pay with French francs. I took all the change out of my pocket.

"But sir, those are pennies!"

I was ashamed by my ignorance and poverty, and apologized at length. I felt completely disoriented. Then I got back on my plane for Paris. I was expecting at any moment to be called on the loud speaker: "Would Mr Rossi please come to the control centre!" But no, the airplane did not turn back to its point of departure, as I feared.

Finally, the plane landed on the runway at the Bourget airport and I, Jacques Rossi, I stepped out onto French soil with my own two feet, which had not rotted away in Siberia.

At the passport control, there were two policemen, one white, the other black, who were chatting together and not paying any attention to me. This pleased me because their relationship conformed with my ideal of racial equality. With the standard gesture, one of them took my passport, glanced at it quickly, and stamped it, without calling attention to anything. I couldn't believe it. The last time I crossed a border, the Soviet customs officers had practically done a careful examination of my anus. And now, for this person who returned from the Gulag and the communist world, here in France, there wasn't the slightest interest in him. Absolutely none!

Jacques does not remember having gone through customs. Once he was in the capital, he knew where to find the subway. He went straight to the address that had been given to him in Warsaw. The apartment was near Alma. It was the home of a Pole who had been in France since the First World War and who welcomed him without much enthusiasm but nevertheless gave him tea. The stone building was grand; the Roux-Combaluzier elevator reminded Jacques of the Paris of his youth. Jacques admired the staircase, so nicely polished by the concierge, with steps of white marble and a red carpet. During the next few hours, he reclaimed the city of his youth, once again.

> I walked through the city. I was like a crazy person. I was astounded. I have never been drunk, but I imagine it was a state similar to mine during those first few days in Paris. I walked endlessly because it is on foot that you can recapture a city. Once I was strolling near the Gare de Lyon. I continued walking and I saw a facade that I didn't recognize. It was the city hall, completely resurfaced and unrecognizable.
>
> In the small street behind city hall, I asked a merchant standing on the doorstep of his shop where I could find the Rue de Rivoli. He answered me very politely, "Of course, when you live in the provinces you forget where certain streets are."
>
> I realized that he thought I was an elderly gentleman who had just arrived from the provinces, from where he hadn't emerged in a long time. I was touched by the impression that he had of me. It was as if he was holding out his hand to help me take a step into my home. It was as if he was reintegrating me into my country!

Jacques contemplated the sights in front of him and around him. This was for him a country of mythical proportions, the memory of which kept him alive in the labour camps of the Far North. And now here he was, in this country where people were going about their affairs, strolling around and living as if nothing had happened.

> All those people didn't give a damn about what had happened to me. Even more, they didn't care about what happened to millions of others. I realized that the suffering of millions of human beings could have no importance. That was almost reassuring. Because at a certain point, when you reach the depths of such misery, you realize that in that ocean of despair, you are but a grain of sand. People tend to think that they shoulder all the world's misery. It is true that in the Gulag there were those who were worse off than I was. I also discovered that in France as in the rest of the world, there were men who weren't at all unhappy and, for the most part, they weren't even aware of this.

After the shock of his return to Paris, Jacques left for Grenoble on his internship. There he, together with students and a Danish secondary school French teacher, was housed with a French family. It was during this stay that he was lucky to receive a letter from an old Gulag comrade, Hans the Austrian.

> I think that he got my address from the famous Adam, a mutual acquaintance. I lost touch with Hans for many years. We had been in contact in Norilsk until about 1947. At that time, we asked each other no questions, but I understood that he also had been a communist patriot. With his gift for cooking he always managed to give me something to eat when I came back to the barracks half dead after my day of labour. He was an electrical engineer by training and, of course, he could rattle on in Russian. As a high-ranking member of the Comintern – he was a bit older than I was – he had often been in Moscow before being sent to the Gulag.
> He wasn't assigned to do forced labour, but with a small team he did repairs in the small mechanical workshop. They brought him radios from outside the camp, which enabled him to listen to forbidden foreign stations. When Hitler attacked the Soviet Union in 1941, he shared that information with me and, at that time, he and I knew more about what was going on than our camp commander. After a new accusation was fabricated against him, as happened with me, he got an extra ten years. In 1947, he was released thanks to his wife, who had not been deported but was only sent with their daughter to Kazakhstan. He found them again in Vienna. When he was still in the Gulag, he was able to correspond with her, and he often shared her letters with me. You cannot imagine what a breath of fresh air those messages from outside were for us in the camps.
> It was Hans the Austrian who wrote to me and proposed that I come to Vienna on my way back to Poland.

It was a providential contact for Jacques. He managed to pass through Vienna despite the suspicions of the Poles, who were in charge of the exchange program. In Vienna, he found Hans, unchanged, with his curly mane now grey and his distinguished features. His wife was still a passionate communist. They were waiting for him in their BMW.

> Erna, his wife, was also the sister of the general secretary of the Austrian communist party. Her influence derived from those family ties. As far as ideology was concerned, nothing had shaken her faith. The day I arrived in Vienna, with a book by Solzhenitsyn, she said sharply: "I refuse to read that literature!"

> She did not participate in our conversations. I quickly understood that she was a believer who would never change religions. So I did not insist. On the other hand, Hans did not admit to me that he was a member of the central committee of the Austrian communist party. I only discovered that later, to my surprise. He had not enlightened me and I had assumed that he shared my views on the Marxist-Leninist system.

This re-established relationship would permit Jacques to return to western Europe and to France regularly over subsequent years. Each time, Hans sent him a ticket and an invitation for two to three months, along with his commitment to provide for the needs of his guest. With these resources and with the support of the university, which did not have to pay for a ticket, Jacques obtained a passport from the Polish authorities with multiple entries valid for all of Europe. Once Jacques was in Vienna, Hans paid his round-trip ticket to France.

At first, and in preparation for writing *The Gulag Handbook*, Jacques decided to do a PhD. He initially considered doing a dissertation on "Gulagology," but that subfield did not exist. He proposed another subject that was less explicit: "The condition of political prisoners during the Jacobin dictatorship of 1792–1794." This subject was approved.

> In the National Archives, I was able to analyse the situation of these prisoners of the French Revolution. I studied almost all the prisons of Paris. I even knew the names of the concierges of the prisons. I made comparisons with what I knew first hand and concluded that it was better to have been a prisoner during the Jacobin terror than during the Soviet terror. Executions, for example, were not decided by the police as they had been in the Soviet Union.

Jacques never finished his dissertation. But the preliminary research helped him to complete a task dearer to his heart and soul. He published in Polish in the revue *Mowia Wieka* (the centuries speak) two articles about the French Revolution and the Paris Commune.[2]

Meanwhile, he had another providential meeting in France when he met Albert Joannon.

> Initially, I left Poland at my own risk with Hans's invitation. I had to get a visa for France and, once in Paris, find lodging, which was always temporary and uncertain, with friends or friends of friends or

in a maid's room. From one year to the next, I tried to find lodging. One time I was given the address of a Polish student whose sister was the wife of a Frenchman from the south of France. Completely by chance, as I was talking with that Pole about the possibility of renting his room the following year, his brother-in-law from the south came by to see him. We started to talk. I told him my story, which interested him, and he invited me to his home among the southern vineyards. It was in this house that I met the oldest daughter of Albert Joannon. She immediately thought that I would get along well with her father, who had spent five years imprisoned in an *Oflag*, a German prison camp.

Jacques and Albert became very close friends. From then on Jacques would spend part of his summers, three weeks at most, between his friend's apartment in Marseilles and his house in the Var.

Albert was a very generous man with exceptionally enlightened views. He was captured by the Germans during the very first days of the Second World War while he was still a young officer. He learned a lot in his Gulag. The prisoners of the *Oflag* had an idea to organize a kind of university in the camp. He was curious by nature, very humane, deeply Catholic, and had high personal ethics. After I had worked on my notes all day, we would talk after dinner with his wife in a café. Since he had training as a lawyer, and I still had my project of a Gulag handbook in French, I asked for his advice on the translations of juridical phrases. On Friday evenings, Albert and his wife would load their car and call me at the last minute. I would join them, the last person to get into the car, with my boxes and the typewriter they had given me. The country house was forty-five miles away. The hospitality of that family lasted for years and years. Through the diplomatic pouch they received packages containing my preparatory notes for *The Gulag Handbook*, and I had my room at their home with my papers that no one touched. I had room and board. My clothes were washed and I had free electricity. When I was there, it was as if I were sitting on top of the world.

This is how Jacques returned to *his* country – on tiptoe through half-opened borders preparing what would become *The Gulag Handbook* and *Fragments of Lives* [first published as *Fragments de vie* and *Qu'elle était belle cette utopie!*]. He persevered like a busy little ant, preparing his notes on communism during his visits to the non-communist world before his great departure for France.

In the meantime, history marched on. Those who were called the "internationalists" of the Polish communist party and to whom Jacques felt the closest were slowly but surely purged. During the political troubles in Poland in March 1968, Jacques was able to help some of his students, who were threatened with expulsion from the university for subversive activities. But he became aware of his lack of power and decided to leave the communist party. He used his age and his ordeals in the Gulag as an excuse. Now that his notes were safe in Albert's house, he no longer feared anything from the Polish communists. His eyes were focused on the future he would have after he retired from the University of Warsaw on 30 September 1977. He accepted an invitation from Misao to spend a year with him in Tokyo. Regina was going to leave Poland too and go to the United States to study for a doctorate in English literature at the University of Alabama.

This time, the doors of the world opened for the man who was then seventy and who had not finished with life, with testifying, and with expressing his gratitude. His membership in the Polish communist party had started in 1926. His voluntary departure from communist Poland took place in 1979. After a short stay in Poland between his return from Japan and his departure for the United States, the man who had been "Jacques the Frenchman" in the Gulag would not return to the country where he first became committed to Marxist-Leninism until after the collapse of communism. By then he had become that which he had for so long desired: the Frenchman Jacques Rossi.

# 35 Life after Communism

I do not regret my journey as a passionate militant, which led me at the end of my life to subsidized housing in the Paris suburbs. The ups and downs of that long path enabled me to discover important social and political falsehoods, whereas my goal had been the search for justice and truth, not my own personal comfort.

Jacques Rossi

When Jacques knocked on the door of my Georgetown office on that November day in 1982, he had already left Poland about six years earlier. This Polish retiree running away from communism had first spent a year in Japan with his "brother" Misao, Misao's wife, and their two daughters.

> Hamako, Misao's wife, could say a few words in Chinese. Nani was twenty and Koulika was fifteen. Koulika guided me around their town because you get lost if you don't speak Japanese. She managed well in English and every time we saw a McDonald's she shouted, "Uncle Jack, Uncle Jack," thinking she was doing me a favour. I liked the atmosphere in my friend's house – the politeness, the graciousness, and the incredible cleanliness.

After a year, Jacques decided to accept an invitation to the United States from Ewa, a former Polish student and a friend of Regina's. Ewa along with her husband had done well in New York in the art market. Before going to the US, Jacques spent two weeks in Poland.

> It was 1980, right in the middle of the Solidarity movement. I was lucky to be able to leave because several weeks after my departure

General Jaruzelski proclaimed a state of emergency and the borders were closed. I offered my studio apartment to a young couple that wasn't able to find lodging. I also left my precious rug from Samarkand. I departed for New York and Ewa's home, where I must have stayed for three months. From there I located an old American friend who lived in the Washington, DC, region. I had met him in Paris in 1976: Jack Platt.

Jacques stayed with Jack Platt for a while, and it was there that he met Father Bradley, a Jesuit and dean of the college at Georgetown University. Father Bradley became friends with Jacques and liked his project. He had him invited to the university. Jacques was granted a small office in the library, offices reserved for certain professors. These small narrow rooms with only space for a tiny table are called "carrels," and they resemble cells. The first time I visited Jacques in his carrel, he welcomed me with these words, all the while shaking the little key to his carrel under my nose sarcastically: "You see, it's like in the Gulag except that I have the key."

With Jack Platt's support, Jacques obtained a research scholarship. These scholarships were granted to persecuted members of the Solidarity movement. He also received financial aid from two Polish sources – the Veterans of the Second World War and the Pilsudski Institute in New York. He taught courses in Soviet history and thereby earned modest sums of money that enabled him to pay for his room in a boarding house and one meal a day.

In all those years, as Jacques travelled around the globe, from Asia to America, he carried his notes with him and was motivated by his obsession to finish his planned *Gulag Handbook*. As the completion and publication of his work approached, he knew that he was committing what the communist world would perceive as a political crime. Didn't former members of the Gulag swear solemnly and under the threat of returning to the Gulag never to reveal anything about their experience in prison and in the camps? When his passport expired for the first time, he renewed it at the Polish embassy in Washington, DC. "I filled out some forms and mentioned the hospitality of the university and then they had me sign a blank sheet of paper. I remember that the civil servant said to me in a mean way: 'Aren't you afraid that I will write something against you?'" Jacques said nothing, but when his passport expired again, he chose not to go back to the embassy. Thus he resided illegally in the United States. Moreover, he was about to publish an anti-Marxist text, an indictment of the communist system. In 1984 he was struck again by bad news. His great friend in Marseilles, Albert

Joannon, had died. "Long before his death he said to me: 'I am still working. You are too. When you have finished your travels, you will come and live in my house with my family. In my home you have your room.' I knew that he had spoken about this with his wife, and I was delighted by the idea."

In 1982, the year we met, Jacques at seventy-three found himself again at a crossroads. In April, he finished his first edition of *The Gulag Handbook* at Georgetown University. An editor in London had just accepted that original version, which would be published in Russian two years later. Georgetown University had started the process of seeking political asylum for Jacques when he received a letter from Pierre Joannon, the son of Albert. Faithful to his father's wishes and desires, Pierre invited Jacques to come and live with him, his wife, and his children in the Drôme. Jacques did not hesitate long in choosing between the United States and France. He chose his mother's country and, with Pierre Joannon's invitation, he requested a long-term visa, which he obtained. He arrived on 25 May 1985, having sent his manuscript to the London editor. He had accomplished the three important projects of his adult life: leaving the Gulag, writing and publishing *The Gulag Handbook*, and returning permanently to his French motherland. He still had to publish *The Gulag Handbook* in French and to acquire French citizenship. That was nothing compared to what he had done already. But a good fifteen years would pass before his work would be published in France and recognized by a large audience.

Upon returning to France, he was welcomed on the train station platform in Montelimar by Pierre's three children, who carried a big sign of welcome. He was housed in their beautiful home, an old stone barn with large, welcoming rooms. "The landscape around the house looked like something you would see in the background of a Renaissance portrait painting – the same light, the same nuances of colour. My room looked to the west, which pleased me greatly because ever since leaving the Soviet Union, I had looked west. Now that I live in Montreuil to the east of Paris I am a bit closer to Russia, but not too close."

Jacques always had his eyes fixed on the capital, where he established contacts with editors and where he met more and more people who were interested in his work.

> I had several connections with the Institute of Social Sciences, thanks to the president of the Academy of Social Sciences in Poland who had come to see me in my "carrel" at Georgetown University during an academic visit to Washington. I would like to stress that this president was elected and not appointed. He was a medievalist

with great intellectual authority, and had never been a communist. I had given him the three volumes of the manuscript for *The Gulag Handbook* in Russian, and he came to my cell at the university to return them to me personally. This exceptional man helped me greatly to obtain some funding and to meet French editors. It was all in vain.

Jacques was up against a wall of incomprehension in his country of origin and choice. Even if French editors showed some interest in his work, most of them were terrified at the prospect of being appropriated by traditional anti-communists. Their view was, "We were not going to provide grist for the mill of the enemy." This was just before the fall of the Berlin Wall and the collapse of the Soviet empire, when the atmosphere was still influenced by the Cold War. Any form of radical anti-communism seemed suspicious, even if the Parisian intellectual milieu had welcomed the work of Solzhenitsyn with a certain enthusiasm. The New Philosophers would try to learn something from it, but their elders were not so willing. The rise of the extreme right was worrisome.

In 1987 Marie-Cécile Antonelli, a French student whom Jacques had met at Georgetown University, founded in Paris "The Association of the Friends of Jacques Rossi," whose objective was to promote his activities and work. It took several years. While Jacques and his friends tried to convince Parisian editors, his work was published by a London press in Russian and, two years later in 1989, by a New York press in English.[1] At the end of October 1989, Leonid Trouss of the human rights organization Memorial wrote a piece in the *Proceedings of the USSR Academy of Sciences*, the Novosibirsk edition, denouncing the Soviet bureaucracy for inventing reasons to prohibit publication of the book in the USSR. He emphasized that this work did not in any way diminish the contribution of Solzhenitsyn's *Gulag Archipelago*. He initiated an appeal in order to acquire funding for its publication. In fact, in 1991, just prior to the collapse of the Soviet Union, a second, improved Russian edition was published in Moscow, which was perhaps the greatest victory for someone who had survived the Siberian camps. In September 1996 a Japanese edition of *The Gulag Handbook* was published.[2] At that time, the book was also being translated by Sophie Benech and Veronique Patte for Le cherche midi in Paris. It was published in 1997 after an unsuccessful attempt with the Swiss publishers Black on White. That same year, Laffont published *The Black Book of Communism* and, shortly thereafter, Francois Furet's *The Passing of an Illusion*. A Czech version of *The Gulag Handbook* was slated to appear in 1999.

In 1990 Jean-Louis Panne wrote an article about the work, and in 1992 Pierre Rigoulot, director of the Institute of Sovereign Social History, referred to Jacques Rossi's book as a work of "great scholarship."³ The Russian edition provoked reactions from numerous Russian and Central European authors. For example: "Roland Barthes proclaimed 'the death of authors in literature.' Yet the pen of Jacques Rossi revives a typically anonymous genre, that of the dictionary, as if a human face has appeared at the louvered window of a cell."⁴ Elsewhere, critics wrote: "In this encyclopedia Rossi, with the precision of a surgeon, dissects the anatomy of the labor camp world and of the Soviet system and reveals the true entrails of that Empire."⁵

Another wrote:

> First of all, it is a handbook. It contains much information about the details and facts of the Gulag, the descriptions of daily reality in the world of the labor camps ... But Jacques Rossi's work is also a historical and geographical guide of the Gulag ... Finally, *The Gulag Handbook* is an analytical dictionary of the language of inmates. So we can correctly describe *The Gulag Handbook* as an encyclopedia of the Gulag world. In this relatively thin volume we can learn everything about the Gulag, its history, its language, its customs ... One of the main qualities of Jacques Rossi's work is that we read it with passion. Perhaps that is because behind the austere language and his scientific approach, one reads the testimony of a man whose detention did not break him. This testimony reveals that the Gulag is an expression of the system that created it. Jacques Rossi's book is not simply another book about the Gulag. It is a history of the terror that was used, from the beginning of Soviet power, and which over a period of decades perpetrated crimes against humanity.⁶

In the course of the 1990s, Jacques's reputation among Russian researchers continued to grow. According to Arsenii Roginsky, "*The Gulag Archipelago* by Aleksandr Solzhenitsyn (1973) and *The Gulag Handbook* by Jacques Rossi (London 1987; Moscow 1991) undoubtedly remain invaluable resources on the culture and the philosophy of the Gulag." This statement appeared in the foreword to the Russian work "The system of corrective-labor camps in the USSR, 1923–1960: A guide."⁷

Two years earlier, in 1995, Jacques Rossi's book *Fragments of Lives*, a volume of short stories in French, was published by Elika. It was published with the help of Sophie Benech. A number of individuals wrote about the book in prominent venues, including the historian Nicolas Werth in *La Quinzaine litteraire*, Bruno de Cessole in *La Revue des deux mondes*, and Nicole Zand in *Le Monde*. At that time, Jacques was invited to Laure Adler's *Cercle de minuit*, where the theme was "Archives of

Espionage." These short stories, which were first called "Gulag snapshots," were written by Jacques with the help of one of the translators of *The Gulag Handbook* after he completed the latter in 1985. In the conclusion of *Fragments of Lives*, Jacques wrote the following:

> Dear Reader,
> These *fragments* you have just read are scenes taken from an immense tragedy I witnessed. I have waited for a rendezvous with the public for a long time. If I survived more than twenty years of intense hardship, it was partly due to my strong will and determination to return to France to tell the tale of what I had seen and learned in the Gulag.
> ....
>   It wasn't until 1985, after my numerous journeys, that I returned to the land of my ancestors to settle down. I discovered, to my great surprise, that the testimony of my experiences interested so few people and was even disturbing to others. "As long as he doesn't fall into the right wing's hands!" some would worry. Others would claim, "It's not right to reveal some questionable facts about the USSR, a country that sacrificed so much to rid Europe of fascism!" Others would interject, persisting in not acknowledging what the critics had suspected for a long time, that if the USSR had helped liberate Europe, it didn't do so out of its own conviction.
>   I had almost given up hope in getting my story out until the day, in 1995, Jean-Michel Marquebielle came to find me and offered to publish some stories from this volume.
>   Seventy years ago, I committed myself body and soul to the Communist movement, genuinely devoted to defending the cause of social justice. Nothing has changed in that respect. Yet, let's face it: I was led astray and it's now my duty to warn honest people everywhere: "Be careful! Don't get involved on a path that will inevitably lead you to economic, social, political, cultural and ecological catastrophe."
>   If it hadn't been for all those years spent in the Gulag, I would have had trouble realizing all this.[8]

"The main subject of *Fragments*," wrote Nicolas Werth, "is the survival of a man under extreme conditions, in a world that is both incomprehensible and absolutely cruel, where everyone is a potential enemy. *Homo homini lupus*. But there's a difference between his and the stories of Shalamov, for whom the experience in the camps was purely negative – 'man only becomes worse.' In … *Fragments*, Jacques Rossi also wrote about lessons of life, not of death."[9] And Nicole Zand wrote: "This collection of short stories, about fifty quick, often vitriolic sketches, offers a view inside the Soviet system. They are rooted in real experiences and in raw language expose the apparently aberrant logic of a machine for crushing lives."[10] *Fragments* would also be published in Japan in August 1997 in Yokohama.

Between 1985, the first time Jacques lived with Albert's son, and 1997, the date when *The Gulag Handbook* was published in French, Jacques was a nomad in France. He was as he had been before, a vagabond moving around the world searching for the way back to his real home. After several months in the Drôme, he spent about a year in Marseilles in a room next to the apartment of Jeanne Joannon, Albert's widow. In the fall of 1987, thanks to the efforts of Amnesty International and, most notably, Lise Weil, he settled in a small room on rue Edgar-Poe in the nineteenth arrondissement of Paris. It was only in November 1988 that he finally settled into an apartment of his own. It was subsidized housing at 32 Avenue de la Résistance in Montreuil-sur-Seine, near the subway station Croix-de-Chavaux (Jacques Duclos square) just beyond the Robespierre station. It was a communist suburb of Paris, with communists in the city hall. "Avenue de la Résistance! I am especially proud of my address. Well, there it is. And here I am." From the time he moved in, his neighbours Mr and Mrs Rabot never missed an opportunity to help him in any way, for example, by carrying his purchases up to his place when he had difficulty getting around.

Jacques was already living in Montreuil when he received the news that his French citizenship had been issued, thanks to friends who were members of Amnesty International and who had taken the time to contact the proper authorities at the chancellery.

> The only paper that I presented was the birth certificate of my mother, born in Bourg-en-Bresse, and my birth certificate. It was simple. I am my mother's son and my mother is very important to me. She was French, so I am French like she was. She was the one who instilled in me that moral conviction from which I never wavered, and which helped me to hold on, despite the circumstances. So I waited. And one day I received a government letter instructing me to come and get my identification card. I was so proud! My dream had finally come true. When I lived in the Norilsk night, a female inmate once said to me cruelly: "You will never see your France again, no more than your ears!" How fortunate that she was wrong!

The naturalization decree was dated 9 August 1990. The new birth certificate that Jacques received stated his Polish names. It indicated in the margins the receipt of Polish authorization for his name change to "Jacques Rossi." The French rendering of his first name was to be "Jacques-François," by decree dated 26 February 1991, thus completing the decree of 9 August 1990.

> The first time that there were elections, I voted, not without a certain satisfaction. I continue to exercise my civic rights all the while knowing that democracy, according to Churchill, is a bad system, but the least bad of all systems. Today I am ninety. I have been very committed. I have fought a lot. I have been through ordeals that were a bit difficult. I still think it is noble to be a militant, but at my age that is finished.

In 1999, the man who endured ordeals that were "a bit difficult" reflected upon the society of the coddled in his country, with a degree of criticism, amusement, and exasperation. He appreciated the fact that the state provided him with a small pension that helped him cover the cost of housing. In addition, he received a very small Polish pension. Up until that time, his royalties had been slim. He was paid modestly for his lectures and his public appearances at universities and high schools and for private groups, when his hosts had the money. If not, he asked only that his train ticket in second class be paid for. The librarians in Brest wanted to pool their resources in order to offer him a first-class ticket, but Jacques refused them outright. As in his youth, he refused to eat the caviar!

With publication of *The Gulag Handbook* in London in 1987, a period of commemoration began. Jacques was a very present witness, gifted with an incredible memory. He was the preferred host for these meetings, which were covered with growing interest by the media. It was the time when Gorbachev was trying to make the Soviet system more humane. Jacques was surprised to receive Russian articles that mentioned *The Gulag Handbook*. In April 1992, he was invited to participate in the first international conference organized by the human rights organization Memorial, which was co-founded by Andrei Sakharov. The conference took place in Warsaw, and included participants from Memorial in Russia and Poland as well as some former Soviet republics. On 1 May 1992, a correspondent from *La pensée russe* wrote, "The appearance of Lev Kopelev ... and Jacques Rossi was truly an important event."

On 19–21 May 1992, the first international convention on the theme "Resistance in the Camps" was organized in Moscow by the organization *Vozvrashchenie* (Return), a group committed to prisoners' "resumption of intellectual activity after time in the Gulag."

Established in 1989 by Semione Vilensky, the organization helped former inmates adjust to life after detention. It was the first time that Jacques returned to Moscow since his eventful departure from the Soviet Union in 1961.

> I was welcomed at the Moscow airport with a bouquet of flowers. Liudmila Sergeevna Novikova came to the airport with two other members of the organization. She was the secretary of *Vozvrashchenie* and a former victim of the Soviet system. Her father had been sent to the Gulag when she was very little. I couldn't believe the welcome. They had a car and received financial support from private banks. We were housed in private homes, typically the homes of people who supported the association.

Liudmila Novikova would later write of Jacques and his work:

> Jacques Rossi is an important friend [of *Vozvrashchenie*]. We met him for the first time in 1992 during our first conference, "Resistance in the Gulag." He impressed us with his intellect, his knowledge and above all his experience in the Gulag. His *Gulag Handbook* is the best book of its kind published in Russia in recent years. We bought several copies to share with those interested in the subject.
>
> His small book of memories, ... *Fragments*, is above all impressive in its laconic narrative style and the surprising elements of each story. It's a great art to be so precise in the choice of words and yet so eloquent. He speaks Russian better than we do. He understands our current problems perhaps better than we do.[11]

Jacques rediscovered Moscow and his youthful memories as a secret agent, as well as the memories of his anxiety and uncertainty following his release from the Gulag. It was nevertheless "with pleasure" that he revisited the city where he was first arrested.

> I walked the streets and reconnected with the city. I discovered that the monuments that had been re-baptized with the names of obscure Soviet communists had been given back their original names, that Dzerzhinsky Square was called Lubianka Square once again. I also spoke with people, old ladies who missed Stalin and who complained, rightly so, that thugs who had been locked up in the Gulag had come back and were spreading terror. In fact, I knew those thugs well, and I shuddered at the thought that those serious criminals were again in the streets. At the same time, I studied those Russians who were

going about their business. Their country was so different from the one that I had known, yet they didn't fully appreciate the changes. I want to stress that I observed this all with pleasure!

The first conference brought together the victims of Soviet and Nazi camps like Germaine Tillon, a member of the French resistance. There were a lot of former Trotskyists with whom I had tough discussions, for they still believed strongly in the Marxist-Leninist project, but just thought it had gone astray during Stalin's time. I was then and remain convinced that this project is an illusion that can only lead to disaster. There were many Germans at this convention, some of whom were former victims of the Nazis and other former communists expelled from the party. There was also a large group of former Gulag prisoners, especially Ukrainians who upon the death of Stalin and Beria had stirred up revolts in the camps. Of course, the Russians for the first time could speak about their pain, too. At the time of the so-called first rehabilitation following the Twentieth Party Congress, all of the pure hardliners declared that they would remain faithful to the communist party. They believed, despite all they had endured. For them, past events were the result of bad luck and the capriciousness of one man. It was only much later that Soviet dissidents started to denounce the system itself.

At this conference, at least they could describe the pain, and speaking about it helped them. What made this conference unique was the presence of officers of the former KGB. They were part of a special department of rehabilitation created by Gorbachev. These officers had once been persecutors and now they were discriminated against. On the whole, at this first conference, we talked a great deal, but we weren't very reflective. We listened to the voices from the Soviet camps because a lot had been already written about the Nazi camps. Work on the Nazi camps was already being done. As soon as a comparison was made, however, we were warned not to confuse the two. But I will say this clearly: an innocent victim is an innocent victim – whether persecuted because of the delirium of a totalitarian regime like the Soviet Union or by the racial delirium of the Nazis. For me, there is no difference!

Jacques doesn't speak to the intense polemical comparisons between the two systems. He does not refute what Tzvetan Todorov stated, that the goal of the Nazi camps was death itself, while in the Soviet system of concentration and labour camps the central feature was that life had no value. He himself did not exaggerate the horror of what he had experienced. That is the strength of his testimony – he avoids all exaggeration. He simply weighs the effectiveness of two contemporary totalitarian systems and ascertains that ideological perversity permitted one, communism, to last longer and be more widespread than the other. He acknowledges the fact that he probably would not have had such a long life had he been detained in Hitler's death camps. He also notes that since Hitler's message was clearer, he and others like him would have never believed in Nazism with body and soul, the way that they embraced communist dogma. Jacques subscribed to the authority of Raymond Aron, who wrote at the end of his life, "Communism is not less odious than Nazism. The argument that I used more than once to distinguish class messianism from racial messianism no longer impresses me. The apparent universality of the former has become, in the last analysis, an illusion."[12]

The "quite noisy" second conference of the organization *Vozvrashchenie* took place in 1993. The Russian editor of *The Gulag Handbook* was there, and Jacques discovered that his work had become more well known in Russia. The third conference that Jacques attended took place in 1994. Meanwhile, he returned to the United States and to Georgetown University, where he spoke of the Gulag as being an "enormous sociopolitical laboratory." In 1995, Jacques participated in two international conferences on the topic "Nazi and Soviet camps." These conferences took place at the Sorbonne in Paris in May and in Vienna, Austria, in December.

On 30 October 1996, the anniversary of the day when a Moscow crowd toppled the statue of Dzerzhinsky, the chief of the security police, another Russian commemoration took place: "The Day of Political Prisoners." Jacques was invited to Norilsk, to that faraway Arctic territory where he had spent the ten most painful years of his life. He was not invited there because of those years, but because he was the author of *The Gulag Handbook*. Jacques was being filmed by a German TV station as he was welcomed once more with a bouquet of flowers, this time in the Arctic cold, which brought back many memories. The guest of honour received a warm welcome from the mayor of Norilsk and the president of the Association of Former Political Prisoners. His hosts were the leaders of Memorial. Memorial worked to establish the truth concerning the Gulag, and one of its objectives was to take care of former members of the Gulag.

> We were taken to the best hotel in the town. Of course, like all hotels in the former Soviet Union, the faucets did not work. But there was a certain comfort there that was different from what I had been used to in the same place! To think that I, a former prisoner, was being housed and fed in this palace, with a good bundle of rubles for

my personal expenses, did not displease me at all. I was not even annoyed when the governor of the province (in Russian, they called him the "chief of administration") excused himself at the last minute. In fact, I wondered what we could have talked about.

I visited the museum of the area. It wasn't called "The Museum on the Exploitation of Prisoners" but, rather, "The Historical Museum of the City of Norilsk." On display there were mainly reindeer, exotic animals, wood and mining extractions. There was only occasional reference to the harsh conditions in which the work had occurred. [Their attitude was] "You know comrades, it's very sad, so we don't speak about it."

In this museum, the fate of millions of my comrades was hidden. There was no way there could be mention of the enormous outrage that had taken place on this territory, in this town that we, the prisoners, built with our blood. However, *The Gulag Handbook* was on display in the Norilsk museum, along with other objects.

I wanted to go to Mount Schmidt, named for the oceanographer. That was where prisoners were buried. Each dead person's grave had been marked with a stick with his number. But the sticks had disappeared, removed during development projects. I only saw a small stone, the presumed foundation for a future monument for the dead.

I was invited to give a speech, to have meetings, and to meet the press and journalists. I said what I believed and continue to believe: that I never was and am not a victim. I was there in a country whose cause I thought I was serving, and I had understood reality. I spoke of how I had started out as a communist and was very responsible for the erroneous project to which I had committed myself. While I was talking, I mentioned my second sentence, when I was sent from Norilsk to Irkutsk. I did not know whether it was in 1949 or in 1950. To my great surprise, I heard one of the staff at the museum affirm decisively that it was 1950. He was writing his thesis on that historical period and on Jacques Rossi, among others. He had obtained permission to work in the KGB archives in Krasnoyarsk and he knew my life, at least for that period, better than I did. But he had to be careful. This information could only be used in his thesis and could not be communicated. Transparency could only go so far!

Afterwards, a journalist wrote a short article about the person he called Monsieur Jacques (using the French word *Monsieur*). Moreover, a German TV station was doing a film that brought the filming crew into the tundra to a place that a former prisoner had located for them, in which summary shootings and executions had taken place in 1953–1955.

Later, they came and filmed me in Montreuil while my Japanese brother was there. But in the final film version many scenes were cut.

German TV accompanied Jacques on other trips back to places of his youth: Berlin from the time he worked for the Comintern, or Poznan in Poland, where he found the very first cell where a communist militant had been imprisoned by Pilsudski. Above all, it went with him to the KGB headquarters, which had opened slightly – then closed – its archives. In the Lubianka archives, Jacques found his own file under the watchful eye of a KGB civil servant responsible for the rehabilitation of its victims. Jacques would later say that he learned nothing new from his file.

The [German] film that was shown in France on the Arte station on 30 October 1997 was not the first film in which Jacques had participated. During this time of increasing media attention, Jacques first appeared on TV in the film *The Breath of Freedom*, produced for Antenne 2 by Daniel Costell and François Furet and shown on 28 September 1989 during the celebration of the bicentennial of the French Revolution. It follows the high and low points in the struggle for human rights that emerged in 1789 and that included Jacques's own odyssey, among others. In addition, on 3 and 10 November 1994, "The Historical Files" on France's Channel 3 scheduled a two-part program by Thibault d'Oiron and Bernard Dufourg entitled *The French in the Gulag*. The film studied the tragedy of the more than three thousand French men and women in the Gulag, of which at least one thousand are believed to have perished in the camps. The film argues that they were "abandoned" by the French government. Alain Besançon explained the abandonment, saying that France wanted to be "realistic," that is to say, "benevolent" towards the USSR according to Georges Bortoli. Thus it closed its eyes to Gulag victims, even if they were French. During that filming, Jacques for the first time had a guided tour of his former Moscow prison and also of the Lubianka.

Then a TV show scheduled a meeting among some French citizens who had survived the Gulag.

What struck me was that the moderator kept asking whether the French government had treated us properly, as if he wanted us to disparage it. Some of the participants did do that. Obviously, it is always easy, when you are used to being spoiled, to consider that you deserved everything. It's easy to criticize the state for not doing enough. I only told the truth. I had not wanted to take advantage of the French ambassador's generosity and create problems for him by begging for political asylum.

During this period, Guillaume Malauri wrote a long article about Jacques in the November 1995 issue of *L'Evénement du jeudi*, with texts by authors and historians, and a portrait in *L'Express*. In the spring of 1997, Jacques was invited by his two Japanese publishers to give a lecture tour in Japan. And *The Gulag Handbook* was finally published by Le cherche midi in France in 1997, ten years after its initial publication in London in Russian. This time, things had changed. Public opinion was ready for Jacques's work and also for *The Black Book of Communism*, which along with *The Gulag Handbook* created a flurry of public interest, polemical discussions, and sales success. His participation in the TV show *L'heure de Vérité* with Jean-Marie Cavada would be crucial. Jean-François Revel, who was invited to the show, titled "85 Million Dead: The Dark History of Communism," told this highly amusing story: "It was the moment when the communist party national secretary pulled out of his sleeve an issue of the Le Pen newspaper *National Hebdo* and waved it in front of the camera. He accused Stéphane Courtois, Jacques Rossi, and myself of playing into the hands of fascists, as if there were this miserable conspiracy of our 'band of three.' Jacques Rossi was accused of having had a particularly crafty ingenious ruse. Had he not exploited the reactionaries to the point where he was imprisoned for nineteen years in the Gulag with the unique scheme of helping, in the future, the anti-communist propaganda of the future Front National, which didn't even exist at the time?"[13]

The print media of all persuasions talked about the publication of *The Gulag Handbook*, from *Le Monde* to the *Canard enchaîné*, including *Le Figaro*, *Libération*, *Télérama*, and many others. According to Nicole Zand, "Whoever is interested in the history of Soviet communism and in the general history of that period will be fascinated by reading this scientific, educational, sarcastic and thoroughly factual work. It is unique, the work of a remarkable man, whose odyssey reveals something quite exemplary."[14] Nathalie Nougayrede also wrote an article about Jacques's life in *Le Monde* on 19 March 1999.

Foreign journalists made trips to Paris to interview the former Gulag prisoner in his subsidized housing in Montreuil. It was an apartment where you took off your shoes upon entering and you sat on the floor. Among those visiting in 1998 were journalists from the *Frankfurter Allegmeine Zeitung* of Frankfurt and *Asahi Shimbun* of Tokyo. *The Gulag Handbook* attracted a good deal of attention, and the publishing house Le cherche midi wanted to buy the rights again for *Fragments of Lives*, which had not been read by a large audience. A revised edition of *Fragments of Lives*, with supplementary passages and a new title, was published in September 2000 and created a wave of intense interest.

Jacques's participation in the television show *Bouillon de culture*, hosted by the well-known journalist and interviewer Bernard Pivot, in December 2000 marked perhaps the high point in recognition and media attention for his work. He would also appear, along with very few others, in the retrospective during Pivot's last show in July 2001. The director, Jacques Sigalla, brought to the stage at the Proscenium in Paris several excerpts from *Fragments of Lives* in January and February 2001. Jacques was invited everywhere, not only by radio stations and televisions channels but also by universities, junior and senior high schools, book stores, and various clubs and associations. He always accepted the invitations. He participated in numerous conferences, received and responded to mail from across the globe, and gave lectures. This ninety-year-old man was everywhere and enormously active, despite his first stroke in 1999, which forced him to use a walker. He was surrounded by friends, from all stages of his long life:

> It seems that I become attached to people for a long time, if not forever. I still think about Julita, my Spanish fiancée whom I have not seen since my arrest in 1937. I have no possessions, but I have the memories of my friends. Men and women are my wealth, the gems of my jewel box. It's true that I have many female friends. I really don't know why.

Jacques sweeps aside with a gesture my weak interpretation of the inexplicable, which concerns his mother or the brutally masculine universe of the Gulag. Since his definitive return to the capital, Jacques took advantage of his freedom in the city that he had longed for. On the RER trains, the metro, and on foot, he criss-crossed Paris and spent time in its suburbs. He walked up and down its streets talking to passersby, asking them questions, helping them cross the street, making small talk and always ready to help. Just as he had been in the camp at Norilsk, Jacques was curious about meeting new people and enthusiastic for new experiences.

> When I lived on Edgar Allen Poe street in the nineteenth arrondissement, I went to a laundromat not very far from my home. One evening I saw a young woman there who was trying to take her laundry out of the washing machine. Since her sheets were longer than her arms, I helped her to fold them. We chatted and exchanged addresses. Her name was Laurence and she was a social worker. It wasn't long before I told her that I was a former Gulag prisoner. Everywhere I lived, for miles around people knew my story.

Laurence's companion was a poet and little Eudora was already growing inside Laurence when I met her, though I did not notice [her pregnancy] when we first met. The couple came to visit me in my room and they agreed to remove their shoes like all my friends did. When Laurence worked at the Saint-Louis hospital she made me come to boost the morale of an ill Englishman with whom she could not communicate. Another time she asked for my advice for a new friend who was going to be on television. She spent her time trying to help others. It was because of Laurence that I finally benefitted from the medical coverage of "social security." She knew how to arrange it.

But most of my encounters took place in the subway, especially after I started to live in Montreuil. For example, a Brazilian soccer player became a very good friend. One of my most beautiful love stories took place at the Croix-de-Chavaux station – my station – three years ago. Seated in front of me was a very pudgy woman, quite short and stocky, with a little girl on her knees. The little girl tried to lean towards me, quite low down because the enormous breasts of her mother were obstacles. First I saw one very black eye. So I made a face at her. At first she was very serious. Then she started her little game and I mine. After two or three times she smiled at me. But the mother scolded her and said she was capricious. Capricious! We continued our little game, and three stations later they got up to leave the subway car. Walking in front of me, that very little girl – she was perhaps three or four – pursed her lips at me and I kissed them. Very red lips and so soft on the delicate, completely black face. A great love of several seconds, but I will never forget it like most of my encounters on the subway.

It was during this life so filled with activity that a second stroke surprised Jacques on 2 March 2001 while he was staying with his friends Pierre and Madeleine Gairet in Saint-Remy-de-Provence. He suffered from hemiplegia and a weak paralysis of the right arm. The aphasia disappeared after three days. To the surprise of the doctors, little by little, his memory of recent events came back. His memory of proper names, which had been damaged in the beginning, also returned. It was in his hospital room in Avignon that Jacques revised all the last chapters of this book. He was happy like Ulysses or like "Jacques the Frenchman." Although he accepted that his life's journey was coming to a close, he continued to give lessons about life to his friends, who came quickly to see him from the four corners of the globe! On 18 May 2001, at his request, Jacques left Avignon for the Cochin hospital in

Paris, from which he was transferred on 28 May to the Ivry-sur-Seine hospital. On 21 June, he moved again to a retirement home operated by a Polish religious institution, this time in the heart of Paris. He was watched over carefully by an inner circle of his friends, especially his doctor-friend Esmeralda Luciolli.

"I will marry my friend," Jacques wrote on the invitation to his marriage with Regina, which was celebrated at city hall of the eighteenth arrondissement on 6 August 2001. In the small garden of the Polish retirement home, his close friends gathered to listen to some poems and to celebrate with champagne a love that had lasted for forty years.

In the spring of 1999, at the end of our interviews, I asked Jacques what he thought, in hindsight, about the crime of those who had taken away his youth and who had profoundly and enduringly wronged him. Did he ever think about that overused word – forgiveness?

> First of all, I would say again that I am not the centre of the universe. What's important is not the injustice that was done to me, but the injustice committed against millions of my comrades who were taken away in the same slave ship. The crime that is impossible to forgive is that of the intellectuals in free countries. They were capable of obtaining information, capable of evaluating the extent of the utopia. Yet in order to please themselves, to show off their wisdom or their intelligence, they continued to encourage others to believe in their dream, a dream that could only lead to the cesspool of iniquity where I and so many others had landed. Of course, I don't hold a grudge against those who were mistaken, and who in the end understood their mistake and regretted it. I am angry with those who did not want to admit that it was a crime to have caused millions of people to suffer so and to die. I often think of what a waste it was, these millions of sacrificed lives. I remember vividly my comrades who, like me, were ready to die for that unrealizable ideal and who paid a high price. Yet all those intellectuals, supposedly the masters of critical thinking, continued for the sake of their own reputation or because of intellectual complacency to praise that wicked system!
>
> Who is responsible? First, there is Lenin. Marx was less responsible because he did not foresee the consequences. But Lenin signed the orders: Hang so many peasants – by the hundreds, the thousands. Stalin only continued that. If there is a trial to be held, it should be of the Soviet communist party that committed crimes against its own people. The Soviet state was also a criminal when it judged the Nazis

at Nuremberg. In fact, Soviet crimes were never publicly condemned like the Nazi crimes.

As for the young men who tortured me in Butyrka or even Oleg P. or François P. who betrayed me – no, I would never have wanted to seek revenge, nor would I have wanted them to be punished. I lived a tragedy that went far beyond me personally and that extended far beyond theirs. I was part of a global tragedy that was not my personal drama nor theirs. I have come to understand since then that if Oleg P. hadn't played the role of the traitor, then someone else, an even closer friend, perhaps, would have in his place. It was the system that perverted men. Not the contrary. Even Stalin. When communists moaned, "I was fooled by Stalin," I would ask, well, why did you let yourself be fooled?

The early Russian Gulag testimonies did not question the system. There were books by former Gulag prisoners before the Twentieth Party Congress and the rehabilitations. They maintained an unshakeable faith in the regime, with no resentment against the party that sent them off to die for nothing. Evgenia Ginsburg, another person arrested in 1937, wrote her first book with great prudence, never questioning the global raison d'être of all that horror. It was only in her last testimony that she wrote more thoughtfully. It was also after de-Stalinization that dissidents started to demonstrate before being sent to psychiatric hospitals. A totalitarian system cannot be organized in a humane fashion. For the rest, the immensity of the evil obliterates any idea of vengeance. The desire for revenge only obstructs the search for the truth and becomes just a miserable settling of personal scores. The struggle to prevent a repeat of the nightmare is a noble endeavour.

# IN PLACE OF AN EPILOGUE

## Paris, Autumn 2001

Death has not come. I have beaten all the odds.

Jacques Rossi

# Afterword to the English Edition: A Man of Secrets

Writing the official biography of Jacques Rossi was not an easy task. Before I tried, several good journalists and writers had had a difficult time and failed. Jacques and I managed to complete the task. Together we were able to conceive, write, and publish this book. Jacques had come to the end of his life, and he felt that time was fleeing. If he delayed it more, he would not fulfil what he felt was his duty: to tell the story of his life.

It was 1999, ten years after the Berlin Wall fell, bringing about the end to the Soviet empire and its influence over part of Europe and other nations of the world. Jacques was ninety years old, already weakened by age and tired after spending incredible energy on the publication in France of first his *Gulag Handbook* and then *Fragments of Lives*.

Jacques and I had been friends since we met at Georgetown University, a meeting that is described at the beginning of this book. In those years, he tried several times in vain to write his autobiography with various interviewers, an autobiography that editors wanted to publish very much. Finally, he asked me to write the book with him. Because I was a novelist, he told me, I would make a novel of his life. I resisted strongly. I thought the book should be a genuine and true testimony, a work of memory and historical research. It had nothing to do with fiction even if the main character and his odyssey were truly novelistic.

But there was great urgency to begin and to finish. Jacques tired easily. His incredible charisma on a television show or around a table in a

---

I would like to express my deepest appreciation to Kersti Colombant for her excellent translation and to Golfo Alexopoulos for her invaluable editing work. All my gratitude to Elisabeth Salina Amorini and Michael David-Fox, who made this English edition possible. I would also like to add a long overdue note of thanks to Catherine Chevallier for her generous assistance in the very first stages of this book.

café resulted in a multitude of invitations, and in spite of his increasing fatigue, he accepted all of them. He was still robust during the weeks when we recorded the main part of the interview. Then during long months, he retained enough intellectual sharpness to revise the texts I sent him, chapter after chapter, and he corrected them feverishly. In particular, he removed passages that were too intimate.

When the book was starting to take its final form of a life story told through dialogue, Jacques suffered his first stroke, in 1999, and had to stop his work for a certain time. When he began to read the manuscript again, he was not quite the same, but he managed to finish his revision. A second stroke in 2001 forced him to leave his apartment on the Avenue de la Résistance – yes, it was his real address! – in Montreuil and move to a home run by the Polish nuns of Saint Casimir in Paris. Close friends took his files from his apartment to the Souvarine Library.

Documents were found in his files that shed important light on certain opaque elements of Jacques's story. Before sending this book to the publisher, I confronted him with some of those details, for example, the name "Franciszek Ksawery Heyman," his name at birth, which was on his official documents. He acknowledged that it was his family name but asked me to replace that name in the text with the initial *H* for Heyman.

When I started to work with Jacques and to record our conversations, I realized why it was impossible to turn this story into a novel. But in the end, I also understood better why Jacques had initially preferred to fictionalize a part of his life rather than write a testimony or historical autobiography. This man who was deeply loyal to himself and to others, who had the courage to recreate in precise detail a reality that had been denied by a powerful political system, did not want to be morally obliged to say everything. It would have entailed revealing the secrets that he had kept during an entire life, secrets that permitted the survival of his comrades and himself.

Yes, the man who lifted the veil, who revealed, who told, who searched for the truth was above all a man of secrets. Let us not forget he had once officially belonged to the Soviet secret services and had not betrayed them.

In what way was he a man of secrets? There are many answers to this question. Perhaps the major explanation appears in this autobiography and is probably of a psychological nature. Jacques's tendency to be secretive was the result of his temperament and life, and it emerged from his early childhood wound caused by his incapacity to grieve the death of his mother, which had been kept hidden from him.

The reader will have discovered what happened afterwards while reading Jacques's story. When he became a member of the Polish communist party in Poznan, at the time a clandestine party, he carefully hid it from his family. Then he left Poland and found himself rapidly involved in the Comintern, an ultra-secret international service, which he would leave only when he was assigned to the secret service of the Red Army. From the clandestine service he went to the Gulag universe, where the slightest word could be turned against you and against others. When he came out of the Gulag briefly after ten years and had the misfortune of communicating with the only French compatriot he ever met in the concentration camp universe, he was denounced by the latter and sent back to hell.

Years later, he managed to leave the great Gulag that the Soviet Union was for him. However, it was not the Western democratic country of France, the country of his mother, to which he would be repatriated, but to communist Poland where he had been raised as a child. It was once more a world of dissimulation and hiding where the slightest confidence, the slightest disclosure, could become a trap. When Jacques finally left that world, he was an old man who had spent his entire life concealing his thoughts and memories. He kept them on tiny cards hidden in parts of his body. He never revealed those memories and thoughts until sometime later when they appeared in his written work. An ironic detail: in the peaceful and democratic Paris of the 2000s, Jacques Rossi maintained his address book in a coded language.

It was that man whom I was asking to be transparent in order to unveil all the mysteries that he had hidden so carefully, using strategies that only he knew during his long, enigmatic life.

Some of those mysteries he would reveal to me drop by drop during the few months that we worked on this book, like the day he confessed to me, during a transatlantic call, that he had been transferred, unknowingly at the time, from the Comintern to the Red Army. On another occasion he told me that in Poland, even though during his twenty-four years in the Soviet Gulag his anti-communism had grown stronger and stronger and finally had become an obsession, in the 1960s he was led to once more request membership in the communist party.

He accepted and even justified this commitment to dissimulation, largely for fear of betraying and harming his comrades who were still in danger. He was afraid to reveal certain techniques used by detainees to hide objects or written testimony during searches in the Gulag, techniques that could still be of use to other detainees.

Another example of vagueness concerns his nationality. In spite of the patriotic enthusiasm that led him in the Gulag to consider himself as French above all else, he himself did not have a precise understanding of his formal legal status. When he talked about it, he remained very unclear. Concerning the episode when he illegally broke into the

French Embassy in Moscow by climbing over the wall in order to claim his "legitimate" French nationality, he explained that he did not want to enter his country through the back door. He thought that might cause trouble for the ambassador. He said he finally realized that the only possible solution was to request political asylum in France, an approach that he refused because of pride and the aforementioned reasons.

At the end of his visit to the embassy, to appease the conscience of the French diplomatic authorities, he received as travel supplies several cans of gourmet food. Yet despite this small present, upon leaving the French embassy, he found himself once more at the mercy of the Soviet authorities.

If he had been legally a French citizen at the time, he would not have had to request asylum in his own country. In fact, his French mother, Leonine Charlotte Goyer, born in Bourg-en-Bresse, had married a foreigner and their son had Polish nationality that was never questioned. This explains why Jacques, when in Samarkand, had asked to be repatriated to Poland and not to France. It is also why he had to again wait many years until, on 9 August 1990, he received by decree naturalization in France, which at last "restored" to him citizenship in his mother's country.

The nationality question is closely related to that of Jacques's origins. As mentioned above, the discovery of his identity papers, moved from his apartment while he was still hospitalized, showed that originally his name was not Jacques Rossi but Franciscek Ksawery Heyman. It is clear, though, that in the Gulag his name was Jacques Robertovitch Rossi and that his ethnicity was recognized by the Soviets as French. A copy of his birth certificate translated into French and found in his files indicates in the margin that Franciscek Heyman "had been authorized to be called Rossi by decision of the town council of Warsaw (Poland) on August 4 1962."[1]

Then how can it be explained that Heyman had the name "Rossi" in the Gulag and was identified by his comrades as Jacques the Frenchman? Was "Jacques Rossi" the name on the passport he received in Paris in exchange for the passport of the South American person he was supposed to be in Valladolid? Another mystery! After the death of Stalin, when Jacques asked for permission to write to his family like the Japanese or German detainees, the answer he received was that under no circumstances could he correspond with family abroad because he was considered to be a Soviet citizen. To protest this decision, he started his second hunger strike.

Franciscek Ksawery Heyman was the third child of Marcin Heyman, whom Jacques called "the stepfather" without ever revealing his name in his testimony. In the first versions of his origins the "stepfather" was a Polish aristocrat. Jacques also said that he was an architect and a man of culture who was well read. It was in his library that young Franciscek became acquainted with the writers of the eighteenth-century Enlightenment and with revolutions. Only later in our collaboration, during one of his unexpected moments of confession to me, did Jacques reveal that the "stepfather" was a German Jewish businessman and architect who had converted to Catholicism and whose family was completely integrated in Poland.

The father's identity was fundamental to Jacques Rossi's psychology and explains why each time a potential biographer risked asking him too many questions about the different versions that he presented concerning his parenthood, that biographer was kicked out.

We discovered during the probing of his files that Marcin and Leontine, legally married, had three children. Jacques did not speak about his siblings, at least in the beginning of his account. Silvia was born in 1906; Piotr Stanislaw was born after Silvia (we do not know the exact date of his birth), and Franciszek Ksawery (alias Jacques) was born in 1909, a short time after his brother. It therefore seems very unlikely that Jacques, born shortly after a brother who always claimed to have the same father and the same mother, could have had a father other than the husband of his mother and the father of his brother.

Concerning the rejection of the "stepfather" whose Jewish origins were obliquely acknowledged later, the account offers several coexisting explanations: that he was strict, rich, and anti-communist. When I asked Jacques to explain the relationships with his Polish relatives after he came back from the Gulag, he admitted that the family had intervened for his repatriation. He spoke easily about his aunt Marie, the sister of Marcin, who had apparently converted to Protestantism. He spoke also of his stepfather's mother, presumably his grandmother, as an "Israelite" woman and a fervent Polish patriot.

Marcin was no longer there to welcome Jacques when he returned to Poland. He had died "during the Occupation" in circumstances that Jacques avoided clarifying. The historical context, however, leaves little doubt concerning the possible circumstances: Marcin Heyman was of Jewish origin in a Poland governed by the Nazis. The victim of twenty-four years of incarceration in the Soviet Gulag, Jacques found it barely tolerable that the horror of the Soviet social extermination was often "minimized" when compared to the Nazi racial extermination. For this reason, he generally refrained from speaking about the Holocaust.

In the prologue I co-signed with Jacques, I foresaw that the book would not be exactly an autobiography of Jacques Rossi because it was written by another person and because certain details of the private and family life remained in the "secret garden" of the witness. It would not be a traditional historical biography because it was largely inspired by the vision the witness had of himself. It would not be a novel either because nothing was completely invented from scratch. Rather, it would be the story of a life where the voice of the witness would be transcribed as precisely as possible with its modulations, its intonations, its rhythm, and also its moments of silence.

Today the most deafening moments of silence have been partially erased, some of the secrets have been unveiled, and the vagueness has partially disappeared. It is understood that for his own reasons Jacques would have liked us to create fiction from an occasionally fabricated life story where phantasms and dreams sometimes replace factual reality. The discovery of this reality does not in any way diminish the truth of the person nor prevent his testimony from enriching history. On the contrary, Jacques has told a story as passionate as it is authentic about his journey as a communist and his odyssey as a *zek*. However, he chose to conceal parts of his genealogy and his origins. The passages of the book that relate to this should therefore be re-read in light of the documents that were later discovered in his personal archives.

*Jacques the Frenchman* finishes with a triumphant phrase from the survivor of so many years in the Gulag: "Death has not come. I have beaten all the odds." It was 2001 and he was ninety-two years old. The end of his life, however, was difficult. When this great returnee from the Gulag, who had fought so hard to continue to survive, found himself dependent on an institution run by the Polish nuns of Saint-Casimir in Paris, he no longer had a zest for life. He spent three years there, waiting and hoping for death as he had waited and hoped for life during nineteen years in the Gulag. He died on 30 June 2004, leaving for posterity a brilliant memoir and an exemplary oeuvre. A few secrets he took to his grave.

Michèle Sarde

# Notes

**Preface**

1 Oleg Khlevniuk, "The Gulag and the Non-Gulag as One Interrelated Whole," in *The Soviet Gulag: Evidence, Interpretation, and Comparison*, ed. Michael David-Fox, trans. Simon Belokowsky (Pittsburgh: Pittsburgh University Press, 2016), 27n11.

**Introduction**

1 On Gulag testimony, see Jehanne M. Gheith and Katherine R. Jolluck, *Gulag Voices: Oral Histories of Soviet Incarceration and Exile* (New York: Palgrave Macmillan, 2011); Leona Toker, *Return from the Archipelago: Narratives of Gulag Survivors* (Bloomington: Indiana University Press, 2000).
2 See Milovan Djilas, *The New Class: An Analysis of the Communist System* (Boston: Mariner, 1982); Marci Shore, *Caviar and Ashes: A Warsaw Generation's Life and Death in Marxism, 1928–1968* (New Haven: Yale University Press, 2009).
3 See, for example, Nanci Adler, *Keeping Faith with the Party: Communist Believers Return from the Gulag* (Bloomington: Indiana University Press, 2012).
4 See, for example, Golfo Alexopoulos, *Illness and Inhumanity in Stalin's Gulag* (New Haven: Yale University Press, 2017); Steven A. Barnes, *Death and Redemption: The Gulag and the Shaping of Soviet Society* (Princeton: Princeton University Press, 2011); Oleg V. Khlevniuk, *History of the Gulag: From Collectivization to the Great Terror* (New Haven: Yale University Press, 2004); Fyodor Vasilevich Mochulsky, *Gulag Boss: A Soviet Memoir*, trans. and ed. Deborah Kaple (New York: Oxford University Press, 2011).
5 See Alan Barenberg, *Gulag Town, Company Town: Forced Labor and Its Legacy in Vorkuta* (New Haven: Yale University Press, 2014); Miriam Dobson, *Khrushchev's Cold Summer: Gulag Returnees, Crime, and the Fate of Reform after Stalin* (Ithaca: Cornell University Press, 2011).

6 Sheila Fitzpatrick, "The Motherland Calls: 'Soft' Repatriation of Soviet Citizens from Europe, 1945–1953," *Journal of Modern History* 90 (June 2018): 323–50.
7 Jacques Rossi, *The Gulag Handbook: An Encyclopedia Dictionary of Soviet Penitentiary Institutions and Terms Related to the Forced Labor Camps*, trans. William A. Burhans (New York: Paragon House, 1989).
8 Quoted in Anne Applebaum, *Gulag: A History* (New York: Anchor, 2004), xix.
9 Tony Judt, *Postwar: A History of Europe since 1945* (New York: Penguin, 2005), 215.
10 In Richard H. Crossman, ed., *The God That Failed* (New York: Columbia University Press, 2001), 71.

**The Meeting**

1 Tzvetan Todorov, *Mémoire du mal, Tentation du bien* (Paris: Robert Laffont, 2000), 43.

**1. Never Again**

1 *Editor*: See "Afterword" for Michèle Sarde's discussion of Jacques's stepfather.

**5. Secret Agent**

1 *Editor*: This *sitz redakteur* served as a kind of fake editor who served time in jail when a German communist party publication was censured, providing protection for the genuinely valuable editors and writers.
2 Jacques Rossi, *Fragments of Lives: Chronicles of the Gulag* (Prague: Karolinum Press, 2018), 187. This book was originally published in French under the titles *Fragments de vies* and *Qu'elle était belle cette utopie*.
3 Stéphane Courtois and Jean-Louis Panné, "The Comintern in Action," in *The Black Book of Communism: Crimes, Terror, Repression*, ed. Stéphane Courtois et al. (Cambridge, MA: Harvard University Press, 1999), 293.

**7. Early Indications of an Announced Arrest**

1 Margarete Buber-Neumann, a German communist, was arrested in Moscow on 19 June 1938 and deported to the Karaganda camp in Kazakhstan. After the signing of the Nazi-Soviet pact, she was turned over to the Nazis by the Soviets on 8 February 1940 and deported to Ravensbrück, where she stayed until April 1945. In order to escape the Red Army, she fled on foot across devastated Germany. Buber-Neumann would testify at the Kravchenko trial in 1949. See her memoir *Under Two Dictators: Prisoner of Stalin and Hitler* (London: Pimlico, 2008).

## 8. The Trap

1 Jacques Rossi, *The Gulag Handbook: An Encyclopedia Dictionary of Soviet Penitentiary Institutions and Terms Related to the Forced Labor Camps*, trans. William A. Burhans (New York: Paragon House, 1989), 43–4.
2 *Editor*: See, for example, Paul Gregory, *Terror by Quota: State Security from Lenin to Stalin* (New Haven: Yale University Press, 2009); Khlevniuk, *The History of the Gulag*.

## 9. From the Dog House to the Train Station

1 *Editor*: Jacques may not have remembered all these proverbs perfectly, and there are many variations on similar themes, for example: "There's no avoiding the beggar's pan nor the prison cell" (Peter Mertvago, *Russian Proverbs and Sayings* [New York: Hippocrene, 1996], 273). See also Alexander Margulis and Asya Kholodnaya, *Russian-English Dictionary of Proverbs and Sayings* (Jefferson: McFarland, 2008).
2 *Editor*: On the arrest of Grigorii Petrovich Kireev, see Vladimir Spartakovich Mil'bakh, "Political Repression of the Pacific Ocean Fleet Commanders and Chiefs in 1936–1939," *Journal of Slavic Military Studies* 21, no. 1 (2008): 53–112.
3 *Editor*: See Rossi, *Gulag Handbook*, 56.
4 *Editor*: Although Solzhenitsyn wrote that the Black Marias were first seen in 1927, these vehicles may have appeared as early as 1923. See Lewis H. Siegelbaum, *Cars for Comrades: The Life of the Soviet Automobile* (Ithaca: Cornell University Press, 2008), 201.
5 *Editor*: See Rossi, *Gulag Handbook*, 28, 502.

## 10. We Don't Torture Foreigners

1 See also Jules Margoline, *La condition inhumaine* (Paris: Calmann-Levy, 1949), 42–3.

## 11. Confess, Filthy Fascist!

1 Rossi, *Fragments of Lives*, 15–17.

## 12. On Interrogations

1 Aleksandr I. Solzhenitsyn, *The Gulag Archipelago, 1918–1956: An Experiment in Literary Investigation*, vols. 1–2, trans. Thomas P. Whitney (New York: Harper & Row, 1973), 97.

## 13. Daily Life at the Butyrka Prison

1 The term *metro* referred to the places on the ground under the bed boards where prisoners could sleep. At the time of Jacques's arrival during the Great Purges, the detainees often had to sleep on the ground in the transit prisons and in the crowded detention centres (although a *zek* with self-respect, especially the hardened criminal offenders, rarely lowered themselves to sleep on the ground). In prison slang, *airplanes* referred to sleeping panels usually made of three or four transverse boards. [*Editor*: On the "metro" and the "airplanes," see Rossi, *Gulag Handbook*, 234, 377.]

## 14. The Story of a Blind Man and Coffee with Milk

1 Rossi, *Fragments of Lives*, 43.
2 *Editor*: See Rossi, *Gulag Handbook*, 455–7.

## 16. Destination Unknown

1 *Editor*: Marie-Claude Vaillant-Couturier gave evidence at Nuremberg about the torture that she endured at the hands of the Nazis when she was a prisoner at Auschwitz and Ravensbrück.
2 Solzhenitsyn, *Gulag Archipelago*, vols. 1–2, 512.
3 Ibid., 513.

## 17. Transit: May Your Memory Be Your Only Travel Bag!

1 *Editor*: On the medical-sanitation department and the system of physical exploitation in the camps, see Alexopoulos, *Illness and Inhumanity in Stalin's Gulag*.
2 *Editor*: The French term that Jacques uses here – *cave* – corresponds to the Russian slang *fraier*, meaning "pigeon." It refers to inmates who did not belong to the criminal underworld of the camps and who occupied the bottom rung of the prisoners' social hierarchy. They often did not understand the rules of survival, and fell victim to the torments of stronger prisoners. See Rossi, *Gulag Handbook*, 477.
3 Solzhenitsyn, *Gulag Archipelago*, vols. 1–2, 516.
4 Honoré de Balzac, *The Magic Skin* (Boston: Roberts Brothers, 1896), 163.

## 20. The Polar Night

1 Rossi, *Fragments of Lives*, 154–5.
2 Ibid., 144–5.

3 Aleksandr I. Solzhenitsyn, *The Gulag Archipelago, 1918–1956: An Experiment in Literary Investigation*, vols. 3–4 (New York: Harper & Row, 1975), 214.
4 Alain Parrau, *Ecrire les camps* (Paris: Belin, 1995), 100.

### 23. How Jacques the Frenchman Ceased to Be a Communist

1 Claude Roy, "Préface," in *Fédor Dostoievski: Souvenirs de la maison des morts* (Paris: Filio, 1997), 22.

### 24. The Friends of the People

1 Grigory Pasko, "Prianik," *Znamia* (1999): 171–2.
2 The Polish prisoner Slavomir Rawicz tells the story of his long escape with a small group of fellow camp inmates across Siberia, China, the Gobi desert, Tibet, the Himalaya, all the way to India, which was then British. See his *The Long Walk* (New York: Lyons Press, 1956).
3 The cookies may have been suspected of being a potential bribe in a possible escape plan.

### 25. Continuing in Spite of Oneself

1 *Editor*: The "continent" was a term that Gulag prisoners used to refer to the Soviet mainland, central Russia, or the non-Gulag regions where most civilians lived. It captured the inmates' feelings of being separate, isolated, and on the periphery.
2 S. Shcheglov, a resident of the Norilsk camp from 1942 to 1961, in "The Language of Hate Concerning the Gulag Dictionary," *Knizhnoe Obozrenie*, no. 11 (March 1991).

### 27. In the Central Prison of Alexandrovsk

1 Thanks to Misao's efforts, the Japanese translation of Jacques Rossi and Michèle Sarde's book *Jacques, le Français: Pour mémoire du Goulag* was published in 2004 by Kegado Publishers, Tokyo.
2 Gohsuke Uchimura, "The Russian Revolution Which Has Gone Through My Body" (Tokyo: Satsuki-sjpbpj Press, 2000). Title and quotation translated into French by Tsuguo Togawa.
3 *Editor*: On prisoner correspondence in the camps, see Arsenii Formakov, *Gulag Letters*, ed. and trans. Emily D. Johnson (New Haven: Yale University Press, 2017).

## 28. The Beginning of the End

1 François Furet, *The Passing of an Illusion: The Idea of Communism in the Twentieth Century* (Chicago: University of Chicago Press, 2000), 444.

## 29. "I *Choose* Samarkand"

1 Nicolas Werth, "A State against Its People: Violence, Repression, and Terror in the Soviet Union," in *The Black Book of Communism: Crimes, Terror, Repression*, ed. Stéphane Courtois et al. (Cambridge, MA: Harvard University Press, 1999), 255.
2 Furet, *Passing of an Illusion*, 455.

## 33. Communist Poland: Origins of *The Gulag Handbook*

1 Rossi, *Gulag Handbook*, 289. For a recent analysis of the camp rations in light of declassified archives, see Alexopoulos, *Illness and Inhumanity in Stalin's Gulag*, 19–44.

## 34. Seeing Paris Again

1 *Translator*: In the sixteenth century, Guy de Jarnac hamstrung an opponent in a duel.
2 See Jacek Rossi, *Les Controverses continuent autour de la Revolution francaise* [Controversy continues concerning the French Revolution], *Mowia Wieki* (Warsaw, March 1972): 19–24; and *Controverses autour de la Commune de Paris* [Controversy concerning the Commune of Paris], *Mowia Wieki* (Warsaw, December 1974): 6–11.

## 35. Life after Communism

1 Jacques Rossi, *Spravochnik po Gulagu* (London: Overseas, 1987); *The Gulag Handbook* was published in 1989 by Paragon House, New York. In the foreword to this English edition, Robert Conquest wrote: "This is an important contribution to the understanding of a major phenomenon, and so of the world we live in" (n.p.).
2 Jacques Rossi, *Rageri kyosei shuyojo chukai jiten* (Tokyo: Keigado, 1996).
3 Jean-Louis Panne, "Manuel du Goulag," *Gavroche* (January–February 1990): 21–6; Pierre Rigoulot, *Les Paupières Lourdes: Les Français face au Goulag* (Paris: Editions universitaires, 1992).
4 S. Lominadze, *Literaturnaia Gazeta* (Moscow, 7 October 1992).

5 Lubovik Martinek and Marie-Noelle Petrrapavlovski, *Respekt* (Prague, 3–9 February 1992).
6 Kirill Podrabinek, *Volya*, 2–3 (Moscow, 1994).
7 *Sistema ispravitel'no-trudovykh lagerei v SSSR, 1923–1960: Spravochnik*, ed. M.B. Smirnov (Moscow: Zven'ya, 1998).
8 Rossi, *Fragments of Lives*, 187–90.
9 Nicolas Werth, "Le Goulag m'a appris," *La Quinzaine littéraire* (16–31 December 1995): 21–2.
10 Nicole Zand, "Le dictionnaire de la civilisation du Goulag," *Le Monde*, 26 July 1996, p. 3.
11 Ludmila Novikova and Semione Vilensky, *Une étrange impression de décalage: Retour de Moscou 1996* (Paris: Le temps du non, 1998).
12 Raymond Aron, *Mémoires* (Paris: Julliard, 1983), 1030.
13 Jean-François Revel, *La Grande Parade* (Paris: Plon, 2000), 91–2.
14 Nicole Zand, "Le dictionnaire de la civilisation du Goulag," *Le Monde*, 14 November 1997.

**Afterword to the English Edition: A Man of Secrets**

1 Fonds Jacques Rossi, Bibliothèque Souvarine, or Bibliothèque de l'Institut d'Histoire Sociale, Nanterre, Archives départementales des Hauts de Seine.

# Index

Akhmatova, Anna, 94
alcohol, 238, 271, 288–9
Americans, 107, 143, 160, 162, 247, 274, 288, 306; communists, 47, 77, 254–5, 262. *See also* diplomats, Georgetown
amnesty, 241, 244, 256
Amnesty International, 311
Amorini, Elisabeth Salina, ix–xi, 325
Andropov, Yuri, 115
Antonelli, Marie-Cécile, 308
archives, 72, 151, 219, 233, 256, 297, 302, 309–10
arrests: prewar 46, 59, 69, 73–5, 81–2, 93–4, 104, 134, 200; postwar, 205, 221, 244, 250. *See also* Gulag; interrogations; prisoners; Rossi

barracks, 169, 171, 177–8, 220, 293, 301; army, 30, 70, 105; camp, 159, 173–4, 181, 187–8, 193–4, 211–13; conditions, 160, 185, 205. *See also* camps; guards; Gulag; prisoners
Berman, Matvei, 90
Beria, Lavrenty, 141, 232, 239, 241, 243–4, 250, 252, 314
blackmail, 115, 184, 195–7, 213. *See also* corruption

body searches, 151, 162, 190, 266, 286, 291, 293. *See also* interrogations; guards; Gulag; prison
bread. *See* rations
Brezhnev, Leonid, 115
Buber-Neumann, Greta, 74, 209, 332

camps: labour, 149, 153–4, 182; Nazi, 5, 74, 87, 164, 205, 314; Solovetsky, 122, 213; special camps, 188, 205, 218–20; theatre, xvi, 197–8; transit, 157, 159–62, 169, 190, 232. *See also* barracks; Gulag; labour; rations
cannibalism, 37, 39, 207, 225
capitalism, 20, 28–9, 42, 57, 255; vs. communism, 48, 61, 231, 264, 298
capitalists, 4, 31, 82, 254, 294; police, 48; press, 73, 202; prisons, 100, 240; regimes, 55, 101, 289, 298; spies, 60. *See also* communist party
censorship, 43, 236, 238, 242; censors, 29, 129, 229, 238, 254, 280
census of 1937, 132–2
Central Asia, 191, 261, 269, 270–81, 285. *See also* Rossi
China, 62, 67, 229–30, 247; Chinese language, 4, 61, 65, 175, 223, 229, 236, 305

citizenship, 256, 272; Chinese, 230; French, 272, 307, 311, 328; Polish, 278; Soviet 243–4. *See also* passports; Rossi
collectivization, 132, 162, 196, 202–3, 259, 278. *See also* peasants; Stalin
Cominform (Communist Information Bureau), 49
Comintern (Communist International), 48–9, 74, 83, 108, 112, 124, 134, 301; intelligence agents, 4–6, 12, 15, 42–51, 57–62, 67, 69, 77, 104, 137, 202–3, 209, 243, 254–5, 317, 327. *See also* Rossi; spies
communal apartments, 262, 290
communism, 20, 48, 56, 69, 116, 146, 174, 178, 250–1, 303–4, 318; anti-communism, 34, 84, 296, 305, 308, 327; belief in, 84, 118, 201, 222, 275, 288, 296; vs. Nazism, 315.
communist party, 26–31, 34, 36, 49, 61, 327; Austrian, 301–2; Czech, 41; French, 48–9, 249, 275, 318; German, 42–3, 61, 67; Polish, 5, 28, 43, 134–5, 138, 281, 294–7, 304, 327. *See also* Comintern; communism; Soviet Union
communist underground. *See* Comintern; spies
communists. *See* Comintern; communist party; Soviet Union
confessions, 82, 101, 106–16, 119–20, 139, 206, 221
corruption, 103, 207, 211; bribery, 290; *tufta*, 102, 132–3, 151, 186. *See also* blackmail; theft
counter-revolutionaries, 83, 90, 109, 122, 209; counter-revolutionary activity, 84, 97, 107–8, 132, 141, 147, 193, 215, 226, 237, 241, 274; counter-revolutionary sabotage, 131, 139, 210. *See also* Gulag; prisoners

criminal code, 118
criminal offenders, 57, 92, 94, 147; 156–7, 171, 189–90; released, 81, 241; work, 205, 208, 213, 228, 238. *See also* criminal recidivists; Gulag; prisoners
criminal recidivists, 90, 127, 133, 147, 151–3, 161, 186, 244; barracks, 168–9; everyday life, 189, 196, 206–14, 225, 247, 288, 290–1, 313; violence, 181, 285, 212–13. *See also* criminal offenders; Gulag; prisoners
Czechoslovakia, 36, 38–9, 42, 229

denunciations, 56, 62, 74, 107–8, 136, 138, 195–7, 206, 220, 225, 228, 231, 327. *See also* informers; interrogations
deportation, 14, 127, 203, 250, 291. *See also* Gulag; prisoners
de-Stalinization, 243, 250–1, 280, 286, 322. *See also* Khrushchev; Stalin
diplomats, 53, 130, 219, 221–2, 230, 253, 294, 303; French 219, 257, 261–6, 268–9, 272–3, 278, 317, 328; German 238; Polish 82, 277–82, 294. *See also* citizenship; Rossi
doctors, 22, 68, 115, 117, 190, 226, 274, 320–1; in camps, 170, 187–8, 246, 270. *See also* hospitals; illness; medicine
Doctors' Plot, 241. *See also* Stalin
Dudinka camp 190, 194–5, 203; harbour, 143, 158, 162, 166, 168–74, 181. *See also* Gulag; Norilsk
Duranty, Walter, 255
Dzerzhinsky, Felix, 234, 315

exile, 5, 18–19, 38, 215. *See also* prisoners
exploitation, 151, 168, 316. *See also* Gulag; labour

Index    341

fascism, 20, 55, 82, 84, 310. *See also* Hitler
First World War, 15, 48, 299
food. *See* rations
forced labour. *See* camps; Gulag; labour
*Fragments of Lives*, 110, 130, 147, 152, 191, 207, 239; publication, 309, 318–19, 325; writing, 179, 200, 303, 310. *See also* Rossi
France, 138, 147, 184, 204, 231, 236, 243, 268, 272, 277; prewar, 23, 33, 41, 44–5, 47–8, 275; postwar, 118, 179, 218–20, 222; Rossi and, 3–4, 15–20, 46–67, 74, 152, 224, 251, 257–69, 290–330. *See also* diplomats; Rossi
French Revolution, 33, 302, 317
Furet, François, 243, 246, 249, 250, 308, 317

Georgetown University, 3–4, 175, 292, 305–8, 315, 325. *See also* Rossi
Germany, 14, 16, 48, 222; Berlin, 4, 12, 25, 42–4, 52, 67, 275, 317; Berlin Wall, 308, 325; Nazi 44, 51, 131, 133, 154–5, 203, 272; postwar 226, 236, 289; Weimar, 30–1, 42–4. *See also* Hitler; Nazis
Ginsburg, Evgenia, 322
Goyet, Leontine Charlotte. *See* Rossi
Great Purges, 44–6, 62, 71–4, 82–3, 148, 193, 197, 237, 241, 250; victims 90, 94, 101, 105, 113, 116–18, 122–4, 127, 130, 139–41, 146, 226; and Rossi, 57, 68–9, 285–6. *See also* arrests; interrogations; Stalin
guards, 96, 106, 205, 214, 239, 244–7, 253; border, 39–42, 50, 286; camp, 158–60, 164, 169, 171–2, 181–5, 190, 194, 206, 209; escort, 79, 94–5, 150, 165–8, 175, 178, 188, 193, 212, 219, 224, 235; prison, 16, 31–7, 110–12, 117–29, 144–5, 152–3, 226–8, 237, 251–2; searches, 97, 162, 293. *See also* body searches; Gulag; interrogations; police
Gulag, 148, 159, 179, 216–7, 227, 252, 327; escapes, 164, 168, 206, 208, 213–14, 221, 236, 335; hunger, 110, 165, 168, 179–80, 183, 189, 193; letters, 81, 145, 175, 218–21, 236, 238, 242, 253–4; mortality, 133, 165, 185, 203; punishment cell (cooler), 119, 156, 181–2, 226, 248; releases, 57, 82, 89, 215–16, 228–9, 231, 243, 252–3, 256–7; returnees, 247–8, 268, 295–304, 330; survival, 4, 7, 43, 45, 58, 66, 74, 85, 93, 117–19, 152, 182–91, 197, 209, 211, 223, 226, 308, 310, 317, 326, 330; transit, 142, 148, 150–67; uprisings, 244, 314. *See also* barracks; body searches; camps; doctors; guards; medicine; memorial; prison; prisoners; rations; Rossi; torture; *Vozvrashchenie*
*Gulag Handbook, The*, 4, 6, 105; contents, 66, 82, 89–91, 94, 152, 161–2, 179, 195, 203, 208, 232, 237; reception, 308–18; writing, 89, 154, 200, 242, 265, 288–96, 302–3, 306–7, 325. *See also* Rossi

health. *See* doctors; hospitals; illness; invalids; medicine
Heyman, Franciszek Ksawery, 326, 328. *See also* Rossi
Hitler, Adolf, 30, 42, 44, 48, 51, 61, 218, 254, 315; agents of, 75, 115, 204–5; invasion of USSR, 211, 215, 231–2, 301; pact with Stalin, 74, 154–5, 204. *See also* Germany; Nazis
hospitals, 131, 154, 187–8, 195, 226, 246, 320–1, 328; psychiatric,

247, 322. *See also* doctors; Gulag; illness; invalids; Rossi
housing. *See also* barracks
Hungary, 11, 15, 38, 40–1, 266; revolution, 251
hunger. *See* Gulag; illness; torture
hunger strikes. *See* Rossi

identity. *See* citizenship; passports; Rossi
illness, 22, 72, 170; bedbugs, 106, 185; blindness, 13, 74, 101, 128, 133–4, 187, 294; dysentery, 164–5, 185; frostbite, 161; malnutrition, 176, 178; self-mutilation, 187, 212. *See also* doctors; Gulag; hospitals; invalids; medicine; prisoners
India, 4, 65
infirmary. *See* hospitals
informers, 53, 110, 119, 132, 144, 148, 194–7, 211, 213, 218, 221–2, 254, 295. *See also* denunciation
intellectuals, 103, 106, 190, 206–7, 217, 285, 308; communist, 61, 77, 82, 140, 202, 209; European, 7, 101, 289, 321. *See also* Rossi
interrogations, 30, 67, 102, 107, 109, 113–20, 263; camp, 225, 230, 232, 243; prison, 12, 45, 71, 80, 105, 125, 127, 136; and torture, 96, 106, 110, 116, 119, 122, 137, 145. *See also* arrests; guards; prisoners
invalids, 147, 182, 187, 267. *See also* hospitals; illness; medicine
investigations, 115–17, 223, 227–8, 230, 295. *See also* body searches; Gulag; interrogations
Irkutsk, 158, 187, 232, 247, 316

Jaruzelski, General Wojciech, 306
Jews, 38–42, 84, 112, 131, 254, 277, 290, 329; Polish, 25, 71, 91, 147, 155, 296
Joannon, Albert, 294, 298, 302–7, 311

KGB (Committee for State Security), 63, 82, 113, 243, 253, 257, 266, 283; agents 54, 242, 264–5, 278, 314; archive, 72, 316–17; methods, 115, 117–18, 218, 228. *See also* NKVD
Khrushchev, Nikita, 249–51, 279, 282–3, 285, 289. *See also* de-Stalinization; secret speech
Kirov, 149, 152, 156, 247; theatre, 198
Kirov, Sergei, 250
Kollontai, Alexandra, 61
Krasnoyarsk, 112, 147, 152, 158–62, 169, 213, 219, 228–33, 247, 284, 316
kulaks, 158, 162, 196, 202–3. *See also* collectivization; peasants

labour, 120, 198, 212; accidents, 47, 176, 179, 186–7; brigade, 176–7, 186, 195, 205; competition, 185; exhaustive, 82, 147, 195, 197, 205–6, 301; labourers, 56, 161, 183, 218, 234; physical, 133, 170–6, 186–7, 194, 210; socially useful, 140. *See also* camps; Gulag; rehabilitation
Lake Baikal, 158, 232, 234, 246
Lenin, Vladimir, 32, 48–9, 63, 69, 83, 102–3, 111, 116, 130, 147, 179, 321. *See also* communist party; Marxism-Leninism; Russian Revolution
letters. *See* Gulag; Rossi

Marx, Karl. *See* Marxism-Leninism
Marxism-Leninism, 64–5, 103, 140, 198, 234, 255; belief in, 23, 26, 200. *See also* communist party; Lenin; Rossi
medicine, 22, 36, 42, 203, 222, 320; medical commission, 151, 170; medical examination, 170, 187. *See also* doctors; Gulag; hospitals; illness; invalids
memorial, 308, 312, 315. See also *Vozvrashchenie*

Mindszenty, Cardinal Joseph, 266
Molotov, Vyacheslav, 82,
Muslims, 271–2, 274, 277
MVD (Ministry of Internal Affairs).
  See NKVD

Naito, Misao, 236, 246, 250–2, 304–5
nationality. See citizenship
Nazis, 44, 116, 133, 155, 165, 203, 232,
  321–2; camps, 5, 74, 87, 164, 202,
  205, 314–15; Germany, 44, 203;
  Nazi-Soviet pact, 203–4; Nazism,
  7, 315, 329; victims, 84, 131, 314;
  and war, 190, 205, 216, 218–9, 296.
  See also Germany; Hitler
NKVD (People's Commissariat of
  Internal Affairs), 49, 57, 78, 80,
  82–3, 92, 104–8, 118, 129, 133, 136,
  138, 141, 197, 209, 215, 221–2, 241,
  256. See also arrests; body searches;
  guards; Gulag; interrogations;
  investigations; sentences; police
Nogtev, A.P., 122
Norilsk, 145, 149, 172–3, 192, 267,
  284, 301; camp, 156–61, 166, 168,
  175, 197, 203–6, 214–29, 233, 244,
  256, 311, 319; industry, 178–81,
  195, 199, 265; Jacques's revisit, 5,
  315–6. See also Dudinka; Rossi
Novosibirsk, 149, 152, 154, 156, 176,
  247, 291, 308

OGPU. See KGB; NKVD; police
Omsk, 152, 156

passports, 45, 49–51, 81, 131, 231,
  265, 299, 328; internal, 213, 272;
  Polish, 281–2, 284–7, 302, 306. See
  also citizenship; Rossi
peasants, 40, 103, 111, 112, 129,
  176, 178, 253, 271–2; Chinese, 62;
  Polish, 18, 21, 26, 28; Russian,
  31, 48, 84, 131, 142, 195, 202–6,
  321. See also collectivization;
  kulaks
People's Commissariat of Internal
  Affairs. See NKVD
Pilsudski, Jozef, 17, 20, 26, 28–9,
  31–2, 34, 37, 91, 288, 306, 317.
  See also Poland
Poland, 312, 327–9; communist,
  6, 16–17, 32, 80, 135, 232, 239,
  265, 267, 277–81, 286–98, 301–2,
  304–7, 317; prewar, 5, 12, 18–20,
  23, 25, 28, 31, 37, 40–3, 83, 91, 229;
  Solidarity movement, 305–6. See
  also citizenship; communist party;
  passports; Pilsudski; Rossi
police, Chinese, 229–30; European,
  21, 29, 31, 37–8, 40–1, 48, 50, 57, 65;
  French, 46, 299, 302; German, 43,
  51; Japanese, 147; Polish, 31, 287,
  289, 294; Spanish, 74
police, Soviet, 42, 131, 140–1, 143,
  152, 159, 166, 176, 181, 193, 199;
  in Central Asia, 261, 272–3, 276,
  279–80, 282, 284; in Moscow, 242,
  263–4, 265–9; in Norilsk, 216, 220,
  222, 224; in Odessa, 213; political,
  49, 54, 71, 78–9, 82, 113–15, 136,
  180, 196, 206, 241, 243, 250, 253,
  256, 280, 294, 315. See also guards;
  KGB; NKVD
prison: Alexandrovsk, 147, 164,
  187–8, 232–240, 244, 246, 247, 249,
  255, 264–5, 291; Butyrka, 12, 16, 45,
  71, 78, 100–6, 112, 118–37, 140, 143,
  145, 151, 181, 185, 194, 286, 322;
  capitalist, 100, 240; high-security,
  15, 129, 157, 232–3, 237–8, 248–50,
  293; Lefortovo, 119; Lubianka,
  79–80, 84, 90, 125, 140, 223, 313,
  317; solitary confinement, 6, 183,
  223, 225; transit, 63, 143–59, 228,
  233–4, 247–8, 255, 290. See also body
  searches; camps; Gulag; prisoners

prisoners, 39, 61, 63, 97, 99, 103–7, 121, 177, 251–2, 291, 316; Baltic, 131, 237; complaints, 120; confession, 119; everyday life, 95–6, 123, 125, 128, 132, 157, 171, 173, 178, 181, 186–90, 197, 237, 249, 256; former, 7, 34, 42, 253, 257, 261–2, 295, 318–19, 322; German, 253, 303; Gulag, 14, 71, 89–90, 137, 168–70, 183, 191, 199, 204–5, 221, 312, 314; hunger, 179, 245–6; Japanese, 15, 235, 250, 252; juvenile offenders, 207; political, 33–4, 84, 109, 118, 124, 127, 198, 212, 302, 315; POWs, 206, 229–30; release, 66, 215, 241–4, 268, 273, 278, 287, 290; Rossi, 5–6, 12, 67–8, 92, 193, 195, 224, 226–8, 231–2; Russian, 16, 40; *Starosta*, 122; torture, 45, 113, 115; transport, 93–4, 141–2, 145–54, 158–67, 182, 234, 247–8. *See also* camps; interrogations; Gulag; prison; rations; rehabilitation; Rossi; sentences

*Qu'elle était belle cette utopie!* See *Fragments of Lives*

rape, 154, 172, 186, 190. *See also* torture; women
rations, 68, 144, 151, 166, 213, 235, 245; bread, 156, 173, 176, 181, 210–11, 226, 293–4; meagre, 120, 180, 223; schedule, 161–2, 237; and work, 195, 205. *See also* prisoners
Red Army, 79, 194, 209, 226, 244; spies, 49, 57, 70–1, 83, 109, 202, 327; wartime, 133, 205–6, 254, 291
refugees, 81, 266
rehabilitation, 54, 72, 140, 185, 191, 196, 206, 209, 243, 252, 278, 286–7, 314, 317, 322
releases. *See* amnesty; Gulag; prisoners
Roginsky, Arsenii, 309

Rossi, Jacques: anti-communism, 57, 84, 200–1, 316, 321; arrest, 69–85; Beaux-Arts, 4, 14, 27, 36, 43, 154, 170, 177; Buddhism, 55; childhood, 11–25; citizenship, 243–4, 272, 278, 307, 311, 328; communist belief, 14, 29–30, 51, 56–7, 66, 70, 83–4, 108, 146, 163, 168, 202, 235, 295; communist underground, 26–68; drawings, 14, 23, 94, 97, 186, 192, 197, 208, 223–4, 255–6; father (Marcin Heyman), 17–22, 24–5, 27, 35, 281, 295, 328–9; Friends of Jacques Rossi, 298, 308; Gulag, 168–225; Gulag release, 249–69; Hunger strikes, 225–32, 244–8, 254, 279–85, 328; languages, 4, 62, 65–6, 175, 223, 229, 236, 272, 274, 305; Marxism-Leninism, 57, 84, 163, 231, 262, 302, 314; mother (Leontine Goyet), 12, 17, 24, 118, 329; petitions, 120, 201; Poland, 11–25, 288–304; prison, 89–141; repatriation, 252–3, 257, 277–9, 288–9, 329; Samarkand, 54, 65–6, 249, 257, 261, 268, 270–87, 290, 306, 328; School of Oriental Languages, 52, 177; sentence, 136–41, 231; siblings (Piotr, Silvia), 17, 24, 35, 329; USSR, 6, 29, 50, 66, 238, 242–3, 254, 268–9, 275, 285–9, 296, 307, 313. *See also Fragments of Lives*; France; Georgetown; Gulag; *Gulag Handbook*; interrogations; Norilsk; Poland; prison; prisoners; Sarde
Russian Revolution, 43, 48, 62–3, 101–2, 124, 130, 193, 202, 236. *See also* Lenin

Sarde, Michèle, 3–8, 325–330. *See also* Georgetown
secret agents. *See* Comintern

secret speech, 249–51. *See also* de-Stalinization; Khrushchev
Second World War, 15, 49, 63, 72, 107, 155, 198, 206, 211, 303, 306. *See also* Hitler; Nazis; Red Army
security police. *See* arrests; body searches; guards; interrogations; KGB; NKVD; police
sentences, 84, 109, 123, 211, 213–33, 261, 294; additional, 134, 154, 187–8, 316; courts, 82, 256; length, 33, 66, 107, 118, 147, 170, 205–6, 210, 238, 277; prisoners, 136–41, 194–8, 251–2. *See also* arrests; Gulag; interrogations; prisoners; Rossi
sex and sexuality, 54, 61, 189–91
Shalamov, Varlam, 182–3, 209–10, 293, 310; *Kolyma Tales*, 131, 158, 192, 207, 212, 288
Solzhenitsyn, Aleksandr, 90, 116, 138, 149, 152, 174, 182–3, 187, 195, 209–10; *First Circle*, 68, 93; *Gulag Archipelago*, 68, 99, 106, 158–9, 201, 215, 301, 308–9
Soviet Union (USSR), 79, 85, 131, 134, 265, 277, 294, 309–10, 317; collapse, 49, 151, 308; communist party, 48–9, 63, 100–3, 116–17, 138, 203, 314, 321; central committee, 48–9, 136, 146; council of people's commissars, 90; life in, 61–3, 68–9, 75, 90, 103–5, 198, 204, 247, 257, 315; politburo, 117, 242–4; terror in, 42, 57–9, 81–3, 143–5, 199, 202, 229–30, 250, 278, 293, 302, 314; and war, 31, 49, 154, 203, 211, 215, 301. *See also* Comintern; communist party; KGB; Lenin; NKVD; Rossi; Stalin
Spanish Civil War, 5, 72–4, 77–8
spies, 54, 59–60, 65, 72, 265. *See also* Comintern

Stalin, Joseph, 64, 69, 102–3, 147, 192, 200, 239, 253, 271; death of, 5, 90, 117, 164, 182, 201, 220, 232–4, 239, 241–3, 246, 328; regime, 49, 196, 210, 280, 313–14; repression, 67, 69, 82–4, 106, 132–3, 145, 159, 162, 249–50, 321–2; resistance to, 22, 262; victims, 80, 285, 297; wartime, 74, 131, 154. *See also* de-Stalinization
survival. *See* Gulag
Sweden, 12, 49
Switzerland, 47, 71

theft, 37, 127, 147, 151–2, 165, 171, 186, 190, 208–11. *See also* corruption; criminal offenders; criminal recidivists
Todorov, Tzvetan, 6, 314
torture, 112–15, 137, 139. *See also* hunger; interrogations; rape
Trans-Siberian railway, 153, 158
Trotsky, Leon, 63, 71, 102; Trotskyist, 134, 314
*tufta*. *See* corruption; theft
Twentieth Party Congress. *See* Khrushchev; secret speech

Uchimura, Gohsuke. *See* Naito
Ukraine, 36, 70, 149, 213, 238; Ukrainians, 29–31, 39, 155, 187, 213, 222, 229, 238, 314

*Vozvrashchenie*, 312–13, 315. *See also* memorial

Werth, Nicolas, 233, 249, 309–10
White Sea–Baltic Sea canal, 90, 108, 213
women, 11–12, 25, 159–60, 210, 267, 271–4, 277, 319; communist, 37, 59–61, 74–5; prisoners, 97, 145, 153–4, 163, 189–90, 212,

217, 252, 317. *See also* prisoners; rape; Rossi
work. *See* labour
World War I. *See* First World War
World War II. *See* Second World War

Yagoda, Genrikh, 90, 134
Yenisei river, 158–72, 179, 198, 213
Yezhov, Nikolai, 83, 241, 252

Zetkin, Clara, 61

www.ingramcontent.com/pod-product-compliance
Lightning Source LLC
Chambersburg PA
CBHW030219100526
44584CB00014BA/969